Algebra
to Go

A Mathematics Handbook

GReaT SouRCe®
EDUCATION GROUP
A Houghton Mifflin Company

Acknowledgments

We gratefully acknowledge the following teachers and mathematics supervisors who helped make *Algebra to Go* a reality.

Senior Consultant:
Robert Fair
*District Math
  Coordinator, K-12*
Cherry Creek Schools
Englewood, Colorado

Senior Consultant:
Dr. Marsha W. Lilly
*Secondary Mathematics
  Coordinator*
Alief ISD
Alief, TX

David J. Bach
*Adjunct Mathematics
  Professor*
Raymond Walters College
Cincinnati, OH

Cynthia Fielder
Mathematics Specialist
*Cobb County School
  District*
Marietta, GA

Dr. Matt Larson
K-12 Math Consultant
Lincoln Public Schools
Lincoln, NE

Alan Q. Lippert
Math Teacher
Lakeside School
*Seattle Independent
  School District*
Seattle, WA

Albert H. Mauthe, Ed.D.
*Supervisor of
  Mathematics*
*Norristown Area School
  District*
Norristown, PA

Barbara Nunn
*Secondary Mathematics
  Curriculum Specialist*
Broward County
Fort Lauderdale, FL

Stephen J. Paterwic
Mathematics Teacher
*High School of Science
  and Technology*
Springfield, MA

Kenneth W. Rowe
*Chairman, Mathematics
  Department*
Kearny High School
San Diego, CA

Ronald Vervaecke
*Mathematics
  Coordinator, K-12*
*Warren Consolidated
  Schools*
Warren, MI

Larry A. Ward
*Secondary Mathematics
  Specialist*
Fort Worth ISD
Fort Worth, TX

Writing: Andrew Kaplan, Ann Petroni-McMullen, Kane Publishing Services, Inc; Edward Manfre
Editorial: Carol DeBold, Justine Dunn, Edward Manfre, Susan Rogalski; Judy Bousquet, Kane Publishing Services, Inc.
Design Management: Richard Spencer
Production Management: Sandra Easton
Design and Production: Bill SMITH STUDIO
Marketing: Lisa Bingen
Illustration credits: see end of index

Printed in the United States of America

International Standard Book Number: [0-669-47152-6] (hardcover)
5 6 7 8 9 0 QW 05

International Standard Book Number: [0-669-47151-8] (softcover)
7 8 9 0 QW 05

Table of Contents

Numeration and Number Theory (001)

Estimating and Computing with Real Numbers (067)

Basic Tools of Algebra (098)

Linear Equations (146)

How This Book Is Organized

Algebra to Go is a reference book. That means you're not expected to read it from cover to cover. Instead, you'll want to keep it handy for those times when you're not clear about a math topic and need someplace to look up definitions, procedures, explanations, and rules.

Because this is a reference book and because there may be more than one entry on a page, we've given each topic an item number (003). So, when you are looking for an item, look for the numbered tab.

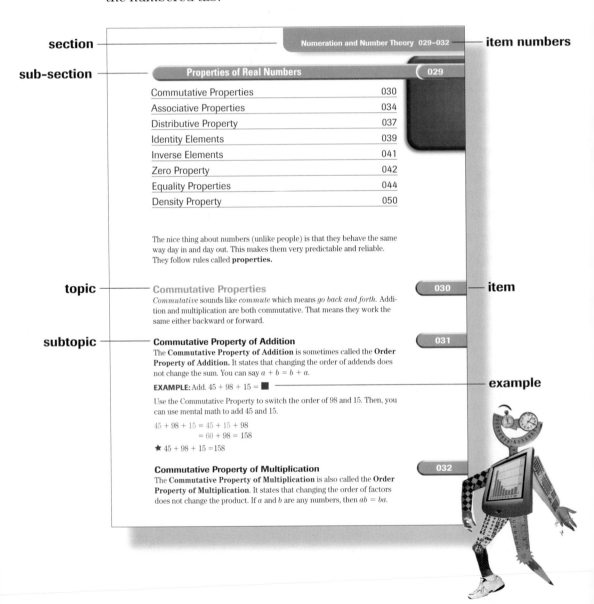

section ——— Numeration and Number Theory 029–032 ——— **item numbers**

sub-section ——— **Properties of Real Numbers** 029

Commutative Properties	030
Associative Properties	034
Distributive Property	037
Identity Elements	039
Inverse Elements	041
Zero Property	042
Equality Properties	044
Density Property	050

The nice thing about numbers (unlike people) is that they behave the same way day in and day out. This makes them very predictable and reliable. They follow rules called **properties.**

topic ——— **Commutative Properties** 030 ——— **item**
Commutative sounds like *commute* which means *go back and forth.* Addition and multiplication are both commutative. That means they work the same either backward or forward.

subtopic ——— **Commutative Property of Addition** 031
The **Commutative Property of Addition** is sometimes called the **Order Property of Addition.** It states that changing the order of addends does not change the sum. You can say $a + b = b + a$.

EXAMPLE: Add. $45 + 98 + 15 = \blacksquare$ ——— **example**

Use the Commutative Property to switch the order of 98 and 15. Then, you can use mental math to add 45 and 15.

$45 + 98 + 15 = 45 + 15 + 98$
$\qquad\qquad\quad = 60 + 98 = 158$

★ $45 + 98 + 15 = 158$

Commutative Property of Multiplication 032
The **Commutative Property of Multiplication** is also called the **Order Property of Multiplication.** It states that changing the order of factors does not change the product. If a and b are any numbers, then $ab = ba$.

A good way to get started in this book is to thumb through the pages. Find these parts:

■ **Table of Contents**
  This lists the major sections and sub-sections of the book.

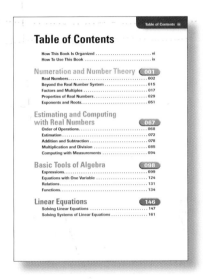

■ **Sections and Sub-Sections**
  Each section of the handbook has a short table of contents so you know what is in the section. Sections have several sub-sections and each of these also has its own short table of contents. Notice the color bars across the top of the pages. Each section has a different color to make it easy to find.

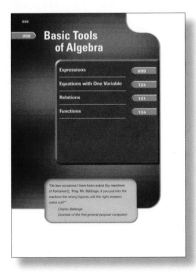

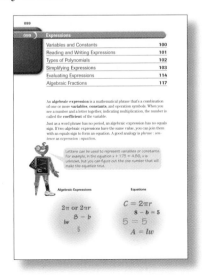

■ Almanac

This includes some very helpful tables and lists. It also has hints on how to study, take a test, and use a graphing calculator. Check out all of the almanac entries—you'll want to refer to them often.

■ Yellow Pages

This part of the handbook has three glossaries. The Glossary of Mathematical Formulas is the place to look if you forget a formula. In the Glossary of Mathematical Terms, you will find math terms that your teacher, your parents, and your textbook use. The Glossary of Mathematical Symbols is a good place to look when you don't remember what a symbol means.

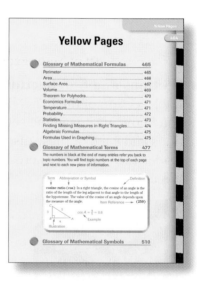

■ Index

This is at the very end of the book.

How to Use This Book

There are three ways to find information about the topic in which you are interested:

1 Look in the Index

We listed items in the index using any word we thought you might use to describe the topic. For example, you'll find absolute value of equations under both *absolute value* and *equations*.

Absolute value, 009–010
 of algebraic expressions, 116
 of equations, 130
 of functions, 141
 of inequalities, 199, 201

Equations, 124–130
 absolute value, 130
 on a graphing calculator, 444
 multi-step, 129
 one-step, 128

Remember that you are being directed to item numbers, not page numbers. Use the item numbers located at the top of each page to help you find the topic you are looking for.

2 Look in the Glossary

The Glossary of Mathematical Terms in this handbook is one of the most extensive high-school algebra glossaries around. Mathematics has a language all its own. Once you learn the language, the rest is much easier. Think of this Glossary as your personal interpreter and turn to this part of the handbook whenever you see an unfamiliar word.

absolute value $(|\ \ |)$: The distance of a number from zero on the number line. For a complex number $(a + bi)$, the absolute value is the distance from the origin of point (a, b). Absolute value is never negative. $|{-}28| = 28; |28| = 28$ **(009)**

Most glossary entries will give you an item number to refer to if you want more information about the topic.

3 Look in the Table of Contents

All the major topics covered in this book are listed in the table of contents. If you're looking for a general topic—like Linear Equations—rather than a very specific one—like Making a Table of Values, the table of contents is a quick way to find it. Notice that the color of each section's item number in the Table of Contents matches the color of the bar across the top of the pages for that section. This makes it easy to locate a section.

Numeration and Number Theory

"There is no smallest among the small and no largest among the large; but always something still smaller and something still larger."

Anaxagoras

When you use something over and over, like a telephone, television, stereo, or microwave oven, you tend to take it for granted. You have used numbers every day for years. You probably don't stop to think much about how ingenious our number system is.

With a few strokes of your pen, you can show how many grains of sand there are on Earth or how many seconds old the universe is. You can also write numbers to describe things too small to see, like the width of an atom. You can even write numbers that are less than nothing. And you can do all that with just ten different digits (0–9) and a few other symbols like a comma, decimal point, and negative sign.

For numbers that you cannot write exactly with the digits 0–9, there are special symbols like $\sqrt{}$ and π. We even have numbers that seem so unreal we call them imaginary. (They're not *really* imaginary—they exist and are applied in such fields as electricity.)

What makes a number real? A **real number** is any number that can be shown on a number line. If a number cannot be shown on the number line, it is not real. It is **imaginary.**

MORE HELP
See 009,
013–014

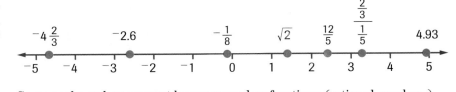

Some real numbers cannot be expressed as fractions (rational numbers), so, real numbers are either rational or irrational.

Real Numbers

> ### Rational Numbers
> real numbers that can be expressed as a ratio of two integers
> Examples: $2\ (2 = \frac{2}{1})$, $^-3$, $\frac{1}{4}$, 0.18, etc.
>
> > ### Integers
> > whole numbers and their opposites
> > Examples: 0, 3, $^-3$, 49, $^-49$, etc.
> >
> > > ### Whole Numbers
> > > zero and natural numbers
> > > Examples: 0, 1, 2, 3, etc.
> > >
> > > > ### Natural Numbers
> > > > all the numbers 1, 2, 3, 4, ... to infinity
>
> ### Irrational Numbers
> real numbers that cannot be expressed as a ratio of integers (a fraction)
> Examples: π, $\sqrt{11}$,
> 0.121121112111112111112...,
> etc.

Rational Numbers

If you say that an idea is *rational*, you probably mean that the idea makes sense. In mathematics, *rational* has a different meaning. A **rational number** is any number that can be written as a fraction, a ratio of two integers $\frac{a}{b}$, where b is never zero.

> The denominator of a fraction can't be zero because division by zero doesn't make sense.

Rational

$$-\frac{19}{7}$$

$$3.6 = 3\frac{3}{5} = \frac{18}{5}$$

$$0.\overline{3}$$

$$8 = \frac{8}{1}$$

Not Rational

$$\sqrt{7} \qquad \pi$$

$$0.25255255525555\ldots$$

MORE HELP
See 041, 043

All rational numbers can be shown on a number line. Each rational number has an **opposite**. Opposite numbers are the same distance from zero in opposite directions.

$4\frac{1}{4}$ and $^-4\frac{1}{4}$ are opposites. $\frac{a}{b}$ and $\frac{^-a}{b}$ are opposites.

1.6 and $^-$1.6 are opposites.   Zero is its own opposite.

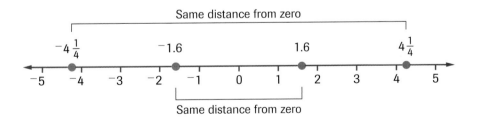

Fractions

A **fraction** is a number (written as a ratio) that represents part of a whole or a set. Since fractions are real numbers, you can place them on a number line.

MORE HELP
See 278–280, 460

In fractions greater than 1 or less than ⁻1, the absolute value of the numerator is greater than the absolute value of the denominator.

Equivalent fractions name the same number.

$$-\frac{5}{4} \quad -\frac{4}{4} \quad -\frac{3}{4} \quad -\frac{2}{4} \quad -\frac{1}{4} \quad \frac{0}{4} \quad \frac{1}{4} \quad \frac{2}{4} \quad \frac{3}{4} \quad \frac{4}{4} \quad \frac{5}{4}$$

$$-\frac{10}{8} \; -\frac{9}{8} \; -\frac{8}{8} \; -\frac{7}{8} \; -\frac{6}{8} \; -\frac{5}{8} \; -\frac{4}{8} \; -\frac{3}{8} \; -\frac{2}{8} \; -\frac{1}{8} \; \frac{0}{8} \; \frac{1}{8} \; \frac{2}{8} \; \frac{3}{8} \; \frac{4}{8} \; \frac{5}{8} \; \frac{6}{8} \; \frac{7}{8} \; \frac{8}{8} \; \frac{9}{8} \; \frac{10}{8}$$

Fractions less than 0 are written with only one negative symbol.

In fractions between ⁻1 and 1, the absolute value of the numerator is smaller than the absolute value of the denominator.

The **denominator of a fraction** tells how many equal parts are in the whole or the set. The **numerator** tells how many parts you're talking about. The fraction bar separating numerator from denominator indicates division.

$$\frac{3}{5}$$ ← numerator (parts you are talking about)
← denominator (equal parts in the whole or set)

EXAMPLE: What fraction of this window is blue?

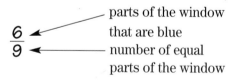

$$\frac{6}{9}$$ ← parts of the window that are blue
← number of equal parts of the window

★ $\frac{6}{9}$, or $\frac{2}{3}$ of the window is blue.

Improper fraction is a term we don't use much, though you may find it on standardized tests. It refers to a fraction with a numerator larger than its denominator. There's really nothing wrong with such a fraction, it just represents a number greater than one.

Complex Fractions

A **complex fraction** is a special kind of fraction in which the numerator, denominator, or both, are fractions.

Complex Fractions   **Simple Fractions**

$$\dfrac{\frac{1}{2}}{6} \qquad \dfrac{\frac{2}{3}}{\frac{3}{4}} \qquad \dfrac{\frac{5}{2}}{5} \qquad\qquad \dfrac{5}{8} \qquad \dfrac{\frac{1}{10}}{} \qquad \dfrac{3}{16}$$

For any complex fraction, you can write a simple fraction by thinking about the division meaning of the fraction bar. Look carefully at the lengths of the fraction bars in a complex fraction. The longest bar indicates the final division.

MORE HELP
See 090

Write: $\dfrac{\frac{3}{5}}{8}$

Say: *three fifths divided by eight*

EXAMPLE: Write $\dfrac{\frac{3}{5}}{8}$ as a simple fraction.

To solve the problem, divide $\frac{3}{5}$ by 8.

$$\frac{3}{5} \div 8 = \frac{3}{5} \times \frac{1}{8}$$

$$\frac{3}{5} \times \frac{1}{8} = \frac{3}{40}$$

★ $\dfrac{\frac{3}{5}}{8} = \dfrac{3}{40}$

006

Decimals

Decimals are numbers that are written using place value based on ten. In our decimal system, each place has ten times the value of the place to its right. You can use place value to help you read, write, and understand decimals.

Sometimes you'll see the word units to mean ones.

Tens	Ones	Tenths	Hundredths	Thousandths	Ten-Thousandths
	6.	3	8	7	5

3. Read the rest of the digits as if they were a whole number. Then read the place value of the last digit.

1. Read the whole number part first.

2. Say the decimal point as and.

Write: 6.3875

Say: *six and three thousand eight hundred seventy-five ten-thousandths*

007

Terminating Decimals

A **terminating decimal** contains a **finite** number of digits. This means you could count the digits.

EXAMPLE: In 1991, Billy Hatcher of the Cincinnati Reds set a World Series record by getting nine hits in 12 times at bat. Write a decimal for $\frac{9}{12}$, Hatcher's batting average for the series. *Source: Associated Press*

Divide. $9 \div 12 = \blacksquare$

$$
\begin{array}{r}
0.75 \\
12\overline{)9.00} \\
-8\ 40 \\
\hline
60 \\
-60 \\
\hline
0
\end{array}
$$

You know the answer will be less than 1, so write a decimal point and some zeros to get started. Keep tacking on zeros until you finish dividing.

When you've divided until there's no remainder, there are digits in two places after the decimal point.

The decimal 0.75 has exactly two decimal places. The decimal is a terminating decimal.

★ Baseball batting averages always include the thousandths place and never include a zero in the ones place. Write .750 for Billy Hatcher's batting average.

Repeating Decimals

A **repeating decimal** has one or more digits to the right of the decimal point that repeat indefinitely.

EXAMPLE: Your favorite CD has a playing time of 52 minutes. There are 12 songs on the CD. About how long is each song?

To solve the problem, divide. $52 \div 12 = \blacksquare$

$$
\begin{array}{r}
4.33... \\
12\overline{)52.00} \\
-48\ 00 \\
\hline
4\ 00 \\
-3\ 60 \\
\hline
40 \\
-36 \\
\hline
4
\end{array}
$$

The digit 3 repeats forever.

Every time you divide, you get the same remainder, so the decimal will repeat.

Write: $4.\overline{3}$

Say: *four point three repeating*

★ The average song length on the CD is a little more than 4 minutes.

Some decimals do not repeat or end. The number 0.122112221112222… continues indefinitely but does not have a repeating pattern. Decimals like this are called **non–repeating, non–terminating decimals.**

MORE HELP
See 013–014

"…" means the digits in the decimal continue without ending.

009

Absolute Value

The **absolute value** of a number is the distance the number is from zero on the number line.

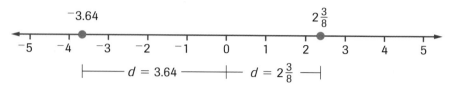

‾3.64 is 3.64 units to the left of zero.

Write: $\left|\,^-3.64\right| = 3.64$

Say: *The absolute value of negative three and sixty-four hundredths is three and sixty-four hundredths.*

Write: $\left|2\frac{3}{8}\right| = 2\frac{3}{8}$

Say: *The absolute value of two and three eighths is two and three eighths.*

Be careful that | | doesn't look like ( ) when written hurriedly.

010

MATH ALERT Absolute Value Is Never Negative

The absolute value of any number except zero is positive. This is because absolute value tells the distance from zero, not the direction from zero. To understand absolute value, think of these rules:

MORE HELP
See 041

- The absolute value of a positive number is itself. $|3| = 3$

- The absolute value of a negative number is its opposite. $\left|\,^-6\right| = 6$

- The absolute value of 0 is 0. $|0| = 0$

- The opposite of the absolute value of a number is negative. $^-|8| = \,^-8.$

Comparing and Ordering Numbers

When you decide which of two numbers is larger, you compare. When you put numbers in order, you compare pairs of numbers until you can define the order.

EXAMPLE: On Monday, a share of Z–Corp stock drops $\frac{7}{8}$ point. On Tuesday, the stock gains 1 point. On Wednesday, the stock loses 0.25 point. On which day does the stock drop the most?

To solve this problem, order the numbers from least to greatest.

ONE WAY   You can use a number line.

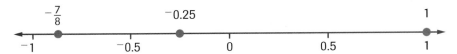

Numbers increase as you go from left to right on the number line. From left to right on the number line, the numbers are: $\frac{-7}{8}$, $^{-}0.25$, 1.

ANOTHER WAY   You can write all the numbers in the same form and then compare.

MORE HELP
See 004

Find the decimal equivalents, then compare.

$$\frac{-7}{8} = {}^{-}0.875$$

$$1 = 1.000$$

$$^{-}0.25 = {}^{-}0.250$$

$$^{-}0.875 < {}^{-}0.250 < 1.000$$

Or find the fraction equivalents, then compare.

$$\frac{-7}{8} = \frac{-7}{8}$$

$$1 = \frac{8}{8}$$

$$^{-}0.25 = {}^{-}\frac{25}{100} = \frac{-2}{8}$$

$$\frac{-7}{8} < \frac{-2}{8} < \frac{8}{8}$$

From least to greatest, the numbers are: $\frac{-7}{8}$, $^{-}0.25$, 1.

★ The stock dropped the most on Monday ($\frac{-7}{8}$ points).

Decimals and Fractions

Think of decimals as fractions with denominators that are powers of 10, such as 10, 100, or 1000. Then all you have to do is say the word name for the decimal aloud to get the fraction name.

Decimal	0.7	3.015
Word name	seven tenths	three and fifteen thousandths
Fraction	$\frac{7}{10}$	$3\frac{15}{1000}$

To write a decimal for a fraction, divide the numerator by the denominator. This works because a fraction is a way of showing division. The bar between the numerator and denominator of a fraction means *is divided by.*

EXAMPLE 1: Write $\frac{1}{4}$ as a decimal.

Think: $\frac{1}{4} = \frac{25}{100}$

$25 \div 100 = 0.25$

★ $\frac{1}{4} = 0.25$

MORE HELP
See 044–048

To write a repeating decimal as a fraction, use what you know about algebra.

EXAMPLE 2: Write $0.\overline{45}$ as a fraction in simplest form.

Since the 45 repeats, you don't know what denominator to use. Use the multiplication property of equality to help you get rid of the part of the decimal that repeats.

❶ Let the variable n equal the number. Multiply n and the number by a power of ten that gives you one complete repeat to the left of the decimal point.	❷ Subtract n from $100n$. You can do this even though the decimals repeat because the repeating digits match exactly and will do so infinitely.	❸ Solve the new equation and simplify the result.
$n = 0.\overline{45}$ $100n = 45.\overline{45}$	$100n = 45.454545\ldots$ $-n = 0.454545\ldots$ ——————— $99n = 45$	$99n = 45$ $n = \frac{45}{99}$ or $\frac{5}{11}$

★ $0.\overline{45}$ as a fraction in simplest form is $\frac{5}{11}$.

Irrational Numbers

A **rational number** is a number that can be represented by a ratio of two integers where the denominator does not equal zero. A rational number can also be expressed as a terminating or repeating decimal.

An **irrational number** is a number that cannot be represented by a ratio of two integers. Often we use special symbols like π and $\sqrt{3}$ to represent irrational numbers. That's because when we try to write irrational numbers as decimals, they don't terminate and they don't repeat the way rational numbers do.

MORE HELP
See 008

Irrational Numbers	Rational Numbers

$$\sqrt{3} \quad 2.6457513...$$
$$\pi$$
$$0.565566555666...$$

$$0.6\overline{13}$$
$$\frac{4}{7} \quad 9$$
$$^-46.2$$

Irrational Numbers on the Number Line

Since any irrational number can be approximated as a decimal, any irrational number can be approximately placed on a number line.

MORE HELP
See 016

$-\sqrt{3} \approx -1.7321 \quad 0.349216... \qquad \pi \approx 3.1416$

Every number on the number line is either irrational or rational. There ARE some numbers that cannot be shown on the number line, like $3\sqrt{^-1}$. Negative numbers have no square root, so, square roots of negative numbers can't be shown on the number line.

Beyond the Real Number System

Have you ever used the words *what if* to imagine situations that weren't real? *What if I could fly? What if I didn't ever have any homework?* This isn't the case with imaginary numbers. Imaginary numbers do exist. Despite their name, they are not really imaginary at all. The name dates back to when they were first introduced. Mathematicians wanted to take the square root of negative numbers. They thought they had used up all the *real-world numbers* already. But as time went on, mathematicians began to realize that i was a useful mathematical concept, especially when modeling electricity, but the term *imaginary* had already stuck.

MORE HELP
See 091–092

> $\sqrt{-3}$ must be imaginary. It sure doesn't seem real to me.

Any real number can be shown on a number line. Square roots of negative numbers can't be shown on a number line because two identical real factors, or roots, whether they're positive or negative, always have a positive product. Square roots of negative real numbers are called **imaginary numbers.**

Imaginary Numbers

An imaginary number is the square root of a negative real number. When you work with imaginary numbers you use the **imaginary unit** i, which is defined by $i = \sqrt{-1}$. This means $i^2 = \sqrt{-1} \cdot \sqrt{-1}$, or just plain -1.

MORE HELP
See 056

EXAMPLE: Simplify $\sqrt{-48}$

$$\sqrt{-48} = \sqrt{48 \cdot -1}$$
$$= \sqrt{16 \cdot 3 \cdot -1}$$
$$= \sqrt{16} \cdot \sqrt{3} \cdot \sqrt{-1}$$
$$= 4i\sqrt{3}$$

★ $\sqrt{-48} = 4i\sqrt{3}$

> You can write any imaginary number as a product of a real number and i.

Factors and Multiples

Think of two numbers that can be multiplied to make a third number. Each of the first two numbers is a **factor** of the third number. The third number is a **multiple** of each of the first two numbers.

$$7 \quad \times \quad 8 \quad = \quad 56$$

factor of 56   factor of 56   multiple of 7 and of 8

Even and Odd Numbers

Even numbers are divisible by two. You can divide any even number of things into two equal-size groups or into pairs, with no leftovers. Every even number is an integer with the digit 0, 2, 4, 6, or 8 in the ones (or units) place. Any even number can be represented by the expression $2n$.

Odd numbers are *not* divisible by two. When you divide an odd number of things into two equal-size groups or into pairs, there is always one item left over. Every odd number is an integer with the digit 1, 3, 5, 7, or 9 in its ones place. Any odd number can be represented by the expression $2n + 1$.

019

Factors

Pick a whole number (24). Now find two integers whose product is your number ($3 \cdot 8 = 24$). You've found two factors of your number.

CASE 1 When you factor a whole number, you're looking for whole-number factors.

EXAMPLE 1: Find all the factors of 18.

MORE HELP
See 182

$18 = 18 \cdot 1$

$18 = 9 \cdot 2$

$18 = 6 \cdot 3$

1, 2, 3, 6, 9, 18
18
18
18

★ The factors of 18 are 1, 2, 3, 6, 9, and 18.

CASE 2 When factoring an expression or expressions, any rational number or expression is an acceptable factor.

For example, $x^2 - 4$ can be factored into $(x - 2)(x + 2)$.

020

Common Factors

A group of two or more numbers may have some factors that are the same and some that are different. Factors that are the same for two or more numbers are their **common factors.**

EXAMPLE 1: Find the common factors of 24, 36, and 40.

Factors of 24: 1, 2, 3, 4, 6, 8, 12, 24

Factors of 36: 1, 2, 3, 4, 6, 9, 12, 18, 36

Factors of 40: 1, 2, 4, 5, 8, 10, 20, 40

★ The common factors of 24, 36, and 40 are 1, 2, and 4.

EXAMPLE 2: Find the common factors of $5x$, $11y$, and $13z$.

MORE HELP
See 023

Factors of $5x$: 1, 5, x

Factors of $11y$: 1, 11, y

Factors of $13z$: 1, 13, z

★ Since 5, 11, and 13 are prime numbers, their only common factor is 1. Since we don't know the values of x, y, and z, we can't assume that there are other common factors of $5x$, $11y$, and $13z$.

Greatest Common Factor

The greatest number that is a factor of two or more whole numbers is the **greatest common factor (GCF)** of the numbers. GCF is very useful in simplifying fractions and algebraic expressions. When looking for GCF or prime factors, you do not need to count 1 as a factor.

EXAMPLE 1: Find the GCF of $4x^3$, $12x^2$, and $8x$.

ONE WAY Use a Venn Diagram to help you understand the GCF.

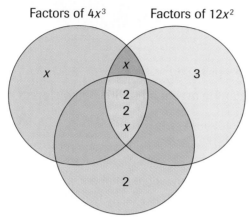

Factors of $4x^3$ Factors of $12x^2$

Factors of $8x$

MORE HELP
See 363

ANOTHER WAY Find the GCF of the terms by listing the prime factors of each expression. Identify the common factors.

Factors of $4x^3$ $= 2 \cdot 2 \cdot x \cdot x \cdot x$

Factors of $12x^2 = 2 \cdot 2 \cdot 3 \cdot x \cdot x$

Factors of $8x$ $= 2 \cdot 2 \cdot 2 \cdot x$

★ Either way, the greatest common factor (GCF) of $4x^3$, $12x^2$, *and* $8x$ is $2 \cdot 2 \cdot x$ or $4x$.

Factorials

Take any whole number and call it n.

Multiply all the positive integers from 1 through n.

$$1 \times 2 \times 3 \times ... \times (n - 1) \times n$$

This product is called **n factorial (n!)**.

Here is a strange mathematical definition.
0! is defined as 1. 1! is also defined as 1.

MORE ▶

EXAMPLE: The Supreme Court has nine justices. How many different ways could the justices line up for an official portrait?

Do we really have to try *every* possible arrangement before we choose one?

MORE HELP
See 317–318

To find the number of possible arrangements (**permutations**) for a number of items, you can find the factorial of the number of items.

$$9! = 9 \cdot 8 \cdot 7 \cdot 6 \cdot 5 \cdot 4 \cdot 3 \cdot 2 \cdot 1 = 362,880$$

★ Nine justices can be arranged in 362,880 different orders.

---

023   Prime Numbers

CASE 1 If you're talking about whole numbers, and most of the time you are, a **prime number** has exactly two different factors, 1 and itself.

For example, $17 = 1 \times 17$. Since there are no other whole-number factors of 17, we know that 17 is a prime number.

MORE HELP
See 024, 026

CASE 2 If you're talking about negative integers, a **negative prime number** has exactly four factors: 1, ⁻1, itself, and its opposite.

For example, $^-7 = {}^-1 \cdot 7$ and $^-7 = 1 \cdot {}^-7$. That is, the only factors of ⁻7 are 1, ⁻1, 7, and ⁻7. Since it has no other factors, ⁻7 is prime.

> **DID YOU KNOW** that any composite number can be written uniquely (except for the order of the terms) as a product of prime numbers?
>
> $93 = 31 \times 3$ $43,165 = 97 \times 89 \times 5$
>
> This is called the **Fundamental Theorem of Arithmetic** or the **Unique Factorization Theory**.

Composite Numbers

A **composite number** is a number that has more than two whole–number factors. Every whole number except 0 and 1 is either a composite number or a prime number.

MORE HELP
See 463

EXAMPLE: Tell whether 37 and 51 are prime or composite.

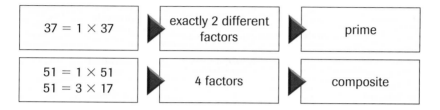

| 37 = 1 × 37 | exactly 2 different factors | prime |
| 51 = 1 × 51
51 = 3 × 17 | 4 factors | composite |

★ 37 has exactly two factors, 1 and 37, so it is a prime number. 51 has four factors, 1, 3, 17, and 51, so it is a composite number.

MATH ALERT One Is Not Prime

The number 1 is neither prime nor composite. The number 1 is not prime because it does not have exactly two different whole–number factors. It's not composite because it does not have more than two whole–number factors.

MORE HELP
See 023

The number ⁻1 is also neither prime nor composite. It does have exactly two factors, 1 and ⁻1, but, since it is negative, it must have exactly four factors in order to be prime.

DID YOU KNOW   that 2 is the only even prime?

Prime Factoring

When you separate a snack mix into different piles of raisins, peanuts, dates, etc., you are breaking it down into its component parts. The component parts of any number are its **prime factors**. A composite number written as the product of prime numbers is called the **prime factorization** of the number.

MORE ▶

EXAMPLE: Find the prime factorization of 260.

ONE WAY You can find the prime factorization of a number by making a factor tree.

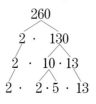

- Write the number you are factoring at the top of the tree.

- Choose any pair of factors as branches. If either of these is not prime, factor again.

- Keep factoring until you have a row of prime factors.

ANOTHER WAY You can find the prime factorization by using division.

2. Keep dividing each quotient by a prime number until the quotient is 1.

1. Divide 260 by a prime number.

$$13\overline{)13}^{1}$$
$$5\overline{)65}$$
$$2\overline{)130}$$
$$2\overline{)260}$$

> If you try a prime number and you get a remainder, that means your dividend is not divisible by that prime. Try a different prime number.

★ Either way, the prime factorization of 260 is $2 \cdot 2 \cdot 5 \cdot 13$, or $2^2 \cdot 5 \cdot 13$.

027 Multiples

Multiples of a number are the products of that number and any other whole number. The product of a number and zero is zero. Since this is always true, you don't usually need to write $0 \cdot n$ on your list of multiples. However, on a test, if you're not sure what's wanted, include it.

028 Least Common Multiple

The smallest positive integer (other than zero) that is a multiple of two or more whole numbers is called the **least common multiple (LCM)** of the numbers.

EXAMPLE: Find the LCM of 6, 12, and 18.

ONE WAY   Find the LCM of numbers by multiplying their common factors.

1 Find the prime factorization of each number and mark the common factors.	**2** Multiply the common factors and the extra factors.
6 = 2 · 3 12 = 2 · 2 · 3 18 = 2 · 3 · 3	2 · 3 · 2 · 3 = 36 common extra factors factors

ANOTHER WAY   Find the LCM of numbers by using prime factorization.

1 Find the prime factorization of each number.	**2** Write the prime factorization in exponential form.	**3** Multiply the highest powers of each prime factor.
6 = 2 · 3 12 = 2 · 2 · 3 18 = 2 · 3 · 3	6 = 2 · 3 12 = 2² · 3 18 = 2 · 3²	2² · 3² = 36 ↑ LCM

ANOTHER WAY   Use a Venn diagram to help you find the LCM.

1 Draw overlapping circles, one for each number. Write the factors for each number in its circle, placing common factors in the intersections.	**2** Multiply all the factors in the diagram.
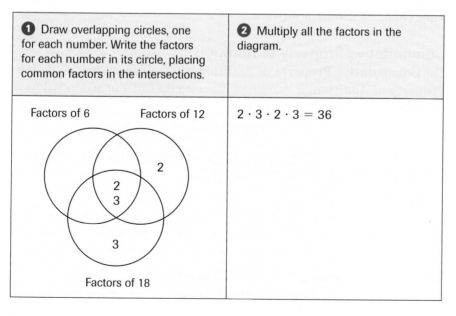	2 · 3 · 2 · 3 = 36

★ Any way you look at it, the LCM of 6, 12, and 18, is 36.

Properties of Real Numbers

The nice thing about numbers (unlike people) is that they behave the same way day in and day out. This makes them very predictable and reliable. They follow rules called **properties.**

030 Commutative Properties

Commutative sounds like *commute* which means *go back and forth.* Addition and multiplication are both commutative. That means they work the same either backward or forward.

031 Commutative Property of Addition

The **Commutative Property of Addition** is sometimes called the **Order Property of Addition.** It states that changing the order of addends does not change the sum. You can say $a + b = b + a$.

EXAMPLE: Add. $45 + 98 + 15 = $ ■

Use the Commutative Property to switch the order of 98 and 15. Then, you can use mental math to add 45 and 15.

$$45 + 98 + 15 = 45 + 15 + 98$$
$$= 60 + 98 = 158$$

★ $45 + 98 + 15 = 158$

032 Commutative Property of Multiplication

The **Commutative Property of Multiplication** is also called the **Order Property of Multiplication.** It states that changing the order of factors does not change the product. If a and b are any numbers, then $ab = ba$.

You can use this property to make it easier to multiply.

EXAMPLE: Multiply. $25x \cdot 212y \cdot 4z = $ ■

Use the Commutative Property to switch the order of $212y$ and $4z$. Then, you can use mental math to multiply $25x \cdot 4z$.

$$25x \cdot 212y \cdot 4z = 25x \cdot 4z \cdot 212y$$
$$= 100xz \cdot 212y$$
$$= 21{,}200xyz$$

★ $25x \cdot 212y \cdot 4z = 21{,}200xyz$

MATH ALERT Subtraction and Division Are Not Commutative!

033

Subtraction and division are not commutative. For example:

$6 - 4 = 2$, but $4 - 6 = {}^{-}2$; subtraction is not commutative.

$6 \div 4 = 1.5$, but $4 \div 6$ is about 0.67; division is not commutative.

CASE 1 You can rewrite a subtraction expression as addition and then use the Commutative Property of Addition.

EXAMPLE 1: Rewrite $15 - 3$ as a commutative expression.

Subtracting 3 is the same as adding $^{-}3$, so $15 + {}^{-}3$ has the same result as $15 - 3$.

MORE HELP
See 079,
082–083

★ $15 - 3$ is equivalent to $15 + {}^{-}3$, which is commutative.

CASE 2 You can also rewrite a division expression as multiplication and then use the Commutative Property of Multiplication.

EXAMPLE 2: Rewrite $15 \div 3$ as a commutative expression.

Dividing by 3 is the same as multiplying by $\frac{1}{3}$, so $15 \times \frac{1}{3}$ has the same result as $15 \div 3$.

MORE HELP
See 086,
091–092

★ $15 \div 3$ is equivalent to $15 \times \frac{1}{3}$, which is commutative.

Associative Properties

You *associate* with friends in groups. The **Associative Properties** are about ways you can group addends and factors. These properties state that you can change the grouping of addends or factors without changing the result.

Associative Property of Addition

The **Associative Property of Addition** states that changing the grouping of addends does not change the sum.

$$(a + b) + c = a + (b + c)$$

The grouping symbols tell you to add in a different order.

EXAMPLE: Add. $146x + 63x + 27x = \blacksquare$

Use the Associative Property to change the grouping so you can use mental math.

$146x + 63x + 27x = 146x + (63x + 27x)$

$\qquad\qquad\qquad = 146x + 90x$

$\qquad\qquad\qquad = 236x$

The 63x associates first with the 146x, then the 27x.

★ $146x + 63x + 27x = 236x$

Associative Property of Multiplication

The **Associative Property of Multiplication** states that changing the grouping of factors does not change the product.

$$(a \cdot b) \cdot c = a \cdot (b \cdot c)$$

The grouping symbols tell you to multiply in a different order.

EXAMPLE: Multiply. $79x \cdot 250y \cdot 4z$

Use the Associative Property to change the grouping so you can use mental math.

$79x \cdot 250y \cdot 4z = 79x \cdot (250y \cdot 4z)$

$\qquad\qquad\qquad = 79x \cdot 1000yz$

$\qquad\qquad\qquad = 79{,}000xyz$

★ $79x \cdot 250y \cdot 4z = 79{,}000xyz$

Distinctive Property

Distributive Property

When you *distribute* something, you separate it into portions. The Distributive Property lets you separate an operation into parts.

The **Distributive Property** states that for any numbers a, b, and c:

$$a \cdot (b + c) = (ab) + (ac)$$

$$a \cdot (b - c) = (ab) - (ac)$$

You can use this property to help you multiply in your head.

EXAMPLE 1: Find the number of one-foot square ceramic tiles needed to tile a terrace that measures 9 feet by 23 feet.

MORE HELP
See 464

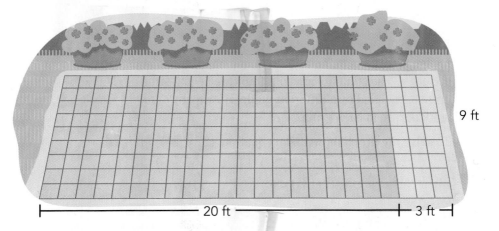

9 ft

20 ft ——— 3 ft

To solve this problem, you need to multiply. It's easy to do this mentally if you think of 23 as $20 + 3$.

$9 \cdot 23 = 9 \cdot (20 + 3)$

$\quad = (9 \cdot 20) + (9 \cdot 3)$

$\quad = 180 + 27$

$\quad = 207$

> Use the Distributive Property to multiply 9 by 23.

★ 207 one-foot square tiles are needed to tile the terrace.

EXAMPLE 2: Multiply. $2(2x + 5)$

$2(2x + 5) = (2 \cdot 2x) + (2 \cdot 5)$

$\quad = 4x + 10$

> Use the Distributive Property. Multiply both terms inside the parentheses by 2.

★ $2(2x + 5) = 4x + 10$

MORE HELP
See 041,
085–087,
091–092

Making Division Distributive

You can use the Distributive Property to help you with division.
First, rewrite the division problem as multiplication, and then use the distributive property.

$$(b + c) \div a = (b + c) \cdot \frac{1}{a}$$
$$= \frac{1}{a}(b + c)$$

> To rewrite division as multiplication, use reciprocals.
> $6 \div 2$ has the same result as $6 \div \frac{2}{1}$, or $6 \times \frac{1}{2}$.

EXAMPLE: Two ninth-grade art classes go to the museum. There are 27 students in one class and 24 in the other. The students are split into three equal-sized groups, each led by a different guide. How many students are in each group?

To solve the problem, write an equation. $(27 + 24) \div 3 = \blacksquare$

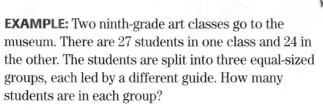

$$(27 + 24) \div 3 = (27 + 24) \cdot \frac{1}{3}$$
$$= \frac{1}{3}(27 + 24)$$
$$= \frac{27}{3} + \frac{24}{3}$$
$$= 9 + 8$$
$$= 17$$

> To see that this works, you can compute without using the Distributive Property:
> $(27 + 24) \div 3$
> $= 51 \div 3$
> $= 17$

★ There are 17 students in each group.

Identity Elements

An identity element is a number that combines with another number (let's call it x), in any order, without changing x. These properties are really common sense.

CASE 1 The Identity Element for Addition is 0 because $a + 0 = a$ and $0 + a = a$.

$4 + 0 = 4$
$0 + 4 = 4$

CASE 2 The Identity Element for Multiplication is 1 because $a \cdot 1 = a$ and $1 \cdot a = a$.

$4 \cdot 1 = 4$
$1 \cdot 4 = 4$

MATH ALERT No Identity Elements for Subtraction and Division

Is $a - 0$ always a? Yes. $1 - 0 = 1, 2 - 0 = 2, 3 - 0 = 3, ...$

Is $0 - a$ always a? No. For example, $0 - 1 = {}^-1$.

Since $0 - a$ is not always a, you can't say that zero is an identity element for subtraction.

Is $a \div 1$ always a? Yes. $1 \div 1 = 1, 2 \div 1 = 2, 3 \div 1 = 3, ...$

Is $1 \div a$ always a? No. For example, $1 \div 5 = \frac{1}{5}$.

Since $1 \div a$ is not always a, you can't say that one is an identity element for division.

Inverse Elements

Inverse elements are numbers that combine with other numbers, in any order, and result in the identity elements of zero or one.

MORE HELP
See 079–083

CASE 1 Additive Inverse

When a number is added to its **additive inverse**, the sum is always zero. Additive inverses are also called **opposites**.

7 and ${}^-7$ are additive inverses.	$7 + {}^-7 = 0$
$\frac{9}{16}$ and $\frac{{}^-9}{16}$ are additive inverses.	$\frac{9}{16} + \frac{{}^-9}{16} = 0$

CASE 2 Multiplicative Inverse

When a number is multiplied by its **multiplicative inverse**, the product is always one. Multiplicative inverses are usually called **reciprocals**. Zero is the only number with no multiplicative inverse.

7 and $\frac{1}{7}$ are reciprocals.	$7 \cdot \frac{1}{7} = 1$
${}^-52.19$ and $\frac{{}^-1}{52.19}$ are reciprocals.	${}^-52.19 \cdot \frac{{}^-1}{52.19} = 1$
0.5 and 2 are reciprocals.	$0.5 \cdot 2 = 1$

042 | Zero Property

The **Zero Property of Multiplication** states that any number multiplied by zero is still zero; $a \cdot 0 = 0$ and $0 \cdot a = 0$, or $7 \cdot 0 = 0$ and $0 \cdot 7 = 0$.

Conversely, if $ab = 0$, then either a or b or both must equal 0.

043 | MATH ALERT Division by Zero is Undefined

To understand why mathematicians say that division by zero is undefined, think about how division is related to multiplication.

EXAMPLE: Try to divide 379 by 0.

To divide, think of related equations.

$379 \div 0 = \blacksquare$

$\dfrac{379}{0} = \blacksquare$

$379 = 0 \cdot \blacksquare$

You can't find a replacement for $\blacksquare$ because any number multiplied by zero is zero! So, mathematicians say that division by zero is undefined.

044 | Equality Properties

If you have two identical skateboards and you put a decal on one of them, they're not identical anymore. If you *want* them to be identical, you must put an identical decal in the same place on the other skateboard.

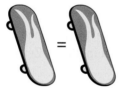 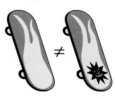 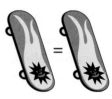

The **equality properties** let you compute with expressions on both sides of an equation. You can do any operation on the expression on one side of the equals sign. But, to keep the equation true, you must balance it by performing the same operation with the same number or expression on the other side of the equals sign.

Addition Property of Equality

If you and a friend had the same amount of money and each of you received $5, you'd still have the same amount of money as your friend.

The **Addition Property of Equality** states that if $a = b$, then $a + c = b + c$. If you add equal to equal you get equal quantities.

To understand this property, think of an equation as a scale that is balanced.

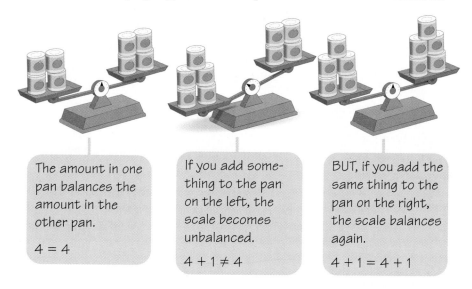

The amount in one pan balances the amount in the other pan.	If you add something to the pan on the left, the scale becomes unbalanced.	BUT, if you add the same thing to the pan on the right, the scale balances again.
$4 = 4$	$4 + 1 \neq 4$	$4 + 1 = 4 + 1$

You can also subtract the same number from both sides of an equation without putting it out of balance.

If $a = b$, then $a - c = b - c$.

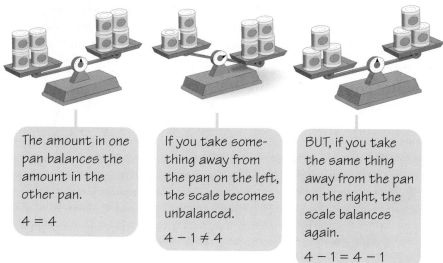

The amount in one pan balances the amount in the other pan.	If you take something away from the pan on the left, the scale becomes unbalanced.	BUT, if you take the same thing away from the pan on the right, the scale balances again.
$4 = 4$	$4 - 1 \neq 4$	$4 - 1 = 4 - 1$

046

Multiplication Property of Equality

The **Multiplication Property of Equality** states that if $a = b$, then $ac = bc$. To understand this property, think of an equation as a scale that is balanced.

MORE HELP
See 041

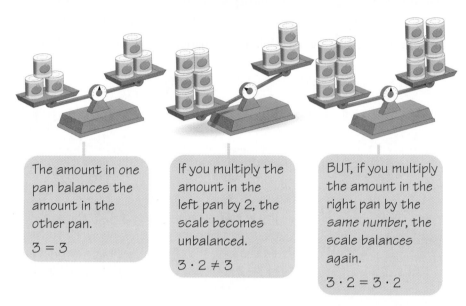

The amount in one pan balances the amount in the other pan.

$3 = 3$

If you multiply the amount in the left pan by 2, the scale becomes unbalanced.

$3 \cdot 2 \neq 3$

BUT, if you multiply the amount in the right pan by the same number, the scale balances again.

$3 \cdot 2 = 3 \cdot 2$

You can also raise to a power, take a root, or divide both sides of an equation by the same number without putting it out of balance.

You can always make a scale balance by putting exactly the same amount in both pans.

047

Reflexive Property of Equality

Whether or not you realize it, you already know the **Reflexive Property of Equality.** This property states that any real number is equal to itself.

$a = a$ and $2.6a = 2.6a$

Symmetric Property of Equality

The **Symmetric Property of Equality** states that, for any real numbers a and b, if $a = b$, then $b = a$. You may think we didn't need to state this. But, in mathematical proofs, you need to be able to say why you do every step.

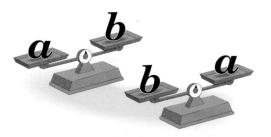

If you switch the contents of the pans in a balanced scale, the scale still balances.

Transitive Relation

The **transitive relation** states that, if $a = b$ and $a = c$, then $b = c$.

If something balances each of two other things, then those two things must balance each other.

Density Property

The **Density Property** states that between every two rational numbers there is another rational number.

MORE HELP
See 003

To understand the Density Property, think of a number line. No matter how densely packed the number line is, there are always more numbers between the numbers that are already shown.

Multiply a number, even a small one like three, by itself over and over and the product gets very large very fast. A few bacteria can grow into a colony of billions in a matter of hours by doubling every 20 minutes. Mathematicians use shortcuts like powers, roots, and logarithms to describe such situations.

A **power** is a number with a base and an exponent, such as 6^4. When you use an exponent, the **base** is a repeated factor. The **exponent** tells how many times the base is used as a factor.

$$6 \cdot 6 \cdot 6 \cdot 6 = 6^4 \leftarrow \text{exponent}$$

$$\uparrow$$

$$\text{base}$$

Write: 6^4

Say: *six to the fourth power* or *the fourth power of six*

MORE HELP
See 056, 059, 066

When you understand powers, you also understand roots. A **root** is the inverse of a power. The square root is one of a number's two equal factors. The cube root is one of a number's three equal factors. $\sqrt[4]{16} = 2$ because $2^4 = 16$.

Patterns in Exponents _____

When you work with exponents with positive bases, you can see patterns. You can use these patterns to understand exponents of 1 and zero, as well as negative exponents.

Look at the pattern at the right. As you can see, when the base is 3, each time you increase the exponent by 1, the product is 3 times as great. Each time you decrease the exponent by 1, the value is $\frac{1}{3}$ as great.

Notice that the pattern shows that $3^0 = 1$. There is an agreement among mathematicians that any number (except zero) to the zero power is equal to one.

Negative exponents turn integers into fractions. For any nonzero number b and integer n, $b^{-n} = \frac{1}{b^n}$.

$$3^5 = 3 \cdot 3 \cdot 3 \cdot 3 \cdot 3 = 243$$

$\times 3 \uparrow \qquad \times \frac{1}{3} \downarrow$

$$3^4 = 3 \cdot 3 \cdot 3 \cdot 3 = 81$$

$\times 3 \uparrow \qquad \times \frac{1}{3} \downarrow$

$$3^3 = 3 \cdot 3 \cdot 3 = 27$$

$\times 3 \uparrow \qquad \times \frac{1}{3} \downarrow$

$$3^2 = 3 \cdot 3 = 9$$

$\times 3 \uparrow \qquad \times \frac{1}{3} \downarrow$

$$3^1 = 3 = 3$$

$\times 3 \uparrow \qquad \times \frac{1}{3} \downarrow$

$$3^0 = 1 = 1$$

$\times 3 \uparrow \qquad \times \frac{1}{3} \downarrow$

$$3^{-1} = \frac{1}{3} = \frac{1}{3}$$

$\times 3 \uparrow \qquad \times \frac{1}{3} \downarrow$

$$3^{-2} = \frac{1}{3 \cdot 3} = \frac{1}{9}$$

The pattern formed by powers of 10 is the basis of our decimal system. In the decimal (or base ten) system, the value of each place is 10 times the value of the place to its right, and $\frac{1}{10}$ of the value to the place to its left. If n is a digit, then its value is shown in the table below.

Thousands	Hundreds	Tens	Ones (Units)	Tenths	Hundredths	Thousandths
$n \cdot 1000$	$n \cdot 100$	$n \cdot 10$	$n \cdot 1$	$n \cdot 0.1$	$n \cdot 0.01$	$n \cdot 0.001$
$n \cdot 10^3$	$n \cdot 10^2$	$n \cdot 10^1$	$n \cdot 10^0$	$n \cdot 10^{-1}$	$n \cdot 10^{-2}$	$n \cdot 10^{-3}$

053

Perfect Powers

Any number that is the product of repeated whole-number factors is a **perfect power.**

Perfect Powers	**Not Perfect Powers**

$$81 = 9^2$$

So, 81 is a **perfect square.**

$$64 = 4^3$$

So, 64 is a **perfect cube.**

$$16 = 2^4$$

So, 16 is a **perfect fourth power.**

$$\sqrt{82} \approx 9.055$$

So, 82 is not a perfect square.

$$\sqrt[3]{65} \approx 4.021$$

So, 65 is not a perfect cube.

$$\sqrt[4]{17} \approx 2.031$$

So, 17 is not a perfect fourth power.

054

Irrational Roots

MORE HELP
See 006–008, 013

A whole number that is not a perfect square has an **irrational** square root. This means that the square root cannot be represented by a ratio of integers. It is represented by a non-repeating, non–terminating decimal.

When a root is irrational, a table or a calculator will give you an approximate value. When you calculate with a root that is not perfect, your answer will also be approximate.

$\sqrt{4} = 2$ perfect square

$\sqrt{5} = 2.236067... \approx 2.236$ ⎫

$\sqrt{6} = 2.449489... \approx 2.449$ ⎬ irrational

$\sqrt{7} = 2.645751... \approx 2.646$ ⎪ roots

$\sqrt{8} = 2.828427... \approx 2.828$ ⎭

$\sqrt{9} = 3$ perfect square

"…" means that the decimal does not end.

Using a Table of Powers and Roots

You can use a table to find powers and roots. This table shows squares, square roots, cubes, and cube roots for the numbers 1 through 10, approximate to the thousandths place.

MORE HELP
See 056, 059, 461

n	n^2	$\sqrt{n}$	n^3	$\sqrt[3]{n}$
1	1	1.000	1	1.000
2	4	1.414	8	1.260
3	9	1.732	27	1.442
4	16	2.000	64	1.587
5	25	2.236	125	1.710
6	36	2.449	216	1.817
7	49	2.646	343	1.913
8	64	2.828	512	2.000
9	81	3.000	729	2.080
10	100	3.162	1000	2.154

EXAMPLE 1: Find the volume of this crate.

To find the volume, you need to find 9^3. So, look for the number 9 in the column labeled n. Then, move along the row to find the number in the column labeled n^3.

★ The volume of the crate is 729 ft³.

Write: 729 ft³
Say: *seven hundred twenty–nine cubic feet*

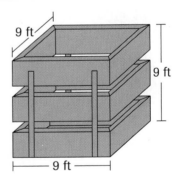

9 ft

9 ft

9 ft

EXAMPLE 2: Find $\sqrt{6}$.

Find the number 6 in the column labeled n. Move along the row to find the number in the column labeled $\sqrt{n}$.

★ $\sqrt{6} \approx 2.449$

MORE HELP
See 053, 054

Remember, non-perfect squares like 6 and non-perfect cubes like 7 have irrational roots. These roots are usually rounded to the thousandths place. $\sqrt{6} \approx 2.449$ and $\sqrt[3]{7} \approx 1.913$.

056

MORE HELP
See 055, 057, 064

Squares and Square Roots

When a number is multiplied by itself, the product is the square of the number. A square room with sides of 12 feet has an area of 144 square feet (ft²).

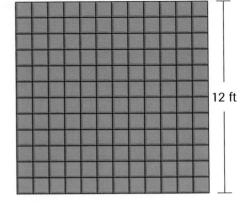

Write: $12^2 = 144$
Say: *Twelve squared equals one hundred forty-four* or *one hundred forty-four is the square of twelve.*

When you look for a number that you can multiply by itself to get a product, you are looking for the **square root** of the product.

Write: $\sqrt{144} = 12$
Say: *The square root of one hundred forty-four equals twelve.*

Note, that $\sqrt{}$ means the principal square root of a number, which is the positive root. However, each positive number also has a negative square root.

057

MATH ALERT Square Roots Can Be Negative

MORE HELP
See 059–060, 086, 092

If you multiply two positive numbers, you get a positive product. But, if you multiply two *negative* numbers you *also* get a positive product.

$$8 \cdot 8 = 64 \qquad {}^-8 \cdot {}^-8 = 64$$

This means that ⁻8 is also a square root of 64. However, $\sqrt{}$ means **the principal square root**, which is the positive root. If you're asked to find x when $\sqrt{64} = x$, then $x = 8$. If you're asked to find x when $64 = x^2$, then $x = \pm8$.

Read this symbol as *plus or minus.*

MATH ALERT Be Careful When Squaring an Expression

Be careful when an exponent appears in a variable expression.

MORE HELP
See 068–070, 464

CASE 1 Sometimes only the variable is squared.

EXAMPLE 1: In $3a^2$, only a is squared.

area of three identical squares $= a^2 + a^2 + a^2$
$$= 3a^2$$

Write: $3a^2$
Say: *three a squared* or *three times the quantity a squared*

CASE 2 Sometimes the whole expression is squared.

EXAMPLE 2: In $(3a)^2$, both the 3 and a are squared.

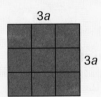

area of one large square $= 3a \cdot 3a$
$$= (3a)^2$$
$$= 3^2 \cdot a^2$$
$$= 9a^2$$

If you want to square a whole expression, use grouping symbols.

Write: $(3a)^2$
Say: *the quantity three a squared*

059 Cubes and Cube Roots

The product of three equal factors is the **cube** of the number. A cube with edges of 4 meters has a volume of 4 m · 4 m · 4m, or 64 m³.

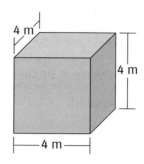

Write: $4^3 = 64$

Say: *Four cubed equals sixty-four* or *sixty-four is the cube of four.*

MORE HELP
See 464

When three equal factors are multiplied to make a product, each equal factor is the **cube root** of the product.

Write: $\sqrt[3]{64} = 4$

Say: *The cube root of sixty-four equals four.*

060 MATH ALERT **Watch the Signs on Cube Roots**

Whenever there is an even number of identical factors, the product will be positive because every pair of identical factors has a positive product. However, when there is an odd number of identical factors, the product will have the same sign as the factors. So, while a negative square root is imaginary, a negative cube root is quite possible.

MORE HELP
See 016, 018

$$5 \cdot 5 = 25 \qquad \text{positive} \cdot \text{positive} = \text{positive}$$

$$^-5 \cdot {}^-5 = 25 \qquad \text{negative} \cdot \text{negative} = \text{positive}$$

$$5 \cdot 5 \cdot 5 = 125 \qquad \text{positive} \cdot \text{positive} \cdot \text{positive} = \text{positive}$$

$$^-5 \cdot {}^-5 \cdot {}^-5 = {}^-125 \quad \text{negative} \cdot \text{negative} \cdot \text{negative} = \text{negative}$$

Negative Numbers in Exponential Expressions _____

Be careful when you work with negative bases and exponents. When
in doubt as to how to show exactly what you mean, use parentheses.

MORE HELP
See 052, 086,
091–092

n^{-a}	$\neq$	$(^-n)^a$	$\neq$	$^-(n^a)$
$3^{-2} = \dfrac{1}{3 \cdot 3}$ $= \dfrac{1}{9}$		$(^-3)^2 = {}^-3 \cdot {}^-3$ $= 9$		$^-(3^2) = {}^-(3 \cdot 3)$ $= {}^-9$

Powers of Fractions _____

Powers of fractions work the same way as powers of integers. The
exponent tells how many times the base is used as a factor.

$$\left(\dfrac{3}{5}\right)^4 \quad \leftarrow \text{exponent}$$
$$\qquad\quad \leftarrow \text{base}$$

Here are two ways to evaluate powers of fractions.

EXAMPLE: Evaluate $\left(\frac{3}{5}\right)^4$.

ONE WAY Multiply the fractions.

MORE HELP
See 012

$$\left(\dfrac{3}{5}\right)^4 = \dfrac{3}{5} \cdot \dfrac{3}{5} \cdot \dfrac{3}{5} \cdot \dfrac{3}{5}$$

$$= \dfrac{81}{625}$$

ANOTHER WAY Write the fraction as a terminating decimal and then multiply.

$$\left(\dfrac{3}{5}\right)^4 = (0.6)^4$$

$$= 0.1296$$

$$\bigstar \left(\dfrac{3}{5}\right)^4 = \dfrac{81}{625} \text{ or } 0.1296.$$

Be careful when you work with powers within fractions.

$\dfrac{x^n}{y}$	$\neq$	$\left(\dfrac{x}{y}\right)^n$	$\neq$	$\dfrac{x}{y^n}$
$\dfrac{3^2}{4} = \dfrac{3 \cdot 3}{4}$ $= \dfrac{9}{4}$		$\left(\dfrac{3}{4}\right)^2 = \dfrac{3}{4} \cdot \dfrac{3}{4}$ $= \dfrac{9}{16}$		$\dfrac{3}{4^2} = \dfrac{3}{4 \cdot 4}$ $= \dfrac{3}{16}$

Fractional Exponents

To understand fractional exponents, think of the base as a product. The denominator of the exponent gives the number of times some factor is used to make that base. Find that factor and raise it to the power in the numerator of the exponent.

MORE HELP
See 051, 052

$$\left(\sqrt[3]{64}\right)^2 = 64^{\frac{2}{3}} \quad \begin{array}{l} \leftarrow \text{exponent} \\ \leftarrow \text{index} \end{array}$$

base

Write: $64^{\frac{2}{3}}$

Say: *sixty-four to the two-thirds power*

EXAMPLE: Evaluate $64^{\frac{2}{3}}$.

ONE WAY

❶ Look at the denominator of the exponent to find the number of factors.	❷ Now look at the numerator of the exponent and raise the factor you found in step 1 to that power.
The denominator of the exponent is 3. So, a factor is used 3 times to make 64. That factor is 4 ⟶ 4 · 4 · 4 = 64	The numerator of the exponent is 2. $4^2 = 16$

ANOTHER WAY Write the expression as a root raised to a power, then evaluate.

$$64^{\frac{2}{3}} = \left(\sqrt[3]{64}\right)^2$$
$$= (4)^2$$
$$= 16$$

In $64^{\frac{2}{3}}$, the exponent's denominator, 3, shows that you are taking the third root, or cube root, of 64. The numerator, 2, shows that you are raising that cube root to the second power.

★ Either way, $64^{\frac{2}{3}} = 16$.

Using a Calculator to Find Powers and Roots

Most calculators have a key for squares $\boxed{x^2}$ and square roots $\boxed{\sqrt{x}}$. You can also use a calculator to evaluate other powers and roots. Remember, different calculators mark their keys differently, so be sure to read the instructions for your calculator if you can't find the keys shown here.

EXAMPLE 1: Evaluate 3^5.

$\boxed{3}\ \boxed{y^x}\ \boxed{5}\ \boxed{=}\qquad 243.$

↑
power key

★ $3^5 = 243$

EXAMPLE 2: Evaluate 4^{-3}.

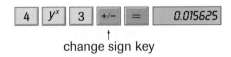

$\boxed{4}\ \boxed{y^x}\ \boxed{3}\ \boxed{+/-}\ \boxed{=}\qquad 0.015625$

↑
change sign key

★ $4^{-3} = 0.015625$

EXAMPLE 3: Evaluate $256^{\frac{3}{4}}$.

$\boxed{2}\ \boxed{5}\ \boxed{6}\ \boxed{y^x}\ \boxed{(}\ \boxed{3}\ \boxed{\div}\ \boxed{4}\ \boxed{)}\qquad 0.75 \quad \boxed{=}\qquad 64.$

MORE HELP
See 063

★ $256^{\frac{3}{4}} = 64$

There are a few ways you can use a calculator to find roots.

EXAMPLE 4: Find $\sqrt[3]{343}$.

ONE WAY You can use the $\boxed{\sqrt[x]{y}}$ key. Press:

$\boxed{3}\ \boxed{4}\ \boxed{3}\ \boxed{\sqrt[x]{y}}\ \boxed{3}\ \boxed{=}\qquad 7.$

ANOTHER WAY Since $\sqrt[3]{343} = 343^{\frac{1}{3}}$, you can press

$\boxed{3}\ \boxed{4}\ \boxed{3}\ \boxed{y^x}\ \boxed{(}\ \boxed{1}\ \boxed{\div}\ \boxed{3}\ \boxed{)}\quad 0.3333333\ \boxed{=}\qquad 7.$

★ The cube root of 343 is 7.

Scientific Notation

Scientists often work with very large or very small numbers. Using zeros to keep track of place value can be tedious with a number like 6,020,000,000,000,000,000,000,000 or 0.000000264. **Scientific notation** uses exponents to make it easier to work with such numbers.

To write a number in scientific notation, write it as a product of two factors:

a decimal greater than or equal to 1 but less than 10 $\times$ a power of 10

Scientific Notation	**Not Scientific Notation**
$3.4 \cdot 10^9$	$3,400,000,000$
$2.75 \cdot 10^5$	$27,500 \cdot 10^2$
$7 \cdot 10^3$	0.00007^2

EXAMPLE 1: In 1998, the United States minted more than 1,860,000,000 dimes. Write this number in scientific notation. *Source: www.usmint.gov*

❶ Move the decimal point to get a number that is greater than or equal to 1 but less than 10. Count how many places you move the decimal point to the left.	❷ For the power of 10, use the number of places that the decimal point moved. If the decimal point moved left, the exponent is positive. If it moved right, the exponent is negative.
1,860,000,000 Move the decimal point 9 places to the left. $1 \leq 1.860000000 < 10$	$1,860,000,000 = 1.86 \cdot 10^9$ The decimal point moved 9 places left.

★ $1,860,000,000 = 1.86 \cdot 10^9$

A very large number requires a positive power of 10. A very small number requires a negative power of 10. This power does not tell you the number of zeros in your result. It tells you the number of places the decimal point moves.

EXAMPLE 2: The width of a human hair can be up to 0.000075 meter. Write this number in scientific notation. *Source: The Sizesaurus*

❶ Move the decimal point so that the number is a number that is greater than or equal to 1 but less than 10. Count how many places you move the decimal point to the right.	❷ If the decimal point moved left, the exponent is positive. If it moved right, the exponent is negative.
0.000075 $1 \leq 7.5 < 10$ Move the decimal point 5 places to the right.	$0.000075 = 7.5 \cdot 10^{-5}$ The decimal point moved 5 places right.

★ $0.000075 = 7.5 \cdot 10^{-5}$

Logarithms

Think of a logarithm as an exponent. A **common logarithm** (or **log**) is just an exponent of 10. If someone asks for the log of 10,000, they're asking for the exponent that would go with 10 to give a value of 10,000. In other words, 10 raised to what power equals to 10,000? The answer is 4.

Write: $\log 10{,}000 = 4$
Say: *The log of ten thousand is four.*

> The log of 10,000 is 4 because 10^4 is 10,000.

Sometimes logarithms indicate exponents of other numbers (called **bases**). If someone asks for the log to the base 2 of 32, they're asking for the exponent that would go with 2 to give a value of 32. In other words, 2 raised to what power equals 32? The answer is 5.

Write: $\log_2 32 = 5$
Say: *The log to the base two of thirty-two is five* or *the log of thiry-two to the base two is five.*

> The log to the base 2 of 32 is 5 because 2^5 is 32.

Any equation in exponential form can also be written with logarithms because if $\log_b a = x$, then $a = b^x$.

Exponential Form	Logarithmic Form
$4^2 = 16$	$\log_4 16 = 2$
$10^6 = 1{,}000{,}000$	$\log 1{,}000{,}000 = 6$
$2^{-5} = \frac{1}{32}$	$\log_2 \frac{1}{32} = -5$

Estimating and Computing with Real Numbers

"Reading and writing, of course, to begin with," the Mock Turtle replied, "and different branches of Arithmetic—Ambition, Distraction, Uglification, and Derision."

The Mock Turtle, when asked about what he took in school. In *Alice's Adventures in Wonderland* by Lewis Carroll (1865)

You may think that computation is a lot of hard work. But then again, many people think that putting dishes into a dishwasher or drilling holes with a power drill is a lot of hard work. We're so accustomed to modern conveniences that we forget how much harder things would be without them. Likewise, we don't think about how tedious things would be without computation. Imagine a stadium with 500 sections, with 12 rows of 15 seats in each section. It sure is a lot easier to multiply $500(12 \cdot 15)$ than to count every single one of those 90,000 seats!

Order of Operations

MORE HELP
See 100

Order of operations is exactly what you'd expect it to be. It tells you the order in which you perform operations in an expression.

EXAMPLE: Evaluate $3 + 6 \div a \cdot 2$, for $a = 3$.

If you worked in order from left to right, you'd do this.	But if you followed the rules for order of operations, you'd do this.
$3 + 6 \div 3 \times 2$ $\quad\downarrow$ $9 \quad \div 3 \times 2$ $\qquad\downarrow$ $3 \quad \times 2 = 6$	$3 + 6 \div 3 \times 2$ $\qquad\downarrow$ $3 + \quad 2 \quad \times 2$ $\qquad\qquad\downarrow$ $3 + \qquad 4 = 7$

★ $3 + 6 \div a \cdot 2$, when $a = 3$, is 7.

Rules for Order of Operations

To make sure that everyone gets the same answer when calculating or evaluating an algebraic expression, we have rules called **order of operations**.

1. Do the operations with grouping symbols: $( )$, $[ ]$, $\frac{x}{y}$
2. Do powers or roots: x^2 or $\sqrt{x}$
3. Multiply or divide in order from left to right: $\times$ or $\div$
4. Add or subtract from left to right: $+$ or $-$

This silly sentence can help you remember order of operations: George's parachute really makes diving almost safe.

EXAMPLE: Simplify $4^2 - 8 \times (6 - 6)$.

To simplify:	$4^2 - 8 \times (6 - 6)$
Simplify within parentheses.	$= 4^2 - 8 \times 0$
Evaluate the exponent.	$= 16 - 8 \times 0$
Multiply or divide left to right.	$= 16 - 0$
Add or subtract left to right.	$= 16$

★ $4^2 - 8 \times (6 - 6) = 16$

Specifying a Different Order of Operations ⎯⎯⎯⎯⎯

When you want calculations to be done in a special order, you can use grouping symbols to say *do this operation first!*

CASE 1 You can use parentheses to group terms.

MORE HELP
See 037, 052

EXAMPLE 1: Show the product of 7 and $y^3 - 8$.

Simply writing $7y^3 - 8$ will not work because the order of operations says that $7y^3 - 8$ means to multiply y^3 by 7, then subtract 8. To show that 8 is subtracted from y^3 first, use parentheses: $7(y^3 - 8)$.

★ $7(y^3 - 8)$

EXAMPLE 2: Evaluate $7(y^3 - 8)$ for $y = 2$.

To evaluate:	$7(y^3 - 8)$
Substitute 2 for y.	$= 7(2^3 - 8)$
Simplify within parentheses:	
Evaluate 2^3.	$= 7(8 - 8)$
Subtract.	$= 7(0)$
Multiply.	$= 0$

CASE 2 You can use nested parentheses (( )), or combinations of parentheses, brackets [ ], and braces { } to group terms. Inner operations get done first, then those in outer grouping symbols.

EXAMPLE 3: Show that $y^3(z - 6) - 5$ is to be multiplied by 9.

★ $9[y^3(z - 6) - 5]$

EXAMPLE 4: Evaluate $9[y^3(z - 6) - 5]$ for $y = 2$ and $z = 8$.

To evaluate:	$9[y^3(z - 6) - 5]$
Substitute.	$= 9[2^3(8 - 6) - 5]$
Simplify within parentheses.	$= 9[2^3(2) - 5]$
Simplify with brackets:	
Evaluate 2^3.	$= 9[8(2) - 5]$
Multiply.	$= 9[16 - 5]$
Subtract.	$= 9[11]$
Multiply.	$= 99$

MORE ▶

CASE 3 Sometimes, the fraction bar is an easy way to show grouping. Since the fraction bar can show division, it almost always replaces the division symbol in algebraic expressions.

EXAMPLE 5: Show that $g^2 + 11$ is to be divided by $6 - g$.

★ $\dfrac{g^2 + 11}{6 - g}$ If you were entering this expression into a calculator, you would need to put parentheses around the numerator and around the denominator.

EXAMPLE 6: Evaluate $\dfrac{g^2 + 11}{6 - g}$ for $g = 4$.

To evaluate:	$\dfrac{g^2 + 11}{6 - g}$
Substitute.	$= \dfrac{4^2 + 11}{6 - 4}$
Evaluate the numerator:	
Evaluate 4^2, then add.	$= \dfrac{16 + 11}{6 - 4} = \dfrac{27}{6 - 4}$
Evaluate the denominator:	
Subtract and simplify.	$= \dfrac{27}{2} = 13\frac{1}{2}$

Order of Operations on the Calculator

Some calculators automatically follow the rules for order of operations. This is known as the **algebraic ordering system** (AOS). Other calculators perform operations in the order that you enter them, even if that order does not follow the rules for order of operations. Does your calculator automatically follow order of operations? Check, using this expression: $16 + 4 \div 2^2$.

If your display shows ⬜ *17.* your calculator follows the rules for order of operations. If it shows ⬜ *100.* it doesn't. If your calculator does not follow the rules for order of operations, you can enter calculations so they are done in the correct order.

When you enter ⬚ **(**, the calculator waits until you enter **)** before it calculates what's between these grouping symbols.

Estimation

Estimating Sums and Differences with Integers — 073

When you don't need an exact numerical answer, you can estimate. You can also use estimates to check your answers.

CASE 1 You can round to estimate sums or differences of integers.

EXAMPLE 1: Your class has $15,856 in its checking account. Your teacher writes three checks and makes one deposit. Is there enough money in the account to pay a class trip bill for $8000?

CHECK NUMBER	DESCRIPTION	PAYMENT/ DEBIT (-)	DEPOSIT/ CREDIT (+)	BALANCE $15,856.00
100	J & M Photo	(-) 7740		
101	Ferris Transport	(-) 2350		
D	Deposit		(+) 880	
102	Opera To Go	(-) 1178		

First, you can estimate how much the balance changes because of the four entries.

‾7740 is about ‾8000.

‾2350 is about ‾3000.

880 is about 1000.

‾1178 is about ‾2000.

The sum of the negative numbers is about ‾13,000. When you add in the positive number, you get about ‾12,000. This represents the most you could have spent because you rounded all your expenses to more than you actually spent. A front-end estimate of $10,000 represents the least you could have spent.

MORE HELP
See 079,
082–083

To find about how much money you have left, estimate the new balance. To the nearest thousand, 15,856 rounds to 16,000. To find the new balance, subtract.

$16,000 − $10,000 = $6000 and $16,000 − $12,000 = $4000

★ You have between $4000 and $6000 left. Your class does not have enough money left to pay a class trip bill for $8000.

CASE 2 You can use front digits to estimate sums or differences of integers.

EXAMPLE 2: Great Western Forum has 17,505 seats. Madison Square Garden has 19,763 seats. About how many more people can attend an event at the Garden than at the Forum? *Source: World Almanac and Book of Facts*

To solve the problem, you can estimate the difference.

$19,763 − 17,505 ≈$ ■

MORE HELP
See 079, 082,
084

For a front-end estimate, you can subtract using one front-end digit. But that may not tell you much.

$$\begin{array}{rcr} 19,763 & \rightarrow & 10,000 \\ -17,505 & \rightarrow & -10,000 \\ \hline & & 0 \end{array}$$

For a closer estimate, you can use two front-end digits.

$$\begin{array}{rcr} 19,763 & \rightarrow & 19,000 \\ -17,505 & \rightarrow & -17,000 \\ \hline & & 2,000 \end{array}$$

★ About 2000 more people can go to an event at the Garden.

074

Estimating Products and Quotients with Integers

You can use rounding and compatible numbers to estimate products and quotients.

CASE 1 Use rounding.

EXAMPLE 1: Is $2000 enough to rent a double room at the Hotel Excelsior for 28 days?

The Hotel **Excelsior**

Daily Rates

Single $69
Double $89
Suites starting at $119

You don't need an exact numerical answer, so estimate. $28 \times 89 \approx$ ■

89 rounds up to 90

28 rounds up to 30

$90 \times 30 = 2700$

The cost for 28 days is about $2700. Since both factors were rounded up, the actual cost is less than $2700. But the rounding wasn't enough for the estimate to be off by $700.

★ $2000 is not enough money.

CASE 2 Use compatible numbers.

One way to estimate quotients is to use number pairs that are easy to divide. These number pairs are called **compatible numbers**.

EXAMPLE 2: Population density can be expressed as the mean number of people per square mile. In 1998, the borough of Manhattan had a population of 1,536,220 packed into 28 square miles. Estimate the population density of the borough of Manhattan.

Source: 1999 The World Almanac

MORE HELP
See 086, 089, 091–092

ONE WAY Write as division, then evaluate. To estimate, use compatible numbers close to 1,536,220 and 28.

$1{,}536{,}220 \div 28$

$1{,}500{,}000 \div 30 = 50{,}000$

MORE HELP
See 086, 093, 119

ANOTHER WAY Write the compatible numbers as a fraction, then simplify.

$$\frac{1{,}536{,}220}{28} \longrightarrow \frac{1{,}500{,}000}{30} = \frac{50{,}000 \times \overset{1}{\cancel{30}}}{\underset{1}{\cancel{30}}} = 50{,}000$$

★ Either way, in 1998, the population density in the borough of Manhattan was about 50,000 people per square mile.

Estimating with Rational Numbers

Estimating with decimals, fractions, and mixed numbers is similar to estimating with integers.

CASE 1 To estimate sums and differences of fractions and mixed numbers, you can use benchmarks. The number line is a good tool for identifying benchmarks.

MORE HELP
See 011

EXAMPLE 1: You live $6\frac{3}{4}$ miles from the Middletown Mall and $3\frac{1}{10}$ miles from the Outback Mall. About how much farther away from you is the Middletown Mall than the Outback Mall?

Use the number line to estimate. $6\frac{3}{4} - 3\frac{1}{10} = \blacksquare$

| 0 | $\frac{1}{10}$ | $\frac{1}{4}$ | $\frac{1}{2}$ | $\frac{3}{4}$ | $\frac{9}{10}$ | 1 |

❶ Determine whether each fraction is closest to 0, $\frac{1}{2}$, or 1. If it is exactly in the middle, round up.	❷ Compute.
$6\frac{3}{4}$ ⟶ $\frac{3}{4}$ rounds to 1. So, $6\frac{3}{4}$ is about 7. $3\frac{1}{10}$ ⟶ $\frac{1}{10}$ is closest to 0. So, $3\frac{1}{10}$ is about 3.	$7 - 3 = 4$

★ The Middletown Mall is about 4 miles farther away from you.

EXAMPLE 2: There are $85\frac{3}{8}$ pounds of dogfood in a sack. The humane society needs about 800 pounds of dogfood. How many sacks should they buy?

These numbers are big enough that you can ignore the fraction altogether and estimate with the whole numbers. $800 \div 80 = 10$.

★ The humane society should buy 10 sacks of dogfood.

CASE 2 Sometimes it makes sense to underestimate. Sometimes it makes sense to overestimate.

EXAMPLE 3: A can of soup makes 2.75 servings of soup. The total number of calories is 228. About how many calories are in one serving?

To estimate, use compatible numbers close to 2.75 and 228.

$$230 \div 2 = 115$$

If your dividend is high and your divisor is low, you will probably get an **overestimate.**

$$210 \div 3 = 70$$

If your dividend is low and you divisor is high, you will probably get an **underestimate.**

★ There are between 70 and 115 (closer to 70), calories in one serving.

EXAMPLE 4: You want to buy books that cost $8.35, $9.95, $7.95, and $9.25. You have $36.15 that you saved and $18.15 you have earned baby-sitting. Do you have enough money to buy the books?

To be sure you have enough money, underestimate the amount you have. To underestimate a sum, do a front-end estimate.

$36.15 ⟶ $30

$18.15 ⟶ $10

$30 + $10 = $40

If you overestimate the cost of books, your estimate will be more than the actual cost. To overestimate a sum, round up.

$8.35 ⟶ $9

$9.95 ⟶ $10

$7.95 ⟶ $8

$9.25 ⟶ $10

$9 + $10 + $8 + $10 = $37

★ Since you have at least $40 and the books cost at most $37, you have enough money to buy the books.

Estimating with Exponents

To estimate with exponents, use powers that are easy to work with.

MORE HELP
See 052, 100

EXAMPLE 1: You use your calculator to evaluate a^5 for $a = 13$. Your calculator display shows | 28,561 |. Is that answer reasonable?

To find whether the answer is reasonable, estimate 13^5. Since 13 is close to 10, use 10^5 to estimate 13^5.

$10^5 = 100,000$

Powers of 10 are easy to work with because the power tells you the number of zeros after the 1.

★ 13^5 is greater than 10^5, so 28,561 is not a reasonable answer for 13^5. You probably multiplied $13 \cdot 13 \cdot 13 \cdot 13$, instead of $13 \cdot 13 \cdot 13 \cdot 13 \cdot 13$.

EXAMPLE 2: Estimate 2^{10}.

You can use what you know to estimate 2^{10}.

If you know that $2^5 = 32$, then $2^{10} = 2^5 \times 2^5 = 32 \times 32$; so a good estimate is 30×30.

$30 \times 30 = 900$

★ 2^{10} is about 900.

EXAMPLE 3: Estimate 301.121^3.

To estimate, find a simpler number that is close to 301.121. Try 300^3.

$300 \times 300 \times 300 = 27,000,000$

301.121 is just a little greater than 300. So, 300^3 will be a little less than 301.121^3.

★ $301.121^3 \approx 27,000,000$

Estimating Square Roots

Suppose you want to find the square root of a number that is not a perfect square. The square root will not be an integer. It will be a non–terminating, non-repeating decimal. You can use a calculator or a square root table to find this kind of square root. You can also estimate.

MORE HELP
See 053, 055, 064

EXAMPLE: Find $\sqrt{29}$ to the nearest hundredth.

❶ Find two consecutive perfect squares with 29 between them.	❷ Pick a value and use the results to pick a closer one.	❸ Continue using your results to pick closer values.
$25 < 29 < 36$ $5^2 < \blacksquare^2 < 6^2$ **Since 29 is closer to 25 than to 36, $\sqrt{29}$ must be closer to 5 than 6.**	$(5.3)^2 = 28.09$ $(5.4)^2 = 29.16$ **So, $\sqrt{29}$ is between 5.3 and 5.4, closer to 5.4.**	$(5.38)^2 = 28.9444$ $(5.39)^2 = 29.0521$ **So, $\sqrt{29}$ is closer to 5.39 than to 5.38.**

The more you refine your estimate, the more accurate your approximation becomes.

★ $\sqrt{29} \approx 5.39$

Always use ≈ instead of = when numbers are approximate.

There are four operations: addition, subtraction, multiplication, and division. Yet, when you learn mathematics, you usually start with addition. Why? Here are just a few reasons.

- Subtraction is inversely related to addition.

- Multiplication often represents repeated addition.

- Division is inversely related to multiplication, so even division is related to addition.

The basic terms that are used in describing addition are **addend** and **sum.**

$$
\begin{array}{r}
47 \\
+\ 261 \\
\hline
308
\end{array}
\begin{array}{l}
\leftarrow \text{addend} \\
\leftarrow \text{addend} \\
\leftarrow \text{sum}
\end{array}
\qquad
47\ +\ 261\ =\ 308
$$

$$
\underset{\text{addend}}{47}\ +\ \underset{\text{addend}}{261}\ =\ \underset{\text{sum}}{308}
$$

You use subtraction for taking away, comparing, and finding a missing addend. The basic terms that may be used in describing subtraction are **minuend, subtrahend** and **difference.**

$$
\begin{array}{r}
308 \\
-\ 261 \\
\hline
47
\end{array}
\begin{array}{l}
\leftarrow \text{minuend} \\
\leftarrow \text{subtrahend} \\
\leftarrow \text{difference}
\end{array}
\qquad
\underset{\text{minuend}}{308}\ -\ \underset{\text{subtrahend}}{261}\ =\ \underset{\text{difference}}{47}
$$

You can see how addition and subtraction are related by thinking about using the descriptive terms for one operation to describe another.

$$
\begin{array}{r}
\text{difference} \\
+\ \text{subtrahend} \\
\hline
\text{minuend}
\end{array}
\qquad
\begin{array}{r}
\text{sum} \\
-\ \text{addend} \\
\hline
\text{addend}
\end{array}
\qquad
\begin{array}{r}
\text{sum} \\
-\ \text{addend} \\
\hline
\text{addend}
\end{array}
$$

079   **Adding and Subtracting with Positive Numbers** _____

Addition and subtraction are inverse relations. A number line shows what happens when you add and subtract positive numbers. When you add a positive number you move to the right on the number line. When you subtract a positive number you do the opposite and move to the left on the number line.

EXAMPLE 1: Use a number line to add. $3 + 5 = $ ■

Begin at 3.

To add 5, move five units to the right.

A space on the number line counts as one unit.

★ The final position is 8, so $3 + 5 = 8$.

EXAMPLE 2: Use a number line to add. $7x + 5x = $ ■

Each unit on this number line represents x instead of 1. Begin at $7x$. To add $5x$, move five units to the right.

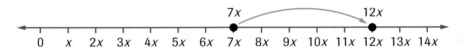

★ The final position is $12x$, so $7x + 5x = 12x$.

EXAMPLE 3: Use a number line to subtract. $7 - 3 = $ ■

Begin at 7.

To subtract 3, move three units to the left.

★ The final position is 4, so $7 - 3 = 4$

EXAMPLE 4: Use a number line to subtract. $7x - 9x = $ ■

Each unit on this number line represents x instead of 1. Begin at $7x$. To subtract $9x$, move nine units to the left.

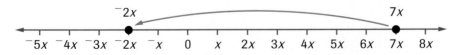

★ The final position is ^-2x, so $7x - 9x = {}^-2x$.

Adding and Subtracting with Decimal Numbers

With both integers and decimals, you add the digits in each place and regroup when necessary.

EXAMPLE 1: Add. 20.59 + 8.7 = ■

Estimate: 20 + 9 = 29, so your sum should be about 29.

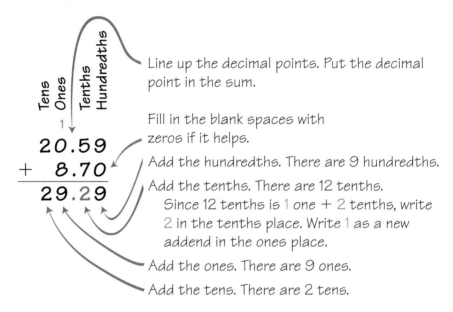

Line up the decimal points. Put the decimal point in the sum.

Fill in the blank spaces with zeros if it helps.

Add the hundredths. There are 9 hundredths.

Add the tenths. There are 12 tenths.
   Since 12 tenths is 1 one + 2 tenths, write 2 in the tenths place. Write 1 as a new addend in the ones place.

Add the ones. There are 9 ones.

Add the tens. There are 2 tens.

$$20.59 + 8.70 = 29.29$$

★ 20.59 + 8.7 = 29.29. This agrees with your estimate.

EXAMPLE 2: Look at the bar graph. How many more hours per week of TV did an average household watch in 1997 than in 1971?

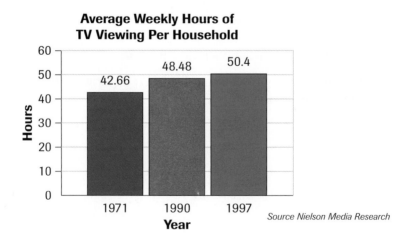

Average Weekly Hours of TV Viewing Per Household

Source Nielson Media Research

Check the bar graph. The number of hours for 1997 is 50.4. The number of hours for 1971 is 42.66. Estimate. 50 − 43 = 7, so your difference should be about 7.

ONE WAY You can use paper and pencil.

Tens	Ones	Tenths	Hundredths

```
          3 10
  5 0 . 4 Ø̶
− 4 2 . 6 6
      .   4
```

Line up the decimal points. Write the decimal point in the difference.

Fill in blank spaces with zeros if it helps.

Try to subtract the hundredths. You need more hundredths. Use a tenth. Change the number of tenths from 4 to 3, and the number of hundredths from 0 to 10. Now subtract the hundredths.

```
  49  13
       3̶ 10
  5̶ 0̶ . 4̶ Ø̶
− 4  2 . 6  6
  7  . 7  4
```

Try to subtract the tenths. You need more tenths. There are no ones to use, so use a ten. Give 9 to the ones place and 1 (as 10 tenths) to the tenths place. Now finish subtracting.

> You can use the same rule in every place:
> Regroup if needed, then subtract.

ANOTHER WAY You can use a calculator.

| 5 | 0 | . | 4 | − | 4 | 2 | . | 6 | 6 | = | 7.74 |

★ Either way, an average household watched 7.74 more hours per week of TV in 1997 than in 1971. This agrees with your estimate.

Adding and Subtracting with Fractions

The method you use to add or subtract fractions depends on whether the fractions have the same denominator.

MORE HELP
See 004

CASE 1 If the fractions have the same denominator, just add or subtract the numerators and keep the same denominator.

EXAMPLE 1: In 1997, about $\frac{4}{25}$ of the recorded music that was sold was on full-length cassettes. About $\frac{1}{25}$ of the recorded music that was sold was on cassette singles. About what part of the recorded music sold was on cassettes? *Source: Recording Industry Association of America*

To solve the problem, add. $\frac{4}{25} + \frac{1}{25} = \blacksquare$

❶ Add the numerators.	$\frac{4}{25} + \frac{1}{25} = \frac{4+1}{25}$
❷ Simplify the numerator.	$\frac{4+1}{25} = \frac{5}{25}$
❸ Simplify the fraction.	$\frac{5 \div 5}{25 \div 5} = \frac{1}{5}$

★ About $\frac{1}{5}$ of the recorded music sold was on cassettes.

MORE HELP
See 464

CASE 2 If the fractions have different denominators, you can rewrite them as fractions with a common denominator.

EXAMPLE 2: What is the length of the remaining side of the triangle?

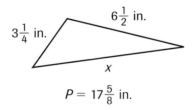

$P = 17\frac{5}{8}$ in.

Write an equation to show what is going on in the problem.

$6\frac{1}{2} + 3\frac{1}{4} + x = 17\frac{5}{8}$

To find x, subtract.

$17\frac{5}{8} - \left(6\frac{1}{2} + 3\frac{1}{4}\right) = x$

Since $6\frac{1}{2} + 3\frac{1}{4} = 9\frac{3}{4}$, you subtract $9\frac{3}{4}$ from $17\frac{5}{8}$ to find x.

MORE HELP
See 004

❶ Find equivalent fractions with a common denominator.	❷ Regroup if needed. Subtract the fractions. Subtract the whole numbers.	❸ Simplify if needed.
$17\frac{5}{8}$ ⟶ $17\frac{5}{8}$ $9\frac{3}{4}$ ⟶ $9\frac{6}{8}$	$17\frac{5}{8} \to 16 + \frac{8}{8} + \frac{5}{8} \to 16\frac{13}{8}$ $-\; 9\frac{3}{4}$ ⟶ $9\frac{6}{8}$ _____ $7\frac{7}{8}$	$7\frac{7}{8}$ is already in simplest form.

★ The remaining side of the triangle measures $7\frac{7}{8}$ inches.

EXAMPLE 3: Use a calculator with fraction capability to add. $\frac{24}{55} + \frac{1}{25} = \blacksquare$

MORE HELP
See 008, 012

| 2 | 4 | / | 5 | 5 | + | 1 | / | 2 | 5 | = | 131/275 |

If your calculator does not handle fractions, you can use the parentheses and division keys, but your result won't be in fraction form.

| (| 2 | 4 | ÷ | 5 | 5 |) | + | (| 1 | ÷ | 2 | 5 |) | = | 0.476363636 |

★ $\dfrac{24}{55} + \dfrac{1}{25} = \dfrac{131}{275}$ or $0.47\overline{63}$

Adding and Subtracting with Negative Numbers ____ 082

You can use a number line to add and subtract with negative numbers. Since addition and subtraction are inverse relations, when you add a negative number move to the left. When you subtract a negative number, do the opposite and move to the right.

Positive 1 and ⁻1 are sometimes called a **zero pair** because their sum is zero. You can use counters to help you make sense of adding and subtracting with negative numbers. To model adding and subtracting with counters, use two colors. One color stands for positive and a different color stands for negative.

positive 1   negative 1   zero pair

Adding with Negative Numbers

Think of the signs (⁺ and ⁻) as directions on a number line: ⁺ means right, or positive, and ⁻ means left, or negative. The operation sign (+) tells you to move in the direction of the sign on the next addend.

EXAMPLE 1: Add. ⁻13 + 16 = ■

> If there is no sign on a number, it is positive.

ONE WAY You can show the addition on a number line.

Place a point above the first addend on the number line. This is your starting point.

The second addend is positive. Draw an arrow as long as the second addend in the positive direction.

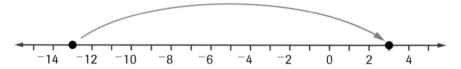

ANOTHER WAY You can show the addition using counters and zero pairs.

❶ Show counters for the first addend.	❷ Add counters for the second addend.	❸ Look for zero pairs of counters. The unpaired counters are the sum.
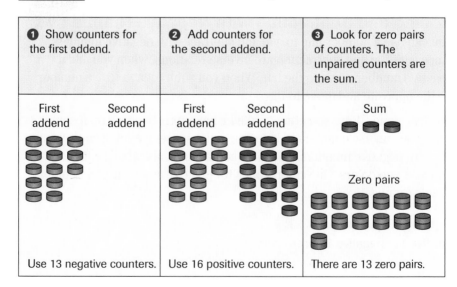		
Use 13 negative counters.	Use 16 positive counters.	There are 13 zero pairs.

All the remaining counters will be one color. Count them. The counters are blue, so the sum is positive.

★ Either way, ⁻13 + 16 = 3.

You can also use absolute value and follow some simple rules to add.

MORE HELP
See 009, 104

Addends	Rules	Example
To add positive + positive	Add absolute values. The sum is positive.	53 + 74 ⟶ 53 + 74 53 + 74 = 127
To add negative + positive or positive + negative	Subtract the smaller absolute value from the greater. The sum has the sign of the number with the greater absolute value.	53 + ⁻74 ⟶ 74 − 53 ⁻74 + 53 = ⁻21
To add negative + negative	Add absolute values. The sum is negative.	⁻53 + ⁻74 ⟶ 53 + 74 ⁻53 + ⁻74 = ⁻127

Since
$|{}^-74| > |53|$,
the sign on the
sum is negative.

Subtracting with Negative Numbers

084

Subtracting a negative number is the same as adding its opposite. To understand how this works, think about using counters to subtract.

EXAMPLE 1: Subtract. $^-2 - {}^-5 = $ ■

ONE WAY You can think of subtraction as taking away.

❶ Show counters for the minuend. Have a collection of zero pairs handy.	❷ Take away from the minuend the number of counters named by the subtrahend. If you don't have enough, break up some zero pairs. The left-over unmatched counters are the difference.
Minuend Zero pairs	Difference Zero pairs

ANOTHER WAY You can think of subtraction as addition. $^-2 - {}^-5 = {}^-2 + 5.$

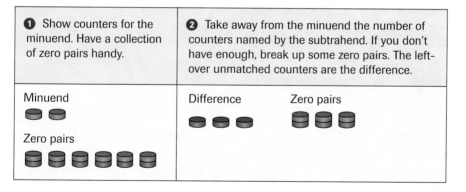

❶ Show counters for the first addend.	❷ Add counters for the second addend.	❸ Look for zero pairs.
Addend Addend	Addend Addend	Sum
Use 2 negative counters.	Use 5 positive counters.	There are 2 zero pairs.

★ Either way, $^-2 - {}^-5 = 3.$

Multiplication is a shortcut for adding the same amount over and over. The basic terms that are used in describing multiplication are **factor** and **product.**

$$750 \longleftarrow \text{factor}$$
$$\times \quad 40 \longleftarrow \text{factor}$$
$$\overline{30,000} \longleftarrow \text{product}$$

$$40 \times 750 = 30,000$$
$$\qquad \uparrow \qquad \uparrow \qquad \qquad \uparrow$$
$$\text{factor} \qquad \text{factor} \qquad \text{product}$$

Division is inversely related to multiplication. Reciprocals are inverses, so division by a number gives the same result as multiplication by its reciprocal. $30,000 \div 40 = 30,000 \times \frac{1}{40}$

The basic terms that are used in describing division are **dividend, divisor,** and **quotient.**

$$\text{divisor} \longrightarrow 40 \overline{)30,000} \begin{array}{l} \longleftarrow \text{quotient} \\ \end{array}$$
$$\phantom{\text{divisor} \longrightarrow 40}\,750 \longleftarrow \text{quotient}$$

$$30,000 \div 40 = 750$$
$$\quad \uparrow \qquad \quad \uparrow \qquad \uparrow$$
$$\text{dividend} \qquad \text{divisor} \quad \text{quotient}$$

MORE HELP
See 089, 119

$$\text{numerator or dividend} \longrightarrow \frac{30,000}{40} = \frac{750 \times \overset{1}{40}}{\underset{1}{40}} = 750 \longleftarrow \text{quotient}$$
$$\text{denominator or divisor} \longrightarrow$$

You can see how multiplication and division are related by thinking about using the descriptive terms for one operation to describe the other.

$$\begin{array}{r} quotient \\ \times \quad divisor \\ \hline dividend \end{array} \qquad \begin{array}{r} factor \\ factor \overline{)product} \end{array}$$

Multiplying and Dividing with Positive Numbers ____

Multiplication and division are *inverse* relations. One *undoes* the other. You can use this relationship to find quotients.

MORE HELP
See 041

Multiplying with Decimal Numbers

To multiply with decimals, first multiply as if you were multiplying with integers. If you first estimate the product, you can easily place the decimal point in your answer.

EXAMPLE 1: Multiply. $1.3 \times 3.5 = $ ■

Estimate. Since $1 \times 4 = 4$, your product should be about 4.

First, multiply the factors as if they were integers.

$$
\begin{array}{r}
1 \\
13 \\
\times\ 35 \\
\hline
65
\end{array}
$$

Multiply by the ones: $5 \times 13 = $ ■
$5 \times 3 = 15 \longrightarrow 5$ ones with 1 ten to regroup
$5 \times 10 = 50 \longrightarrow 5$ tens $+ 1$ ten $= 6$ tens
So, $5 \times 13 = 65$

$$
\begin{array}{r}
1 \\
13 \\
\times\ 35 \\
\hline
65 \\
+390 \\
\hline
455
\end{array}
$$

Multiply by the tens: $30 \times 13 = $ ■
$30 \times 3 = 90 \longrightarrow 9$ tens $+ 0$ ones
$30 \times 10 = 300 \longrightarrow 3$ hundreds
So, $30 \times 13 = 390$

Add the partial products.

Your estimate is 4, so the decimal goes between the 4 and the first 5.

★ $1.3 \times 3.5 = 4.55$

You can also decide the number of places after the decimal point by adding:

    number of places in first factor
  + number of places in second factor
    number of places in product

EXAMPLE 2: How fast does the Zapline Internet Service claim to be in kilobytes per second?

To find the answer, multiply.
$12.4 \times 57.6 = $ ■

GET ZAPPED!

Zapline Internet Service is 12.4 times as fast as the 57.6 kilobytes per second service you're probably stuck with now!

ONE WAY You can use paper and pencil.

❶ Estimate.	❷ Multiply as if the factors were integers.	❸ Place the decimal in the product based on your estimate.
$12 \times 60 = 720$	576 $\times$ 124 　2304　Multiply by the ones. 11520　Multiply by the tens. +57600　Multiply by the hundreds. 71424　Add partial products.	720 is close to 714, so the product is 714.24.

ANOTHER WAY You can use a calculator.

| 1 | 2 | . | 4 | × | 5 | 7 | . | 6 | = | 714.24 |

★ Either way, Zapline Internet Service claims to have a speed of 714.24 kilobytes per second.

DID YOU KNOW The first modem ran at 1200 bits per second and improved modems ran at 2400, then 9600, then 14,400, then 28,800, then 57,600.

Dividing with Decimal Numbers

Division is inversely related to multiplication. If you multiply to estimate, finding quotients is easy.

EXAMPLE 1: Divide. $75 \div 0.5 = \blacksquare$

MORE HELP
See 004, 044

First, estimate the quotient. How many halves are in 75? There are 160 halves in 80, so 160 is a good estimate.

$75 \div 0.5$ can be written as $\frac{75}{0.5}$. To make the division easier, you can simplify this fraction by multiplying numerator and denominator (dividend and divisor) by 10. This will not change the result of the division because multiplying by $\frac{10}{10}$ is the same as multiplying by 1.

$$\frac{75 \times 10}{0.5 \times 10} = \frac{750}{5}$$

Now set up your division framework and divide.

---

❶ Divide the hundreds.
7 hundreds $\div 5 = \blacksquare$

Multiply to estimate.
  5×1 hundred $= 500$
  5×2 hundreds $= 1000$
    Use 5×1 hundred.
  Write 1 in the hundreds place.
  Write 500 below 750.

Subtract and compare.
  $750 - 500 = 250$
  $250 > 5$
  You have enough to keep dividing.

$$
\begin{array}{r}
1 \\
5\overline{)750} \\
-\,500 \quad \longleftarrow \quad 5 \times 1 \text{ hundred} \\
\hline
250 \quad \longleftarrow \quad 750 - 500
\end{array}
$$

---

❷ Divide the tens.
25 tens $\div 5 = \blacksquare$

Multiply to estimate.
  5×5 tens $= 25$ tens
  Write 5 in the tens place.
  Write 250 under 250.

Subtract and compare.
  $250 - 250 = 0$
  There is no remainder.
  You have no ones to divide, so write 0 in the ones place of your quotient.

$$
\begin{array}{r}
150 \\
5\overline{)750} \\
-\,500 \\
\hline
250 \\
-\,250 \quad \longleftarrow \quad 5 \times 5 \text{ tens} \\
\hline
0 \quad \longleftarrow \quad 250 - 250
\end{array}
$$

If you still have a remainder after you've run out of places in your dividend, tack on a decimal point and some zeros and keep dividing. Don't forget to put the decimal point in the quotient straight above the one in the dividend.

★ Either way, $75 \div 0.5 = 150$. This is close to your estimate.

Multiplying with Fractions

Sometimes you need to multiply fractions and expressions involving fractions. There are a few ways you can do this.

MORE HELP
See 004

EXAMPLE 1: Multiply. $\frac{3}{8} \times \frac{2}{3} =$ ■

ONE WAY A diagram may help you to understand multiplying with fractions.

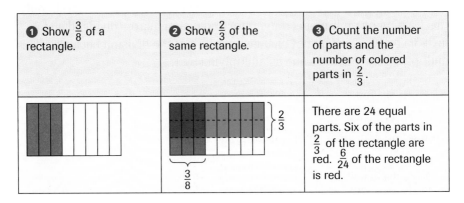

❶ Show $\frac{3}{8}$ of a rectangle.	❷ Show $\frac{2}{3}$ of the same rectangle.	❸ Count the number of parts and the number of colored parts in $\frac{2}{3}$.
	$\left.\right\}\frac{2}{3}$ $\underbrace{}_{\frac{3}{8}}$	There are 24 equal parts. Six of the parts in $\frac{2}{3}$ of the rectangle are red. $\frac{6}{24}$ of the rectangle is red.

ANOTHER WAY You can use paper and pencil.

❶ Multiply the numerators. Multiply the denominators.	❷ Write the product in simplest form.
$\frac{3}{8} \times \frac{2}{3} = \frac{6}{24}$	$\frac{6 \div 6}{24 \div 6} = \frac{1}{4}$

ANOTHER WAY You can use a calculator.

| 3 | / | 8 | × | 2 | / | 3 | = | 6/24 | simp | = | 3/12 | simp | = | 1/4 |

★ Any way you look at it, $\frac{3}{8} \times \frac{2}{3} = \frac{1}{4}$.

SHORTCUT

You can simplify the fractions *before* multiplying them. This is called *canceling*.

Divide the numerator of one fraction and the denominator of the other by a common factor. Then multiply.

$$\frac{{}^1 2}{{}_1 3} \times \frac{3^1}{8_4} = \frac{1}{4}$$
Divide the 3s by 3.
Divide 2 and 8 by 2.

Dividing with Fractions

Sometimes you need to divide fractions and expressions involving fractions.

MORE HELP
See 004, 041

EXAMPLE 1: How many $\frac{3}{8}$-yard pieces of fabric can you cut from $\frac{3}{4}$ yard of fabric?

To solve the problem, divide. $\frac{3}{4} \div \frac{3}{8} = $ ■

| ONE WAY | You can use mental math.

A fourth is twice as big as an eighth, so $\frac{3}{4}$ is twice $\frac{3}{8}$.

| ANOTHER WAY | You can diagram the problem.

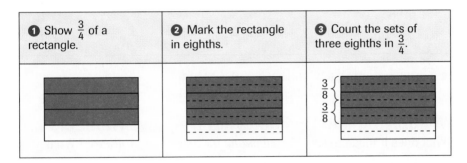

| ❶ Show $\frac{3}{4}$ of a rectangle. | ❷ Mark the rectangle in eighths. | ❸ Count the sets of three eighths in $\frac{3}{4}$. |

| ANOTHER WAY | You can use paper and pencil.

❶ Multiply by the reciprocal of the divisor.	❷ Write the product in simplest form.
$\frac{3}{4} \div \frac{3}{8}$ $\downarrow$ $\frac{3}{4} \times \frac{8}{3} = \frac{24}{12}$	$\frac{24}{12} = 2$

★ No matter which way you choose, you can cut the fabric into two $\frac{3}{8}$-yard pieces.

EXAMPLE 2: Chicago gets an average of $2\frac{7}{10}$ inches of precipitation in March and $3\frac{3}{5}$ inches of precipitation in April. In Chicago, how many times as wet is it in April as in March? *Source: NOAA National Climate Data Center*

To find out how many times as wet it is in April, you can divide the amount of rain in April by the amount of rain in March. $3\frac{3}{5} \div 2\frac{7}{10} = \blacksquare$

❶ Write each mixed number as a fraction.	❷ Multiply by the reciprocal of the divisor.	❸ Write the product in simplest form.
$3\frac{3}{5} \div 2\frac{7}{10}$ $\downarrow$ $\left(\frac{15}{5} + \frac{3}{5}\right) \div \left(\frac{20}{10} + \frac{7}{10}\right)$ $\downarrow$ $\frac{18}{5} \div \frac{27}{10}$	$\frac{18}{5} \div \frac{27}{10}$ $\downarrow$ $\frac{18}{5} \times \frac{10}{27} = \frac{180}{135}$	$\frac{180}{135} = 1\frac{45}{135}$ $= 1\frac{1}{3}$

★ In Chicago, April is $1\frac{1}{3}$ times as wet as March.

Multiplying and Dividing with Negative Numbers

What does it mean to say, *My telephone number is not unlisted?* What does it mean to say, *My telephone bill is not unpaid?* In ordinary language, having the word *not* followed by a word beginning with the prefix *un-* can be like multiplying two negative numbers. The result is positive.

One way you can understand multiplying and dividing with negative numbers is to use colored counters. For example, use counters to multiply ⁻3 times 2.

Begin by making a collection of red and blue counters.

You need to get three negative counters from your collection twice.

You have six negative counters with no positive partners, so your result is ⁻6.

Multiplying with Negative Numbers

The process for multiplying negative numbers is the same as for multiplying positive numbers, except that you must determine the sign of the result.

One way you can think about multiplying negative numbers is to use a number line.

EXAMPLE 1: Multiply. $3 \times {}^-\frac{1}{2} = $ ■

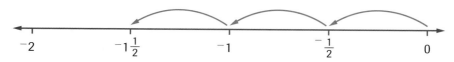

$3 \times {}^-\frac{1}{2} + {}^-\frac{1}{2} + {}^-\frac{1}{2}$

★ $3 \times {}^-\frac{1}{2} = {}^-1\frac{1}{2}$

To understand how signs work when you multiply, you can use patterns.

CASE 1 This pattern shows that when two factors have different signs, the product is negative.

$5 \times 2 \ = 10$

$5 \times 1 \ = 5$

$5 \times 0 \ = 0$

$5 \times {}^-1 = {}^-5$

$5 \times {}^-2 = {}^-10$

It makes sense that $5 \times {}^-1 = {}^-5$ because if you lose five $1 bills, you lose $5.

MORE ▶

CASE 2 This pattern shows that when two factors are negative, their product is positive.

$2 \times {}^-5 = {}^-10$

$1 \times {}^-5 = {}^-5$

$0 \times {}^-5 = 0$

${}^-1 \times {}^-5 = 5$

${}^-2 \times {}^-5 = 10$

${}^-3 \times {}^-5 = 15$

> When multiplying two factors, if the signs are the same, the product is positive. If the signs are different, the product is negative. A product of zero is neither positive nor negative.

You can also use absolute value and some rules to multiply integers.

Factors	Rules	Examples	
To multiply positive · positive or negative · negative	Multiply the absolute values.	$24 \cdot 5$ $\downarrow$ $24 \cdot 5 = 120$	${}^-9c \cdot {}^-5$ $\downarrow$ $9c \cdot 5 = 45c$
	The product is positive.	$24 \cdot 5 = 120$	${}^-9c \cdot {}^-5 = 45c$
To multiply negative · positive or positive · negative	Multiply the absolute values.	${}^-24 \cdot 5$ $\downarrow$ $24 \cdot 5 = 120$	$9c \cdot {}^-5$ $\downarrow$ $9c \cdot 5 = 45c$
	The product is negative.	${}^-24 \cdot 5 = {}^-120$	$9c \cdot {}^-5 = {}^-45c$

Dividing with Negative Numbers

To understand how signs work when you divide, you can use what you know about multiplying. Look at the pattern below.

Multiplication Equation	Related Division Equation
$8 \cdot 6 = 48$	$48 \div 6 = 8$
$^-8 \cdot 6 = {}^-48$	$^-48 \div 6 = {}^-8$
$8 \cdot {}^-6 = {}^-48$	$^-48 \div {}^-6 = 8$
$^-8 \cdot {}^-6 = 48$	$48 \div {}^-6 = {}^-8$

In any multiplication or division equation, there are either no negative numbers or an even number of negative numbers. You can use this fact to help you place the negative signs in your products and quotients.

EXAMPLE 1: Divide. $^-29x \div 6 = $ ■

Since your dividend is negative and your divisor is not, your quotient must be negative. Divide as if you had positive numbers, then place the negative sign on your quotient.

$$29x \div 6 = 4\tfrac{5}{6}x$$
$$^-29x \div 6 = {}^-4\tfrac{5}{6}x$$

★ $^-29x \div 6 = {}^-4\tfrac{5}{6}x$

EXAMPLE 2: Compute. $^-6(7 - 9) \div {}^-4 = $ ■

Follow the rules for order of operations, keeping your eye on the signs.

MORE HELP
See 069

To solve:	$^-6(7 - 9) \div {}^-4$
Work inside the parentheses.	$= {}^-6(^-2) \div {}^-4$
Multiply and divide left to right.	$= 12 \div {}^-4$ $= {}^-3$

Double check the signs. When you were ready to start multiplying and dividing, you had three negative numbers, two of them cancel each other out and the leftover one means your answer should be negative.

★ $^-6(7 - 9) \div {}^-4 = {}^-3$

094

Computing with Measurements

Measures like 5 ft 3 in. and 1 lb 8 oz are called **mixed measures**, because they mix two units together to specify the measure of one thing. When you compute with mixed measures, use your math sense to help you decide what to do.

095

Adding and Subtracting with Mixed Measures

EXAMPLE 1: Find the length of the fence around the garden.

MORE HELP
See 079,
082–083, 464

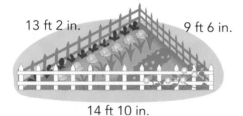

13 ft 2 in.   9 ft 6 in.

14 ft 10 in.

ONE WAY You can change to one unit and then compute.

Change to all inches.	Or, change to all feet.
13 ft 2 in. → 156 in. + 2 in. → 158 in. 9 ft 6 in. → 108 in. + 6 in. → 114 in. + 14 ft 10 in. → 168 in. + 10 in. → 178 in. 450 in. 450 in. = $37\frac{1}{2}$ ft	13 ft 2 in. → $13\frac{2}{12}$ ft 9 ft 6 in. → $9\frac{6}{12}$ ft + 14 ft 10 in. → $14\frac{10}{12}$ ft $36\frac{18}{12}$ ft $36\frac{18}{12} = 37\frac{6}{12}$, or $37\frac{1}{2}$ ft

ANOTHER WAY You can operate on like units, regrouping when necessary.

MORE HELP
See 079, 081

❶ Add inches.	❷ Add feet.	❸ Regroup
13 ft 2 in. 9 ft 6 in. + 14 ft 10 in. ──────── 18 in.	13 ft 2 in. 9 ft 6 in. + 14 ft 10 in. ──────── 36 ft 18 in.	36 ft 18 in. ↓ 36 ft + 12 in. + 6 in. = 36 ft + 1 ft + 6 in. = 37 ft + 6 in.

★ Either way, the length of the fence is 37 feet 6 inches, or $37\frac{1}{2}$ feet.

Subtracting mixed measures is just like adding mixed measures except that you may need to regroup *before* computing.

EXAMPLE 2: Subtract. 3 ft 4 in. − 1 ft 9 in. = ■

ONE WAY You can change to one unit and then compute.

Change all to inches.	3 ft 4 in. ⟶ 36 in. + 4 in. ⟶ 40 in. − 1 ft 9 in. ⟶ 12 in. + 9 in. ⟶ 21 in. ───────── 19 in. 19 in. = 1 ft 7 in.
Or, change all to feet.	3 ft 4 in. ⟶ $3\frac{4}{12}$ ft ⟶ $2\frac{16}{12}$ ft − 1 ft 9 in. ⟶ $1\frac{9}{12}$ ft ⟶ $1\frac{9}{12}$ ft ───────── $1\frac{7}{12}$ ft

MORE HELP
See 079

ANOTHER WAY You can operate on like units, regrouping when necessary.

MORE HELP
See 079

❶ Regroup.	❷ Subtract the inches.	❸ Subtract the feet.
3 ft 4 in. ↓ 2 ft + 12 in. + 4 in. ↓ 2 ft 16 in.	2 ft 16 in. − 1 ft 9 in. ──────── 7 in.	2 ft 16 in. − 1 ft 9 in. ──────── 1 ft 7 in.

★ Either way, 3 ft 4 in. − 1 ft 9 in. = 1 ft 7 in. or $1\frac{7}{12}$ ft.

Multiplying and Dividing with Mixed Measures

When you multiply or divide measures, what you do depends on whether you are multiplying or dividing a measure by a number, or by another measure.

CASE 1 Sometimes you multiply or divide a measure by a number.

EXAMPLE 1: Suppose you add 4 of these weights to a barbell. What is the total amount of weight that you add to the barbell?

ONE WAY You can multiply each unit of the measure separately, regrouping when necessary.

MORE HELP
See 086, 089, 091–092, 456

❶ Multiply ounces.	❷ Multiply pounds.	❸ Regroup.
7 lb 8 oz $\times$ 4 ——— 32 oz	7 lb 8 oz $\times$ 4 ——— 28 lb 32 oz	28 lb 32 oz ↓ 28 lb + 2 lb = 30 lb

ANOTHER WAY You can change to one unit and then compute.

Change to all ounces. Multiply, then change back to a mixed measure.	**Or, change to all pounds.** Multiply, then change back to a mixed measure.
7 lb 8 oz → 112 oz + 8 oz → 120 oz 120 oz $\times$ 4 = 480 oz 480 oz $\div \frac{16 \text{ oz}}{1 \text{ lb}} = \frac{480 \text{ oz}}{1} \times \frac{1 \text{ lb}}{16 \text{ oz}} = 30$ lb	7 lb 8 oz → $7\frac{8}{16}$ lb → $7\frac{1}{2}$ lb $7\frac{1}{2}$ lb $\times$ 4 = 30 lb

When you divide by a measurement rate, like ounces or pounds or miles per hour, it may be easier to see what you're doing if you rewrite division as multiplication and cancel measurements that appear in both numerator and denominator.

★ Any way you look at it, a total of 30 pounds is added.

CASE 2 To multiply or divide a measure by a measure, be sure that all measures are the same before computing.

MORE HELP
See 089

EXAMPLE 2: You have 6 pounds 12 ounces of peanuts. How many 12–ounce bags of peanuts can you fill?

Change to all ounces.	**Or, change to all pounds.**
6 lb 12 oz ⟶ 96 oz + 12 oz ⟶ 108 oz	6 lb 12 oz ⟶ $6\frac{12}{16}$ lb ⟶ $6\frac{3}{4}$ lb
$\dfrac{108 \text{ oz}}{12 \text{ oz}} = 9$	12 oz ⟶ $\frac{12}{16}$ lb ⟶ $\frac{3}{4}$ lb
When you divide ounces by ounces, you get a number (in this case a number of bags), not a number of ounces.	$6\frac{3}{4}$ lb ÷ $\frac{3}{4}$ lb = $\dfrac{6\frac{3}{4} \text{ lb}}{\frac{3}{4} \text{ lb}}$
	$\dfrac{6\frac{3}{4}}{\frac{3}{4}} = \dfrac{27}{4} ÷ \dfrac{3}{4}$
	$\dfrac{27}{4} \times \dfrac{4}{3} = \dfrac{108}{12}$
	$= 9$

★ Either way, you can fill nine bags.

When you divide pounds by pounds, you get a number, not a number of pounds.

Precision

Precision is an indication of how finely a measurement was made. When you calculate, you must round to the smallest unit in the actual measurement. It doesn't make sense to have an answer with more decimal places than the measures you computed with.

For example, you run a marathon in exactly 5.5 hours. To find your average hourly rate, you divide 26.2 miles by 5.5 hours and your calculator display shows 4.763636364 . Since the original measurements were in tenths, the hourly rate is precise only to the tenths place: 4.8 miles per hour.

098

Basic Tools of Algebra

"On two occasions I have been asked [by members of Parliament], 'Pray, Mr. Babbage, if you put into the machine the wrong figures, will the right answers come out?'"

Charles Babbage
(inventor of the first general-purpose computer)

Whether it's rockets, buildings, or phone calls, if you add four of them and five of the same thing, you get nine of them. The equation $4 + 5 = 9$ works for all objects. That's why arithmetic is so useful.

But arithmetic alone will not put people into space. Nor will it build skyscrapers or route telephone calls. For that we need a way to describe things that change, a precise way that will help us predict whether a rocket will escape Earth's gravity, whether a skyscraper will stay up, or whether your friend's call will get through to you. We need algebra.

To see how algebra works, first imagine trying to describe precisely how the distance your car travels relates to how fast you're going and to how long you drive. You might generate a long list of the possible relations: If you go 40 mph for $\frac{1}{2}$ hour, you'll travel 20 miles; if you go 41 mph for $\frac{1}{2}$ hour, you'll travel $20\frac{1}{2}$ miles; and so forth.

An easier way is to describe the relationship with a single general statement: The number of miles you go equals your rate of speed in miles per hour multiplied by the number of hours you travel.

And, yes, there's even an easier way. Use letters instead of words to stand for distance, rate, and time. Then, you could write something short and sweet like $d = r \cdot t$.

When you see all those letters, think of them as tools—tools that help launch rockets, construct skyscrapers, and make your telephone ring.

An **algebraic expression** is a mathematical phrase that's a combination of one or more **variables**, **constants**, and operation symbols. When you see a number and a letter together, indicating multiplication, the number is called the **coefficient** of the variable.

Just as a word phrase has no period, an algebraic expression has no equals sign. If two algebraic expressions have the same value, you can join them with an equals sign to form an equation. A good analogy is *phrase : sentence* as *expression : equation*.

Letters can be used to represent variables or constants. For example, in the equation x + 1.73 = 4.86, x is unknown, but you can figure out the one number that will make the equation true.

Algebraic Expressions

$$2\pi \text{ or } 2\pi r$$

$$8 - b$$

$$lw$$

$$5$$

Equations

$$C = 2\pi r$$

$$8 - b = 5$$

$$5 = 5$$

$$A = lw$$

Variables and Constants

A **constant** is a quantity that stays the same, like the number of cents in a dollar. A **variable** is a quantity that can change, like the cost of a carton of orange juice or a piece of data in a formula. A **coefficient** is a number that multiplies a variable: in the equation $P = 4s$, the four is the coefficient of s.

When you write algebraic expressions or equations, you can use a letter to stand for a variable. You can choose any letter you like. Often, people choose the first letters of the important words to make the meanings of the variables easier to remember.

Volume = (area of base) × height

$V = Bh$

> To avoid confusion with the variable x, you usually don't use the X symbol to show multiplication in variable expressions. Instead, to show that V is the product of B and h, you can write:
> $V = Bh$, $V = B(h)$ or $V = B \cdot h$.

Reading and Writing Expressions

A **monomial** is an expression in which variables and constants may stand alone or be multiplied. Some monomials include 8, x^2, $2x^2$, and $\frac{4a}{3}$. Monomials can be combined by addition or subtraction into larger expressions called **binomials** and **multinomials** or **polynomials**. The **terms** of an algebraic expression are its monomials.

MORE HELP
See 082

Quantity Expressed in Words	Algebraic Expression for that Quantity		
The value in cents of a given number of quarters, dimes, and nickels	25*q* + Term (value of quarters)	10*d* + Term (value of dimes)	5*n* Term (value of nickels)
4, 8, 12, 16, 20, . . . The first number is 4 • 1, the second number is 4 • 2, and so on. So, the *n*th number of the pattern is	4*n* Term	A subtraction or addition operation sign between monomials is considered part of the term on its right.	

102 · Types of Polynomials

A **polynomial** is either a monomial or a sum of monomials. Some polynomials have special names.

Name	Examples	
Monomial (one term)	$7x$	$3x^2y$
Binomial (two terms)	$5x + 3$	$x^2 + 2x$
Trinomial (three terms)	$\frac{1}{2}x^2 - 5x + 11$	$x^2 - 5x + 11$
Other polynomials	$x^4 + 4x^3 - x^2 + x$	$3x^2y + 4x^2 + 8y + 12$

> $x^2 - 5x + 11$ can be called a sum of monomials because it's the same as $x^2 + {}^-5x + 11$.

103 · Simplifying Expressions

When you combine like terms or use properties to make polynomial expressions easier to work with, you are **simplifying**.

104 · Combining Like Terms to Simplify Expressions

Think about adding four dogs, three cats, two dogs, and four more cats. If you combine the *dog* terms and the *cat* terms you have a simpler expression.

4 dogs + 2 dogs + 3 cats + 4 cats = 6 dogs + 7 cats

In algebra, **like terms** are terms that have the same variable raised to the same power. $6x^3$ and $3x^3$ are like terms. $3z^3$ and $3z^2$ are *not* like terms because z^3 and z^2 have different exponents.

To see how this works, think about substituting 3 for x in the expression $2x^2 + 5x^2$.

$2 \cdot 3^2 + 5 \cdot 3^2 = 2 \cdot 9 + 5 \cdot 9$

$(2 + 5) \cdot 3^2 = 18 + 45$

$63 = 63$

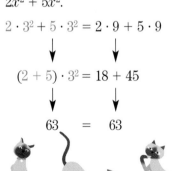

EXAMPLE: Simplify $3x^2 - 3 - x^2 + 2x + 5 - 5x$ by combining like terms.

You can use Algebra Tiles to model polynomials and combine like terms. Group all the added terms in degree order: squared variable, variable with no exponent, no variable. Then change colors and group the subtracted terms in the same order. Same size light and dark tiles are opposites and zero each other out.

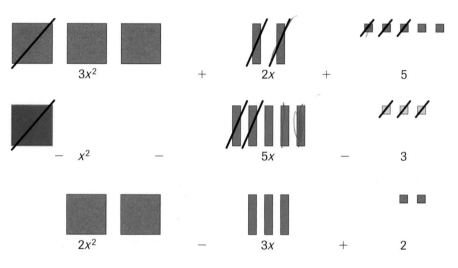

$\bigstar$ $3x^2 - 3 - x^2 + 2x + 5 - 5x = 2x^2 - 3x + 2$

Using Properties to Simplify Expressions

105

You can use Commutative, Associative, and Distributive Properties to simplify expressions.

It may be easier to work with subtracted terms if you make them into added terms: Subtracting ^+n is the same as adding ^-n and subtracting ^-n is the same as adding ^+n.

EXAMPLE: Simplify $10y - 2(4y + 5)$.

To Simplify:	$10y - 2(4y + 5)$
Rewrite as addition.	$10y + {}^-2(4y + 5)$
Use the Distributive Property to get rid of the parentheses.	$10y + {}^-8y + {}^-10$
Use the Distributive Property to combine the y terms.	$(10 + {}^-8)y + {}^-10 = 2y + {}^-10$

MORE HELP
See 030–031, 034–035, 037

$\bigstar$ $10y - 2(4y + 5) = 2y + {}^-10$ or $2y - 10$.

MORE HELP
See 037

Adding and Subtracting with Roots

You can add or subtract roots of any given number. Treat them as you do variables: If they are the same or can be made the same by factoring, you can combine them by adding or subtracting.

CASE 1 When the roots are the same, use the Distributive Property.

EXAMPLE 1: Find the sum. $\sqrt{2} + 3\sqrt{2} = $ ■

To find the sum, use the Distributive Property to combine expressions that include the same root.

$$\sqrt{2} + 3\sqrt{2}$$
$$\downarrow \qquad \downarrow$$
$$1\sqrt{2} + 3\sqrt{2}$$
$$\downarrow$$
$$(1 + 3)\,\sqrt{2} = 4\sqrt{2}$$
$$\bigstar\ \sqrt{2} + 3\sqrt{2} = 4\sqrt{2}$$

CASE 2 When the roots are not the same, try to simplify so that they are. If you can't, don't try to compute unless you are estimating the roots.

EXAMPLE 2: Find the difference. $5\sqrt{8} - 3\sqrt{2} = $ ■

$$5\sqrt{8} - 3\sqrt{2}$$
$$\downarrow$$
$$5\sqrt{4 \cdot 2} - 3\sqrt{2}$$
$$\downarrow$$
$$5\sqrt{4} \cdot \sqrt{2} - 3\sqrt{2}$$
$$\downarrow$$
$$\left(5 \cdot 2 \cdot \sqrt{2}\right) - 3\sqrt{2}$$
$$\downarrow$$
$$10\sqrt{2} - 3\sqrt{2}$$
$$\downarrow$$
$$(10 - 3)\sqrt{2} = 7\sqrt{2}$$
$$\bigstar\ 5\sqrt{8} - 3\sqrt{2} = 7\sqrt{2}$$

MATH ALERT: Be Careful When You Compute with Roots and Powers

- When you add or subtract expressions with roots, don't add or subtract the numbers under different radical signs!

For example, $\sqrt{a} - \sqrt{b}$ does not equal $\sqrt{a - b}$.

To see how this works, try evaluating each expression for $a = 16$ and $b = 9$.

$$\sqrt{a} - \sqrt{b} = \sqrt{16} - \sqrt{9} \qquad\qquad \sqrt{a - b} = \sqrt{16 - 9}$$

$$= 4 - 3 \qquad\qquad\qquad = \sqrt{7}$$

$$= 1 \qquad\qquad\qquad\qquad \approx 2.646$$

$1 \ne 2.646$, so $\sqrt{a} - \sqrt{b} \ne \sqrt{a - b}$.

- When you add or subtract terms with the same exponents and bases, add or subtract the coefficients only.

For example, $5t^2 + 3t^2 = 8t^2$, not $8t^4$.

To see how this works, try evaluating each expression for $t = 4$.

Work it out without simplifying.	Add only coefficients.	Add coefficients and exponents.
$5t^2 + 3t^2 = 5(4^2) + 3(4^2)$	$8t^2 = 8(4^2)$	$8t^4 = 8(4^4)$
$= 5(16) + 3(16)$	$= 8(16)$	$= 8(256)$
$= 80 + 42$	$= 128$	$= 2048$
$= 128$	Yes, this works.	No, this doesn't work.

MORE HELP
See 037

Multiplying Binomials

Sometimes, when you simplify expressions, you need to multiply a binomial by another binomial. In this case, you need to be very careful that each term in one binomial gets multiplied by each term in the other.

EXAMPLE 1: Multiply $(x + 2)$ by $(x + 3)$.

ONE WAY You can use Algebra Tiles to understand how to multiply binomials.

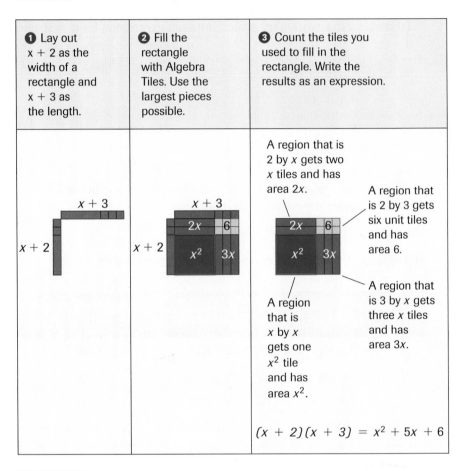

❶ Lay out x + 2 as the width of a rectangle and x + 3 as the length.	❷ Fill the rectangle with Algebra Tiles. Use the largest pieces possible.	❸ Count the tiles you used to fill in the rectangle. Write the results as an expression.

A region that is 2 by x gets two x tiles and has area $2x$.

A region that is 2 by 3 gets six unit tiles and has area 6.

A region that is x by x gets one x^2 tile and has area x^2.

A region that is 3 by x gets three x tiles and has area $3x$.

$(x + 2)(x + 3) = x^2 + 5x + 6$

ANOTHER WAY You can use the Distributive Property to multiply binomials. Multiply the second factor by each term of the first factor.

$$(x + 2)(x + 3) = x(x + 3) + 2(x + 3)$$
$$= x^2 + 3x + 2x + 6$$
$$= x^2 + 5x + 6$$

★ Either way, $(x + 2)(x + 3) = x^2 + 5x + 6$.

EXAMPLE 2: Multiply. $(2x + 3)(x - 2) =$ ■

Use the Distributive Property to be sure all the multiplication gets done.

$$(2x + 3)(x - 2) = \boxed{2x(x - 2)} + \boxed{3(x - 2)}$$
$$= \boxed{2x^2 \boxed{- 4x}} + \boxed{3x} - 6$$
$$= 2x^2 \boxed{- x} - 6$$

★ $(2x + 3)(x - 2) = 2x^2 - x - 6$

> Since adding the negative of a number is the same as subtracting the number, $2x^2 - x - 6$ is the same as $2x^2 + {}^-x + {}^-6$. It may be less confusing to write it with fewer symbols.

SHORTCUT

You can use this shortcut to multiply binomials.

1. Multiply the first terms.

   $(2x + 3)(x - 2)$ $2x^2$

2. Multiply the outer terms.

   $(2x + 3)(x - 2)$ ^-4x

3. Multiply the inner terms.

   $(2x + 3)(x - 2)$ ^+3x

4. Multiply the last terms.

   $(2x + 3)(x - 2)$ $^-6$

5. Combine like terms. $2x^2 + (^-4 + 3)x - 6 = 2x^2 - x - 6$

> To memorize this shortcut, you can use the acronym FOIL (First, Outer, Inner, Last).

109 MATH ALERT: When You Operate on a Term, Operate on the Whole Term

Be careful when you operate on terms in variable expressions. Remember to operate on each part of the term.

EXAMPLE 1: Find the product. $^-2(a + 6) = \blacksquare$

$$^-2(a + 6) = {}^-2a + {}^-2(6)$$
$$= {}^-2a + {}^-12$$

> Distribute $^-2$ to each term. Multiply both a and 6 by $^-2$.

★ $^-2(a + 6) = {}^-2a + {}^-12$ or $^-2a - 12$

EXAMPLE 2: Simplify $(2xy)^3$.

$$(2xy)^3 = 2xy \cdot 2xy \cdot 2xy$$
$$= 2 \cdot 2 \cdot 2 \cdot x \cdot x \cdot x \cdot y \cdot y \cdot y$$
$$= 2^3 \cdot x^3 \cdot y^3$$
$$= 8x^3y^3$$

> Cube 2, x, and y.

★ $(2xy)^3 = 8x^3y^3$

110 Finding the Product of the Sum and Difference of Two Terms

When you multiply binomials, you will find some patterns. These patterns can help you use shortcuts when you factor quadratic polynomials and when you solve quadratic equations.

MORE HELP
See 174, 181, 188

One pattern is produced by multiplying the sum of two terms by the difference of the same two terms. In this situation multiplying two binomials results in a binomial.

EXAMPLE 1: Multiply the binomials. $(x + 4)(x - 4) = \blacksquare$

$$(x + 4)(x - 4) = x^2 + 4x - 4x - 16$$
$$= x^2 - 16$$

> The middle terms zero each other out.

★ $(x + 4)(x - 4) = x^2 - 16$

EXAMPLE 2: Use what you know about finding the product of the sum and difference of two terms to multiply 54 by 46.

These two numbers are four more and four less than 50, so you could write the product as $(50 + 4)(50 - 4)$, the sum and difference of two terms! This gives you a great mental–math way to find the product.

$$(50 + 4)(50 - 4) = 2500 - 16$$
$$= 2484$$

★ $54 \times 46 = 2484$

> It sure is a lot shorter to express things algebraically. When you multiply the sum of two terms by the difference of the same two terms, the product is the difference of the squares of the two terms: $(a + b)(a - b) = a^2 - b^2$.

Squaring a Binomial

111

If you square a binomial, you get a **perfect square trinomial**. If you learn to recognize perfect square trinomials, you can save a lot of time when you factor quadratic polynomials, and when you solve quadratic equations.

EXAMPLE 1: Multiply. $(x + 4)^2 =$

$$(x + 4)^2 = (x + 4)(x + 4)$$
$$= x^2 + 4x + 4x + 16$$
$$= x^2 + 8x + 16$$

★ $(x + 4)^2 = x^2 + 8x + 16$

MORE HELP
See 108, 174, 181

> When the coefficient of the first term is one, the coefficient of the middle term in the product is twice the constant term in the original expression. $8 = 2(4)$

EXAMPLE 2: Multiply. $(2x - 4)^2 =$

$$(2x - 4)^2 = (2x - 4)(2x - 4)$$
$$= 4x^2 - 8x - 8x + 16$$
$$= 4x^2 - 16x + 16$$

★ $(2x - 4)^2 = 4x^2 - 16x + 16$

> When you square binomials, you find these patterns:
>
> $(a \oplus b)^2 = a^2 \oplus 2ab + b^2$ and
> $(a \ominus b)^2 = a^2 \ominus 2ab + b^2$

Multiplying and Dividing with Powers

MORE HELP
See 051

CASE 1 To multiply non–negative powers of the same base, add their exponents. To divide non–negative powers of the same base, subtract their exponents.

EXAMPLE 1: Multiply. $b^3 \cdot b^5 = \blacksquare$

$b^3 \cdot b^5 = (b \cdot b \cdot b) \cdot (b \cdot b \cdot b \cdot b \cdot b)$
$\qquad = b^8$

> The general rule is $b^m \cdot b^n = b^{m+n}$.

★ $b^3 \cdot b^5 = b^8$

EXAMPLE 2: Divide. $z^6 \div z^2 = \blacksquare$

$z^6 \div z^2 = \dfrac{z \cdot z \cdot \overset{1}{\cancel{z}} \cdot \overset{1}{\cancel{z}} \cdot z \cdot z}{\underset{1}{\cancel{z}} \cdot \underset{1}{\cancel{z}}}$

$\qquad = z^4$

> The general rule is $b^m \div b^n = b^{m-n}$ or $\dfrac{b^m}{b^n} = b^{m-n}$.

★ $z^6 \div z^2 = z^4$

CASE 2 To raise a non–negative power to a non–negative power, multiply the two powers and use the product as the exponent: $(a^m)^n = a^{mn}$. This is also called finding a power of a power.

Write: $(p^3)^2$
Say: *the second power of p cubed*

EXAMPLE 3: Simplify $(p^3)^2$.

$(p^3)^2 = p^3 \cdot p^3$
$\qquad = p \cdot p \cdot p \cdot p \cdot p \cdot p$
$\qquad = p^6$

★ $(p^3)^2 = p^6$

Multiplying with Roots

You can use the Distributive Property to multiply with roots.

For any positive real numbers x and y, and any real number n,
$n\sqrt{x} \cdot n\sqrt{y} = n^2\sqrt{xy}$.

To see how this works, try multiplying $2\sqrt{4}$ by $2\sqrt{16}$ two different ways.

$2\sqrt{4} \cdot 2\sqrt{16} = 2(2) \cdot 2(4)$ or $2\sqrt{4} \cdot 2\sqrt{16} = 2^2\sqrt{4 \cdot 16}$

$\qquad = 4 \cdot 8 \qquad\qquad\qquad\qquad = 4\sqrt{64}$

$\qquad = 32 \qquad\qquad\qquad\qquad\quad = 4 \cdot 8$

$\qquad\qquad\qquad\qquad\qquad\qquad\quad = 32$

This fact comes in handy when you need to factor and find multiples of perfect powers under a radical sign.

Evaluating Expressions _____

To **evaluate** an algebraic expression, you substitute (replace) numbers for the variables and carry out the computation.

Many fitness experts believe that the key to effective workouts is paying attention to heart rate. In workouts, the optimal training zone is 65% to 85% of maximum heart rate. Although maximum heart rate is different for different people, you can estimate your maximum heart rate by using the expression, $220 - a$, where a is your age in years. To find the upper limit of your optimal training zone, you would use the expression $0.85(220 - a)$.

Source: www.fitnesszone.com

MORE HELP
See 464

EXAMPLE 1: Use the expression to find the upper limit of the optimal training zone of a 20-year-old.

To solve the problem, evaluate the expression $0.85(220 - a)$ for $a = 20$. Substitute 20 for a and compute.

$$0.85(220 - a) = 0.85(220 - 20)$$
$$= 0.85(200)$$
$$= 170$$

★ The upper heart rate limit for the optimal training zone of a 20-year-old is 170 beats per minute.

EXAMPLE 2: Find the area of a circle with a radius of three centimeters.

Substitute 3 for r and 3.14 for π in the formula for the area of a circle. Then compute.

Since 3.14 is an approximate value for π, you must indicate that your calculation is approximate by using the wavy equals symbol.

$$A = \pi r^2$$
$$\approx 3.14 \cdot 3 \cdot 3$$
$$\approx 28.26$$

★ The area of the circle is about 28.26 square centimeters.

Replacement Sets

Before you evaluate a variable expression, you need to know what values a variable can have. Otherwise, you might substitute a number that doesn't make sense. The set of meaningful values that can be substituted for a variable is called the **replacement set** for the variable.

EXAMPLE: Suppose you are paid $3.00 for each 1-year magazine subscription that you sell. This means that the number of dollars you earn is given by the variable expression $3n$, where n is the number of subscriptions you sell. What is the replacement set for n?

MORE ▶

You can't sell a negative number of subscriptions. You also can't sell a fractional number of subscriptions. This means that, in the expression $3n$, the replacement set for the variable, n, is the set of whole numbers.

I sold ⁻4 subscriptions.

You mean you went door to door and bought subscriptions?

★ The replacement set for n is $n = 0, 1, 2, 3, ...$

Suppose that, in addition to $3.00 per subscription, you get an extra $0.75 bonus for each subscription after the first 50 that you sell. This means that when you sell more than 50 subscriptions, the number of dollars that you earn is given by this variable expression.

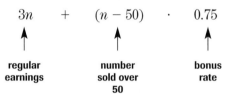

$$3n \quad + \quad (n - 50) \quad \cdot \quad 0.75$$

regular earnings   number sold over 50   bonus rate

If you substitute a number less than 50 for n, $n - 50$ produces a negative value. Since you won't get penalized if you sell fewer than 50 subscriptions, the replacement set for $3n + (n - 50)(0.75)$ is the set of whole numbers greater than or equal to 50: $n = 50, 51, 52, ...$ If you sell fewer than 50 subscriptions, you use the expression $3n$ to represent earnings.

116 Evaluating Expressions Involving Absolute Value

MORE HELP
See 009, 079

Some expressions involve absolute value. The **absolute value** of a number, which is written as $|n|$, is the distance between the number and zero on the number line. Distance is always positive.

EXAMPLE 1: Evaluate the expression $|x| + 1$ for $x = 5$; $x = 0$; $x = {}^-5$.

For $x = 5$:

$$|x| + 1 = |5| + 1$$
$$= 5 + 1$$
$$= 6$$

For $x = 0$:

$$|x| + 1 = |0| + 1$$
$$= 0 + 1$$
$$= 1$$

For $x = {}^-5$

$$|x| + 1 = |{}^-5| + 1$$
$$= 5 + 1$$
$$= 6$$

★ $|5| + 1 = 6; |0| + 1 = 1; |{}^-5| + 1 = 6$

EXAMPLE 2: Evaluate the expression $|x + 1|$ for $x = 5$, $x = 0$, and $x = {}^-5$.

For $x = 5$:

$$|x + 1| = |5 + 1|$$
$$= |6|$$
$$= 6$$

For $x = 0$:

$$|x + 1| = |0 + 1|$$
$$= |1|$$
$$= 1$$

For $x = {}^-5$

$$|x + 1| = |{}^-5 + 1|$$
$$= |{}^-4|$$
$$= 4$$

★ $|5 + 1| = 6$; $|0 + 1| = 1$; $|{}^-5 + 1| = 4$

Algebraic Fractions

An **algebraic fraction** (also called a **rational expression**) is like any other fraction—it has a numerator and a denominator, and it's written in the form $\frac{a}{b}$. It looks different than other fractions when a and/or b are polynomials.

EXAMPLE: To find the number of diagonals in any polygon, you can use the expression $\frac{n^2 - 3n}{2}$, where n represents the number of sides of the polygon. What happens to the number of diagonals as the number of sides increases?

Since n represents the number of sides of a polygon, the possible replacements for n are whole numbers greater than two.

For a square, $n = 4$. The number of diagonals is two.

$$\frac{n^2 - 3n}{2} = \frac{4^2 - 3(4)}{2}$$
$$= \frac{16 - 12}{2}$$
$$= \frac{4}{2} = 2$$

For a pentagon, $n = 5$. The number of diagonals is five.

$$\frac{n^2 - 3n}{2} = \frac{5^2 - 3(5)}{2}$$
$$= \frac{25 - 15}{2}$$
$$= \frac{10}{2} = 5$$

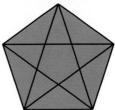

For a hexagon, $n = 6$. The number of diagonals is nine.

$$\frac{n^2 - 3n}{2} = \frac{6^2 - 3(6)}{2}$$
$$= \frac{36 - 18}{2}$$
$$= \frac{18}{2} = 9$$

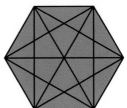

★ The number of diagonals increases as the number of sides increases.

MORE HELP
See 012, 020,
026, 037, 464

Simplifying Algebraic Fractions

Any fraction is in simplest form if the only common factor of the numerator and denominator is 1 or $^-1$. This is just as true for algebraic fractions as it is for other fractions. To simplify a fraction, look for factors common to both the numerator and denominator.

$\frac{abcd}{abg}$ is equivalent to $\frac{a \cdot b \cdot c \cdot d}{a \cdot b \cdot g}$.

You could also write this as $\frac{a}{a} \cdot \frac{b}{b} \cdot \frac{cd}{g}$. Since $\frac{a}{a}$ and $\frac{b}{b}$ are each equivalent to one, the simplified form of the fraction is $\frac{cd}{g}$.

CASE 1 If you think about an algebraic fraction as a group of fractions multiplied by each other, you can see why pairs of matching factors, one in the numerator and one in the denominator, help you to quickly simplify fractions.

EXAMPLE 1: Write in simplest form the ratio of the area of the rectangle to the area of the trapezoid.

The fractional expression of the ratio is:

$$\frac{\text{Area of rectangle}}{\text{Area of trapezoid}}$$

$$= \frac{lw}{\frac{1}{2}h(b_1 + b_2)}$$

$$= \frac{4a(3a)}{\frac{1}{2}(3a)(4a + 4a + 4 + 6)}$$

$$= \frac{12a^2}{12a^2 + 15a}$$

To simplify the expression, follow these steps.

❶ Find the prime factors of the numerator and denominator.	❷ Divide out all the factors common to both numerator and denominator.
$\frac{12a^2}{12a^2 + 15a} \longrightarrow \frac{2 \cdot 2 \cdot 3 \cdot a \cdot a}{3 \cdot a \cdot (4a + 5)}$	$\frac{2 \cdot 2 \cdot \cancel{3} \cdot \cancel{a} \cdot a}{\cancel{3} \cdot \cancel{a} \cdot (4a + 5)}$

★ The ratio in simplest form is $\frac{4a}{4a + 5}$.

You could think of this expression as $\frac{3}{3} \cdot \frac{4a}{(4a + 5)} \cdot \frac{a}{a}$. Since $\frac{3}{3}$ and $\frac{a}{a}$ are equivalent to 1, the identity element states that the expressions $\frac{12a^2}{12a^2 + 15a}$ and $\frac{4a}{(4a + 5)}$ have the same value.

EXAMPLE 2: Simplify $\frac{2x^2 - 6x}{6x^2}$.

❶ Find the prime factors of the numerator and denominator.		❷ Divide out all the factors common to both numerator and denominator.
$\dfrac{2x^2 - 6x}{6x^2}$ $\longrightarrow$	$\dfrac{2x(x - 3)}{2 \cdot 3 \cdot x \cdot x}$	$\dfrac{\overset{1}{\cancel{2}} \cdot \overset{1}{\cancel{x}} \cdot (x - 3)}{\underset{1}{\cancel{2}} \cdot 3 \cdot \underset{1}{\cancel{x}} \cdot x}$

★ $\dfrac{2x^2 - 6x}{6x^2} = \dfrac{x - 3}{3x}$

CASE 2 When the denominator of an algebraic fraction is not a monomial, you may be able to use a process of polynomial division to simplify the fraction.

EXAMPLE 3: Use polynomial division to simplify $\frac{6x^2 + 7x + 2}{2x + 1}$.

Polynomial division is a lot like ordinary long division. Compare the polynomial division on the left with the long division on the right. The main difference is that, in polynomial division, the quotient isn't based on our base-ten place value system.

Be sure to write the dividend in order from highest degree to lowest.

Polynomial division   **Long Division**

Step 1

$$
\begin{array}{r}
3x \\
2x + 1\overline{)6x^2 + 7x + 2} \\
-(6x^2 + 3x) \\
\hline
4x + 2
\end{array}
$$

Divide.

Multiply.
Subtract and bring down.

$$
\begin{array}{r}
3 \\
21\overline{)672} \\
-63 \\
\hline
42
\end{array}
$$

Step 2

$$
\begin{array}{r}
3x + 2 \\
2x + 1\overline{)6x^2 + 7x + 2} \\
-(6x^2 + 3x) \\
\hline
4x + 2 \\
-(4x + 2) \\
\hline
0
\end{array}
$$

Divide.

Multiply.
Subtract and bring down.

$$
\begin{array}{r}
32 \\
21\overline{)672} \\
-63 \\
\hline
42 \\
-42 \\
\hline
0
\end{array}
$$

★ $\dfrac{6x^2 + 7x + 2}{2x + 1} = 3x + 2$

119 MATH ALERT Cancel Only Factors

When you divide out factors common to the numerator and denominator to simplify fractions, you are **canceling**. When a factor in the
numerator of a fraction matches a factor in the denominator of that
fraction, they cancel each other because their quotient is one. Be sure
that when you cancel, you are matching factors, not terms.

EXAMPLE: Name factors that will cancel each other in this fraction.

numerator ──────▶ $\dfrac{3xy}{12x + 6y}$
denominator ──────▶

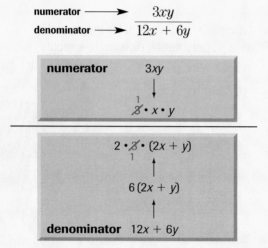

There is only one matching pair of factors. Even though the numerator and the denominator have the same variables, these variables do
not match up as factors, so they do not cancel.

★ The numerator and denominator each have a factor of 3. These
threes cancel each other.

120 Common Denominators for Algebraic Fractions

If you need to add or subtract fractions, you must first write them as fractions with a common denominator before you compute. You know how to
do this with fractions whose numerators and denominators are numbers.
To do it with fractions whose numerators and denominators are polynomials, you follow the same steps.

EXAMPLE 1: Write $\frac{3}{8}$ and $\frac{1}{6}$ as fractions with a common denominator.

ONE WAY You can find the least common denominator.

❶ Find the least common multiple of the denominators. This is the least common denominator.	The denominators are 8 and 6. 8: 8, 16, 24 6: 6, 12, 18, 24
❷ Multiply the numerator and denominator of each fraction by a factor that will result in the least common denominator.	$\frac{3}{8} = \frac{3 \times 3}{8 \times 3} = \frac{9}{24}$ $\frac{1}{6} = \frac{1 \times 4}{6 \times 4} = \frac{4}{24}$

When you multiply both the numerator and denominator of a fraction by the same number, you are multiplying the entire fraction by one ($\frac{a}{a}$). You are not changing the value of the fraction.

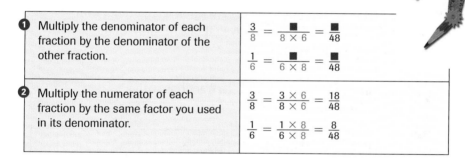

ANOTHER WAY You can use any common denominator.

❶ Multiply the denominator of each fraction by the denominator of the other fraction.	$\frac{3}{8} = \frac{\blacksquare}{8 \times 6} = \frac{\blacksquare}{48}$ $\frac{1}{6} = \frac{\blacksquare}{6 \times 8} = \frac{\blacksquare}{48}$
❷ Multiply the numerator of each fraction by the same factor you used in its denominator.	$\frac{3}{8} = \frac{3 \times 6}{8 \times 6} = \frac{18}{48}$ $\frac{1}{6} = \frac{1 \times 8}{6 \times 8} = \frac{8}{48}$

★ Two possible ways to write $\frac{3}{8}$ and $\frac{1}{6}$ with common denominators are $\frac{9}{24}$ and $\frac{4}{24}$, or $\frac{18}{48}$ and $\frac{8}{48}$.

EXAMPLE 2: Write $\frac{3x^2}{6x}$ and $\frac{5x^2}{8x}$ as fractions with a common denominator.

ONE WAY You can find the least common denominator.

❶ Find the least common multiple of the denominators. This is the least common denominator.	The denominators are $6x$ and $8x$. $6x$: $6x$, $12x$, $18x$, $24x$ $8x$: $8x$, $16x$, $24x$
❷ Multiply the numerator and denominator of each fraction by a factor that will result in the least common denominator.	$\frac{3x^2}{6x} = \frac{3x^2 \cdot 4}{6x \cdot 4} = \frac{12x^2}{24x}$ $\frac{5x^2}{8x} = \frac{5x^2 \cdot 3}{8x \cdot 3} = \frac{15x^2}{24x}$

MORE ▶

ANOTHER WAY You can use any common denominator.

❶ Multiply the denominator of each fraction by the denominator of the other fraction.	$\frac{3x^2}{6x} = \frac{\blacksquare}{6x \cdot 8x} = \frac{\blacksquare}{48x^2}$ $\frac{5x^2}{8x} = \frac{\blacksquare}{8x \cdot 6x} = \frac{\blacksquare}{48x^2}$
❷ Multiply the numerator of each fraction by the same factor you used in its denominator.	$\frac{3x^2}{6x} = \frac{3x^2 \cdot 8x}{48x^2} = \frac{24x^3}{48x^2}$ $\frac{5x^2}{8x} = \frac{5x^2 \cdot 6x}{48x^2} = \frac{30x^3}{48x^2}$

★ Two possible ways to write $\frac{3x^2}{6x}$ and $\frac{5x^2}{8x}$ with common denominators are $\frac{12x^2}{24x}$ and $\frac{15x^2}{24x}$ or $\frac{24x^3}{48x^2}$ and $\frac{30x^3}{48x^2}$.

121

MATH ALERT Any Polynomial Can Be Expressed as a Fraction

Any two numbers or expressions can be written as fractions with common denominators. This is true even if one or more of the numbers or expressions is irrational.

EXAMPLE: Write $\frac{3n + 5}{2n^2 - 1}$ and $5 + n\sqrt{7}$ as fractions with a common denominator.

❶ Write each expression as a fraction.	$\frac{3n + 5}{2n^2 - 1}$ $5 + n\sqrt{7} = \frac{5 + n\sqrt{7}}{1}$
❷ Multiply the numerator and denominator of the fraction whose denominator is 1 by the other denominator.	$\frac{3n + 5}{2n^2 - 1} = \frac{3n + 5}{2n^2 - 1}$ $\frac{5 + n\sqrt{7}}{1} = \frac{(5 + n\sqrt{7})(2n^2 - 1)}{1(2n^2 - 1)}$

This is the same method as multiplying the denominator of each fraction by the denominator of the other, then multiplying each numerator by the factor used in its denominator.

★ One possible answer: $\frac{3n + 5}{2n^2 - 1} = \frac{3n + 5}{2n^2 - 1}$; $5 + n\sqrt{7} = \frac{(5 + n\sqrt{7})(2n^2 - 1)}{2n^2 - 1}$.

Multiplying and Dividing Algebraic Fractions

To multiply or divide algebraic fractions, follow the steps you use with simple fractions. Then, follow the steps for simplifying algebraic fractions.

EXAMPLE 1: Multiply. $\frac{2x^2}{9} \cdot \frac{3}{2x^4} =$ ■

MORE HELP
See 089–090, 117–119, 182, 188

ONE WAY Simplify first, then multiply.

① Find the prime factorization for both numerator and denominator.	$\frac{2x^2}{9} \cdot \frac{3}{2x^4} \longrightarrow \frac{2 \cdot x \cdot x \cdot 3}{3 \cdot 3 \cdot 2 \cdot x \cdot x \cdot x \cdot x}$
② Divide out factors common to the numerator and denominator, then multiply.	$\frac{\overset{1}{\cancel{2}} \cdot \overset{1}{\cancel{x}} \cdot \overset{1}{\cancel{x}} \cdot \overset{1}{\cancel{3}}}{3 \cdot \underset{1}{\cancel{3}} \cdot \underset{1}{\cancel{2}} \cdot \underset{1}{\cancel{x}} \cdot \underset{1}{\cancel{x}} \cdot x \cdot x} = \frac{1}{3 \cdot x \cdot x} = \frac{1}{3x^2}$

ANOTHER WAY Multiply first, then simplify.

① Multiply the numerators. Multiply the denominators.	$\frac{2x^2}{9} \cdot \frac{3}{2x^4} = \frac{6x^2}{18x^4}$
② Find the prime factorization for both numerator and denominator.	$\frac{6x^2}{18x^4} \longrightarrow \frac{2 \cdot 3 \cdot x \cdot x}{2 \cdot 3 \cdot 3 \cdot x \cdot x \cdot x \cdot x}$
③ Divide out the factors common to the numerator and denominator, then multiply.	$\frac{\overset{1}{\cancel{2}} \cdot \overset{1}{\cancel{3}} \cdot \overset{1}{\cancel{x}} \cdot \overset{1}{\cancel{x}}}{\underset{1}{\cancel{2}} \cdot \underset{1}{\cancel{3}} \cdot 3 \cdot \underset{1}{\cancel{x}} \cdot \underset{1}{\cancel{x}} \cdot x \cdot x} = \frac{1}{3 \cdot x \cdot x} = \frac{1}{3x^2}$

★ Either way, the product is $\frac{1}{3x^2}$.

To divide algebraic fractions, multiply the dividend by the reciprocal of the divisor. Then, follow the steps for multiplying fractions.

MORE HELP
see 041

EXAMPLE 2: Divide. $\frac{2y^2}{3} \div \frac{8y}{5} =$ ■

ONE WAY Simplify first.

① Rewrite the division as multiplication by the reciprocal of the divisor.	$\frac{2y^2}{3} \div \frac{8y}{5} \longrightarrow \frac{2y^2}{3} \cdot \frac{5}{8y}$
② Find the prime factorization for both numerators and denominators.	$\frac{2 \cdot y \cdot y}{3} \cdot \frac{5}{2 \cdot 2 \cdot 2 \cdot y}$
③ Divide out factors common to the numerator and denominator, then multiply.	$\frac{\overset{1}{\cancel{2}} \cdot \overset{1}{\cancel{y}} \cdot y}{3} \cdot \frac{5}{\underset{1}{\cancel{2}} \cdot 2 \cdot 2 \cdot \underset{1}{\cancel{y}}} = \frac{5y}{12}$

MORE ▶

ANOTHER WAY Multiply $\frac{2y^2}{3}$ by the reciprocal of $\frac{8y}{5}$, then simplify.

❶ Rewrite the division as multiplication by the reciprocal of the divisor.	$\frac{2y^2}{3} \div \frac{8y}{5} \longrightarrow \frac{2y^2}{3} \cdot \frac{5}{8y}$
❷ Multiply the numerators. Multiply the denominators.	$\frac{2y^2}{3} \cdot \frac{5}{8y} = \frac{10y^2}{24y}$
❸ Find the prime factorization for both numerator and denominator.	$\frac{10y^2}{24y} \longrightarrow \frac{2 \cdot 5 \cdot y \cdot y}{2 \cdot 2 \cdot 2 \cdot 3 \cdot y}$
❹ Divide out factors common to the numerator and denominator, then multiply.	$\frac{\overset{1}{\cancel{2}} \cdot 5 \cdot \overset{1}{\cancel{y}} \cdot y}{\underset{1}{\cancel{2}} \cdot 2 \cdot 2 \cdot 3 \cdot \underset{1}{\cancel{y}}} = \frac{5 \cdot y}{2 \cdot 2 \cdot 3} = \frac{5y}{12}$

★ Either way, the quotient is $\frac{5y}{12}$.

MORE HELP
See 294, 464 **EXAMPLE 3:** What percent of the area of the rectangle is the area of the square?

Use the formulas for area of a rectangle and area of a square.

x $2x$ $\frac{xy}{2}$ $\frac{xy}{2}$

$A \text{ (rectangle)} = 2x \cdot 1x = 2x^2$

$A \text{ (square)} = \frac{xy}{2} \cdot \frac{xy}{2} = \frac{x^2y^2}{4}$

To find the percent $\frac{x^2y^2}{4}$ is of $2x^2$, divide. $\frac{x^2y^2}{4} \div 2x^2 = \blacksquare$

❶ Rewrite the division as multiplication by the reciprocal of the divisor.	$\frac{x^2y^2}{4} \div 2x^2 \longrightarrow \frac{x^2y^2}{4} \cdot \frac{1}{2x^2}$
❷ Find the prime factorization for both numerators and denominators.	$\frac{x \cdot x \cdot y \cdot y}{2 \cdot 2} \cdot \frac{1}{2 \cdot x \cdot x}$
❸ Divide out factors common to the numerator and denominator, then multiply.	$\frac{\overset{1}{\cancel{x}} \cdot \overset{1}{\cancel{x}} \cdot y \cdot y}{2 \cdot 2} \cdot \frac{1}{2 \cdot \underset{1}{\cancel{x}} \cdot \underset{1}{\cancel{x}}} = \frac{y^2}{8}$
❹ Rewrite as a fraction times the variable. Divide the numerator by the denominator, then multiply that quotient by 100 to find the percent.	$\frac{y^2}{8} = \frac{1}{8}y^2$ $= 0.125y^2$ $= 12.5y^2\%$

★ The square is $12.5y^2\%$ of the rectangle.

Adding and Subtracting Algebraic Fractions

To add or subtract algebraic fractions, follow the steps you use to add or subtract fractions that have numerators and denominators that are numbers. Then, follow the steps for simplifying algebraic fractions.

MORE HELP
See 082,
089–090,111,
118, 120

CASE 1 To add or subtract algebraic fractions with the same denominator, add or subtract the numerators and use the common denominator.

EXAMPLE 1: Add. $\dfrac{x^2 + 4x}{x + 3} + \dfrac{2x + 9}{x + 3} = $ ■

❶ Add the numerators.	$\dfrac{x^2 + 4x}{x + 3} + \dfrac{2x + 9}{x + 3} = \dfrac{x^2 + 4x + 2x + 9}{x + 3}$
❷ Simplify the numerator by combining like terms.	$\dfrac{x^2 + 4x + 2x + 9}{x + 3} = \dfrac{x^2 + 6x + 9}{x + 3}$
❸ Factor the numerator and/or the denominator, if possible.	$\dfrac{x^2 + 6x + 9}{x + 3} = \dfrac{(x + 3)(x + 3)}{x + 3}$
❹ Simplify, if possible.	$\dfrac{\overset{1}{\cancel{(x + 3)}}(x + 3)}{\underset{1}{\cancel{x + 3}}} = x + 3$

★ The sum is $x + 3$.

EXAMPLE 2: Subtract. $\dfrac{6a^2 - 16a}{a^2 - 3a} - \dfrac{a^2 + 4a}{a^2 - 3a} = $ ■

❶ Subtract the numerators.	$\dfrac{6a^2 - 16a}{a^2 - 3a} \ominus \dfrac{a^2 + 4a}{a^2 - 3a} = \dfrac{6a^2 - 16a \ominus (a^2 + 4a)}{a^2 - 3a}$
❷ Simplify the numerator by combining like terms.	$\dfrac{6a^2 - 16a - (a^2 + 4a)}{a^2 - 3a} = \dfrac{6a^2 - 16a - a^2 - 4a}{a^2 - 3a}$ $= \dfrac{5a^2 - 20a}{a^2 - 3a}$ $^-16a + {^-4a} = {^-}\lvert 16a + 4a\rvert$
❸ Factor the numerator and/or the denominator, if possible.	$\dfrac{5a^2 - 20a}{a^2 - 3a} = \dfrac{5a\,(a - 4)}{a\,(a - 3)}$
❹ Simplify, if possible.	$\dfrac{\overset{1}{\cancel{5a}}(a - 4)}{\underset{1}{\cancel{a}}(a - 3)} = \dfrac{5\,(a - 4)}{a - 3}$

★ The difference is $\dfrac{5(a - 4)}{a - 3}$.

MORE HELP
See 082, 110, 120

CASE 2 To add or subtract algebraic fractions with different denominators, express the fractions with a common denominator. Then, add or subtract the numerators.

EXAMPLE 3: Add. $\dfrac{7b}{4b+12} + \dfrac{5+b}{b^2-9} = \blacksquare$

❶ Factor the numerators and/or the denominators.	$\dfrac{7b}{4b+12} + \dfrac{5+b}{b^2-9} = \dfrac{7b}{4(b+3)} + \dfrac{5+b}{(b+3)(b-3)}$
❷ Rewrite each fraction using the least common denominator.	$\dfrac{7b}{4(b+3)} + \dfrac{5+b}{(b+3)(b-3)} = \dfrac{7b(b-3)}{4(b+3)(b-3)} + \dfrac{4(5+b)}{4(b+3)(b-3)}$ $= \dfrac{7b^2-21b}{4(b+3)(b-3)} + \dfrac{20+4b}{4(b+3)(b-3)}$
❸ Add the numerators.	$\dfrac{7b^2-21b}{4(b+3)(b-3)} + \dfrac{20+4b}{4(b+3)(b-3)} = \dfrac{7b^2-21b+20+4b}{4(b+3)(b-3)}$
❹ Simplify.	$\dfrac{7b^2-21b+20+4b}{4(b+3)(b-3)} = \dfrac{7b^2-17b+20}{4(b+3)(b-3)}$

★ The sum is $\dfrac{7b^2-17b+20}{4(b+3)(b-3)}$.

EXAMPLE 4: Subtract. $\dfrac{2x+5}{x^2-2x} - \dfrac{2x-3}{x^2-4} = \blacksquare$

❶ Factor the numerators and/or the denominators.	$\dfrac{2x+5}{x^2-2x} - \dfrac{2x-3}{x^2-4} = \dfrac{2x+5}{x(x-2)} - \dfrac{2x-3}{(x-2)(x+2)}$
❷ Rewrite each fraction using the least common denominator.	$\dfrac{2x+5}{x(x-2)} - \dfrac{2x-3}{(x-2)(x+2)} = \dfrac{(2x+5)(x+2)}{x(x-2)(x+2)} - \dfrac{x(2x-3)}{x(x-2)(x+2)}$ $= \dfrac{2x^2+5x+4x+10}{x(x-2)(x+2)} - \dfrac{2x^2-3x}{x(x-2)(x+2)}$
❸ Subtract the numerators.	$\dfrac{2x^2+5x+4x+10}{x(x-2)(x+2)} - \dfrac{2x^2-3x}{x(x-2)(x+2)}$ $= \dfrac{2x^2+5x+4x+10-(2x^2 \ominus 3x)}{x(x-2)(x+2)}$ $= \dfrac{2x^2+5x+4x+10-2x^2 \oplus 3x}{x(x-2)(x+2)}$
❹ Simplify.	$\dfrac{2x^2+5x+4x+10-2x^2+3x}{x(x-2)(x+2)} = \dfrac{12x+10}{x(x-2)(x+2)}$

★ The difference is $\dfrac{12x+10}{x(x-2)(x+2)}$ or $\dfrac{2(6x+5)}{x(x-2)(x+2)}$.

Equations with One Variable

An **equation** is a statement that two mathematical expressions represent the same quantity—they are equal.

Equations	Not Equations
$x + 3 = 10$	$x + 3 \quad 25$
$7y - 5 = 4y + 7$	$7n < 3x^2 + 2$
$x^2 + 5x + 6 = 0$	$15 + 25$
$15 + 25 = 40$	

Reading and Writing Equations

An equation shows the equal relationship between two expressions. Sometimes, you know all the numbers in an equation. Sometimes, you know only how the numbers are related. Either way, you can translate words into symbols so that finding any missing information is easier.

Words	Algebraic Equations
Eleven less than $\frac{1}{3}$ of a number is 15.	$\frac{1}{3}n - 11 = 15$
An adult ticket costs $1\frac{1}{3}$ times as much as a child's ticket. The total cost of an adult ticket and a child's ticket is $17.50.	adult's ticket + child's ticket = total cost $1\frac{1}{3}n + n = \$17.50$

Simplifying Equations

You often simplify equations as you get ready to solve them, or in the midst of solving them. To simplify equations, use the steps you already know for simplifying expressions.

MORE HELP
See 030–031,
034–035, 037,
103, 127

EXAMPLE: Simplify $7a - 4(3a + 6) + 8 = 46$.

ONE WAY Rewrite as addition.

To Simplify:	$7a - 4(3a + 6) + 8 = 46$
Rewrite as an addition equation if you find this easier.	$7a + \boxed{{}^-4(3a + 6)} + 8 = 46$
Use the Distributive Property to get rid of the parentheses.	$7a + \boxed{{}^-12a + {}^-24} + 8 = 46$
If there are like terms on one side of the equals sign, combine them.	${}^-5a + {}^-16 = 46$

ANOTHER WAY Don't rewrite as addition.

To Simplify:	$7a \boxed{- 4(3a + 6)} + 8 = 46$
Use the Distributive Property.	$7a \boxed{- 12a - 24} + 8 = 46$
If there are like terms on one side of the equals sign, combine them.	${}^-5a - 16 = 46$

★ Either way, $7a - 4(3a + 6) + 8 = 46$ simplifies to ${}^-5a + {}^-16 = 46$ or ${}^-5a - 16 = 46$.

This equation is ready for you to solve it—each side is as simple as you can make it without factoring or finding a way to get the variable by itself on one side of the equals sign.

Solving Equations with One Variable _____

To solve an equation that has one variable, you need to find the solution set for the equation. The **solution set** for an equation is the set of values that makes the equation true. One way to find the solution set is to **isolate the variable**—get it by itself on one side of the equation.

To understand the process of isolating the variable, think of an equation as a balanced scale. On a balanced scale, each side has an equal weight. In an equation, there is an equal quantity on each side of the equals sign.

EXAMPLE: Look at the scale to the right. Suppose that a represents the weight of one laptop computer. Then $a + 6 = 9$ represents the relationship shown on the scale.

To find the weight of the computer, you want to get it alone on one side of the scale so you can tell what weight balances it.

If you remove the 5-pound weight and one 1–pound weight from one side, you have to remove six pounds from the other side, too, to keep the scale in balance.

MORE HELP
See 044–046

★ The weight of the laptop computer is 3 pounds.

Of course, you don't need to carry around a balance and weights to solve equations. You can use the Addition and Multiplication Properties of Equality. The items that follow show how. Some of the problems you can solve in your head, but the methods shown help you save time when you are working with complicated equations.

One-Step Equations

Some equations can be solved in one step using the Equality Properties.

MORE HELP
See 044

CASE 1 To solve one-step equations involving addition, you can use the Addition Property of Equality.

EXAMPLE 1: In 1997, 906 new lipsticks were introduced. This number is 201 greater than the number of new lipsticks introduced in 1996. How many new lipsticks were introduced in 1996?

Source: Marketing Intelligence Service, LTD.

Words	Algebraic Expression or Equation
new lipsticks introduced in 1996	n
906 is 201 greater than n	$n + 201 = 906$

To find the number of new lipsticks introduced in 1996, solve for n in the equation.

To Solve:	$n + 201 = 906$
Isolate n: Undo the addition in $n + 201$. The Addition Property of Equality lets you add $^-201$ to (or subtract 201 from) each side.	$n + 201 + {}^-201 = 906 + {}^-201$ or $n + 201 - 201 = 906 - 201$
Simplify.	$n = 705$

Think of the solution process as getting rid of the clutter at each step. Use a property or simplify or compute to get rid of stuff you don't want.

★ The number of new lipsticks introduced in 1996 was 705.

CASE 2 To solve one-step equations involving subtraction, you can also use the Addition Property of Equality.

EXAMPLE 2: You withdraw $80 from an automated teller machine. The screen tells you that your new bank balance is $220. What was your bank balance before you made the withdrawal?

Words	Algebraic Expression or Equation
original bank balance	b
$220 is left after subtracting $80 from b	$b - 80 = 220$

To Solve:	$b - 80 = 220$
Isolate b: Undo the subtraction in $b - 80$. The Addition Property of Equality lets you add 80 to each side.	$b - 80 + 80 = 220 + 80$
Simplify.	$b = 300$

★ Your original bank balance was $300.

CASE 3 To solve one-step equations involving multiplication, you can use the Multiplication Property of Equality.

EXAMPLE 3: You buy five oranges for $2.45. What is the cost per orange?

Words	Algebraic Expression or Equation
price of one orange	p
five oranges cost $2.45	$5p = 2.45$

To Solve:	$5p = 2.45$
Isolate p: Undo the multiplication in $5p$. The Multiplication Property of Equality lets you multiply each side by $\frac{1}{5}$ (or divide each side by 5).	$5p \cdot \dfrac{1}{5} = 2.45 \cdot \dfrac{1}{5}$ or $\dfrac{5p}{5} = \dfrac{2.45}{5}$
Simplify.	$p = 0.49$

★ The cost per orange is $0.49.

MORE ▶

CASE 4 To solve one-step equations involving division, you can also use the Multiplication Property of Equality.

EXAMPLE 4: The cost of a bicycle is $180. You plan to buy the bicycle 15 weeks from now. You have no money set aside for this purchase. If you plan to save the same amount each week, how much money must you save per week?

Words	Algebraic Expression or Equation
amount of money you must save per week	m
in fifteen weeks, savings must be $180	$15m = 180$

To Solve:	$15m = 180$
Isolate m: Undo the multiplication in $15m$. Divide both sides by 15.	$\dfrac{15m}{15} = \dfrac{180}{15}$
Simplify.	$m = 12$

★ You must save $12 per week in order to have enough money to buy the bicycle in 15 weeks.

Multi-Step Equations

Sometimes, it takes more than one step to simplify and solve an equation. In that case, first clear any fractions, then follow the order of operations in reverse.

MORE HELP
See 003, 068

EXAMPLE 1: The sum of three consecutive integers is 24. Find the numbers.

Consecutive integers are integers that follow each other in natural order, such as 20, 21, 22.

Words	Algebraic Expression or Equation
first integer	n
second integer	$n + 1$
third integer	$n + 2$
sum of integers is 24	$n + (n + 1) + (n + 2) = 24$

To solve the problem, solve for n in the equation,
$n + (n + 1) + (n + 2) = 24$.

To Solve:	$n + (n + 1) + (n + 2) = 24$
Combine like terms.	$3n + 3 = 24$
Isolate n: Undo the addition by subtracting 3 from each side of the equation.	$3n + 3 - 3 = 24 - 3$
Simplify.	$3n = 21$
Next, undo the multiplication by dividing both sides of the equation by 3.	$\dfrac{3n}{3} = \dfrac{21}{3}$
Simplify.	$n = 7$

Since $n = 7$, then $n + 1 = 8$ and $n + 2 = 9$. Check this solution in the original problem. $7 + 8 + 9 = 24$. Your work checks.

★ The three consecutive integers are 7, 8, and 9.

MORE ▶

EXAMPLE 2: Used alone, a pipe will fill a tank in two hours. A second pipe used alone will fill the same tank in three hours. If both pipes are used at the same time, how long will it take to fill the tank?

To solve the problem, let x represent the number of hours needed to fill the tank.

MORE HELP
See 120

Pipe	Time Needed to Complete Job (in hours)	Part of Job Done in One Hour	Part of Job Done in x Hours
first pipe	2	$\frac{1}{2}$	$\frac{1}{2}x = \frac{x}{2}$
second pipe	3	$\frac{1}{3}$	$\frac{1}{3}x = \frac{x}{3}$
both pipes	■	■	1

In x hours, the first pipe will complete $\frac{x}{2}$ of the job and the second pipe will complete $\frac{x}{3}$ of the job. Together, the pipes will complete the job when $\frac{x}{2} + \frac{x}{3}$ equals the whole job (1). To solve the problem, solve the equation, $\frac{x}{2} + \frac{x}{3} = 1$.

To Solve:	$\frac{x}{2} + \frac{x}{3} = 1$
Clear the fractions: Multiply each term by the product of the denominators.	$6\left(\frac{x}{2}\right) + 6\left(\frac{x}{3}\right) = 6(1)$
Simplify.	$3x + 2x = 6$
Combine like terms.	$5x = 6$
Undo the multiplication by dividing both sides of the equation by 5.	$\frac{5x}{5} = \frac{6}{5}$
Simplify.	$x = 1\frac{1}{5}$

★ If both pipes are used to fill the tank, they will take a total of $1\frac{1}{5}$ hours, or 1 hour and 12 minutes.

Absolute Value Equations with One Variable

Some equations involve absolute value. Then you must remember that two numbers can have the same absolute value.

EXAMPLE: In a poll, 52% of town residents said that they are against building a new mall. The results of the poll have a probable margin of error of plus or minus 3%. Write and solve an equation that gives you the most likely greatest and least percent of people who are against the new mall.

MORE HELP
See 009, 084

Let n represent the most likely percent of people who are against the new mall. The situation is represented by the equation $|n - 52| = 3$.

ONE WAY Use a number line.

On a number line, the predicted greatest and least values for n are each a distance of 3 units away from 52.

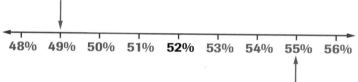

Actual percent is not likely to be lower than this

48% 49% 50% 51% **52%** 53% 54% 55% 56%

Actual percent is not likely to be higher than this

ANOTHER WAY Think about the meaning of absolute value.

For $|n - 52| = 3$ to be true, $n - 52$ must equal 3 or ⁻3 because $|3| = 3$ and $|{}^{-}3| = 3$.

Greatest Value	Least Value
$n - 52 = 3$	$n - 52 = {}^{-}3$
$n - 52 + 52 = 3 + 52$	$n - 52 + 52 = {}^{-}3 + 52$
$n = 55$	$n = 49$

To check, substitute each solution into the original equation

$$|n - 52| = \blacksquare \qquad\qquad |n - 52| = \blacksquare$$
$$|55 - 52| = \blacksquare \qquad\qquad |49 - 52| = \blacksquare$$
$$|3| = 3 \qquad\qquad\qquad |{}^{-}3| = 3$$

★ Either way, the likely percent of people against the new mall is at least 49% and at most 55%.

A **relation** is a set of ordered pairs. The members of the set can be pairs of things (like socks), or people (like husbands and wives), or people and things (like representatives and the states that they represent), or numbers (like 5 and 10).

Here are several ways to show how the elements in two sets are related.

- a word description
- an algebraic rule or equation
- a table
- a graph
- a list of ordered pairs
- an arrow diagram

The first item in an ordered pair comes from a set of elements called the **domain**. The second item in the ordered pair comes from a set of elements called the **range**. If the relation is between two sets of numbers, the domain contains the values of the **independent variable**. The range contains the values of the **dependent variable**. The value of the dependent variable is determined by the independent variable.

MORE HELP
See 137

EXAMPLE 1: How can you show the relation between a set of vehicles (boat, bicycle, motorcycle, car, light van, truck) and the number of wheels each vehicle has?

Domain: boat, bicycle, motorcycle, car, light van, truck

Range: zero and the even whole numbers; 0, 2, 4, 6, . . .

You can show this relation in different ways.

ONE WAY Use a table to show a relation.

Vehicle	boat	bicycle	motorcycle	car	light van	truck
Number of Wheels	0	2	2	4	4	even numbers from 4 through 22

ANOTHER WAY List the ordered pairs to show a relation.

(boat, 0), (bicycle, 2), (motorcycle, 2), (car, 4), (light van, 4), (truck, 4),…, (truck, 22)

ANOTHER WAY Use an arrow diagram to show the relation.

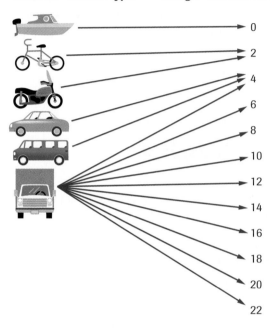

Domain—Vehicle Type   **Range—Number of Wheels**

EXAMPLE 2: Here are two ways to show the relation, *the second number is one more than twice the first number.*

ONE WAY You can use a table to show the relation.

x = first number y = second number

x	0	1	2	3	4	5	6	7	8
y	1	3	5	7	9	11	13	15	17

ANOTHER WAY You can use an equation to show the relation.

words:	the second number	is	one more than	twice the first
equation:	y	=	$1 +$	$2x$

Kinds of Relations

There are several kinds of relations.

CASE 1 In a *one-to-many* relation, some pairs show the same first value paired with different second values. The first value can repeat.

EXAMPLE 1: The relation containing the pairs (truck, 4 wheels), (truck, 6 wheels), (truck, 8 wheels),…, (truck, 22 wheels) is *one-to-many* because there are many possibilities for the number of wheels on a truck.

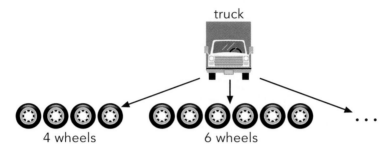

truck

4 wheels   6 wheels   . . .

CASE 2 A *many-to-one* relation shows different first values paired with the same second value. The second value can repeat.

EXAMPLE 2: The relation containing the pairs (car, 4 wheels), (van, 4 wheels), and (truck, 4 wheels) is *many-to-one* because the three vehicles are paired with the same number of wheels.

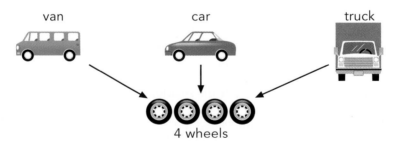

van   car   truck

4 wheels

CASE 3 In a *many-to-many* relation, a first value may be paired with different second values and a second value may be paired with different first values. The first value can repeat and the second value can repeat.

EXAMPLE 3: A relation between the number of bedrooms in an apartment and the number of people living in an apartment, (1, 1), (1, 2) (2, 1), (2, 2), (2, 3), (2, 4), (3, 1), (3, 2), (3, 3), (3, 4) is *many-to-many* because the numbers of bedrooms (1, 2, and 3) repeat and the numbers of people living in an apartment (1, 2, 3, and 4) repeat.

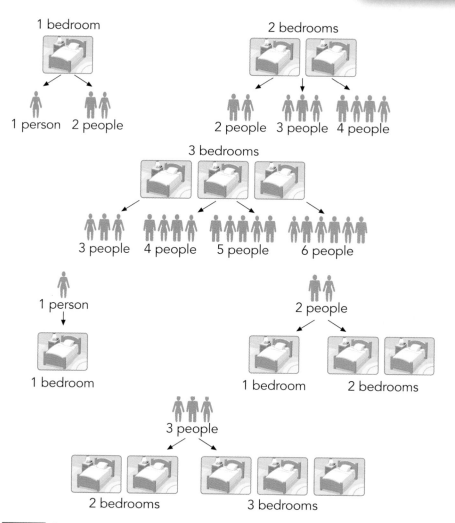

1 bedroom

1 person   2 people

2 bedrooms

2 people   3 people   4 people

3 bedrooms

3 people   4 people   5 people   6 people

1 person

1 bedroom

2 people

1 bedroom   2 bedrooms

3 people

2 bedrooms   3 bedrooms

CASE 4 A *one-to-one* relation shows that each first value is paired with only one second value and each second value is paired with only one first value. No first values can repeat and no second values can repeat.

EXAMPLE 4: The relation in which the dollars earned by the video store clerk is determined by the number of hours worked is *one-to-one*. This is because any number of hours may be paired with just one number of dollars earned, and a particular number of dollars earned may be paired with just one number of hours worked.

1 hour	2 hours	3 hours
↕	↕	↕
$5	$10	$15

Graphing Relations

You can use a graph to show a relation by plotting the ordered pairs in the relation.

MORE HELP
See 139, 219

EXAMPLE 1: A video store charges $5.00 to rent a video for a weekend. The store gives a $5.00 discount if four or more videos are rented. Graph the relation between the number of videos rented and the total cost for up to six videos.

First, use a table to show this many–to–one relation.

Number of Videos (x)	0	1	2	3	4	5	6
Total Cost (y)	0	$5.00	$10.00	$15.00	$15.00	$20.00	$25.00

★ Graph the ordered pairs: (0, 0), (1, 5), (2, 10), (3, 15), (4, 15), (5, 20), (6, 25).

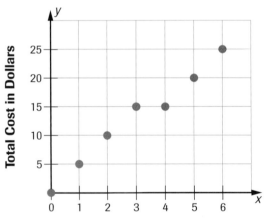

The points are not connected, because you can't rent a fractional number of videos! You can only rent a whole number of videos.

VILLAGE VIDEO

WEEKEND RENTAL
$5.00

$5 discount for rental of 4 or more videos.

EXAMPLE 2: The clerk at the video store earns $6.00 per hour. Graph the relation between hours worked and amount earned, up to five hours.

First, use a table to show this one–to–one relation.

Hours Worked (*x*)	0	1	2	3	4	5
Dollars Earned (*y*)	0	$6.00	$12.00	$18.00	$24.00	$30.00

★ Graph the ordered pairs: (0, 0), (1, 6), (2, 12), (3, 18), (4, 24), (5, 30).

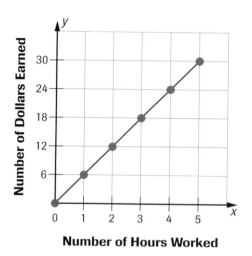

The points are connected, because the graph can tell you the amount earned at any number of hours. The number of hours does not need to be a whole number. Every point on the connecting line has meaning because each tells you the amount earned for that number of hours.

Functions

How fast can you get from your home to your school? That depends on your speed, and your speed depends on whether you walk, ride your bike, take the bus, or go by car. You could say that the length of time it takes you to get to school is a function of your method of transport.

A **function** is a special kind of relation in which the value of one variable depends on the value of another variable. Like a relation, it is a set of ordered pairs. However, in a function, each first value may be paired with one and only one second value. A function is a relation that is *many-to-one* or *one-to-one*.

135 ## Kinds of Functions

CASE 1 In many-to-one functions each second value can have more than one first value.

In most suburban commuter transit systems, ticket price is a *function* of distance traveled. In many of these systems, distances fall into zones, and there is one price for different trips that fall within a particular zone. This function is a *many-to-one* relationship.

Station/Distance from NYC (mi)		Zone	Round Trip
Newark	10.3	2	$4.50
East Orange	12.5	4	5.50
Brick Church	13.1	4	5.50
Orange	14.0	4	5.50
Highland Avenue	14.7	5	6.00
Mountain Station	15.6	5	6.00
South Orange	16.4	5	6.00

Source: New Jersey Transit

CASE 2 In one-to-one functions every first or second value has only one corresponding second or first value.

Suppose you are on a cliff. You drop a coin onto the rocks below. The distance that the coin has fallen is a *function* of the time that passes between when you drop the coin and when it hits the rocks and stops. For each elapsed time, there is one distance. For each distance, there is one elapsed time. This function is a *one-to-one* relationship.

You can use function notation to describe this function.

Suppose x = time. Then, distance fallen is a *function* of x, or $f(x)$.

MORE HELP
See 137

Write: $f(x)$
Say: *f of x* or *function of x*

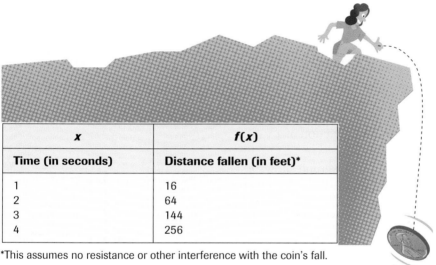

x	f(x)
Time (in seconds)	Distance fallen (in feet)*
1	16
2	64
3	144
4	256

*This assumes no resistance or other interference with the coin's fall.

According to the table, when time (x) is given in seconds, the distance fallen in feet is $16x^2$ seconds.

You could use d to stand for distance and write $d = 16x^2$. You could use y to stand for distance, since the most common notation for the dependent variable is y. However, to emphasize that one quantity is a function of the other, use $f(x)$ instead of d or y: $f(x) = 16x^2$.

The Vertical Line Test

When you graph a relation, you can use the **vertical line test** to determine whether the relation is a function. According to the **vertical line test**, if each vertical line drawn through any point on the graph of a relation intersects the graph at no more than one point, then that relation is a function.

EXAMPLE 1: The graph shows $y = x^2$.
Is y a function of x?

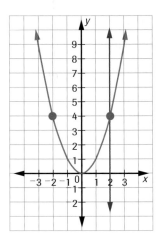

★ Any vertical line intersects the graph of $y = x^2$ at no more than one point, so y is a function of x^2.

EXAMPLE 2: The graph shows $y^2 = x$.
Is y a function of x?

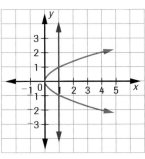

★ Some vertical lines intersect the graph of $y^2 = x$ in two places, so y is not a function of x.

Dependent and Independent Variables

When you work for an hourly wage, the total amount of money you earn depends on the number of hours that you work. If you express time (x) and amount earned (y) as a set of ordered pairs in the form (x, y), then x is the **independent variable** and y is the **dependent variable.** This means that the value of y depends on the value of x.

EXAMPLE: If you apply the function, $f(x) = 3x + 4$, for the x values 1, 2, and 3, what are the $f(x)$ values? Use ordered pairs to describe your answer.

x-Value	Function Rule: $f(x) = 3x + 4$	$f(x)$ Value	Ordered Pair
1	$f(x) = 3(1) + 4$	7	(1, 7)
2	$f(x) = 3(2) + 4$	10	(2, 10)
3	$f(x) = 3(3) + 4$	13	(3, 13)

★ Three ordered pairs of the function, $f(x) = 3x + 4$, are: (1, 7), (2, 10), and (3, 13).

MATH ALERT How to Tell When There Is One Solution or Many Solutions

138

Suppose you need to graph $y = 70$. What would the graph look like? The answer depends on the question for which $y = 70$ is the answer. Suppose the question is, *I've stopped growing, and I'm 70 inches tall. Graph my height against my age for the next 5 years.* Then, the answer is a line.

Suppose the question is, *What number added to itself equals 140?* This question is represented by the equation $2y = 140$ or $y = 70$. Then, the answer is a point on a number line.

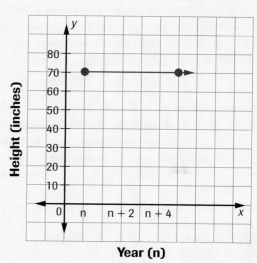

Discrete and Continuous Functions

Imagine a plane flying at a constant speed. The distance traveled has no gaps and you can say that the distance is a **continuous function** of time. If you plotted a few ordered pairs for this function, you could connect the dots. Any point on the line would have meaning. It would tell you how far the plane had traveled at that point in time.

This is a graph of a continuous function that describes a plane flying at 600 miles per hour, and has points plotted at intervals of one hour. You can connect the points that you're given and know that any other points on the line also answer the question: *How many miles have been traveled at this point in time?*

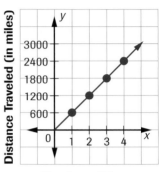

Number of Hours

Now imagine buying souvenir T-shirts to bring back from a trip. The total price you pay for the T-shirts is a function of the number of T-shirts you buy. But this function is *not* continuous, because you can't buy a fractional number of T-shirts. This function is a **discrete function**. If you graphed this function, you would not connect the dots, because the graph would have no meaning between the points.

This graph shows the total cost of x T-shirts, when the T-shirts cost $12.00 each. If you connected the points to make a line, you'd be saying that any point between the ones you plotted would give you a cost for a number of shirts. That means that the point $(2\frac{1}{2}, 30)$ would work. But it wouldn't make sense to say that $2\frac{1}{2}$ shirts would cost $30.00.

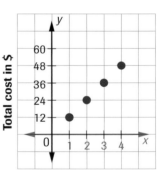

Number of T-shirts

The standard way to set up a graph is to put the independent variable along the x axis. In this graph, the total cost depends on the number of shirts, so number of shirts is the independent variable.

Linear Functions

A **linear function** is a function that is graphed as a straight line. You may be able to tell whether a function is linear by looking at its graph.

This graph shows the number of carbohydrates consumed as a function of ounces of Oat-O's cereal eaten. The graph is represented by the equation, $y = 23x$. The graph is a straight line. The function is linear.

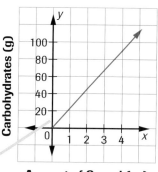

Carbohydrates (g) / Amount of Cereal (oz)

> In a linear function, a change in x causes proportional change in y. If you double x, you double y.

This graph shows three different-sized boxes of Oat-O's cereal and the prices of these boxes. There aren't any sizes of Oat-O's cereal in between these three sizes of boxes, so this is a discrete graph. However, you can use a straightedge to see that the points do not lie along a straight line.

The most reliable way to tell whether a function is linear is by looking at the equation. A linear equation contains one or two variables, each in the first power. It can be written in slope-intercept form, $y = mx + b$. If either variable is raised to a power other than 0 or 1, its graph is not linear.

> In a function that is not linear, a change in the x-value does not always cause a proportional change in the y-value.

MORE HELP
See 061, 149–152

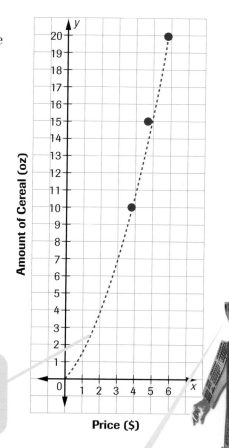

Amount of Cereal (oz) / Price ($)

> It's always best to decide whether a graph is linear by means other than just looking at it.

MORE ▶

CASE 1 Here are some equations that represent linear functions. They are first degree equations with one or two variables.

$$y = 2x + 4 \qquad n = 23 \qquad d = 4.5t$$

CASE 2 Here are some equations that do not represent linear functions. If you graphed them, they would not be straight lines.

$A = 5x^2$ ⟵ This does not represent a linear function because x^2 is a variable raised to the second power.

$y = \dfrac{1}{x} + 6$ ⟵ This does not represent a linear function because $y = \frac{1}{x} + 6$ is the same as $y = x^{-1} + 6$. The variable is raised to the $^-1$ power.

141

Absolute Value Functions

Here are some absolute value functions and their graphs.

MORE HELP
See 009, 114

$$y = |x|$$

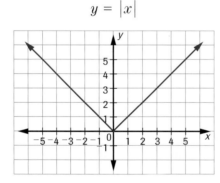

You can spot an absolute value function just by looking at its graph. The graph of an absolute value function always forms a V-shape!

$$y = |x| - 3$$

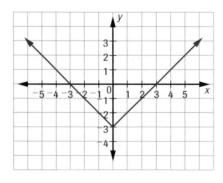

$$y = |x + 3|$$

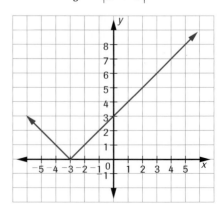

Quadratic Functions

Many relations in the physical world are quadratic functions. The relationships between distance and time, area and length, and kinetic energy and speed are all quadratic. When a function has a **degree of two**, it has a variable that is squared and is called a **quadratic function**. Quadratic functions have a degree of 2 and the exponents are all positive.

The graph of a quadratic function is a parabola. The standard form for the equation of a quadratic function is $y = ax^2 + bx + c$ where a, b, and c are constants and $a \neq 0$.

MORE HELP
See 176–178

To imagine the shape of a **parabola**, think of the path of a ball thrown into the air. When something travels through the air, and has no additional force or help to keep it in the air, the force of gravity causes that object to follow a parabolic path.

Some parabolas open upward and some open downward.

When a parabola opens upward, it has a minimum value. A high-diver's path into a pool and back to the surface looks a bit like a parabola—it's a curve with a minimum value. The **minimum value**, or lower bound, is the lowest point the diver reaches.

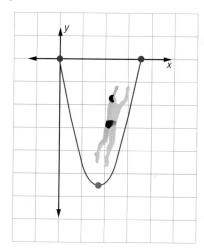

When a parabola opens downward, it has a maximum value. An example of such a curve would be the arc of an arrow shot into the air. The **maximum value**, or upper bound, is the top of the arc.

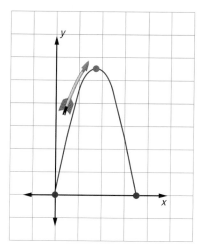

Greatest Integer Functions

You don't want to buy half of a CD or a third of a car. Sometimes, fractional amounts just won't do. In those situations, you can use a function called the GIF. The **greatest integer function** is the function, f, such that $f(x) = [x]$ where $[x]$ is the greatest integer less than or equal to a real number, x. For example, when $x = 2.7$, $[x] = 2$. When $x = {}^-2.7$, $[x] = {}^-3$.

x	$f(x) = [x]$
$^-4 \leq x < {}^-3$	$^-4$
$^-3 \leq x < {}^-2$	$^-3$
$^-2 \leq x < {}^-1$	$^-2$
$^-1 \leq x < 0$	$^-1$
$0 \leq x < 1$	0
$1 \leq x < 2$	1
$2 \leq x < 3$	2
$3 \leq x < 4$	3

When you see [ ] bracketing a variable, read *greatest integer of.*

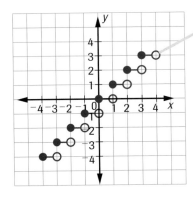

When you see an open circle, the point in the circle is not included in the graph.

The graph of the greatest integer function looks like a series of steps. That's why it's sometimes called a **step function.**

You can use greatest integer notation and graphs based on the greatest integer function to describe a variety of situations.

EXAMPLE: In a storewide sale, all CDs are priced at $8.00, including sales tax. Write a formula for the nth number of CDs you can purchase at $8.00 each if you have d dollars. Then, graph this function for values of d from 0 through 40.

To find the number of CDs (n) you can purchase, you need to divide the number of dollars (d) you have by the price per CD, $8.00. So, $n = \left[\frac{d}{8}\right]$.

d	$n = \left[\frac{d}{8}\right]$
$0 \le d < 8$	0
$8 \le d < 16$	1
$16 \le d < 24$	2
$24 \le d < 32$	3
$32 \le d < 40$	4
$d = 40$	5

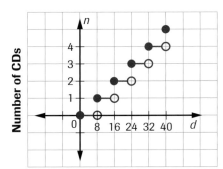

Number of Dollars

To figure out where the graph will be discontinuous, look for points where $\frac{d}{8}$ will be an integer: 8, 16, 32, 40. Each time you reach these amounts, you can buy an additional CD.

Inverse Functions

Suppose you drive 120 miles. The time your trip takes in t hours at an average speed, or rate, of r miles per hour is given by the equation, $120 = rt$.

Rate r (miles per hour)	Time t (hours)
10	12
20	6
30	4
40	3
50	$2\frac{2}{5}$
60	2

As your speed increases, your time decreases proportionally, and vice versa. You can say that the time that your trip takes varies inversely as your speed, or is **inversely proportional** to your speed.

MORE ▶

MORE HELP
See 293

An **inverse function** is a function in which two variables are inversely proportional. Two variables are **inversely proportional** if their product is always the same. An inverse function is defined by these equations:

$xy = k$, or $y = \frac{k}{x}$, where k does not equal zero.

EXAMPLE: Graph the equation $xy = 1$.

$xy = 1$ is an inverse function (if x gets bigger, y gets smaller proportionally), so the product will always stay the same. The graph of such a function is a **hyperbola.**

x	-3	-2	-1	$-\frac{1}{2}$	$-\frac{1}{3}$	$\frac{1}{3}$	$\frac{1}{2}$	1	2	3
y	$-\frac{1}{3}$	$-\frac{1}{2}$	-1	-2	-3	3	2	1	$\frac{1}{2}$	$\frac{1}{3}$

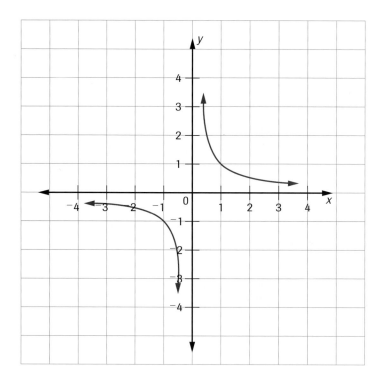

Periodic Functions

When scientists study sound, electricity, light, and other physical phenomena, they often run into functions that show a repeating or **periodic** pattern.

MORE HELP
See 249

The graph shows the function $y = \sin x$. As you can see, the graph of $y = \sin x$ shows a pattern in which the curve is repeated in each interval of 2π.

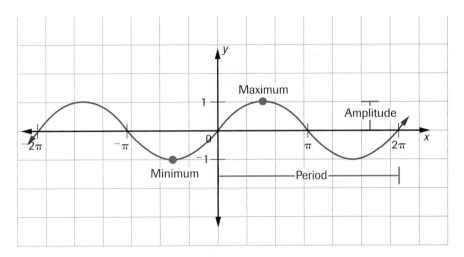

When a function has this type of repeating pattern, it is called a **periodic function**. A periodic function repeats itself at regular intervals. The **period** (p) of the function is the length of one repetition of the pattern. The **amplitude** of the function is the greatest absolute value of the function.

Linear Equations

"If mathematically, you end up with the wrong answer, try multiplying by the page number."

Anonymous

You probably have noticed the sizes and prices of drinks in a movie theater. The small 12–ounce cup might cost $2.50, the medium 18–ounce cup $3.50, and the large 32–ounce cup $4.50. If you buy a medium instead of a small, you get six more ounces for the extra dollar. But if you buy a large instead of a medium, you get 14 more ounces for the extra dollar. The relationship between size and price is not a linear relationship. Changes in one quantity (size) don't always result in the proportional change in the other quantity (price).

On the other hand, suppose you're buying CDs for $15 each and you're using a coupon good for $5 off your total purchase. One CD will cost you $10, two will cost $25, and three $40. Naturally, after the first CD, every time the number of CDs increases by one, the total cost increases by $15. The relationship between the number of CDs and the total cost is a linear relationship. Not only does the cost depend on the number of CDs, but also a given change in one quantity (number of CDs) always results in the corresponding proportional change in the other quantity (total cost).

Linear relationships can be described with **linear equations**. It makes sense to use the word *linear* for these equations because their graphs are lines. In this section you'll see how to solve equations and sets of equations that represent linear relationships, like buying CDs with a coupon, but not like buying drinks in a movie theater.

MORE HELP
See 140

To solve an equation, you find the values for variables that make the equation true. A linear equation, such as $y = 3x + 2$, has an infinite number of pairs of values (x, y) that make the equation true. The graph of these number pairs is a line. Any point along the line described by the equation $y = 3x + 2$ is a solution to the equation. We say that each of these points **satisfies** the equation.

There are many ways to find solutions to linear equations. For example, you can make a table of values by substituting values for x to find the corresponding values for y. You can also draw a graph of the equation, and find points along that line.

148

Making a Table of Values

According to the United States Coast Guard, only about $\frac{1}{8}$ of the mass of an iceberg is above the surface of the ocean. The other $\frac{7}{8}$ is below the ocean's surface. The relationship between the submerged part of the iceberg and the tip is given by the equation, $u = 7t$, where t represents the mass of the tip of the iceberg, and u represents the mass of the submerged part.

Source: www.uscg.mil

To complete a table of values for $u = 7t$, substitute each value of t into the equation. Then, write the corresponding value of u in the table.

Mass of Tip in tons (t)	Mass of Submerged Part in tons (u)
50,000	350,000
60,000	420,000
70,000	490,000

If $t = 50,000$, then
$u = 7 \cdot 50,000$, or $350,000$.

Writing Linear Equations

Suppose you have data about two variables. You can analyze those data to determine whether the two variables are linearly related. If so, you can write a linear equation that describes that relationship.

EXAMPLE 1: The table shows how room size and recommended air-conditioner size are related. Write an equation that gives the number of BTUs recommended for a room of any size.

Room Size in Square Feet (r)	300	400	500	600
Air Conditioner Size in BTUs (b)	6000	8000	10,000	12,000

Source: U.S. Department of Energy

To find the recommended number of BTUs per square foot, choose several pairs of values and look for relationships—can you add, subtract, multiply, or divide to get consistently from r to b? In this case it looks like b is a multiple of r. Check to see whether the relationship holds with other pairs of values.

$$300 \times 20 = 6000 \qquad 500 \times 20 = 10,000$$
$$400 \times 20 = 8000 \qquad 600 \times 20 = 12,000$$

★ To find the number of BTUs recommended for a room of any size, multiply the room size in square feet by 20: $b = 20r$.

EXAMPLE 2: The ad shows the rates for Internet access at Kathy's Coffee Shop. Write an equation that gives the cost in dollars (c) for a given number of minutes (m) of Internet access.

Cost = \$0.16 per minute · number of minutes + \$3.00

$$c = 0.16m + 3$$

★ The situation is represented by the equation, $c = 0.16m + 3$.

Surf and Swig!

Browse the Internet while you drink jolting java at Kathy's Coffee Shop.

Internet Access:
Just \$3.00
plus16¢ per minute!

Writing Linear Equations in Slope-Intercept Form

Suppose you know the slope of a line. Suppose you also know the distance from the origin $(0, 0)$ to the point where the line crosses the y–axis. This distance is the **y-intercept,** the value of y when $x = 0$. Anytime you know these two pieces of information, you can write the equation of the line very easily, using **slope–intercept** form.

Sometimes you may see y-intercept de-fined as the point $(0, b)$.

MORE HELP
See 157,
221–222

EXAMPLE 1: Look at the graph. Write the equation for the line.

$y = mx + b$, where m = slope and b = y-intercept

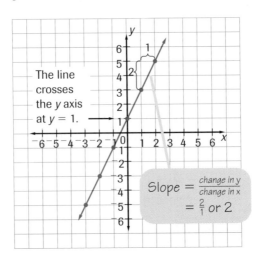

The line crosses the y axis at y = 1.

$$\text{Slope} = \frac{\text{change in } y}{\text{change in } x}$$
$$= \frac{2}{1} \text{ or } 2$$

When you use a graphing calculator to graph a line, you must enter the equation in slope-intercept form.

★ The slope of the line is two, so $m = 2$. The y-intercept is 1, so $b = 1$. The equation of the line is $y = 2x + 1$.

EXAMPLE 2: Write the equation for the line.

To write the equation for the line, find the slope and the y-intercept, then substitute these values into the equation $y = mx + b$.

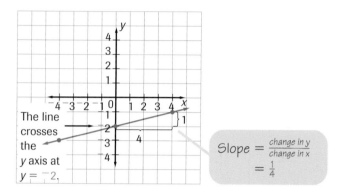

The line crosses the y axis at $y = {}^-2$,

$$\text{Slope} = \frac{\text{change in } y}{\text{change in } x}$$
$$= \frac{1}{4}$$

★ The equation of the line is $y = \frac{1}{4}x + {}^-2$, or $y = \frac{x}{4} - 2$.

EXAMPLE 3: Write the equation for the line. This line has a negative slope. How does its equation differ from the equation in example 2, above, which has a positive slope?

MORE HELP
See 099,
221–222

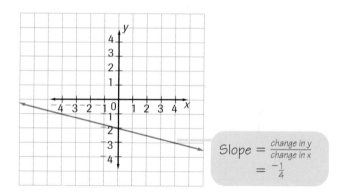

$$\text{Slope} = \frac{\text{change in } y}{\text{change in } x}$$
$$= \frac{{}^-1}{4}$$

★ The equation of the line is $y = {}^-\frac{1}{4}x + {}^-2$. The only difference between the equations for example 2 and example 3 is in the sign on the coefficient of x. The line with negative slope has a negative coefficient of x.

Writing Linear Equations When You Know a Point and the Slope

151

If you know the slope of a line and any point on the line, you can write the equation of the line. That makes sense, since through any point, there can be only one line with a given slope.

MORE ▶

MORE HELP
See 150–151,
127, 220–221

EXAMPLE: Find the equation of the line with a slope of $\frac{1}{3}$ that passes through the point (6, 1).

> **ONE WAY** Graph the line and use the graph to write the equation.

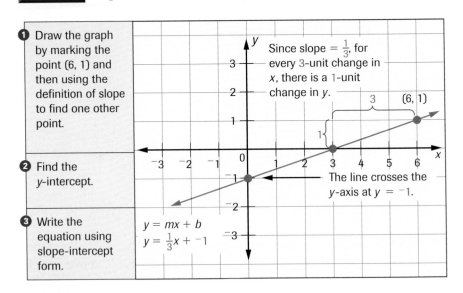

❶ Draw the graph by marking the point (6, 1) and then using the definition of slope to find one other point.	Since slope = $\frac{1}{3}$, for every 3-unit change in x, there is a 1-unit change in y.
❷ Find the y-intercept.	The line crosses the y-axis at $y = {}^-1$.
❸ Write the equation using slope-intercept form.	$y = mx + b$ $y = \frac{1}{3}x + {}^-1$

> **ANOTHER WAY** You can find the slope and the y–intercept and use them to write the equation.

❶ Find the y-intercept by substituting slope, $\frac{1}{3}$, and the x- and y- coordinates of the point (6, 1) into the slope-intercept form.	$y = mx + b$ $1 = \frac{1}{3}(6) + b$	Step 1 works because you know that (6, 1) is on the line, so it must be a solution to the equation that you are trying to find.
❷ Solve for b.	$1 = 2 + b$ ${}^-1 = b$	
❸ Substitute b and m into the slope-intercept equation.	$y = mx + b$ $y = \frac{1}{3}x + {}^-1$	

★ Either way, the equation of the line is $y = \frac{1}{3}x + {}^-1$, or $y = \frac{x}{3} - 1$.

Writing Linear Equations in Standard Form

Standard form for a linear equation is: $ax + by + c = 0$, where a, b, and c are integers and $a > 0$.

CASE 1 If you know the slope-intercept form of a linear equation, you can write the equation in standard form.

MORE HELP
See 103, 150, 156, 221

EXAMPLE 1: Write the linear equation $y = {}^-5x + 6$ in standard form.

❶ Write the equation in slope-intercept form.	$y = mx + b$ $y = {}^-5x + 6$
❷ Rewrite the equation as a variable expression equal to zero.	$y - y = {}^-5x - y + 6$ $0 = {}^-5x - y + 6$
❸ If necessary, multiply both sides of the equation by ${}^-1$ to make a positive.	$5x + y - 6 = 0$

★ The equation in standard form is $5x + y - 6 = 0$.

CASE 2 If you know the slope and the y-intercept of a line, you can write the equation of the line in standard form.

EXAMPLE 2: Write a linear equation in standard form for a line that has slope $m = 3$ and y-intercept $b = {}^-4$.

❶ Write the equation in slope-intercept form.	$y = mx + b$ $y = 3x + {}^-4$
❷ Rewrite the equation as a variable expression equal to zero.	$y - y = 3x - y + {}^-4$ $0 = 3x - y + {}^-4$
❸ If necessary, multiply both sides of the equation by ${}^-1$ to make a positive.	a is already positive.

★ The equation in standard form is $3x - y - 4 = 0$.

MORE ▶

CASE 3 If you know the slope of a line and any point on the line, you can write the equation of the line in standard form.

EXAMPLE 3: Write a linear equation in standard form for the line with slope $m = {}^-2$ that passes through the point $({}^-3, {}^-1,)$.

❶ Find b, the y-intercept.	$y = mx + b$
	$^-1 = {}^-2({}^-3) + b \longleftarrow$ Substitute $m = {}^-2$,
	$^-b = 7 \qquad\qquad\qquad x = {}^-3, y = {}^-1.$
	$b = {}^-7 \longleftarrow\qquad\qquad$ Solve for b.
❷ Write the equation in slope-intercept form using the values you have for m and b.	$y = mx + b$ $y = {}^-2x + {}^-7$
❸ Rewrite the equation in standard form.	$2x + y + 7 = 0$

★ The equation is $2x + y + 7 = 0$.

153 Graphing Linear Equations

A **linear equation** is an equation whose graph is a straight line. To tell whether an equation is a linear equation, you need to inspect the equation itself. If you can write it in slope-intercept form, and if the slope is the same everywhere, an equation is linear. Following are several ways to graph a linear equation.

154 Using a Graphing Calculator to Graph Linear Equations

To use a graphing calculator to graph the linear equation, $y = 2x - 3$, you must first enter the equation in slope-intercept form.

MORE HELP
See 140

Press: (Y=)

Press:

(2) (x,T,ø,n) (—) (3)

Press: (GRAPH)

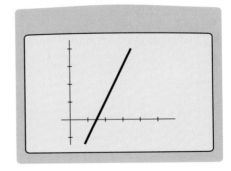

Using a Table of Values to Graph a Linear Equation

You can use a table of values to graph a linear equation.

EXAMPLE: A purse contains 40¢, all in dimes and nickels. Write an equation whose solution would include all the different possible combinations of dimes and nickels that could be in the purse. Graph the equation and use the graph to find all of the possible combinations.

First, write an equation.

Words	Algebraic Expression or Equation
value of one nickel × the number of nickles	$5n$
value of one dime × the number of dimes	$10d$
Total value is 40.	$5n + 10d = 40$

MORE HELP
See 139, 220

Next, make a table of values (remember $5n + 10d$ must equal 40, so $d = 4 - \frac{n}{2}$).

n	d
8	0
6	1
4	2

You really only need to find two points in order to define the line of a linear equation. The third point is just a check.

Last, plot points on the graph.

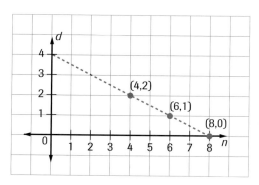

There can't be any fractional parts of dimes or nickels, so this is a discrete graph. But, you can dot in the line or use a straightedge to find other ordered pairs that are whole numbers. There can't be a negative number of either coin. So your graph must be in the first quadrant.

★ There are five possible combinations of nickels and dimes: 8 and 0, 6 and 1, 4 and 2, 2 and 3, and 0 and 4.

Using the Slope and a Point to Graph Linear Equations

If you know the slope of a line and any point on the line, you can graph that line on the coordinate plane.

EXAMPLE: Graph the line with a slope of $\frac{2}{3}$ that passes through ($^-2$, $^-2$).

MORE HELP
See 139,
150–151,
220–221

Plot the given point: ($^-2$, $^-2$).

Then, use the definition of slope to find another point. Use these two points to draw the line.

Since slope $= \frac{\text{change in } y}{\text{change in } x}$ find a point 2 units in the positive direction along y from $^-2$ and 3 units in the positive direction along x from $^-2$.

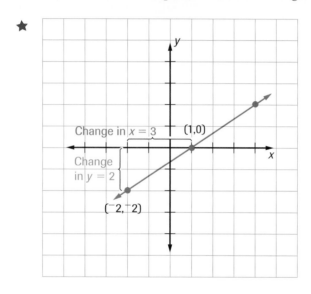

Change in $x = 3$ (1,0)

Change in $y = 2$

($^-2$, $^-2$)

You can check your work using **point-slope form**: $y - y_1 = m(x - x_1)$.

Pick any two points on the graph. Try $(4, 2)$ and $(1, 0)$. Is it true that $2 - 0 = \frac{2}{3}(4 - 1)$? Yes, $2 = 2$, so your graph satisfies the conditions of the problem.

If you need to write the equation of your graph, use the slope and a point to find the y-intercept.

$y = \frac{2}{3}x + b$

$^-2 = \frac{2}{3}(^-2) + b$

$^-2 + \frac{4}{3} = b$

$^-\frac{2}{3} = b$

So, $y = \frac{2}{3}x - \frac{2}{3}$

Using Slope-Intercept Form to Graph Linear Equations

The **slope-intercept** form of a linear equation is $y = mx + b$. In this form, m is the slope of the line and b is the value of y when $x = 0$. This value, b, is called the **y-intercept**. When an equation is in slope-intercept form, you can tell the slope and the y-intercept just by looking at the equation. This makes slope-intercept form a convenient tool for graphing linear equations.

MORE HELP
See 150,
220–221

EXAMPLE: Find the slope and the y-intercept of $y = 4x - 3$. Graph the equation.

By looking at the equation, you can tell that the slope, m, is 4 and the y-intercept, b, is ⁻3.

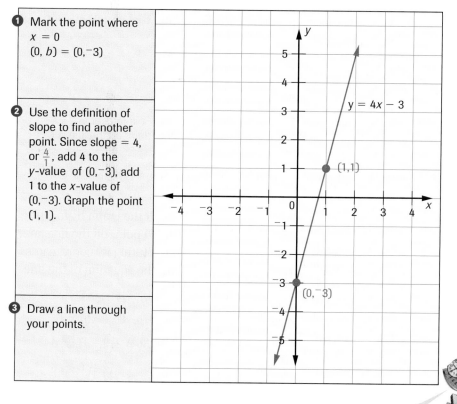

① Mark the point where
$x = 0$
$(0, b) = (0, ⁻3)$

② Use the definition of slope to find another point. Since slope = 4, or $\frac{4}{1}$, add 4 to the y-value of $(0, ⁻3)$, add 1 to the x-value of $(0, ⁻3)$. Graph the point $(1, 1)$.

MORE HELP
See 155, 156

③ Draw a line through your points.

$y = 4x - 3$

$(1,1)$

$(0, ⁻3)$

You could also make a table of values and plot the points. Draw a line through the points, then use it to find the slope and the y-intercept.

Finding the Intercepts to Graph a Linear Equation

You only need two points to determine a line, so one quick way to graph a line is to find the x- and y-intercepts. To find these, find the points where the line crosses the y-axis ($x = 0$) and the x-axis ($y = 0$).

MORE HELP
See 160

It's always easy to find the intercepts. To find the y-intercept, substitute 0 for x and solve for y. To find the x-intercept, substitute 0 for y and solve for x.

EXAMPLE: Find the x- and y-intercepts of $3x + 2y = 6$. Then, graph the equation.

First, find the intercepts.

❶ Find the y-intercept. Let $x = 0$.	❷ Find the x-intercept. Let $y = 0$.
$3x + 2y = 6$ $3(0) + 2y = 6$ $2y = 6$ $y = 3$ ⟶ y-intercept $= 3$ So, one point on the line is (0, 3).	$3x + 2y = 6$ $3x + 2(0) = 6$ $3x = 6$ $x = 2$ ⟶ x-intercept $= 2$ So, another point on the line is (2, 0).

★ The x-intercept for this graph is 2. The y-intercept is 3.

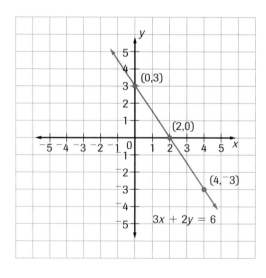

Check the graph by locating a third point on the line and substituting its coordinates into the equation of the line.

Try $(4, {}^{-}3)$.

$$3x + 2y = 6$$
$$3(4) + 2({}^{-}3) \;\blacksquare\; 6$$
$$12 - 6 \;\blacksquare\; 6$$
$$6 = 6$$

$(4, {}^{-}3)$ is a solution to the equation. So, the graph is correct.

Slope of Zero and Undefined Slope

What's the difference between a line with a slope of zero and a line with undefined slope (sometimes called no slope)? Isn't zero the same as nothing? The answer to the second question is *no*, when you're talking about slope.

CASE 1 A line with a slope of zero is a horizontal line.

To understand the idea of a **slope of zero**, think of the slope-intercept form of an equation, $y = mx + b$. When the slope, m, equals 0, the equation becomes $y = 0x + b$, or $y = b$. This is the equation for a line that always has the same y–value, a horizontal line. So, any equation in the form $y = b$ has a graph with a slope of zero.

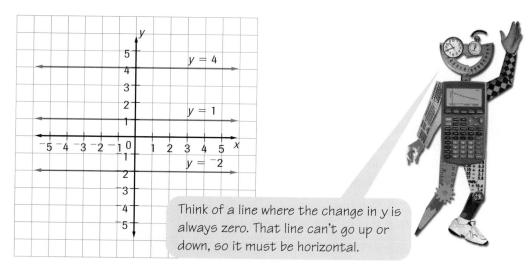

Think of a line where the change in y is always zero. That line can't go up or down, so it must be horizontal.

These graphs all have a slope of zero. The graph of a line with zero slope is a horizontal line.

MORE ▶

CASE 2 A line with undefined slope is a vertical line.

To understand the idea of **undefined slope**, think of the definition of

slope: $\dfrac{\text{Change in } y\text{-value}}{\text{Change in } x\text{-value}}$.

A fraction with a denominator of zero is undefined, so if a line has an x-value that does not change, the slope of the line is undefined because division by zero is undefined. Any equation in the form of $x = k$, where k is a constant, will graph as a line with undefined slope.

The graph of a line with undefined slope is a vertical line.

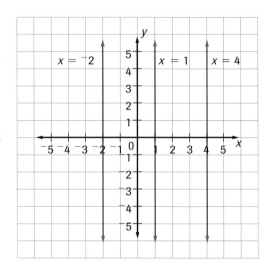

Checking Solutions to Linear Equations

To see whether a pair of x and y values (x, y) is a solution for an equation, substitute those values into the equation. If the equation is true, that pair of x and y values is a **solution** and the ordered pair lies on the graph of the equation.

EXAMPLE 1: Is $(3, 2)$ a solution to $4x + 3y = 18$?

To check:	$4x + 3y = 18$
Replace x with 3 and y with 2.	$4(3) + 3(2) \ \blacksquare \ 18$
Simplify.	$12 + 6 \ \blacksquare \ 18$
Check.	$18 = 18$

★ $(3, 2)$ is a solution to $4x + 3y = 18$.

EXAMPLE 2: Is $(8, \ ^-5)$ a solution to $y = \frac{x}{4} - 6$?

To check:	$y = \frac{x}{4} - 6$
Replace x with 8 and y with $^-5$.	$^-5 \ \blacksquare \ \frac{8}{4} - 6$
Simplify.	$^-5 \ \blacksquare \ 2 - 6$
Check.	$^-5 \neq \ ^-4$

Replacing x with 8 and y with $^-5$ makes a false statement ($^-5 = \ ^-4$ is false).

★ $(8, \ ^-5)$ is *not* a solution to $y = \frac{x}{4} - 6$.

Solving Systems of Linear Equations

Would it be cheaper, over the course of four years to pay more for a newer car and spend less for gasoline or pay less for a junker that uses a lot of gas? When would the cost of new windows in your home be paid for by the savings in heating and air conditioning costs? Should you take a job that pays less but has great benefits?

Sometimes, you need a bit of information that's described by two or more related linear equations, called a **system of equations**. The point at which the graphs for these equations intersect is a solution to all of the equations. It's also the solution to the system of equations. You can solve these systems by hand or with a graphing calculator. Just look for the common point.

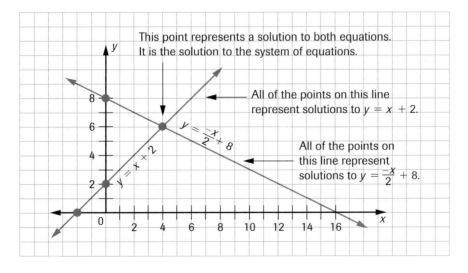

This point represents a solution to both equations. It is the solution to the system of equations.

All of the points on this line represent solutions to $y = x + 2$.

All of the points on this line represent solutions to $y = \frac{-x}{2} + 8$.

$y = \frac{-x}{2} + 8$

$y = x + 2$

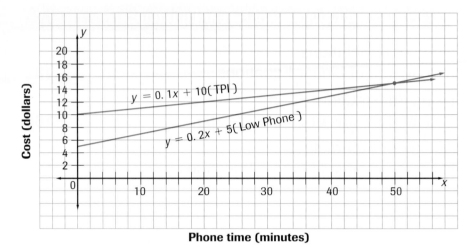

Phone time (minutes)

This graph shows the monthly pricing plans of two long-distance telephone companies.

Let y represent the total cost in dollars and let x represent the number of minutes of phone time used.

LowPhone's monthly billing plan is given by the equation $y = 0.2x + 5$, or 20¢ per minute plus a $5 charge. TPI's monthly billing plan is given by the equation $y = 0.1x + 10$, or 10¢ per minute plus a $10 charge.

The solution to the system of linear equations is the point where the graphs intersect. At this point, (50, 15), the cost for both plans is the same: $15 for 50 minutes. An analysis of the graph shows that if you use less than 50 minutes of phone time each month, LowPhone's pricing system is less expensive. If you use more than 50 minutes in a month, TPI is less expensive.

162

Number of Solutions to a System of Linear Equations

A system of linear equations can have no solutions, one solution, or many solutions.

163

No Solution

If two or more graphed lines are parallel, they have no intersection point. This means there is no point (x, y) that satisfies both equations, so there is no solution for their system of equations.

EXAMPLE: Solve this system of equations by graphing.

$$y = x + 2$$
$$y = x - 1$$

MORE HELP
See 220–221

You can tell from the equations that both lines have a slope of 1, which indicates they are parallel.

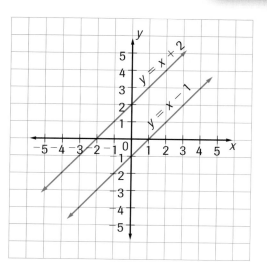

★ The lines do not intersect. There is no solution for this system of equations.

One Solution

164

If two or more graphed lines intersect in one point, that point is the only solution for their system of equations.

EXAMPLE: Solve this system of equations by graphing.

$$y = x + 1$$
$$y = \frac{x}{2} + 2$$

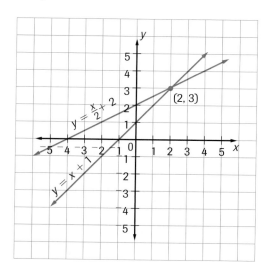

In systems that have only one solution, the lines must have different slopes.

★ The lines intersect in exactly one point, $(2, 3)$. $(2, 3)$ is the only solution for this system of equations.

Many Solutions

If the graphs of two or more linear equations intersect in more than one point, they are the same line (they are **collinear**) and the solution to their system of equations is all the points on the line.

EXAMPLE: Solve this system of equations by graphing.

$$y = -x$$

$$2y = -2x$$

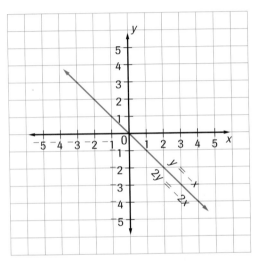

If you divide both sides of the second equation by 2 you get the first equation. So, the two equations are equivalent. No wonder their graphs are the same line!

★ The two lines are the same line. Every point on the line is a solution to the system of equations and every ordered pair that satisfies one equation also satisfies the other.

Using Substitution to Solve a System of Linear Equations

Sometimes a graph is not the best way to solve a system of equations. Maybe the solution values are not whole numbers and would be hard to read from a graph. Maybe the lines intersect far from the origin. Fortunately, for cases like these, there are a few ways to solve a system of equations without graphing. One of these methods is the **substitution method,** where one equation is solved for one variable and that solution is *substituted* into the second equation.

EXAMPLE: Use the substitution method to solve this system of equations.

MORE HELP
See 126, 128, 129

$$y - 6x = {}^-5$$

$$2y + 3x = 0$$

❶ Solve one of the equations for one variable.	$y - 6x = {}^-5$ ⟵ Solve $y - 6x = {}^-5$ for y. $y = 6x - 5$	
❷ Substitute the expression from Step 1 for its equivalent variable in the other equation.	$2y + 3x = 0$ $2(6x - 5) + 3x = 0$ ⟵ $12x - 10 + 3x = 0$ $15x - 10 = 0$	Substitute $6x - 5$ for y in the second equation.
❸ Solve for the second variable.	$15x - 10 = 0$ $15x = 10$ $x = \frac{10}{15}$, or $\frac{2}{3}$	
❹ Substitute this value of x into either of the original equations and solve for y. Both will give the same y value.	$y - 6x = {}^-5$ $y - 6(\frac{2}{3}) = {}^-5$ $y - 4 = {}^-5$ $y = {}^-1$	
❺ Write an ordered pair that describes your solution.	$(x, y) = (\frac{2}{3}, {}^-1)$	
❻ Check by substituting your solution into the equation you didn't use for Step 4.	$2y + 3x = 0$ $2({}^-1) + 3(\frac{2}{3})$ ■ 0 ${}^-2 + 2$ ■ 0 $0 = 0$	The solution checks.

★ The solution to the system of equations is $(\frac{2}{3}, {}^-1)$

Adding or Subtracting to Solve Systems of Linear Equations

MORE HELP
See 126,
128–129

To solve a system of equations, you can add or subtract the two equations. This method is called the **linear combination method**. If two equations have the same term in one variable (for instance, $3x$ and $3x$) or a pair of opposite terms in one variable (for instance, $3x$ and ^-3x), the linear combination method is simple. Just subtract or add the equations. This eliminates one variable. Then you can solve the system.

CASE 1 When two equations have opposite terms in one variable, add to solve the system.

EXAMPLE 1: The perimeter of a rectangle is 48 inches. If you subtract twice the width from the length, you get 1 foot. What are the dimensions of the rectangle?

Let l represent the length in inches and let w represent the width in inches.

The perimeter is 48 inches. ⟶ $2l + 2w = 48$

The length minus twice the width is 12 inches. ⟶ $l - 2w = 12$

Since $2w$ and ^-2w are opposites, add the equations to eliminate w and solve the system.

❶ Add the similar terms of the two equations.	$2\ell + 2w = 48$ $+\ \ell - 2w = 12$ $\overline{3\ell + 0w = 60}$
❷ Solve the equation.	$3\ell = 60$ $\ell = 20$
❸ Substitute the value of ℓ from Step 2 into either original equation and solve for w.	$2\ell + 2w = 48$ $2(20) + 2w = 48$ $40 + 2w = 48$ $2w = 8$ $w = 4$
❹ Check by substituting your solution into the other original equation.	$\ell - 2w = 12$ $20 - 2(4)\ \blacksquare\ 12$ $20 - 8\ \blacksquare\ 12$ $12 = 12$

★ The rectangle's length is 20 inches and its width is four inches.

CASE 2 When two equations have the same term in one variable, subtract to solve the system.

MORE HELP
See 082

EXAMPLE 2: Solve the system.

$$\tfrac{1}{2}x - 5y = 30$$
$$\tfrac{1}{2}x + 7y = 6$$

Since the two equations have the same term, $\tfrac{1}{2}x$, subtract to eliminate x and solve the system.

❶ Subtract the similar terms of the two equations.	$\tfrac{1}{2}x - 5y = 30$ $- (\tfrac{1}{2}x + 7y = 6)$ $0x - 12y = 24$	When you subtract an expression, subtract each term of the expression.
❷ Solve the equation.	$-12y = 24$ $y = {}^-2$	
❸ Substitute the solution from Step 2 into either original equation to find the value of the other variable.	$\tfrac{1}{2}x - 5y = 30$ $\tfrac{1}{2}x - 5({}^-2) = 30$ $\tfrac{1}{2}x + 10 = 30$ $\tfrac{1}{2}x = 20$ $x = 40$	
❹ Write the possible solutions as an ordered pair.	$(x, y) = (40, {}^-2)$	
❺ Check by substituting your solution into the other original equation.	$\tfrac{1}{2}x + 7y = 6$ $\tfrac{1}{2}(40) + 7({}^-2) \blacksquare 6$ $20 - 14 \blacksquare 6$ $6 = 6$ The solution checks.	

★ The solution to the system of equations is $(40, {}^-2)$.

Using Multiplication with Linear Combinations

168

Sometimes a pair of equations does not have a pair of variable terms that are the same (like $4y$ and $4y$) or opposites (like $4y$ and ${}^-4y$). This type of system can't be solved simply by adding or subtracting the two equations. However, you can use multiplication to create an equivalent system that *can* be solved by using addition or subtraction.

MORE ▶

CASE 1 Sometimes you need to multiply only one linear equation before you add or subtract to solve a system of equations.

EXAMPLE 1: The Maplewood Symphony Orchestra sold 146 tickets and collected a total of $1036 in ticket sales. Admission was $5 for children and $8 for adults. How many children's tickets were sold? How many adult tickets were sold? Write two equations and use linear combinations to solve the system.

Let x represent the number of children's tickets sold and let y represent the number of adult tickets sold. Then $5x$ represents the dollar value of children's tickets and $8y$ represents the dollar value of adult tickets.

$$x + y = 146 \longleftarrow \text{total number of tickets sold}$$

$$5x + 8y = 1036 \longleftarrow \text{total value of sales}$$

❶ Multiply one of the equations so that one term is the same as, or opposite to, a term in the other equation.	$x + y = 146$ $\downarrow$ $5(x + y) = 5(146) \longrightarrow \begin{aligned} 5x + 5y &= 730 \\ 5x + 8y &= 1036 \end{aligned}$ $5x + 8y = 1036$
❷ Add or subtract similar terms to eliminate one variable.	$\begin{aligned} 5x + 5y &= 730 \\ -(5x + 8y &= 1036) \\ \hline {}^-3y &= {}^-306 \end{aligned}$ Since the two equations now have one matching term, $5x$, subtract.
❸ Solve the equation.	${}^-3y = {}^-306$ $y = 102$
❹ Substitute the value of y from Step 3 into either of the original equations to find the value of x.	$x + y = 146$ $x + 102 = 146$ $x = 44$
❺ Write the possible solution as an ordered pair.	$(x, y) = (44, 102)$
❻ Check by substituting your solution into the other original equation.	$5x + 8y = 1036$ $5(44) + 8(102) \blacksquare 1036$ $220 + 816 \blacksquare 1036$ $1036 = 1036$ The solution checks.

★ The solution is (44, 102). The Maplewood Symphony sold 44 children's tickets and 102 adult tickets.

CASE 2 Sometimes you need to multiply two or more linear equations before you add or subtract to solve a system of equations.

EXAMPLE 2: Use linear combinations to solve the system:

$$2x + 5y = 26$$

$$^-3x - 4y = {}^-25$$

❶ Multiply both equations so that the terms in one variable are the same or the opposite. For simplicity, use the least common multiple of the term.	*If you make fewer mistakes when you add, then always multiply by a factor that will give you a pair of opposite terms.* $^-3(2x + 5y) = {}^-3(26) \longrightarrow {}^-6x - 15y = {}^-78$ $2({}^-3x - 4y) = 2({}^-25) \longrightarrow {}^-6x - 8y = {}^-50$
❷ Add or subtract similar terms to eliminate one variable.	$\begin{aligned}{}^-6x - 15y &= {}^-78 \\ -\ ({}^-6x - 8y &= {}^-50) \\ \hline 0x - 7y &= {}^-28\end{aligned}$ Since the two equations have the same term, ^-6x, subtract.
❸ Solve the equation.	$^-7y = {}^-28$ $y = 4$
❹ Substitute the value of *y* from Step 3 into either of the original equations to find the value of *x*.	$2x + 5y = 26$ $2x + 5(4) = 26$ $2x + 20 = 26$ $2x = 6$ $x = 3$
❺ Write the possible solution as an ordered pair.	$(x, y) = (3, 4)$
❻ Check by substituting your solution into the other original equation.	$^-3x - 4y = {}^-25$ $^-3(3) - 4(4) \ \blacksquare \ {}^-25$ $^-9 - 16 \ \blacksquare \ {}^-25$ $^-25 = {}^-25$ The solution checks.

★ The solution is $(3, 4)$.

Non-Linear Equations and Functions

"A man is like a fraction whose numerator is what he is and whose denominator is what he thinks of himself. The larger the denominator, the smaller the fraction."

Count Lev Nikolayevich Tolstoy

Gina's trip down the ski jump was just like a non-linear relationship—at least, until she crashed.

If you've studied guitar, played baseball, or done any activity that requires practice, you know that the more you practice, the better you get. You also know this: In the beginning, a little practice—even one session—makes a big difference. After a year of regular practice, a single practice session doesn't do nearly as much. The relationship between practice and improvement is nonlinear. If you graphed the relationship, you would not get a straight line. In fact, that's why the rate of improvement is called a learning curve and not a learning line.

Non-linear relationships are everywhere. When you drop a penny, the distance it falls in the first moment of its descent is much less than the distance it plummets in the moment before it hits the ground. When you take a drink from a water fountain, the stream forms a smooth curve, not a straight line.

Fortunately, there are ways to solve non-linear equations. The methods may be a bit more complicated than the ones for linear equations, but they open new possibilities. You can plot the path of a falling penny, a stream of water, or an orbiting satellite. You can even design better guitars and baseball stadiums.

The mathematical term *rational* comes from *ratio*. A **rational expression** looks like a ratio of expressions in fraction form. A **rational equation** is an equation involving rational expressions.

Rational Expressions

Rational Equations

$$\frac{a^2 - 3a - 4}{9a(a-2)}$$

$$\frac{x}{5}$$

$$\frac{b^2 - 4}{b - 2}$$

$$\frac{x}{5} + \frac{1}{x^2} - 4 = \frac{1}{4}$$

$$\frac{a}{a-1} = \frac{2}{a^2 - 1}$$

$$\frac{4}{b^2 - 4} + \frac{b}{b - 8} = \frac{b}{b - 4}$$

Some rational equations look so complicated that you might think solving them would make you irrational. But no matter how complicated a rational equation appears, there are methods you can use to solve it. One method uses the least common denominator; another uses cross products.

171

Solving Rational Equations Using Common Denominators

MORE HELP
See 108, 120,
174–175, 181, 189

One way to solve rational equations is to use the least common denominator.

In an electrical circuit, conductors (called resistors) provide resistance to a flow of current. In a parallel circuit, the total resistance is related to the individual resistors by this equation, $\frac{1}{R} = \frac{1}{r_1} + \frac{1}{r_2} + \ldots + \frac{1}{r_n}$, where $r_1, r_2, \ldots, r_n$ represent the resistance (in ohms) of each of the n resistors.

Source: Physics Made Simple

EXAMPLE 1: A resistor with a resistance of r ohms is connected in parallel with a 2.5 ohm resistor to give a total resistance of 2 ohms. What is the resistance, r?

First, write the equation, filling in the information you have. $\frac{1}{r} + \frac{1}{2.5} = \frac{1}{2}$

> Before you try to clear the fractions, first find an equivalent fraction for $\frac{1}{2.5}$ whose denominator is an integer.
>
> $$\frac{1}{2.5} = \frac{1 \times \boxed{2}}{2.5 \times \boxed{2}} = \frac{2}{5}$$

To solve:	$\frac{1}{r} + \frac{1}{2.5} = \frac{1}{2}$
Rewrite the equation with integral denominators.	$\frac{1}{r} + \frac{2}{5} = \frac{1}{2}$
Clear the fractions: Multiply both sides of the equation by the product of the denominators.	$10r\left(\frac{1}{r} + \frac{2}{5}\right) = 10r\left(\frac{1}{2}\right)$
Simplify.	$10 + 4r = 5r$
Solve for r.	$10 = r$

> If you multiply both sides of an equation by a denominator, you'll clear that denominator from its fraction.

★ The resistance is 10 ohms.

EXAMPLE 2: Solve. $1 + \frac{4}{x} = \frac{12}{x^2}$

ONE WAY Find the least common multiple for every denominator in the equation. Multiply each term by the LCM to clear the fractions.

To solve:	$1 + \frac{4}{x} = \frac{12}{x^2}$
Multiply each side by the LCM.	$x^2\left(1 + \frac{4}{x}\right) = x^2\left(\frac{12}{x^2}\right)$
Use the Distributive Property.	$x^2(1) + x^2\left(\frac{4}{x}\right) = x^2\left(\frac{12}{x^2}\right)$
Simplify.	$x^2 + 4x = 12$
Write in standard form.	$x^2 + 4x - 12 = 0$
Factor.	$(x + 6)(x - 2) = 0$
Set each factor equal to zero.	$x + 6 = 0$ or $x - 2 = 0$
Solve for x.	$x = {}^-6$ or $x = 2$

MORE ▶

ANOTHER WAY Find a way to write the expression on each side of the equation as one fraction. Multiply each expression by the LCM to clear the fractions.

To solve:	$1 + \dfrac{4}{x} = \dfrac{12}{x^2}$
Write 1 as a fraction whose denominator is x, then add.	$\dfrac{x}{x} + \dfrac{4}{x} = \dfrac{12}{x^2}$
	$\dfrac{x + 4}{x} = \dfrac{12}{x^2}$
Multiply each side by the LCM, x^2.	$x^2\left(\dfrac{x + 4}{x}\right) = x^2\left(\dfrac{12}{x^2}\right)$
Simplify.	$x^2 + 4x = 12$
Write in standard form.	$x^2 + 4x - 12 = 0$
Factor.	$(x + 6)(x - 2) = 0$
Set each factor equal to zero.	$x + 6 = 0$ or $x - 2 = 0$
Solve for x.	$x = {}^-6$ or $x = 2$

★ Either way, $x = {}^-6$ or $x = 2$.

172 Solving Rational Equations Using Cross Products

When an equation shows one rational expression equal to another $\left(\frac{a}{b} = \frac{c}{d}\right)$, you have a proportion. You can use cross products to solve the equation.

EXAMPLE 1: The speed of a boat in still water is 20 miles per hour. The boat can travel 80 miles against a river current in the same time that it takes to travel 120 miles with the current. Find the speed of the current.

Let x represent the speed of the current in miles per hour. Then use the distance formula, $(d) = $ rate $(r) \cdot$ time (t), to write an equation that represents the situation. If $d = rt$, then $t = \frac{d}{r}$.

MORE HELP
See 126, 128–129, 289

	r (mph)	d (miles)	$t = \dfrac{d}{r}$ (hours)
Traveling with current increases rate.	$20 + x$	120	$t = \dfrac{120}{20 + x}$
Traveling against current decreases rate.	$20 - x$	80	$t = \dfrac{80}{20 - x}$

Since the time spent traveling with the current is the same as the time traveling against the current, solve the equation, $\frac{120}{20 + x} = \frac{80}{20 - x}$.

If two ratios are equal, their cross products are equal. In the equation $\frac{a}{b} = \frac{c}{d}$, the cross products are $a \cdot d$ and $c \cdot b$.

To solve for x:	$\dfrac{120}{20 + x} = \dfrac{80}{20 - x}$
Set the cross products equal to each other.	$120(20 - x) = 80(20 + x)$
Use the Distributive Property.	$2400 - 120x = 1600 + 80x$ $800 = 200x$
Use the Equality Property to isolate x.	$4 = x$

The solution, $x = 4$, checks when you substitute 4 for x in the original equation.

Check your solution in the original problem. If the current is four miles per hour, a boat will travel 24 miles per hour with the current and 16 miles per hour against it. You can travel 120 miles in $\frac{120}{24}$ hours with the current and you can travel 80 miles in $\frac{80}{16}$ hours against it. $\frac{120}{24} = \frac{80}{16}$, so the solution satisfies the problem.

When you solve a word problem, it's wise to check your solution against the original problem instead of just substituting into the equation you wrote, just in case your equation is faulty.

★ The speed of the current is 4 miles per hour.

MORE ▶

MORE HELP
See 108, 174,
181, 188, 189

EXAMPLE 2: Solve. $\dfrac{3}{2x + 3} = \dfrac{2x - 3}{9}$

To solve:	$\dfrac{3}{2x + 3} = \dfrac{2x - 3}{9}$
Set the cross products equal to each other.	$3(9) = (2x + 3)(2x - 3)$
Use the Distributive Property.	$27 = 4x^2 - 9$
Write the equation in standard form.	$4x^2 - 36 = 0$
Factor.	$4(x^2 - 9) = 0$ $4(x + 3)(x - 3) = 0$
Solve for x.	$x = {}^-3 \text{ or } x = 3$

Test these values in the original equation.

$$\dfrac{3}{2({}^-3) + 3} \ \blacksquare \ \dfrac{2({}^-3) - 3}{9}$$

$$\dfrac{3}{{}^-3} = \dfrac{{}^-9}{9}$$

$$\dfrac{3}{2(3) + 3} \ \blacksquare \ \dfrac{2(3) - 3}{9}$$

$$\dfrac{3}{9} = \dfrac{3}{9}$$

★ Both $x = {}^-3$ and $x = 3$ are solutions to the equation.

173

MATH ALERT: The Denominator of a Rational Expression Is Always Non-Zero

MORE HELP
See 043

When a fraction has a denominator of zero, it is undefined because division by zero is undefined. The solution to a rational equation is only truly the answer to the problem after you've checked the values in the original equation. If a value produces a denominator of zero in the original equation, that value is not a solution to the original equation.

CASE 1 Some equations have no solutions.

EXAMPLE 1: Solve. $\frac{x}{x-2} = 2 + \frac{2}{x-2}$

MORE HELP
See 103, 117

To solve for x:	$\dfrac{x}{x-2} = 2 + \dfrac{2}{x-2}$
Clear the fractions: Multiply both expressions by the common denominator.	$\dfrac{(x-2)x}{x-2} = (x-2)\left(2 + \dfrac{2}{x-2}\right)$
Simplify.	$x = 2x - 4 + 2$ $x = 2x - 2$ $2 = x$

Substitute 2 for x in the original equation.

$$\frac{x}{x-2} = 2 + \frac{2}{x-2} \longrightarrow \frac{2}{2-2} = 2 + \frac{2}{2-2}$$

$$\frac{2}{0} = 2 + \frac{2}{0}$$

You can't divide by zero; 2 is not a solution to the equation.

★ The equation has *no solution*. It is undefined.

CASE 2 When you factor a quadratic equation, one or both of the factors may not provide a solution.

EXAMPLE 2: Solve. $\frac{x}{4} + \frac{x}{x-4} = \frac{4}{x-4}$

To solve:	$\dfrac{x}{4} + \dfrac{x}{x-4} = \dfrac{4}{x-4}$
Multiply each side of the equation by the product of different denominators.	$4(x-4)\left(\dfrac{x}{4} + \dfrac{x}{x-4}\right) = 4(x-4)\left(\dfrac{4}{x-4}\right)$
Simplify.	$x^2 - 4x + 4x = 16$ $x^2 = 16$
Solve for x.	$x = 4 \text{ or } x = {}^{-}4$

When you substitute $x = 4$ into the original equation, $\frac{x}{4} + \frac{x}{x-4} = \frac{4}{x-4}$, it produces a denominator of 0, so $x = 4$ is not a solution. When you substitute $x = {}^{-}4$, the equation checks, so, $x = {}^{-}4$ is the only solution.

★ The solution is $x = {}^{-}4$.

174) Solving Quadratic Equations

When an expression or an equation has a degree of two, it is a **quadratic** expression or equation. The **standard form** for a quadratic equation is $ax^2 + bx + c = 0$. The **roots** or **solutions** of any quadratic equation are the x-intercepts of the graph of $y = ax^2 + bx + c$.

Remember, the **degree** of an equation in one variable tells you the highest exponent of the variable. If the degree is two, the highest power is 2. To remember which equations are quadratic, think that a square is a quadrilateral whose area is s^2.

Quadratic Equations

$$x^2 - 3x - 4 = 0$$

$$\frac{x^2}{4} - 16 = 0$$

$$2x^2 + 4x = 5$$

Not Quadratic Equations

$$x^3 + x^2 + x + 1 = 0$$

$$x^{\frac{1}{2}} = \frac{1}{4}$$

$$75 + 25 = 100$$

The chart below shows some ways of solving quadratic equations. The method that you choose will depend on the problem and what's easiest for you.

MORE HELP
See 175–184

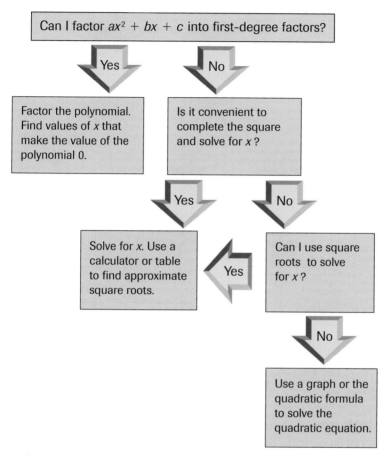

Can I factor $ax^2 + bx + c$ into first-degree factors?

Yes

No

Factor the polynomial. Find values of x that make the value of the polynomial 0.

Is it convenient to complete the square and solve for x?

Yes

No

Solve for x. Use a calculator or table to find approximate square roots.

Yes

Can I use square roots to solve for x?

No

Use a graph or the quadratic formula to solve the quadratic equation.

Writing Quadratic Equations in Standard Form

175

To write a quadratic equation in standard form, you need to write it so that 0 is alone on one side of the equals sign: $ax^2 + bx + c = 0$.

MORE HELP
See 103

EXAMPLE: Write in standard form. $2x^2 + 4x = 5 + x$

To write in standard form:	$2x^2 + 4x = 5 + x$
Use the Equality Properties to isolate 0.	$2x^2 + 4x - (5 + x) = 5 + x - (5 + x)$
Combine like terms.	$2x^2 + 3x - 5 = 0$

★ $2x^2 + 4x = 5 + x \rightarrow 2x^2 + 3x - 5 = 0$

Graphing Quadratic Equations

Think of the graph of an equation as a picture of all of the solutions to the equation. That can be very useful because you often want to find certain special solutions—like the value of x when $y = 0$. When you have a graph, all you need to do is look for the point where the graph crosses the x-axis.

The graph of a quadratic function is a symmetric curve called a **parabola**. Knowing how to find the vertex and line of symmetry of a parabola can help you sketch the graph.

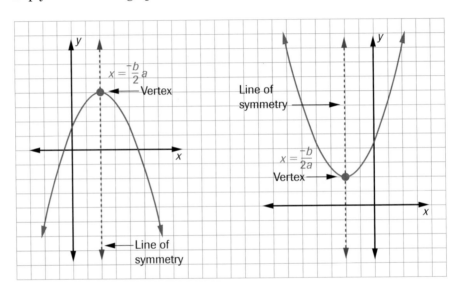

Locating a Vertex

If a parabola opens upward, the vertex is a point whose y-coordinate is the minimum y-value, or **lower bound**. If a parabola opens downward, the y-coordinate of the vertex is the maximum y-value, or **upper bound**.

> In the equation, $y = ax^2 + bx + c$, if a is positive, the parabola opens upward. If a is negative, the parabola opens downward.

For a parabola given by the equation, $y = ax^2 + bx + c$, the x-coordinate of the vertex is $\frac{-b}{2a}$. To see that this works, think about a simple parabola: $y = x^2$. The formula for the x-coordinate of the vertex $\left(\frac{-b}{2a}\right)$, tells you that it should be at $x = 0$. In this equation, if $x = 0$, then $y = 0$.

EXAMPLE 1: Find the vertex of the graph of the equation, $y = x^2 - 4x - 2$.

ONE WAY One way to locate the vertex of a parabola is to look at the graph of the parabola.

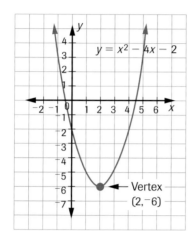

★ Since the graph opens upward, the vertex, $(2, {}^-6)$, contains the lower bound of the parabola, $^-6$.

ANOTHER WAY You can also find the vertex by using the equation of a parabola.

To find the y-coordinate of the vertex, use the formula $x = \frac{^-b}{2a}$, then substitute the value of the x-coordinate into the equation.

For $y = x^2 - 4x - 2$, $a = 1$ and $b = {}^-4$:

x-coordinate of vertex

$$x = \frac{^-b}{2a}$$

$$= \frac{-({}^-4)}{2(1)}$$

$$= 2$$

y-coordinate of vertex

$$y = x^2 - 4x - 2$$

$$= (2)^2 - 4(2) - 2$$

$$= {}^-6$$

★ Either way, the vertex of the graph given by the equation, $y = x^2 - 4x - 2$, is $(2, {}^-6)$.

MORE ▶

EXAMPLE 2: Find the vertex of the parabola given by the equation, $y = \frac{-x^2}{2} + 1$.

ONE WAY Look at the graph. The graph opens downward. The vertex is the maximum point, (0, 1).

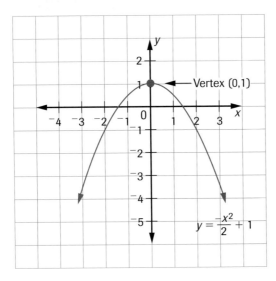

ANOTHER WAY Use the equation of the parabola.

For $y = \frac{-x^2}{2} + 1$, $a = \frac{-1}{2}$, and $b = 0$. Find the coordinates of the vertex.

$$x = \frac{-b}{2a} \qquad y = \frac{-x^2}{2} + 1$$

$$= \frac{0}{2\left(\frac{-1}{2}\right)} \qquad = \frac{0^2}{2} + 1$$

$$= 0 \qquad\qquad = 1$$

★ Either way, the vertex of the parabola given by the equation, $y = \frac{-x^2}{2} + 1$ is (0, 1).

Line of Symmetry

Every parabola has a **line of symmetry** that goes through its vertex. This means that each point of the parabola on one side of the line of symmetry has a reflection on the other side which is also on the parabola.

The line of symmetry is also called the **axis of symmetry.**

EXAMPLE: Find the line of symmetry of the graph, $y = x^2 - 6x + 7$.
Identify the line of symmetry, three points on the graph, and their reflec-
tions on the graph. Then, sketch the graph.

MORE HELP
See 273–274

Look at the equation of the graph. The line of symmetry is a vertical line
through the vertex of a parabola. Since the x–value of the vertex is $\frac{-b}{2a}$, the
equation for the line of symmetry is $x = \frac{-b}{2a}$.

Line of Symmetry:

$$x = \frac{-b}{2a}$$

$$= \frac{-(^-6)}{2(1)}$$

$$= 3$$

Table of Values:

x	y
0	7
6	7
1	2
5	2
2	$^-1$
4	$^-1$

You could also write the
equation in standard form
and then solve it, trace it,
and zoom in on your graphing calculator to identify
the line of symmetry and
reflection points.

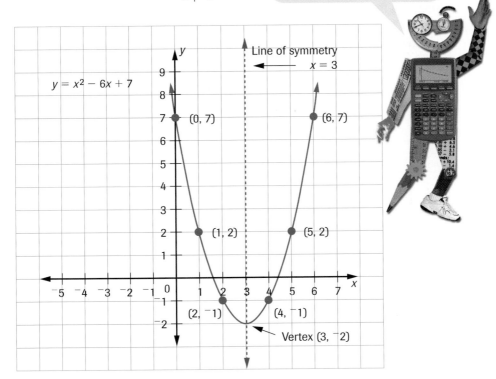

★ The equation for the line of symmetry is $x = 3$. Some points on the
graph will be $(0, 7)$, $(6, 7)$, $(1, 2)$, $(5, 2)$, $(2, ^-1)$, $(4, ^-1)$.

Using the Vertex and the Line of Symmetry to Graph Quadratic Equations

EXAMPLE 1: Graph. $y = x^2 + 2x + 1$

First, use the equation of the graph to find the vertex and the line of symmetry. For $y = x^2 + 2x + 1$, $a = 1$ and $b = 2$. Find the coordinates of the vertex.

$$x = \frac{-b}{2a} \qquad\qquad y = x^2 + 2x + 1$$

$$= \frac{-2}{2(1)} \qquad\qquad = (^-1)^2 + 2(^-1) + 1$$

$$= -1 \qquad\qquad = 0$$

Since the equation for the line of symmetry is $x = \frac{-b}{2a}$, you already know that the equation for the line of symmetry is $x = {}^-1$.

Next, plot the vertex and the line of symmetry on the graph. Make a table of values. Choose three x-values to the left of the vertex and pair them with three x-values to the right of the vertex so you have three pairs of reflection points.

x	y
⁻4	9
⁻3	4
⁻2	1
⁻1	0
0	1
1	4
2	9

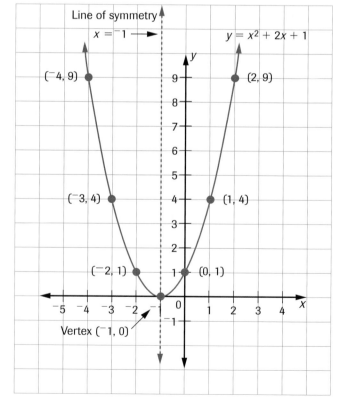

★ Finally, plot the points and sketch the graph.

Using Square Roots to Solve Quadratic Equations

You can use square roots to solve quadratic equations. This method is useful in quadratic equations in the form $ax^2 + c = 0$ (or $ax^2 - c = 0$), quadratic equations in which there is no variable term in the first degree.

MORE HELP
See 016, 103

EXAMPLE 1: A construction worker accidentally drops a wrench from a height of 160 feet. Use the equation $16t^2 - 160 = 0$ to find how many seconds it will take for the wrench to hit the ground.

To solve:	$16t^2 - 160 = 0$
Isolate the variable term.	$16t^2 = 160$ $t^2 = 10$
Solve for t.	$t = \pm \sqrt{10}$
Find the approximate value of t.	$t \approx \pm 3.162$

Don't forget to try your solution in the original problem.
$16t^2 - 160 = 0 \longrightarrow 16 \cdot 10 - 160 = 0$. Since the wrench is not traveling back in time, $t \approx {}^-3.162$ is not a solution.

★ It will take about 3.162 seconds to hit the ground.

EXAMPLE 2: Solve. $3x^2 + 2 = {}^-1$

To solve:	$3x^2 + 2 = {}^-1$
Isolate the variable term.	$3x^2 = {}^-3$
Isolate x.	$x^2 = {}^-1$
Solve for x.	$x = \pm \sqrt{{}^-1}$
Check.	$3\left(\sqrt{{}^-1}\right)^2 + 2 = 3\left({}^-\sqrt{{}^-1}\right)^2 + 2 = {}^-1$

★ Since $\sqrt{{}^-1}$ is an imaginary number, there are no real solutions to this equation.

181

Monomial Factors of Quadratic Polynomials _____

When you try to factor a quadratic polynomial, try to factor out a monomial that contains the greatest common integer factor and the greatest common variable factor.

MORE HELP
See 019–021

EXAMPLE 1: Use the GCF to factor $9x^2 + 6x$.

The GCF of $9x^2$ and $6x$ is $3x$.

To factor:	$9x^2 + 6x$
Factor the GCF from each term.	$9x^2 + 6x = 3x(3x) + 3x(2)$
Use the Distributive Property in reverse to write in factored form.	$= 3x(3x + 2)$

If there is no way to factor further, you're done.

★ $9x^2 + 6x = 3x(3x + 2)$

EXAMPLE 2: Use the GCF to factor $4x^2 - 4x - 8$.

The GCF of $4x^2$, ^-4x, and $^-8$ is 4.

To factor:	$4x^2 - 4x - 8$
Factor the GCF from each term.	$4x^2 - 4x - 8 = 4(x^2) - 4(x) - 4(2)$
Use the Distributive Property in reverse to write in factored form.	$= 4(x^2 - x - 2)$

If there is no way to factor further, you're done.

★ $4x^2 - 4x - 8 = 4(x^2 - x - 2)$. The grouped factor can be factored further, but not by finding a monomial factor.

182

Factoring Polynomials _____

One way to find the solutions to a quadratic equation is to rewrite the polynomial expression as a product. This is called **factoring**. For example, think of $x^2 + 6x + 5$ as a rectangle for which you want to find the lengths of the sides. Use Algebra Tiles for x^2, $6x$, and 5 to make the rectangle.

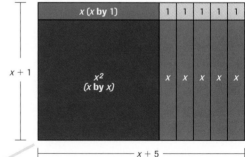

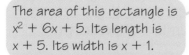

The area of this rectangle is $x^2 + 6x + 5$. Its length is $x + 5$. Its width is $x + 1$.

Writing the quadratic polynomial in factored form makes the equation, $x^2 + 6x + 5 = 0$, easy to solve. For the product $(x + 5)(x + 1)$ to equal zero, either $x + 5$ or $x + 1$ must equal zero. The solutions are $x = {}^-5$ or $x = {}^-1$.

MORE HELP
See 019–021,
108, 110–111,
174, 181,
183–189, 435

This flowchart shows a series of questions you can ask to help you factor a polynomial.

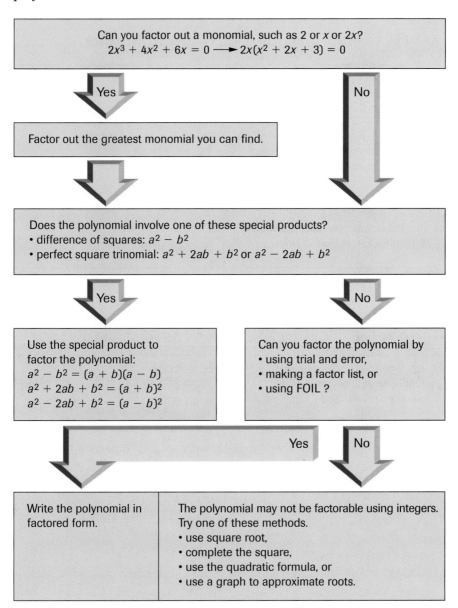

Can you factor out a monomial, such as 2 or x or $2x$?
$$2x^3 + 4x^2 + 6x = 0 \longrightarrow 2x(x^2 + 2x + 3) = 0$$

Yes

No

Factor out the greatest monomial you can find.

Does the polynomial involve one of these special products?
• difference of squares: $a^2 - b^2$
• perfect square trinomial: $a^2 + 2ab + b^2$ or $a^2 - 2ab + b^2$

Yes

No

Use the special product to factor the polynomial:
$a^2 - b^2 = (a + b)(a - b)$
$a^2 + 2ab + b^2 = (a + b)^2$
$a^2 - 2ab + b^2 = (a - b)^2$

Can you factor the polynomial by
• using trial and error,
• making a factor list, or
• using FOIL ?

Yes

No

Write the polynomial in factored form.

The polynomial may not be factorable using integers. Try one of these methods.
• use square root,
• complete the square,
• use the quadratic formula, or
• use a graph to approximate roots.

MORE HELP
See 180,
188–189

Completing the Square

Some quadratic equations in the form of $ax^2 + bx + c = 0$ can be solved easily by factoring. For example, the equation, $x^2 + 6x - 16 = 0$, factors easily to $(x + 8)(x - 2) = 0$. This gives the solution $x = {}^-8$ or $x = 2$.

When a quadratic equation cannot be factored using integers, you can sometimes use a method called **completing the square** to solve the equation. This works best when $a = 1$.

EXAMPLE 1: Solve $x^2 + 8x - 10 = 0$ by completing the square.

❶ Write the equation in the form $ax^2 + bx = c$. (Make sure that $a = 1$.)	$x^2 + 8x - 10 = 0$ $x^2 + 8x = 10$
❷ Find $\frac{1}{2}$ of b in $ax^2 + bx = c$. Add the square of that number $(\frac{b}{2})^2$, to both sides of the equation.	**Think** $b = 8$ $\frac{1}{2}b = 4$ $4^2 = 16$ $x^2 + 8x + 16 = 10 + 16$
❸ The left side is now a perfect square trinomial. Factor the left side.	$x^2 + 8x + 16 = 26$ $(x + 4)^2 = 26$
❹ Find the square root of each side.	$(x + 4)^2 = 26$ $x + 4 = \pm\sqrt{26}$
❺ Solve for x.	$x = {}^-4 \pm \sqrt{26}$
❻ Use a calculator or a square root table to approximate the solutions, if necessary.	$\sqrt{26} \approx 5.099$ $x \approx {}^-4 + 5.099$ or $x \approx {}^-4 - 5.099$ $x \approx 1.099$ $\qquad$ $x \approx {}^-9.099$

★ The solutions are $x = {}^-4 + \sqrt{26}$ and $x = {}^-4 - \sqrt{26}$. Using an approximation for $\sqrt{26}$, the solutions are $x \approx 1.099$ and $x \approx {}^-9.099$.

EXAMPLE 2: A golfer hits a ball with an upward speed of 20 meters per second. The expression, $^-5t^2 + 20t$, gives the approximate height in meters of the golf ball after t seconds. The solution to the equation $^-5t^2 + 20t = 5$ gives the time at which the golf ball is 5 meters above the ground. Find the time, or times, at which the golf ball is 5 meters above the ground.

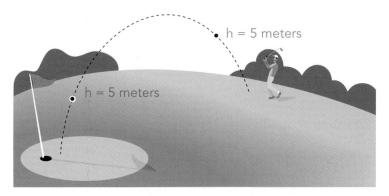

❶ Make sure that $a = 1$. Divide both sides of the equation by $^-5$.	$^-5t^2 + 20t = 5$ $t^2 - 4t = ^-1$
❷ Find $\frac{1}{2}$ of b in $ax^2 + bx = c$. Add the square of that number to both sides of the equation.	$t^2 - 4t + 4 = ^-1 + 4$ $b = ^-4$ $\left(\frac{b}{2}\right)^2 = 4$
❸ The left side is now a perfect square. Factor the left side.	$t^2 - 4t + 4 = 3$ $(t - 2)^2 = 3$
❹ Find the square root of each side.	$(t - 2)^2 = 3$ $t - 2 = \pm\sqrt{3}$
❺ Solve for t.	$t = 2 \pm \sqrt{3}$
❻ Use a calculator or a square root table to simplify the solutions, if necessary.	$\sqrt{3} \approx 1.732$ $t = 2 + \sqrt{3}$ or $t = 2 - \sqrt{3}$ $t \approx 3.732$ $t \approx 0.268$

★ The golf ball is 5 meters off the ground at about 0.3 seconds and at about 3.7 seconds.

It makes sense to use both solutions since the ball is 5 meters high on the way up and again on the way down.

The Quadratic Formula

The **Quadratic Formula** can be used to solve *any* quadratic equation. It states:

MORE HELP
See 120, 123, 183

If $ax^2 + bx + c = 0$, and $a \neq 0$, then

$$x = \frac{-b \pm \sqrt{b^2 - 4ac}}{2a}$$

You can use the completing-the-square method to see why the quadratic formula works.

To solve:	$ax^2 + bx + c = 0$
Subtract c from each side.	$ax^2 + bx = -c$
Divide each side by a.	$x^2 + \left(\dfrac{b}{a}\right)x = \dfrac{-c}{a}$
Complete the square by adding $\left(\dfrac{b}{2a}\right)^2$ to both sides.	$x^2 + \left(\dfrac{b}{a}\right)x + \left(\dfrac{b}{2a}\right)^2 = \dfrac{-c}{a} + \left(\dfrac{b}{2a}\right)^2$
Factor the left side. Simplify the right side.	$\left(x + \dfrac{b}{2a}\right)^2 = \dfrac{b^2 - 4ac}{4a^2}$
Take the square root of each side.	$x + \dfrac{b}{2a} = \pm\sqrt{\dfrac{b^2 - 4ac}{4a^2}}$
Isolate x.	$x = \dfrac{-b}{2a} \pm \sqrt{\dfrac{b^2 - 4ac}{4a^2}}$
Simplify and express as a single fraction.	$x = \dfrac{-b}{2a} \pm \dfrac{\sqrt{b^2 - 4ac}}{2a}$ $x = \dfrac{-b \pm \sqrt{b^2 - 4ac}}{2a}$

Using the Quadratic Formula to Solve Quadratic Equations

You can use the quadratic formula to solve any quadratic equation.

MORE HELP
See 118

The Highway Code of Great Britain uses a formula for the stopping distance of an average car. The formula is based on the speed of the car, the time it takes a driver to apply the brakes, and the braking distance of the car.   *Source: Highway Code of Great Britain*

$$\frac{x^2}{20} + x = s$$

x represents speed in miles per hour   **s represents stopping distance in feet**

EXAMPLE: Suppose a car is 50 feet from an intersection at which it must stop. What is the maximum speed at which it can be traveling?

The maximum speed at which the car can be traveling and still be able to stop in time is given by the equation $\frac{x^2}{20} + x = 50$. You can use the quadratic formula to solve this equation.

❶ Write the equation in standard form, $ax^2 + bx + c = 0$, where $a \neq 0$.	$\frac{x^2}{20} + x = 50$ $\frac{1}{20}x^2 + x - 50 = 0$
❷ Clear all fractions.	$20\left(\frac{1}{20}x^2 + x - 50\right) = 20 \cdot 0$ $x^2 + 20x - 1000 = 0$
❸ Find the values for a, b, and c.	$x^2 + 20x - 1000 = 0$ $a = 1, b = 20, c = {}^{-}1000$
❹ Substitute the values for a, b, and c into the quadratic formula and solve.	$x = \dfrac{-b \pm \sqrt{b^2 - 4ac}}{2a}$ $= \dfrac{{}^{-}20 \pm \sqrt{(20)^2 - 4(1)({}^{-}1000)}}{2(1)}$ $= \dfrac{{}^{-}20 \pm \sqrt{400 + 4000}}{2}$ $= \dfrac{{}^{-}20 \pm \sqrt{4400}}{2}$ $x \approx \dfrac{{}^{-}20 + 66.332}{2}$ or $x \approx \dfrac{{}^{-}20 - 66.332}{2}$ $x \approx 23.166$ or $x \approx {}^{-}43.166$

> If you multiply both sides of an equation by a denominator, you clear that denominator from its fraction.

The solutions are $x \approx 23.166$ or $x \approx {}^{-}43.166$. Since a negative speed doesn't make sense, $x \approx {}^{-}43.166$ is not a solution. Check the solution in the original equation.

$s = \frac{x^2}{20} + x$

$50 \approx \frac{23.166^2}{20} + 23.166$

★ To be able to stop in 50 feet, the maximum speed at which a car can travel at is about 23 miles per hour.

Finding the *x*-Intercepts

The roots, or solutions, of any quadratic equation of the form $ax^2 + bx + c = 0$ are the **x-intercepts** of the graph, $y = ax^2 + bx + c$.

EXAMPLE: Find the *x*-intercepts of the graph of $y = 2x^2 - 5x + 2$.

You can use the quadratic formula. The roots of the equation will give you the *x*-intercepts of the graph of $y = 2x^2 - 5x + 2$ because an equation's roots are the values of x when $y = 0$.

In $2x^2 - 5x + 2 = 0$:
$a = 2, b = {}^-5$, and $c = 2$.

$$x = \frac{-b \pm \sqrt{b^2 - 4ac}}{2a}$$

$$= \frac{{}^-({}^-5) \pm \sqrt{({}^-5)^2 - 4(2)(2)}}{2(2)}$$

$$= \frac{5 \pm \sqrt{9}}{4}$$

$$x = \frac{5 + 3}{4} \text{ or } x = \frac{5 - 3}{4}$$

$$x = 2 \qquad \text{ or } x = \tfrac{1}{2}$$

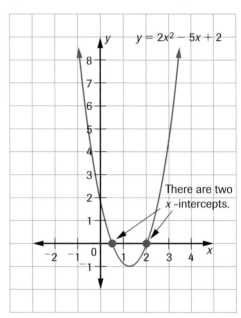

$y = 2x^2 - 5x + 2$

There are two *x*-intercepts.

Substitute these solutions into the original equation to be sure they work.

$$y = 2x^2 - 5x + 2$$

$$y = 2(2)^2 - 5(2) + 2 \qquad\qquad y = 2\left(\frac{1}{2}\right)^2 - 5\left(\frac{1}{2}\right) + 2$$

$$= 8 - 10 + 2 \qquad\qquad\qquad = \frac{1}{2} - \frac{5}{2} + 2$$

$$= 0 \qquad\qquad\qquad\qquad\qquad = 0$$

★ The graph of $y = 2x^2 - 5x + 2$ crosses the *x*-axis at $(\frac{1}{2}, 0)$ and $(2, 0)$. The *x* intercepts are $\frac{1}{2}$ and 2.

Using the Discriminant to Describe Solutions

A quadratic equation can have two real solutions, one real solution, or no real solutions. One way to tell how many real solutions a quadratic equation has is to look at the graph of the corresponding function. Another way is to evaluate the **discriminant**, $b^2 - 4ac$, for any quadratic equation, $ax^2 + bx + c = 0$.

MORE HELP
See 002, 175

The expression, $b^2 - 4ac$, is called the discriminant because it's the part of the quadratic formula that helps you discriminate among possibilities.

	What the Discriminant Can Tell You		
	Value of $b^2 - 4ac$	**Number of Different Real Roots of** $ax^2 + bx + c = 0$	**Number of x-Intercepts of the Graph of** $y = ax^2 + bx + c$
Case 1	positive, but not a perfect square	2	2
Case 2	positive, and a perfect square	2 These roots are also rational.	2
Case 3	zero	1 This root is also called a **double root.**	1
Case 4	negative	0	0

MORE ▶

CASE 1 If the discriminant, $b^2 - 4ac$, is positive, but not a perfect square, there are two real, irrational roots.

EXAMPLE 1: Use the discriminant to tell the number and type of roots in the equation, $x^2 + 4x - 2 = 0$. Compare that answer with the results given by the quadratic formula and to the graph of the related function, $y = x^2 + 4x - 2$.

In $x^2 + 4x - 2 = 0$, $a = 1$, $b = 4$, and $c = {}^-2$.

Find the discriminant.

$$b^2 - 4ac = (4)^2 - 4(1)({}^-2)$$

$$= 16 - {}^-8$$

$$= 24$$

Use the discriminant in the quadratic formula.

$$x = \frac{-b \pm \sqrt{b^2 - 4ac}}{2a}$$

$$= \frac{{}^-4 \pm \sqrt{24}}{2}$$

$x \approx 0.450$ and $x \approx {}^-4.450$

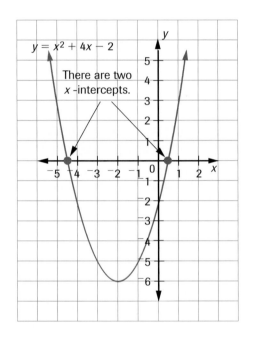

$y = x^2 + 4x - 2$

There are two x-intercepts.

★ Since the discriminant, 24, is positive but not a perfect square, there are two real, irrational roots. This result describes the two roots given by the quadratic formula, $x \approx 0.450$ and $x \approx {}^-4.450$. The results also match the graph of the corresponding function, which crosses the x-axis twice at non-integral intercepts.

CASE 2 If the discriminant, $b^2 - 4ac$, is positive and a perfect square, there are two real, rational roots.

EXAMPLE 2: Use the discriminant to tell the number and type of roots in the equation, $x^2 - 2x - 3 = 0$. Compare that answer with the results given by the quadratic formula and to the graph of the related function, $y = x^2 - 2x - 3$.

In $x^2 - 2x - 3 = 0$, $a = 1$, $b = {}^-2$, and $c = {}^-3$.

Find the discriminant.

$$b^2 - 4ac = ({}^-2)^2 - 4(1)({}^-3)$$

$$= 4 - {}^-12$$

$$= 16$$

Use the discriminant in the quadratic formula.

$$x = \frac{2 \pm \sqrt{16}}{2}$$

$$x = \frac{2 + 4}{2} \text{ or } x = \frac{2 - 4}{2}$$

$$x = 3 \qquad \text{ or } x = {}^-1$$

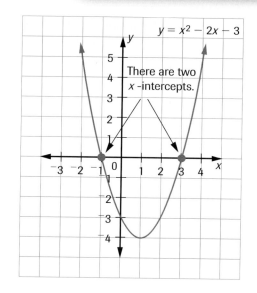

★ Since the discriminant, 16, is positive and a perfect square, there are two real, rational roots. The two roots given by the quadratic formula, $x = 3$ or $x = {}^-1$, are real and rational, as you'd expect from the form of the discriminant. The graph crosses the x-axis twice.

CASE 3 If the discriminant, $b^2 - 4ac$, is zero, there is one real root.

EXAMPLE 3: Use the discriminant to tell the number and type of roots in the equation, $x^2 - 6x + 9 = 0$. Compare that answer with the results given by the quadratic formula and to the graph of the related function, $y = x^2 - 6x + 9$.

In $x^2 - 6x + 9 = 0$, $a = 1$, $b = {}^-6$, and $c = 9$.

Find the discriminant:

$$b^2 - 4ac = ({}^-6)^2 - 4(1)(9)$$

$$= 36 - 36$$

$$= 0$$

Use the discriminant in the quadratic formula:

$$x = \frac{6 \pm \sqrt{0}}{2}$$

$$= 3$$

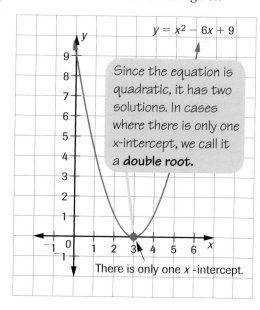

MORE HELP
See 055

★ Since the discriminant is zero, there is one real root. As expected, the single root given by the quadratic formula, $x = 3$, is real. The graph of the corresponding function shows one x-intercept.

CASE 4 If the discriminant, $b^2 - 4ac$, is negative, there are no real roots.

EXAMPLE 4: Use the discriminant to tell the number and type of roots in the equation, $x^2 - 4x + 5 = 0$. Compare that answer with the results given by the quadratic formula and to the graph of the related function, $y = x^2 - 4x + 5$.

In $x^2 - 4x + 5 = 0$, $a = 1$, $b = {}^-4$, and $c = 5$.

Find the discriminant.

$$b^2 - 4ac = ({}^-4)^2 - 4(1)(5)$$
$$= 16 - 20$$
$$= {}^-4$$

Use the discriminant in the quadratic formula:

$$= \frac{4 \pm \sqrt{{}^-4}}{4}$$

$$= \frac{4 \pm 2\sqrt{{}^-1}}{4}$$

$$= \frac{2 \pm \sqrt{{}^-1}}{2}$$

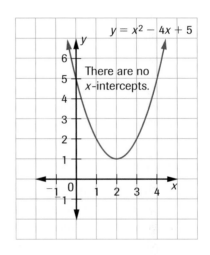

$y = x^2 - 4x + 5$

There are no x-intercepts.

★ Since the discriminant is negative, there are no real roots. This result describes the two roots given by the quadratic formula, $\frac{2 \pm \sqrt{{}^-1}}{2}$, which are not real roots because $\sqrt{{}^-1}$ is not a real number. The results also match the graph of the corresponding function, which does not cross the x-axis.

Using Special Products of Polynomials

Some polynomials fit special patterns. You can use these patterns to factor polynomials.

MORE HELP
See 019–021, 108, 110, 111, 189

CASE 1 To use the difference of two squares pattern, use this relationship:
$$a^2 - b^2 = (a - b)(a + b)$$

EXAMPLE 1: Factor $9x^2 - 25$.

You can tell this is a difference of two squares because both 9 and 25 are perfect squares and x^2 is the square of x. To factor $9x^2 - 25$ using the pattern, identify a^2 and b^2, find a and b, and then substitute those values into the pattern.

$a^2 - b^2 = (a - b)(a + b)$

$a^2 = 9x^2$, so $a = 3x$

$b^2 = 25$, so $b = 5$

★ $9x^2 - 25 = (3x - 5)(3x + 5)$

CASE 2 To factor a perfect square trinomial product, use these relationships:
$$a^2 + 2ab + b^2 = (a + b)^2$$
$$a^2 - 2ab + b^2 = (a - b)^2$$

EXAMPLE 2: Factor $x^2 + 6x + 9$.

You can tell this is a perfect square trinomial.

- Both 1 (the coefficient of x^2) and 9 (the constant) are perfect squares.
- x^2 is the square of x.
- The middle term is twice the product of the square roots of the first and last terms.

To factor $x^2 + 6x + 9$ using the pattern, identify a^2 and b^2, find a and b, and then substitute those values into the pattern.

$a^2 + 2ab + b^2 = (a + b)^2$

$a^2 = x^2$, so $a = x$

$b^2 = 9$, so $b = 3$

$2ab = 2 \cdot x \cdot 3$, or $6x$

★ $x^2 + 6x + 9 = (x + 3)^2$

Sometimes when the coefficient of x^2 is 1, laying out a and b in this way helps with factoring.

product

sum

MORE ▶

EXAMPLE 3: Factor $16x^2 - 40x + 25$.

You can tell this is a perfect square trinomial:

- both 16 and 25 are perfect squares,
- x^2 is the square of x,
- and the middle term is twice the product of the square roots of the first and last terms.

To factor using the pattern, identify a^2 and b^2, find a and b, and then substitute those values into the pattern.

$$a^2 = 16x^2, \text{ so } a = 4x$$
$$b^2 = 25, \text{ so } b = 5$$
$$2ab = 2 \cdot 4x \cdot 5, \text{ or } 40x$$

Look at the sign of the middle term. If the middle term is negative, use the $(a - b)^2$ form.

$$a^2 - 2ab + b^2 = (a - b)^2$$

★ $16x^2 - 40x + 25 = (4x - 5)^2$

It takes some practice to easily recognize this pattern, so here are some more examples you can study:

$a^2 + 2ab + b^2 = (a + b)^2$	$a^2 - 2ab + b^2 = (a - b)^2$
$9x^2 + 24x + 16 = (3x + 4)^2$	$9x^2 - 24x + 16 = (3x - 4)^2$
$8x^2 + {}^-64x + 128 = 8(x + {}^-4)^2$	$8x^2 - 64x + 128 = 8(x - 4)^2$
$8x^3 + 24x^2 + 18x = 2x(2x + 3)^2$	$8x^3 - 24x^2 + 18x = 2x(2x - 3)^2$

Using FOIL when Factoring Quadratic Polynomials

When you multiply two binomials, you multiply their first terms, then their outside terms, then their inside terms, and then their last terms—first, outside, inside, last = FOIL.

MORE HELP
See 108

$$(i + o)(n + f) = in + if + on + of$$

You can use a list of factors and what you know about multiplying binomials to help you factor polynomials that have the form $ax^2 + bx + c$.

CASE 1 In $ax^2 + bx + c$, when $a = 1$, you're looking for factors of c whose sum is b.

EXAMPLE 1: Factor $x^2 + 7x + 12$.

❶ Identify b and c.	In $x^2 + 7x + 12$, $b = 7$, and $c = 12$.
❷ List pairs of factors of c. Find a pair that has a sum of b.	**Factors of 12** **Sum** 12 and 1 13 $^-$12 and $^-$1 $^-$13 6 and 2 8 $^-$6 and $^-$2 $^-$8 4 and 3 7 $^-$4 and $^-$3 $^-$7
❸ Set up a pair of factors with first terms. Use the factor pair from Step 2 as the last terms.	$(x \quad)(x \quad)$ $(x + 4)(x + 3)$
❹ Use FOIL to check your answer.	$(x + 4)(x + 3) = x^2 + 3x + 4x + 12$ $= x^2 + 7x + 12$

★ $x^2 + 7x + 12 = (x + 4)(x + 3)$

MORE ▶

EXAMPLE 2: Factor $x^2 + 5x - 24$.

❶ Identify b and c.	In $x^2 + 5x - 24$, $b = 5$, and $c = {}^-24$.
❷ List pairs of factors of c. Find a pair that has a sum of b. You really don't need to inspect all possibilities; just search until you find a number pair that works.	**Factors of $^-24$** **Sum** $^-24$ and 1 $^-23$ 24 and $^-1$ 23 $^-12$ and 2 $^-10$ 12 and $^-2$ 10 $^-8$ and 3 $^-5$ 8 and $^-3$ 5 $^-6$ and 4 $^-2$ 6 and $^-4$ 2
❸ Set up a pair of factors with first terms. Use the factor pair from Step 2 to complete the factors.	$(x \quad)(x \quad)$ $(x + 8)(x - 3)$
❹ Use FOIL to check your answer.	$(x + 8)(x - 3)$ $= x^2 - 3x + 8x - 24$ $= x^2 + 5x - 24$

★ $x^2 + 5x - 24 = (x + 8)(x - 3)$

CASE 2 In $ax^2 + bx + c$, when $a \neq 1$, you're looking for pairs of factors of a and of c. The sum of the first factor in each pair and the last factor in each pair is b.

EXAMPLE 3: Factor $6x^2 + 5x - 4$.

ONE WAY You can use a version of the guess-check-and-revise strategy.

❶ Identify a and c.	In $6x^2 + 5x - 4$, $a = 6$, and $c = {}^-4$
❷ List pairs of positive factors of ax^2.	$6x$ and $1x$ $1x$ and $6x$ $3x$ and $2x$ $2x$ and $3x$

❸ List factors of c.	$^-4$ and 1 $\quad$ 4 and $^-1$ $^-2$ and 2 $\quad$ 2 and $^-2$ $^-1$ and 4 $\quad$ 1 and $^-4$
❹ Analyze these factor pairs by testing sums of outside and inside products against $b = 5$.	$(6x \cdot 1) + (1x \cdot {}^-4) = 2x \quad$ too low $(1x \cdot {}^-2) + (6x \cdot 2) = 10x \;$ too high $(3x \cdot {}^-1) + (2x \cdot 4) = 5x \quad$ just right
❺ The outside terms in your factored expression will be $3x$ and 1. The inside terms will be 4 and $2x$.	$(3x + 4)(2x - 1)$

ANOTHER WAY You can narrow down the range of factors you need to test.

❶ Multiply the coefficient of the first term by the constant term. $(ac = \blacksquare)$	$6x^2 + 5x - 4$ $6 \times {}^-4 = {}^-24$ Coefficient of first term is 6. Constant term is $^-4$.
❷ Find the factors of this product whose sum is the coefficient of the second term, b.	Factors of $^-24$ with sum of 5 are 8 and $^-3$.
❸ Take the factors you found and use them as the numerators of fractions with a denominator of ^-a. These are the values of x.	$x = \dfrac{8}{^-a} \quad$ or $\quad x = \dfrac{^-3}{^-a}$ $\downarrow \qquad\qquad\quad \downarrow$ $x = \dfrac{8}{^-6} \quad$ or $\quad x = \dfrac{^-3}{^-6}$ $x = \dfrac{^-4}{3} \qquad\qquad x = \dfrac{1}{2}$
❹ Work backward to find the factors of the equation.	$x = \dfrac{^-4}{3} \qquad\qquad x = \dfrac{1}{2}$ $3x = {}^-4 \qquad\qquad 2x = 1$ $3x + 4 = 0 \qquad 2x - 1 = 0$ The factors are $3x + 4$ and $2x - 1$.

★ Either way, $6x^2 + 5x - 4 = (3x + 4)(2x - 1)$

Inequalities

"One and one does not necessarily make 11."

Anonymous

Y ou don't usually need exact change. You can purchase an $8 movie
ticket if you have $12 or $21 or $50. How would you describe all the
amounts of money that are enough to buy a ticket? Not by listing them all.
It's much easier to use a statement like *Any amount $8 or more.* This is a
statement of inequality.

If your cafeteria is allowed to hold up to 450 people, how would you describe the different numbers of people allowed in the room? You could list
all the whole numbers from 0 to 450, but it would be a lot quicker to say
Any whole number less than or equal to 450. This, too, is a statement of
inequality.

Inequalities come in handy because things are not always equal. Statements of equality, like equations, don't always apply. But you can solve
and display inequalities by using methods like the ones you know for
equations. You'll see how in this section.

You have no more than $50 to spend today at BOOKS.COM and you are not a member. You could say that the cost for all your books plus the membership fee must be less than or equal to $50.

That is an **inequality statement**. In algebra, there is a shorter way to write the same thing. If n is the number of books you buy, then $4n$ is the cost of those books. You can write an algebraic inequality statement to represent the situation.

$$4n \quad + \quad 10 \quad \leq \quad 50$$

cost   membership   budget
of books   fee

Write: $\leq$

Say: *is less than or equal to*

Placing the bottom half of an *equals* symbol below an inequality symbol adds *or equal to* to the way you read the symbol.

If you want to spend exactly $50, there is just one way to do it—join and order 10 books. Since you are willing to spend $50, or less than that amount, there are a few ways to do it. You can join and buy any number of books from 0 through 10. Or, you can choose not to join the club.

Graphing Inequalities on the Number Line

Sometimes you need a way to show many values that could be solutions to an inequality. For example, there are an infinite number of real numbers less than 15. A practical way to show these values is to graph them on a number line.

MORE HELP
See 139

CASE 1 For some inequalities, the solution is a continuous graph. In a **continuous graph**, all points on the graph represent solutions to the inequality.

EXAMPLE 1: At what temperatures Fahrenheit will the ice in a skating pond remain frozen? Use a number line to graph your answer.

Ice begins to melt when the temperature of the surrounding atmosphere becomes greater than 32°F. So, at *any* temperature less than or equal to 32°F, the ice in the skating pond will remain frozen.

★ $x \leq 32$

> The solid line shows that all numbers less than or equal to 32 are solutions. The solid dot on 32 shows that 32 is part of the solution.

0° 2° 4° 6° 8° 10° 12° 14° 16° 18° 20° 22° 24° 26° 28° 30° 32° 34° 36°

CASE 2 For some inequalities, the solution is a discrete graph. In a **discrete graph**, only *some* points on the graph are solutions to the inequality.

EXAMPLE 2: To be approved as an official school club, a club needs to have 25 or more members. Use a graph to show the number of members a school club can have.

★ $x \geq 25$

20   21   22   23   24   25   26   27   28   29   30

> Since the club can't have fractional members, only the whole numbers 25 or greater are shown on the graph.

Is Less Than (<) or Is Greater Than (>)

To compare quantities when they are not equal, use inequality symbols *is less than* (<) or *is greater than* (>).

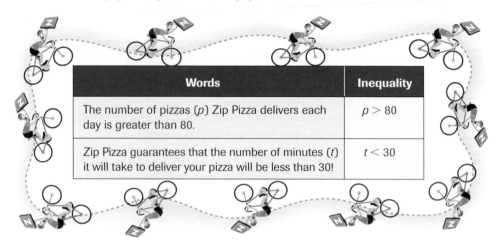

Words	Inequality
The number of pizzas (p) Zip Pizza delivers each day is greater than 80.	$p > 80$
Zip Pizza guarantees that the number of minutes (t) it will take to deliver your pizza will be less than 30!	$t < 30$

On the number line, the graph of an inequality with < or > shows a circle around the starting point. This means that the circled value is *not* included in the solution set.

EXAMPLE: Graph the solutions for $t < 30$ on the number line.

★ $t < 30$

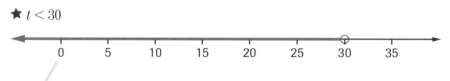

0   5   10   15   20   25   30   35

$t < 0$ makes no sense in this problem because the pizza can't arrive before you order it. Numbers < 0 are not possible times, even though they are solutions to the inequality.

Is Less Than or Equal To (≤) or Is Greater Than or Equal To (≥)

To compare quantities when they may or may not be equal use *is less than or equal to* (≤) or *is greater than or equal to* (≥).

On the number line, the graph of an inequality with ≤ or ≥ shows a solid dot at the starting point. This means that the value at that position is included in the solution set.

Words	Inequality
The FDA recommends that refrigerated foods be kept at a temperature (*T*), which is less than or equal to 45°F.	$T \le 45$ −30° −20° −10° 0 10° 20° 30° 40° 50°
To protect against illness, the FDA recommends that raw foods be cooked to an internal temperature (*T*), which is greater than or equal to 160°F.	$T \ge 160$ 0° 20° 40° 60° 80° 100° 120° 140° 160° 180° 200°

Source: U.S. Food and Drug Administration

EXAMPLE: Graph the solutions for $t \ge {}^-6$ on the number line.

★ $t \ge {}^-6$

Writing and Graphing Compound Inequalities

A **compound inequality** is made by combining two inequalities with *and* or with *or*.

You can use a **compound inequality** to describe the permitted speeds. The sign indicates that speed must be greater than or equal to 45 mph *and* less than or equal to 55 mph. Using symbols, the inequality can be written in either of these ways:

SPEED LIMIT **55** MINIMUM **45**

$45 \le s$ and $s \le 55$ $45 \le s \le 55$

To solve a compound inequality with *and*, you find the values for which *both* inequalities are true. The graph for $45 \le s \le 55$ includes all numbers greater than or equal to 45 *and at the same time* less than or equal to 55.

$45 \le s \le 55$

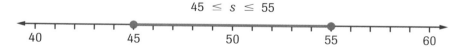

MORE ▶

You can use a **compound inequality** to describe the ages of people who pay half price.

The sign indicates that a person's age (x) must be less than or equal to 6 *or* greater than or equal to 70 to pay half price.

$x \leq 6$ or $x \geq 70$

To solve a compound inequality with *or*, you find the values for which *either* of the sentences is true. The graph of $x \leq 6$ or $x \geq 70$ includes all numbers less than or equal to 6 *or* greater than or equal to 70.

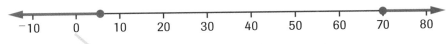

No points less than 0 are solutions to the problem even though they are solutions to the inequality. It doesn't make sense to sell a ticket to a person whose age is less than 0.

196

Solving Inequalities with One Variable

MORE HELP
See 127

If you know how to solve equations, you know how to solve inequalities. You just need to combine like terms and use what you know about the properties of addition, subtraction, multiplication, and division.

CASE 1 Sometimes, only one step is needed to solve an inequality.

EXAMPLE 1: In 1999, the Metropolitan Transit Authority in New York City offered a monthly subway pass for $63. A single subway fare cost $1.50. For what number of monthly rides was a pass less expensive?

Source: Metropolitan Transit Authority

Let x represent the number of subway rides taken each month. Then $1.5x$ represents the total amount of money paid for single fares.

To solve for x:	$63 < 1.5x$
Divide both sides by 1.5	$42 < x$

★ In one month, for any number of rides greater than 42, the monthly pass was less expensive than paying for single fares.

CASE 2 Sometimes, it takes more than one step to solve an inequality.

EXAMPLE 2: Suppose you get two job offers. Ben's Sound Studio offers a salary of $400 per week plus a 5% commission on sales. Crazy Cal's offers $200 per week plus a 7% commission. For what amounts of weekly sales will you earn more at Crazy Cal's than at Ben's?

Let x represent weekly sales in dollars. Then $\frac{5}{100}x$ represents the weekly commissions at Ben's Sound Studio and $\frac{7}{100}x$ represents the weekly commissions at Crazy Cal's. To solve the problem, you need to find the values for x that make this inequality true: $200 + \frac{7}{100}x > 400 + \frac{5}{100}x$.

To solve:	$200 + \dfrac{7}{100}x > 400 + \dfrac{5}{100}x$
Clear the fractions.	$20{,}000 + 7x > 40{,}000 + 5x$
Subtract 20,000 and $5x$ from both sides.	$2x > 20{,}000$
Divide both sides by 2.	$x > 10{,}000$

Any number greater than 10,000 is a solution.

★ You will earn more at Crazy Cal's than at Ben's Sound Studio if your weekly sales are greater than $10,000.

> You could also solve this problem by graphing both expressions on your graphing calculator and looking at their intersection.

197

MATH ALERT Be Careful with Negative Numbers in Inequalities

Sometimes you have to multiply or divide to isolate the variable. In both inequalities and equations, you can multiply or divide both sides by the same number.

■ **If you multiply or divide both sides of the inequality by the *same negative number*, the direction of the inequality reverses.** This is because multiplying a number by $^{-}1$ moves it to the other side of zero on the number line. Think: $n \cdot -a = -1(na)$ and $n \div -a = -1\left(\frac{n}{a}\right)$.

EXAMPLE: $-8n < 32$

$$-8n \div {}^{-}8 \; \blacksquare \; 32 \div {}^{-}8$$

$$n > {}^{-}4$$

★ $n > {}^{-}4$

> Watch out! If you forget to change the inequality sign, you'll be saying that numbers less than $^{-}4$ solve the inequality. You know that $^{-}5$ is less than $^{-}4$, so try it out in the original inequality. Is $^{-}8 \cdot {}^{-}5 < 32$? It's not! So, flip the inequality sign.

Solving Compound Inequalities

To solve a compound inequality, solve a pair of inequalities and then combine those solutions. How you combine the solutions depends on whether the pair of inequalities is joined with the word *and* or with the word *or*.

MORE HELP
See 195–196

CASE 1 To solve an inequality with the word *and*, you must solve each inequality, then find solutions that make *both* sentences true.

EXAMPLE 1: In 24 years, John will be between two and three times his current age. What are the possible ages he could be now?

> In mathematics, x is between a and b means $a < x < b$. In such an inequality a and b are not included.

Let n represent John's age now. Then $n + 24$ represents his age 24 years from now. To solve this problem you need to find the values for n that make this compound inequality true: $2n < n + 24$ *and* $n + 24 < 3n$.

Solve each inequality.

$2n < n + 24 \longrightarrow n < 24$

$n + 24 < 3n \longrightarrow 12 < n$

$12 < n < 24$

★ John is now more than 12 but less than 24 years old.

CASE 2 To solve an inequality with the word *or*, you must solve each inequality, then find all solutions that make *either* sentence true.

EXAMPLE 2: Which graph illustrates the solution to $2x - 5 \geq 11$ *or* $3x + 7 < 13$?

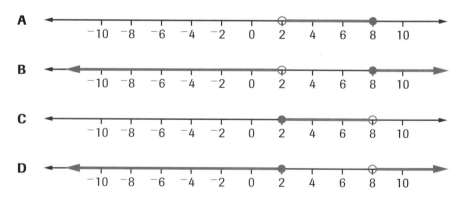

Solve each inequality independently.

$2x - 5 \geq 11 \longrightarrow x \geq 8$

$3x + 7 < 13 \longrightarrow x < 2$

Study the question to decide what the graph should look like. Look especially at the symbols to decide whether the starting points for each path
should be open or closed and in which direction each path should point.

$x \geq 8$ ———▶ The starting point should be closed and the path goes right
from 8.

$x < 2$ ———▶ The starting point should be open and the path goes left
from 2.

★ Number line B illustrates $2x - 5 \geq 11$ *or* $3x + 7 < 13$.

Absolute Value Inequalities on the Number Line

To understand inequalities involving absolute value, think about the definition of **absolute value**—the absolute value of a number is its distance
from 0 on the number line. To solve an inequality involving absolute value,
you use a compound inequality involving *and* or *or*.

CASE 1 To solve an inequality in which the absolute value of a number is
less than another number ($|x| < a$), or less than or equal to an-
other number ($|x| \leq a$), use a compound inequality involving *and*.

MORE HELP
See 009, 116,
130

The *equation* $|x| = 2$ has two solutions, $x = 2$ and $x = {}^-2$.

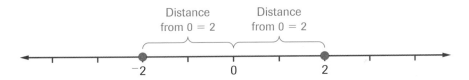

The *inequality* $|x| < 2$ is true for any number whose distance from 0 is
less than 2. This means that $|x| < 2$ has the same meaning as:

$^-2 < x$ *and* $x < 2$

$^-2 < x < 2$

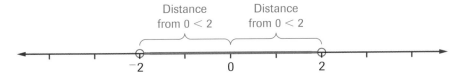

MORE ▶

CASE 2 To solve an inequality in which the absolute value of a number is greater than another number ($|x| > a$), or greater than or equal to another number ($|x| \geq a$), use a compound inequality involving *or*.

MORE HELP
See 196

The inequality $|x| > 2$ is true for any number whose distance from zero

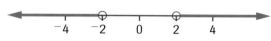

is greater than 2. So, $|x| > 2$ has the same meaning as: $x < {}^-2 \ or \ x > 2$

EXAMPLE: Solve and graph the inequality, $|4x - 6| > 18$.

To solve $|4x - 6| > 18$, solve $4x - 6 < {}^-18 \ or \ 4x - 6 > 18$.

$4x - 6 < {}^-18 \longrightarrow x < {}^-3$

$4x - 6 > 18 \longrightarrow x > 6$

★ The solution is: $x < {}^-3 \ or \ x > 6$.

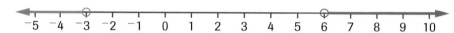

200

Checking Solutions to Inequalities

After you solve an inequality, it's a good idea to check your solution. The best way to check is to substitute a sample number or two into the original inequality. You should also examine the original question to make sure you're not including some numbers that work in the inequality but make no sense in the problem.

EXAMPLE: Solve and graph the inequality. $50h + 75 \leq 300$

To solve:	$50h + 75 \leq 300$
Subtract 75 from each side.	$50h \leq 225$
Divide each side by 50.	$h \leq 4.5$

Check. Try two numbers less than 4.5, like 3 and $^-1$, as h in the original inequality:

Is $50(3) + 75 \leq 300$? Yes, 225 is less than or equal to 300.

Is $50({}^-1) + 75 \leq 300$? Yes, 25 is less than or equal to 300.

★ The solution is $h \leq 4.5$.

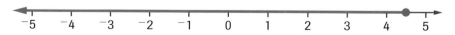

Inequalities with Solutions on the Coordinate Plane 201

When an inequality has two variables, each solution consists of a pair of values. Making a graph on a coordinate plane is a practical way to represent sets of ordered pairs.

MORE HELP
See 130,
146–160,
174–177

■ **Linear Inequalities**: The graph of a linear inequality (an inequality, like $ax + by < c$, in which both variables have degree one), shows a line graphed on a plane. The solutions may involve points on either side of the line, and maybe the line itself, depending on the inequality.

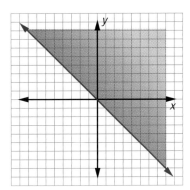

■ **Quadratic Inequalities**: The graph of a quadratic inequality (an inequality with two variables, one of degree two, one of degree one) shows a parabola. The solutions may involve points inside or outside of the parabola, and maybe on the parabola itself.

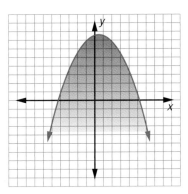

■ **Absolute Value Inequalities:** The graph of an absolute value inequality shows a V-shape. The solutions may involve points on the inside or outside of the V, and maybe on the V itself.

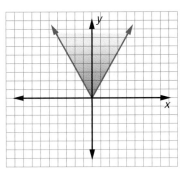

202   Graphing Linear Inequalities _____

To graph a linear inequality (such as $y \leq x + 2$), you start by graphing the related linear equation $(y = x + 2)$. This graph is called the **boundary line,** or **plane divider**, because it divides the plane. Once you have a boundary line, you have to decide which side of that line contains the solutions to the inequality. You also have to decide whether the plane divider itself includes solutions.

203   Plane Divider

In the graph of a linear inequality, the **plane divider** divides the plane.

CASE 1 An inequality with $\leq$ or $\geq$ has a plane divider that is a solid line because the line represents the *is equal to* part of the comparison.

EXAMPLE 1: Your parents allow you to work at a part-time job for a maximum of 12 hours a week as long as your grades don't fall. You can work on weekday afternoons or on weekends. Draw the plane divider of the graph that represents the number of weekly hours and weekend hours you can work.

Let x represent the number of weekday hours and let y represent the number of weekend hours. Since you can work up to 12 hours per week, $x + y \leq 12$ describes this situation.

To draw the plane divider, graph the related linear equation: $x + y = 12$.

Since the solutions of $x + y \leq 12$ include the solutions of $x + y = 12$, draw a solid line for $x + y = 12$. This shows that the points on the line are part of the solution.

The rest of the solutions are on only one side of the plane divider. Look at item 204 to figure out which side of the divider contains the solutions!

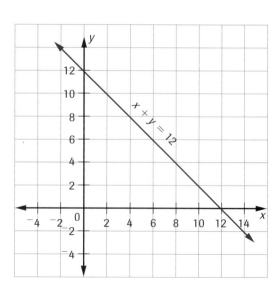

CASE 2 An inequality with $<$ or $>$ has a plane divider that is a dashed line because this inequality does not have an *is equal to* part, which would be the line.

EXAMPLE 2: The bonus level of a computer game occurs after you have earned 400 points. Draw the plane divider of the inequality that shows points beyond bonus level.

To draw the plane divider, graph the related linear equation, $y = x + 400$.

Since the solutions to $y > x + 400$ don't include the solutions of $y = x + 400$, draw a dashed line for $y = x + 400$. This shows that the points on the line are *not* part of the solution.

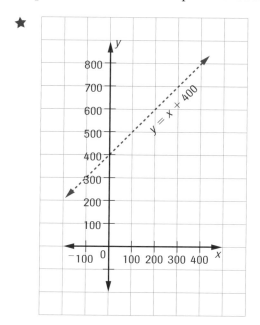

Choosing the Relevant Half-Plane

MORE HELP
See 203

In the graph of an inequality, the plane divider separates the plane into two regions. These are sometimes called **half-planes**. One of these regions contains solutions to the inequality. To find out which one does, test points on each side of the plane divider.

Consider the inequality describing the situation in which you can work up to 12 hours and split the time between weekdays and weekends. The inequality $x + y \leq 12$ describes the situation. The plane divider is the graph of $x + y = 12$, and is a solid line because points on the line are part of the solution.

Pick a test-point on each side of the plane divider. Check to see whether it is a solution to the inequality, $x + y \leq 12$. If the result is true, shade the region which contains the test point.

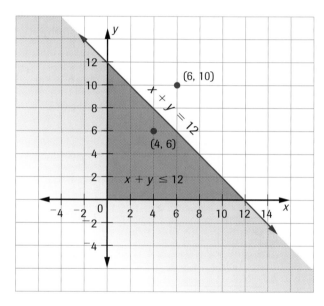

Try point (6, 10). Is $6 + 10 \leq 12$?

$16 \leq 12$ is false, so (6, 10) is *not* a solution.

Try point (4, 6). Is $4 + 6 \leq 12$? $10 \leq 12$ is true, so (4, 6) is a solution. All the points in the half-plane that contains (4, 6) are solutions to the inequality.

When you give a solution to the problem (not the inequality, but the original problem) be careful! Be sure your answer is reasonable. You can only work a positive number of hours, so both x and y must be positive for a point to be a solution to the original problem. There are many different combinations of weekday and weekend hours you can work. Use points in the darker-shaded region, where both times are positive.

Graphing Quadratic Inequalities

The graph of a quadratic inequality shows a parabola. The solutions may involve points inside or outside of the parabola, and maybe also on the parabola itself.

The inequality $y > \frac{x^2}{20} + x$, where x represents speed in miles per hour, is a function used to determine stopping distance. *Source: Highway Code of Great Britain*

MORE HELP
See 005,
176–179

Suppose you want to make a graph that relates speed and stopping distances of a car. You want the graph to show distances (in feet) at which it is impossible to stop, given particular speeds.

Graph the related quadratic equation, $y = \frac{x^2}{20} + x$.

❶ Use the equation to find the vertex and the line of symmetry.	$x = \frac{-b}{2a} \qquad y = \frac{(^-10)^2}{20} + {}^-10$ $\quad = {}^-10 \qquad\qquad = {}^-5$ The coordinates of the vertex are $(^-10, {}^-5)$. The line of symmetry is $x = {}^-10$.
❷ Make a table of values for the vertex and a few points on each side of the vertex.	<table><tr><td>x</td><td>$^-20$</td><td>$^-10$</td><td>0</td><td>10</td></tr><tr><td>y</td><td>0</td><td>$^-5$</td><td>0</td><td>15</td></tr></table>
❸ Plot the graph. Since the solutions of $y > \frac{x^2}{20} + x$ don't include the solutions of $y = \frac{x^2}{20} + x$, draw a dashed parabola.	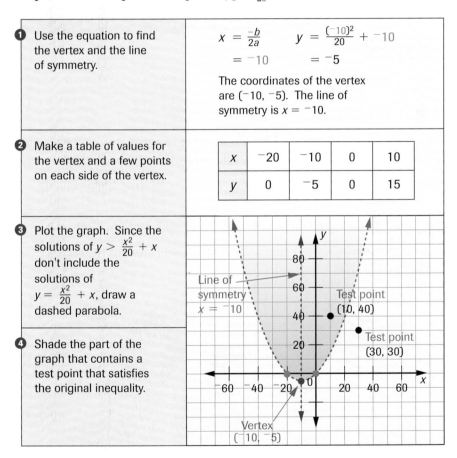
❹ Shade the part of the graph that contains a test point that satisfies the original inequality.	

All the points inside the parabola are solutions. To find solutions that make sense in the real world, look at x-values (speeds) greater than 0.

Graphing Systems of Inequalities _____

Sometimes, you need to find regions on a graph in which the points make two or more *different* inequalities true. When you do this, you are solving a **system of inequalities**.

EXAMPLE: A craftsperson makes flat kites and box kites from nylon and aluminum rods. A flat kite requires three yards of aluminum and four yards of nylon. A box kite requires six yards of aluminum and three yards of nylon. The person has 30 yards of aluminum and 24 yards of nylon. Use a graph to find the different possible combinations of kites that can be made.

First, make a table to show the information.

	Flat Kite	Box Kite	Total
Yards of aluminum	3	6	30
Yards of nylon	4	3	24

Next, model the situation algebraically.

Let x represent the number of flat kites. Let y represent the number of box kites. Yards of aluminum $= 3x + 6y$ and yards of nylon $= 4x + 3y$.

Since there are only 30 yards of aluminum, you can write the inequality $3x + 6y \le 30$.

The yards of nylon used must satisfy the inequality $4x + 3y \le 24$.

To solve the problem, graph each inequality. Then, look for the region where the two solutions overlap.

$3x + 6y \le 30$ is shown in red on this graph.

$4x + 3y \le 24$ is shown in blue on this graph.

The solutions to the system are in the overlapping purple region.

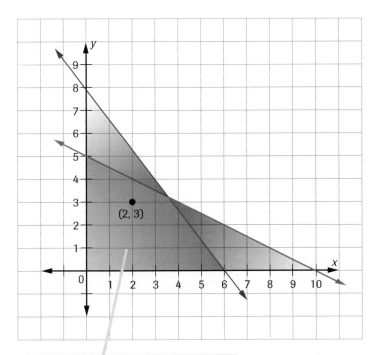

This purple region is called the **region of flexible solutions.**

Check a solution such as $(2, 3)$, which represents two flat kites and three box kites. Does this solution work?

Is $3(2) + 6(3) \le 30$? Yes.

Is $4(2) + 3(3) \le 24$? Yes.

You might also try several points not in the purple region to be absolutely sure they do not satisfy both equations.

★ Any point in the purple region shows a combination of flat kites and box kites that can be made if it is okay to partially complete a kite. Since it's probably not okay to count parts of kites, you should look for points that represent whole numbers of kites.

Elements of Geometric Figures

"I advise my students to listen carefully the moment they decide to take no more mathematics courses. They might be able to hear the sound of closing doors."

James Caballero

ook closely enough at a chalkboard, or any surface, no matter how smooth, and you can find scratches, dents, and bumps. Examine the sidelines of a football field, the rails of a train track, or even the pinpoint beam of a laser and you can find a little bending. Check out the edge of a penny or a corner of this page and you can feel some rounding. If you want a world of perfectly smooth surfaces, perfectly straight lines, and perfectly sharp corners, enter the world of geometry. Although it's inhabited by the abstraction of perfection, geometry is quite useful in the real and imperfect world.

By imagining perfect points, lines, and planes you can understand why things look the way they do, how they fit together, and what paths they take when they move. These elements of geometry help in designing bridges and ballparks, rockets and rollerskates, and stereos and street signs.

Look in this section and you'll find out about the building blocks of geometry. Don't look too closely—you might get distracted by the imperfections in the paper.

Points, lines, curves, and planes are mathematical abstractions. You can, however, use models of points, lines, and curves to draw anything. They can help you construct triangles, rectangles, buildings, or anything else that you want. They also help you describe shape, position, direction, and the relationships among shapes.

209

Points

MORE HELP
See 219

In geometry, a **point** is a place in space. You can't touch a point. It has no size, only location. You can draw a dot to represent a point. You can use numbers to describe its exact position, and you can name it, usually with a capital letter.

Where two lines **intersect** (cross), there is a point. If you name any two distinct points, there is exactly one line that passes through them.

If you name any three points that are not on the same line (that is, they are not **collinear**), then,

- they can be the vertices of a triangle,
- there is a circle that goes through them all,
- and there is a plane that contains them all.

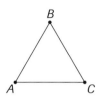

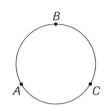

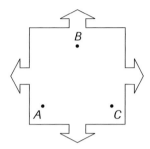

Lines

A **line** is a straight path of points that has no endpoints. It goes on infinitely in two directions but it has no thickness. If you take any two points, you can always draw a line (and only one line) through them. Mathematicians say that two points **determine** a line.

To name a line, you can mark any two points on the line with capital letters and then name the line with those letters. You can also use a single lowercase letter.

This symbol means the figure is a line.

Write: $\overleftrightarrow{JK}$, or $\overleftrightarrow{KJ}$, or *c*

Say: *line J K, line K J, or line c*

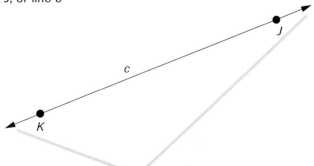

The arrowheads mean that the line goes on infinitely without stopping. You cannot measure the length of a line.

211 Rays

Suppose you cut a line and separate the two parts. Each part has an end-point and goes on infinitely in one direction. What you have are two rays.

A **ray** is a part of a line that has one endpoint and continues in one direction infinitely. You cannot measure the length of a ray. To name a ray, you use the endpoint and any other point on the ray.

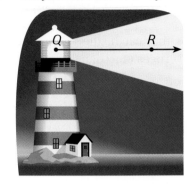

> This symbol means that the figure is a ray. Always write the name of the endpoint first.

Write: $\overrightarrow{QR}$

Say: *ray Q R*

212 Line Segments

A **line segment** is part of a line. It has two endpoints and includes all the points between those two endpoints. You can measure the length of a line segment. To name a line segment, use its endpoints.

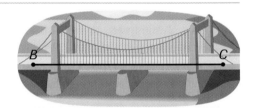

> This symbol means that the figure is a line segment. If you don't use the symbol or the words *line segment*, BC means the distance between point B and point C.

Write: $\overline{BC}$ or $\overline{CB}$

Say: *line segment B C* or *line segment C B* or *segment B C* or *segment C B*

213 Midpoints

The **midpoint** of a line segment is a point that divides the segment into two congruent parts.

Point M divides $\overline{AB}$ into two segments of equal length.

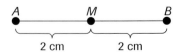

M is the midpoint of $\overline{AB}$. $AM = MB = \frac{1}{2} AB$

> Remember, if you do not indicate that two letters refer to a segment, you are referring to the distance between two points named by the letters.

If you know the coordinates of the endpoints, you can use this formula to find the midpoint. For any two points (x_1, y_1) and (x_2, y_2), the coordinates of the midpoint are the mean of the x-coordinates and the mean of the y-coordinates.

$$\text{midpoint} = \left(\frac{x_1 + x_2}{2}, \frac{y_1 + y_2}{2}\right)$$

MORE HELP
See 219–220

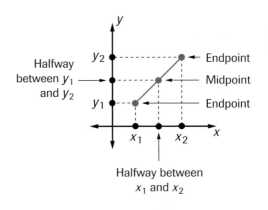

(x_1, y_1) is a short way of writing (first value of x, first value of y). (x_2, y_2) is a short way of writing (second value of x, second value of y).

EXAMPLE: Find the midpoint of $\overline{CD}$.

Use the coordinates of C for (x_1, y_1). Use the coordinates of D for (x_2, y_2).

$(x_1, y_1) = (^-2, ^-1)$

$(x_2, y_2) = (4, 1)$

$$\text{Midpoint} = \left(\frac{x_1 + x_2}{2}, \frac{y_1 + y_2}{2}\right)$$

$$= \left(\frac{^-2 + 4}{2}, \frac{^-1 + 1}{2}\right)$$

$$= \left(\frac{2}{2}, \frac{0}{2}\right)$$

$$= (1, 0)$$

★ The midpoint of $\overline{CD}$ is $(1, 0)$.

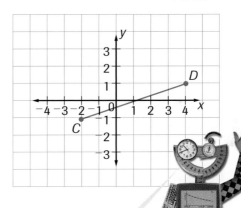

You could also count to find the value halfway between ⁻2 and 4 and the value halfway between ⁻1 and 1.

Parallel, Intersecting, and Skew Lines

MORE HELP
See 218

Parallel lines are lines in the same plane that never cross because they are always the same distance apart. Since they don't cross, they don't have any points in common. Segments of parallel lines are also parallel.

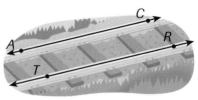

Write: $\overleftrightarrow{TR} \parallel \overleftrightarrow{AC}$

This symbol means is parallel to.

Say: *Line T R is parallel to line A C.*

Intersecting lines are lines that cross. They either have one point in common (the point where they cross) or all points in common. If they have all points in common, they are the same line. If two different lines intersect, then there is only one plane that contains them both. Segments of intersecting lines can also intersect. $\overleftrightarrow{PA}$ and $\overleftrightarrow{NE}$ intersect.

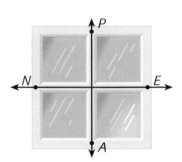

Skew lines are lines that are not parallel and that do not intersect. If lines are skew, there is no single plane that contains them both. Segments of skew lines are skew, too.

$\overleftrightarrow{RA}$ and $\overleftrightarrow{MP}$ are not in the same plane. They are skew.

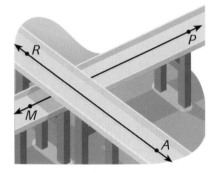

Perpendicular Lines

Perpendicular lines are lines that form right angles when they meet. Segments formed by two perpendicular lines are perpendicular.

Perpendicular

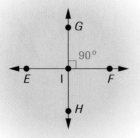

Not Perpendicular

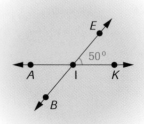

This means *is perpendicular to.*

Write: $\overleftrightarrow{EF} \perp \overleftrightarrow{GH}$, or $\overline{EF} \perp \overline{GH}$

Say: *Line E F is perpendicular to line G H,* or *segment E F is perpendicular to segment G H.*

The angles formed where $\overline{AK}$ and $\overline{BE}$ intersect are not right angles. $\overline{AK}$ and $\overline{BE}$ are not perpendicular.

Just because something looks perpendicular, doesn't mean that it is. To decide, look for clues such as the symbols ⊥ or ∟. Also use what you know about rectangles and squares.

Perpendicular Bisector

A **perpendicular bisector** of a line segment is a line, line segment, ray, or plane that forms a right angle with the line segment and divides it into two congruent parts. It intersects the line segment at its midpoint.

216

MORE HELP
See 213

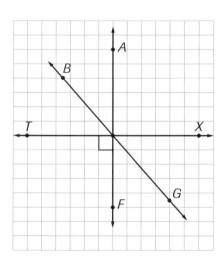

EXAMPLE: Find the perpendicular bisector of $\overline{TX}$.

Both $\overline{AF}$ and $\overline{BG}$ bisect $\overline{TX}$. However, only $\overline{AF}$ is perpendicular to $\overline{TX}$.

★ $\overline{AF}$ is the perpendicular bisector of $\overline{TX}$.

217

Curves

A line is just a straight curve. Curves are paths of points with no thickness, just length and direction.

Open Curves

Closed Curves

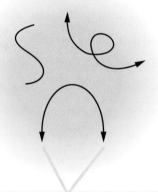

The arrowheads mean the curve continues without stopping.

218

Planes

A plane is a set of points that forms a flat surface infinitely wide and infinitely long with no thickness. This means that you can't measure the length and width of a plane. It also means that you can't count the number of points or lines in a plane, because there is an infinite number of them.

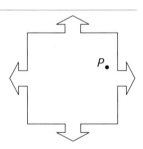

$P_\bullet$

CASE 1 Planes can intersect each other, and where they do, there is a line. This line is the vertex of a **dihedral angle**.

CASE 2 Two planes can be parallel to each other. When they are, they have no points in common. A line in one is either parallel or skew to a line in the other.

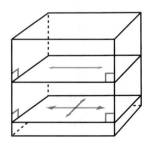

The Coordinate Plane

Grids help you organize space and find locations. One place you've probably seen grids is on maps. In the map index, you can look up a place, like a
city, a town, or a street. A pair of grid coordinates, like C-4, helps you find
the place on the map.

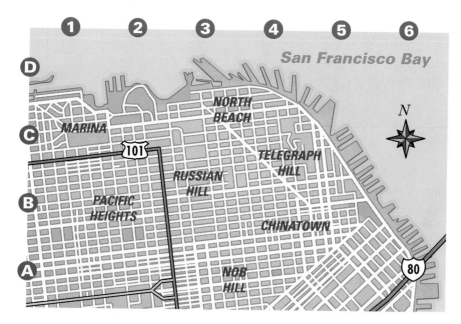

In mathematics, a **coordinate grid** is a way to locate points in a plane
instead of regions on a map. A coordinate grid consists of a horizontal number line called the **x-axis** and a vertical number line called the **y-axis**. These
two lines intersect at a point called the **origin**. The x-axis and the y-axis
divide the plane into four sections called **quadrants**.

You can name any point on
a coordinate plane with two
numbers called **coordinates**.
The first number is the
x-coordinate (or abscissa).
The second number is the
y-coordinate (or ordinate).
Since the pair is always
named in order (first x,
then y), it's called an
ordered pair.

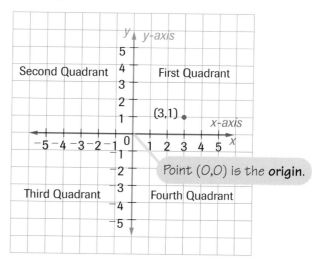

Write: (3, 1)
Say: *point three one*

Plotting and Naming Points

The sign of each coordinate of a point tells the direction to move from the origin when you plot the point. The absolute value of each coordinate tells the number of units to move. When one or both of the numbers in an ordered pair (x, y) is negative, the point is not in the first quadrant.

MORE HELP
See 009

- A positive x-coordinate means *go right*.

- A negative x-coordinate means *go left*.

- A positive y-coordinate means *go up*.

- A negative y-coordinate means *go down*.

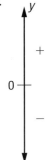

You can identify the quadrant in which a point is located by looking at the coordinates of the point.

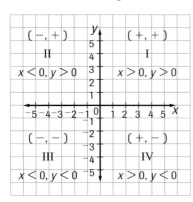

A mathematical convention is to name the quadrants with Roman numerals, I, II, III, IV.

EXAMPLE 1: Plot point Q at $(2, 3)$. Plot point R at $(^-2, 3)$. Plot point S at $(^-2, ^-3)$.

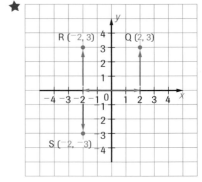

EXAMPLE 2: Point T is at $(2, ^-3)$. In which quadrant is point T?

The x-coordinate is positive, so the point is to the right of the y-axis. The y-coordinate is negative, so the point is below the x-axis.

★ Point T is in the fourth quadrant.

Slope

Suppose you go skiing. In what ways would you expect the advanced slope to be different from the beginner's slope? One difference you would probably find is in the steepness of the hill. The advanced slope would probably be much steeper than the beginner's slope.

MORE HELP
See 146, 159

In mathematics, **slope** measures the steepness of a line. A line that moves upward from left to right has a **positive slope**. A line that moves downward from left to right has a **negative slope**. If a line is **horizontal**, (flat from left to right), it has a slope of 0. If a line is **vertical**, (goes straight up and down), we say that its slope is undefined.

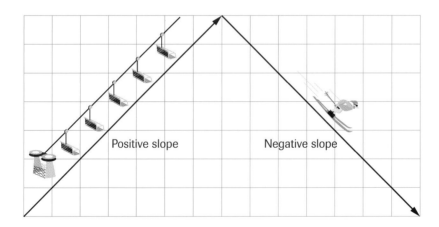

Positive slope   Negative slope

Finding the Slope of a Line

The slope of a line tells you how the value of y changes as the value of x changes. To find the slope of any line, choose two points on the line, then use this formula.

$$\text{Slope} = \frac{\text{change in } y\text{-value}}{\text{change in } x\text{-value}}$$

$$= \frac{\text{second } y - \text{first } y}{\text{second } x - \text{first } x}, \text{ or } \frac{y_2 - y_1}{x_2 - x_1}$$

It is also correct to find slope this way: $\frac{y_1 - y_2}{x_1 - x_2}$. Another way to remember slope is to think of the change in y as **rise** and the change in x as **run**. Slope $= \frac{rise}{run}$.

MORE ▶

MORE HELP
See 127–129

EXAMPLE 1: Find the slope of the line for $3x - y = 3$. Compare to the slope of the line for $3x - y = {}^{-}3$.

Choose two points on each line. Find the slope by finding the change in y-value and the change in x-value between those two points.

$$\text{Slope} = \frac{\text{change in } y\text{-value}}{\text{change in } x\text{-value}} = \frac{y_2 - y_1}{x_2 - x_1}$$

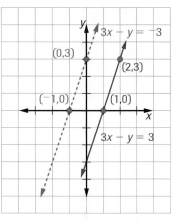

Slope of $3x - y = 3$ $\longrightarrow$ $\dfrac{3 - 0}{2 - 1} = 3$

Slope of $3x - y = {}^{-}3$ $\longrightarrow$ $\dfrac{3 - 0}{0 - {}^{-}1} = 3$

This means that, for both lines when the x-value changes by 1, the y-value changes by 3. Because the slope of each line is positive, the lines slant upward from left to right.

★ The slope of $3x - y = 3$ is 3. This is also the slope of $3x - y = {}^{-}3$. Note that the two lines are parallel and the coefficient of x is the same.

EXAMPLE 2: Find and compare the slopes of these two lines:
${}^{-}3x - y = {}^{-}3$ and $\frac{-1}{3}x - y = {}^{-}3$.

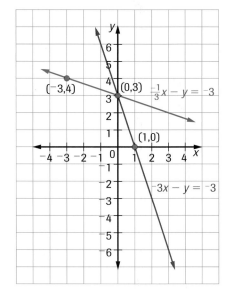

Choose two points on each line and find the slope.

$$\text{Slope} = \frac{\text{change in } y\text{-value}}{\text{change in } x\text{-value}} = \frac{y_2 - y_1}{x_2 - x_1}$$

Slope of ${}^{-}3x - y = {}^{-}3$ $\longrightarrow$ $\dfrac{0 - 3}{1 - 0} = {}^{-}3$

Slope of $\frac{-1}{3}x - y = {}^{-}3$ $\longrightarrow$ $\dfrac{3 - 4}{0 - {}^{-}3} = \dfrac{{}^{-}1}{3}$

★ The slope of $^-3x - y = ^-3$ is $^-3$ and the slope of $\frac{^-1}{3}x - y = ^-3$ is $\frac{^-1}{3}$. They have negative coefficients of x and both have negative slopes. Note that the slope of the line with the smaller coefficient of x is much steeper than the slope of the line with the larger coefficient of x.

MORE HELP
See 157

> When an equation is in slope-intercept form, $y = mx + b$, the coefficient of x is the slope.

Rate of Change

223

When you look at slope, you can see the rate at which the quantity represented by y increases or decreases with respect to a change in x. In other words, you can see the **rate of change** of the quantity represented by y.

EXAMPLE: The graph shows the numbers of people age 7 or older who participated in basketball and inline skating in given years. Between 1990 and 1995, in which sport did the number of participants grow at a greater rate?

The steepness of a line or line segment tells you the rate of change of the quantity. To solve the problem, compare the line segments that represent each sport from 1990 to 1995. The steeper segment shows a greater rate of growth.

★ For the interval from 1990 to 1995, the segment for inline skating is steeper than the segment for basketball. For those years, the number of inline skaters grew at a greater rate than the number of basketball players.

Growth of Basketball and Inline Skating, 1985–1995

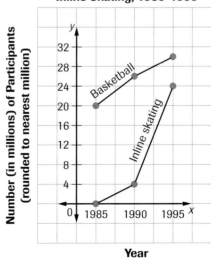

Source: National Sporting Goods Association

Suppose you were to shoot a movie. How should you turn the camera to get the shot you want? Suppose you are designing a house. How steep should the stairs be? What kind of corners will the roof form? All of these questions are about angles. When you think about turns or corners, you are thinking about angles.

225)

Parts of Angles

Angles are formed by two rays that have the same **endpoint**. This point is called the **vertex**. Angles occur wherever lines and line segments intersect. You can name an angle in three different ways.

- Use three letters in this order: a point on one ray, the vertex, a point on the other ray.

  Write: $\angle NAP$ or $\angle PAN$
  Say: *angle N A P,* or *angle P A N*

- Use one letter at the vertex if there's no chance for confusion.

  Write: $\angle A$
  Say: *angle A*

- Use a number or lowercase letter written inside the rays of the angle.

  Write: $\angle 1$ or $\angle a$
  Say: *angle one* or *angle a*

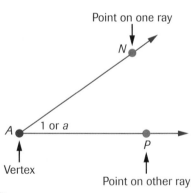

Point on one ray

N

A 1 or *a*

P

Vertex

Point on other ray

The symbol $\angle$ means angle.

Classifying Angles by Measure _____

Angles are named for the way they relate to 90° or to 180°.

Moving counterclockwise from 0°:

- less than 90°   Acute

- exactly 90°   Right

- greater than 90°   Obtuse
  and less than 180°

- exactly 180°   Straight

- greater than 180°
  and less than 360°   Reflex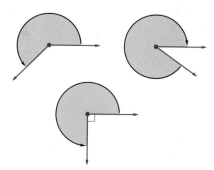

You can use this sentence to remember the way angles are named. A Rocket Orbits Saturn's Rings.

Angles in Polygons

Polygons are simple closed figures in a plane, whose line segments meet only at their endpoints. Where the sides of the polygons intersect, angles are formed. The angles can be on the inside of the figure or the outside of the figure.

When you draw segments from a point inside a polygon to each of the vertices, you form angles around that point. The sum of the measures of these angles is always 360°.

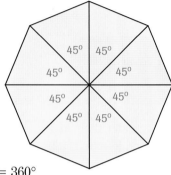

$$45° + 45° + 45° + 45° + 45° + 45° + 45° + 45° = 360°$$

Interior Angles

An **interior angle** is an angle formed by the sides of a polygon. It is inside the figure.

EXAMPLE: How many interior angles are in the square? How many are in the hexagon? Relate the number of interior angles to the number of sides in a polygon.

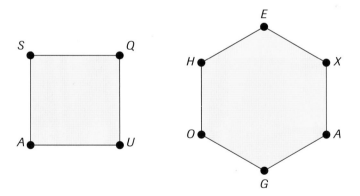

★ There are four interior angles in the square: $\angle SQU$, $\angle QUA$, $\angle UAS$, and $\angle ASQ$. There are six interior angles in the hexagon: $\angle HEX$, $\angle EXA$, $\angle XAG$, $\angle AGO$, $\angle GOH$, and $\angle OHE$. The number of interior angles in a polygon is the same as the number of sides.

Exterior Angles

To see an **exterior angle** of a polygon, extend one of the sides of the polygon. Then measure the angle between that extension and the adjacent side of the polygon. For every vertex of a polygon, there are two exterior angles because either side of the angle can be extended.

MORE HELP
See 242

EXAMPLE: Look at the exterior angles (∠1 and ∠2) at vertex U. What is the relationship between each of these angles and the interior angle ∠TUV? What is their relationship to each other?

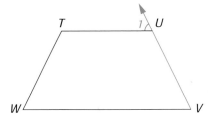 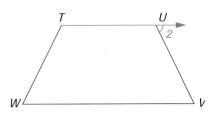

Look at angle 1. It forms a straight angle with ∠TUV. These two angles are supplementary. Now look at ∠2. It is also supplementary to ∠TUV. Write and solve an equation to model the situation.

MORE HELP
See 233

$$m\angle 1 + m\angle TUV = m\angle 2 + m\angle TUV$$

$$m\angle 1 + m\angle TUV - m\angle TUV = m\angle 2 + m\angle TUV - m\angle TUV$$

$$m\angle 1 = m\angle 2$$

The *m* written before the angle-name means *the measure of.*

★ ∠1 and ∠2 have the same measure. They are both supplementary to ∠TUV.

230

Geometric Relationships

"A round man cannot be reasonably expected to fit into a square hole right away."

Mark Twain

In some ways, you can think of geometry as the language of shape. That means there are lots of terms to know, like triangle, rectangle, and curve. You'll find the definitions of these terms and many others in the Glossary.

But geometry is not just the language of shape; it is also the study of shape. Are triangles strong because you can't change their shape without changing the length of a side? Are rectangles easier than other shapes to place in straight rows without gaps? Does bending a beam help it support its own weight? The next time you cross a bridge, stand outside your school, or watch a ball game played at Safeco Field or the Silverdome, take a moment to look closely at these structures. Why does a bridge have so many triangles? Why are bricks rectangular? Why do covered stadiums have curved roofs? The answers are in geometry.

If you look at windows, fences, ballfields, or anything with angles, you'll see that angles are connected to other angles. In many cases, the measure of one affects the measures of others.

232

Congruent Angles

Congruent angles are angles that have the same measure. *Any* two angles with the same measure are congruent. If two angles are congruent, either angle can fit exactly over the other angle.

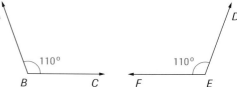

Write: $\angle ABC \cong \angle DEF$

Say: *Angle A B C is congruent to angle D E F.*

233

Supplementary Angles

Two angles are **supplementary** if the sum of their measures is 180°. If two angles can or do form a straight line, then they are supplementary.

Supplementary   **Not Supplementary**

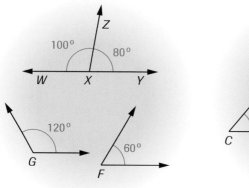

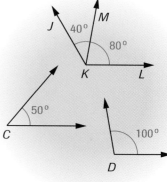

Complementary Angles

Two angles are **complementary** if the sum of their measures is 90°. If two angles can or do form a right angle, then they are complementary.

Complementary

Not Complementary

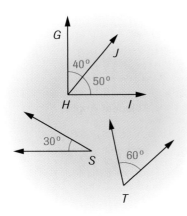

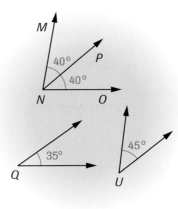

Angle Bisectors

An **angle bisector** is a segment or ray that separates an angle into two congruent angles.

EXAMPLE: Segment AC bisects angle BCD in this parallelogram. Find the measure of angle CAB.

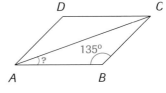

MORE HELP
See 127–129

You know that opposite angles in a parallelogram are congruent and that the sum of the measures of the angles in a quadrilateral is 360°. Use this information to write an equation that describes the situation.

360° is twice the measure of angle B plus twice the measure of angle BCD.

$$360 = 2(m\angle B) + 2(m\angle BCD)$$

> The m in front of an angle symbol is read, the measure of.

$$360 = 2(m\angle B) + 2(m\angle BCD)$$

$$\left. \begin{array}{l} 360 - 2(m\angle B) = 2(m\angle BCD) \\ 360 - 2(m\angle B) = 4(m\angle CAB) \end{array} \right\}$$

> Angle BCD has twice the measure of the angle you're looking for.

$$\frac{360 - 2(m\angle B)}{4} = m\angle CAB$$

$$\frac{360 - 2(135)}{4} = m\angle CAB = 22.5$$

★ The measure of angle CAB is 22.5°.

Angles Formed by Intersecting Lines

When two lines intersect, they form four angles that each measure less than 180°. When angles are formed by two intersecting lines, any two angles next to each other are called **adjacent angles**. Any two angles that are not next to each other are called **vertical angles**.

Vertical angles don't go straight up and down. The word *vertical* in this case is related to the word *vertex*—vertical angles share a vertex.

Vertical Angles   **Adjacent Angles**

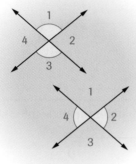
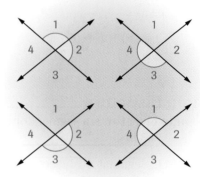

When two lines intersect, the adjacent angles are supplementary and the vertical angles are congruent. This means that if you know the measure of one of the four angles, you know the measures of the others.

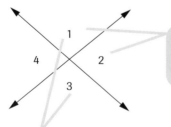

A pair of adjacent angles form a straight angle, so the adjacent angles must be supplementary.

Each of the two vertical angles is supplementary to the same angle. For example, both ∠1 and ∠3 are supplementary to ∠2. Vertical angles are always congruent.

Angles Formed by Lines Cut by a Transversal

A **transversal** is a line that intersects two or more other lines in different points. When a transversal intersects two lines, it forms four angles with each line, or eight angles in all.

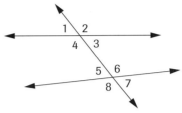

- **Corresponding angles** are in the same position from one line to the other. There are four pairs of corresponding angles: ∠1 and ∠5; ∠2 and ∠6; ∠3 and ∠7; and ∠4 and ∠8.

- **Alternate exterior angles** are on the opposite sides of the transversal and on the *outside* of the lines it intersects. There are two pairs of alternate exterior angles: ∠1 and ∠7; and ∠2 and ∠8.

- **Alternate interior angles** are on the opposite sides of the transversal and on the *inside* of the lines it intersects. There are two pairs of alternate interior angles: ∠3 and ∠5; and ∠4 and ∠6.

Parallel Lines Cut by a Transversal

If a transversal intersects two *parallel* lines, the angles that are formed by the transversal have special relationships.

MORE HELP
See 407

- Corresponding angles are congruent.

- Alternate exterior angles are congruent.

- Alternate interior angles are congruent.

To understand these congruencies, imagine sliding one of the parallel lines along the transversal. The line would fit exactly on top of the other parallel line with all the angles matching.

EXAMPLE: In the figure, a transversal intersects two parallel lines and m∠1 = 60°. Use this measure to find the measures of angles 2–8.

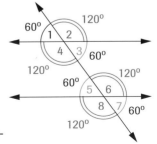

- ∠1 and ∠5 are corresponding angles.
  If m∠1 = 60°, then m∠5 = 60°.

- ∠1 and ∠7 are alternate exterior angles.
  If m∠1 = 60°, then m∠7 = 60°.

- ∠5 and ∠3 are alternate interior angles.
  If m∠5 = 60°, then m∠3 = 60°.

- Each one of the remaining angles is supplementary to an angle that measures 60°, so they must all measure 120°.

★ Angles 1, 3, 5, and 7 measure 60°. Angles 2, 4, 6, and 8 measure 120°.

MORE HELP
See 249

What do the Eiffel Tower, a geodesic dome, and the gate at the right all have in common? They were made using triangles. Architects and builders use triangles because triangles are rigid and can carry heavy loads. A triangle cannot collapse or change in shape unless one of its sides is changed. This is not true of other polygons. If you press on a square or another quadrilateral, you can change its shape without bending or changing the lengths of its sides.

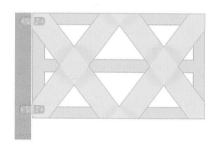

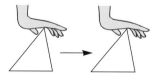 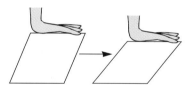

240) **Parts of Triangles**

Any side of a triangle can be called the **base**. The line segment that starts at a vertex and is perpendicular to that base (or the line that contains it) is called the **height**, or **altitude**. Every triangle has three different height-and-base pairs, but the product of the height and base is the same no matter which pair you choose.

> Sometimes the height is outside the triangle. You can extend a side to draw the height.

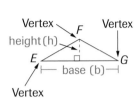

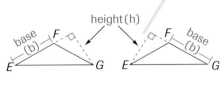

MORE HELP
See 215

EXAMPLE: The area of this triangle is 12 square units. Its perimeter is 16 units. Find the length of segment *MN*.

The formula for the area of a triangle is $A = \frac{1}{2}bh$. The perimeter of a triangle is the sum of the lengths of its sides. From this information, you can write and solve equations that describe the situation.

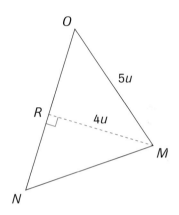

MORE HELP
See 129, 465

First, solve:	$A = \frac{1}{2}bh$
Substitute the length of $\overline{MR}$ for h in the area formula.	$12 = \frac{1}{2} \cdot b \cdot 4$
Solve for b, the length of $\overline{ON}$.	$6 = b$
You now have two sides and the perimeter, so you can find the third side.	$6 + 5 + MN = 16$ $MN = 5$

★ Segment *MN* is five units long.

Right triangles are special, so there are special words to describe their sides. The **legs** are the two sides that form a right angle. The legs are always shorter than the third side, which is called the **hypotenuse** and is always opposite the right triangle.

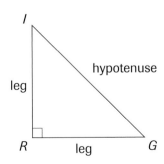

241

Triangle Inequality Theorem

Look at the triangle formed by points F, G, and H. Which is the shorter path from F to H, going directly from F to H, or going from F to G to H?

You can tell just by looking that the direct path from F to H is shorter than the path from F to G to H. The sum of the lengths of sides FG and GH is greater than the length of side FH. In fact, the sum of the lengths of *any* two sides of a triangle is greater than the length of the third side. This statement is called the **Triangle Inequality Theorem**. To test this theorem, try to make a triangle with one side longer than the other two combined—for example 2, 3, and 6 centimeters.

242

Sum of the Angles of a Triangle

A triangle has three **interior angles**, one at each vertex. To find the sum of the measures of these interior angles, you can do an experiment. Tear off each corner of the triangle and then line up the angles so that they are adjacent.

MORE HELP
See 229

For any triangle, the interior angles can form a straight angle, so the sum of the measures of the interior angles of any triangle is 180°.

A triangle also has three pairs of exterior angles. The exterior angles at each vertex are congruent to each other. The measure of either is equal to the sum of the two non-adjacent interior angles of the triangle.

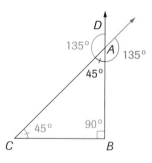

> You can see why this must be true. An exterior angle is supplementary to its adjacent interior angle. The interior angle is one of three angles whose sum is 180°.
> $m\angle CAB + m\angle CBA + m\angle ACB = 180°$
> $m\angle CAB + m\angle CAD = 180°$
> Two quantities equal to the same quantity are equal to each other, so, $m\angle CAD = m\angle CBA + m\angle ACB$.

Classifying Triangles _____

CASE 1 You can classify triangles by side length.

MORE HELP
See 265

Name	Description	Example
Equilateral Triangle	all sides congruent	
Isosceles Triangle	two sides congruent	
Scalene Triangle	no sides congruent	

> There is some disagreement about whether an isosceles triangle has *at least* two congruent sides or *exactly* two congruent sides. Ask your teacher what definition will be used in your class.

CASE 2 You can classify triangles by angle size.

Name	Description	Example
Acute Triangle	all interior angles measure less than 90°	
Equiangular Triangle	each interior angle measures exactly 60°	60° 60° 60°
Obtuse Triangle	one interior angle measures more than 90°	
Right Triangle	one interior angle measures exactly 90°	90°

MORE HELP
See 226

Overlapping Classifications of Triangles

You can classify any triangle according to its sides (equilateral, isosceles, or scalene) and according to its angles (acute, right, or obtuse). This means that you can describe every triangle in more than one way.

	Equilateral	Isosceles	Scalene
Acute	✓	✓	✓
Right		✓	✓
Obtuse		✓	✓

The only way a triangle can be equilateral is if it's equiangular. All angles of an equiangular triangle measure 60°.

If you define an isosceles triangle as having at least two congruent sides, then equilateral triangles are also isosceles.

To read the diagram above, think about the phrases *is always*, *may be*, or *is never*. For example, an obtuse triangle *may be* scalene or isosceles, but *is never* equilateral.

Pythagorean Theorem

In about 2000 B.C., Egyptians devised a way to lay out square corners for their fields. Workers knotted a loop of rope into 12 equal parts. Then they put the rope around stakes to make a triangle that had sides of three, four, and five units. The angle opposite the longest side was always a right angle.

About 1500 years later, a group of Greek philosophers, called Pythagoreans, studied the 3-4-5 right triangle. They noticed a special relationship which is true for any right triangle. They named this relationship the Pythagorean Theorem.

The **Pythagorean Theorem** states that, in a right triangle, the square of the length of the hypotenuse equals the sum of the squares of the lengths of the legs. The converse is also true: If the sum of the squares of the lengths of two sides of a triangle equals the square of the length of the third side, then the triangle is a right triangle.

MORE HELP
See 056,
127–129

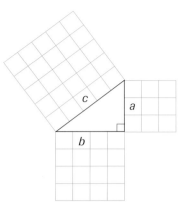

CASE 1 When you know the lengths of two sides of a right triangle, you can use the Pythagorean Theorem to find the length of the third side.

EXAMPLE 1: You place the base of a 30-foot ladder 18 feet from a tree. How high does the ladder reach?

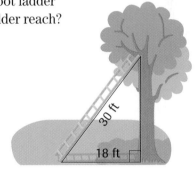

30 ft

18 ft

$$a^2 + b^2 = c^2$$
$$18^2 + b^2 = 30^2$$
$$324 + b^2 = 900$$
$$b^2 = 576$$
$$b = \sqrt{576}$$
$$b = 24$$

★ The ladder reaches 24 feet high.

CASE 2 You can also use the Pythagorean Theorem to tell whether you can make a right triangle from three given line segments.

EXAMPLE 2: Can you make a right triangle with sides 8 m, 10 m, and 12 m?

$$a^2 + b^2 = c^2$$
Does $8^2 + 10^2 = 12^2$?
$$64 + 100 \neq 144$$

Remember, the side that is not part of the right angle is the hypotenuse, c.

★ Since $8^2 + 10^2 \neq 12^2$, you can't make a right triangle with sides of 8 meters, 10 meters and 12 meters.

Pythagorean Triples

The whole numbers 3, 4, and 5 work in the Pythagorean Theorem. They make the statement $a^2 + b^2 = c^2$ true. Other sets of whole numbers that work include 5, 12, and 13; and 7, 24, and 25.

Sets of positive integers that satisfy the equation $a^2 + b^2 = c^2$ are called **Pythagorean Triples.** Common multiples of 3, 4, and 5, like 6, 8, and 10, are Pythagorean Triples. You can also use a table to generate Pythagorean Triples. In this table, $2n$ and $n^2 - 1$ are leg 1 and leg 2; $n^2 + 1$ is the hypotenuse.

	Leg 1	Leg 2	Hypotenuse
n	$2n$	$n^2 - 1$	$n^2 + 1$
3	6	8	10
4	8	15	17
5	10	24	26

To find more Pythagorean Triples, choose any two integers, m and n, with $m > n$, and use these formulas.

leg 1 $= m^2 - n^2$ leg 2 $= 2mn$ hypotenuse $= m^2 + n^2$

EXAMPLE: Use the formula to find a Pythagorean Triple.

Choose any two integers, m and n, with $m > n$.

For $m = 5$ and $n = 2$:

leg 1 $= m^2 - n^2$	leg 2 $= 2mn$	hypotenuse $= m^2 + n^2$
$= 5^2 - 2^2$	$= 2(5)(2)$	$= 5^2 + 2^2$
$= 25 - 4$	$= 20$	$= 25 + 4$
$= 21$		$= 29$

★ 21, 20, and 29 are Pythagorean Triples.

This means that you can draw a right triangle with legs of 21 units and 20 units, and a hypotenuse of 29 units. Try this triple in the Pythagorean Theorem and make sure it works.

30°-60°-90° Triangles

In some right triangles, the sides have special relationships. The 30°–60°–90° triangle is one of those right triangles.

In any 30°–60°–90° triangle:

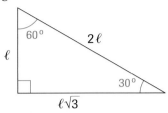

- the hypotenuse is twice as long as the shorter leg.

- the longer leg is $\sqrt{3}$ times as long as the shorter leg.

EXAMPLE: A kite string is 100 feet long. The angle the string makes with the ground is 60°. About how high is the kite?

The string, the height of the kite, and the distance on the ground from the end of the string to the altitude of the triangle form a 30°–60°–90°triangle.

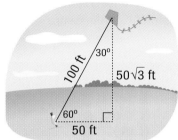

Since $\sqrt{3} \approx 1.7321$, then $50\sqrt{3} \approx 86.605$.

★ The kite is about 87 feet high.

45°–45°–90° Triangles

The sides of the 45°–45°–90° triangle have special relationships.

In any 45°–45°–90° triangle:

- both legs have the same length.

- the hypotenuse is $\sqrt{2}$ times as long as a leg.

MORE HELP
See 056

EXAMPLE: A square garden has sides of 30 meters. About how long is the diagonal path across the garden?

The sides of the garden are the legs of a 45°–45°–90° triangle. Since the diagonal path is the hypotenuse of the triangle, the path is $\sqrt{2}$ times as long as either leg.

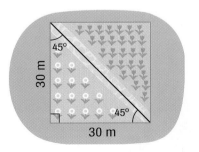

Since $\sqrt{2} \approx 1.4142$, then $30\sqrt{2} \approx 42.426$.

★ The path is about 42 meters long.

Trigonometric Ratios

MORE HELP
See 278–279

DID YOU KNOW Over 2000 years ago, a Greek astronomer named Hipparchus charted the position of the stars in the sky. He did so without a telescope or any other scientific instruments. How did he do it?

Hipparchus used **trigonometric ratios**, which are ratios comparing the legs and the hypotenuse of a right triangle. Today, astronomers and engineers still use trigonometric ratios to find distances that are impossible or impractical to measure directly. The word **trigonometry** originally meant *triangle measurement*.

Name of Ratio (always refer to one of the acute angles)	Ratio	Example
Sine of ∠A (sin A)	length of leg opposite ∠A / length of hypotenuse	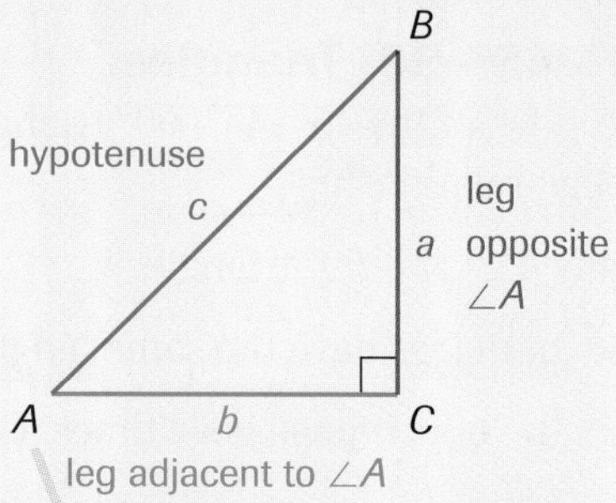
Cosine of ∠A (cos A)	length of leg adjacent to ∠A / length of hypotenuse	
Tangent of ∠A (tan A)	length of leg opposite ∠A / length of leg adjacent to ∠A	

In this diagram, ∠A is the **reference angle** because the legs are named by referring to ∠A.

To remember these ratios, you can use the mnemonic device SOHCAHTOA:

sine = opposite over hypotenuse

cosine = adjacent over hypotenuse

tangent = opposite over adjacent

Using Trigonometric Ratios for Indirect Measurement

You can use trigonometric ratios
to find distances.

MORE HELP
See 249

EXAMPLE: To the nearest foot,
what is the height of the
monument?

Look at the right triangle in the
picture. The length of the side
opposite the 62° angle is represented by x. The adjacent side is
10 feet long. You can use the
tangent ratio and the values you
know to find the height.

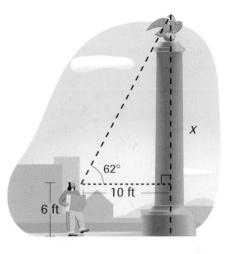

$$\tan A = \frac{\text{side opposite } \angle A}{\text{side adjacent to } \angle A}$$

❶ Write an equation for the tangent of 62°.	$\tan 62° = \frac{x}{10}$	
❷ Use a calculator or table to find the tangent of 62°.	$1.8807 \approx \frac{x}{10}$	
❸ Solve the equation.	$18.807 \approx x$	

To the nearest foot, the top of the monument is 19 feet higher than the
engineer's eye level. To find the height of the monument, the engineer adds
her own eye-level height, 6 feet.

★ The height of the monument is about 25 feet.

Quadrilaterals

A **quadrilateral** is a closed two-dimensional figure with four sides that are line segments—a four-sided polygon.

> There is some disagreement about whether a trapezoid has *at least* one pair of parallel sides or *exactly* one pair of parallel sides. Ask your teacher what definition will be used in your class.

Classifying Quadrilaterals by Properties _____

Some quadrilaterals are classified according to characteristics of their sides and/or angles.

MORE HELP
See 214, 226, 228, 264–265

Name	Description	Example
Trapezoid Sides marked with the same number of arrow notches are parallel.	quadrilateral with exactly one pair of parallel sides	
Parallelogram	quadrilateral with both pairs of opposite sides the same length and parallel	
Rectangle	parallelogram with four right angles	
Rhombus	parallelogram with four congruent sides	
Square	rhombus with four right angles	
Trapezium	quadrilateral with no parallel sides	Kite

Overlapping Classifications of Quadrilaterals

You often have more than one name for something. For example, you might call your dream car a sports car or a convertible depending on what aspect of it you want to emphasize to your listener.

Look at the park to the right. How many different names could you give to its shape?

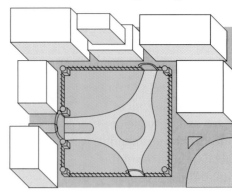

You'd probably start by calling it a square. But you could also call it a quadrilateral, a parallelogram, a rectangle, or a rhombus.

Many quadrilaterals can be described using more than one name. This diagram shows the relationships among different quadrilaterals.

> This diagram uses the *exactly one pair of parallel sides* definition of trapezoid.

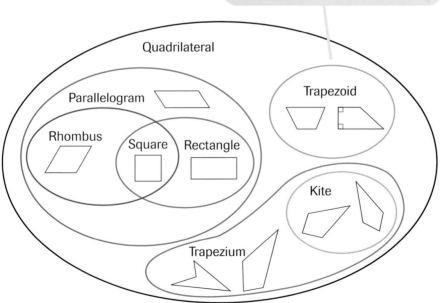

To read the diagram above, think about the phrases *is always, may be,* or *is never.* For example, a rectangle *is always* a parallelogram, *may be* a square or a rhombus, but *is never* a kite.

A **circle** is a set of points in a given plane, all of which are the same distance from a given point called the **center** of the circle. You can use the center, which is not *on* the circle, to name the circle.

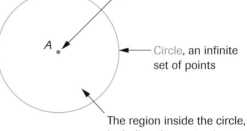

Center

Circle, an infinite set of points

The region inside the circle, including the center, is not part of the circle.

Write: ⊙A

Say: *circle A*

---

255 Lines and Segments Related to Circles

When you work with circles, there are special lines and segments that you will use and special relationships that come in handy when solving problems. These special relationships include:

- a radius to the point of tangency is perpendicular to the tangent.

- when diameters intersect, the angles formed have the same angle measure as the arcs they define.

- an inscribed triangle with one side a diameter is a right triangle.

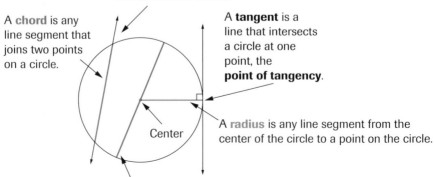

A **secant** is a line that contains a **chord**.

A **chord** is any line segment that joins two points on a circle.

A **tangent** is a line that intersects a circle at one point, the **point of tangency**.

A **radius** is any line segment from the center of the circle to a point on the circle.

Center

A **diameter** is a chord that passes through the center of the circle and divides it into two **semicircles**.

Angles Related to Circles

When you draw radii of a circle, you form **central angles** in that circle. Their vertices are at the center, and their sides intersect the circle. Remember, when you turn a complete revolution, you turn 360°, so when you add the measures of all the central angles in any circle, the sum is 360°.

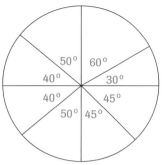

MORE HELP
See 227,
255–256

$$40° + 50° + 60° + 30° + 45° + 45° + 50° + 40° = 360°$$

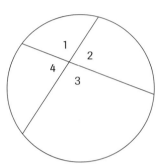

It is also true that chords intersecting any-where in a circle form angles whose sum is 360°. You can see that this must be true be-cause line segments intersect at a point, and you already know that the sum of the angles about a point must be 360°.

$$m \angle 1 + m \angle 2 + m \angle 3 + m \angle 4 = 360°$$

Arcs and Sectors

Each central angle of a circle splits the circle into two parts, a major arc and a minor arc. An arc greater than a semicircle is a **major arc**. An arc less than a semicircle is a **minor arc**. The region inside the circle formed by a central angle and an arc is called a **sector**.

$\overarc{ADC}$ is a major arc. The measure of a major arc is 360° minus the measure of its associated minor arc, so $\overarc{ADC}$ measures 360° − 60°, or 300°.

$\overarc{AC}$ is a minor arc. Its central angle (∠*ABC*) measures 60°, so its measure is also 60°.

The shaded region is sector *ABC*, the sector formed by radii *BA* and *BC*, and arc *AC*.

You name an arc by its endpoints. To name a major arc, you need a third point so that you don't confuse it with a minor arc.

Write: $\overarc{ADC}$
Say: arc A D C

MORE ▶

You use sectors, arcs, and central angles when you work with circle graphs.

MORE HELP
See 294

EXAMPLE: In 1998, the National Soccer Participation Survey showed that in the United States, 61% of soccer participants were male and 39% of soccer participants were female. Make a circle graph that shows these data.

Source: Soccer Industry Council of America

To make the circle graph, draw a sector that is 39% of the circle, or 39% of 360°.

MORE HELP
See 296, 351

❶ Write and solve an equation that describes the situation.	$a\%$ of $b = c$ 39% of 360 = the measure of the sector for female soccer participants $0.39 \times 360 = 140.4$
❷ Draw a central angle that measures about 140°. Label this sector: *Female 39%*. Then label the other sector: *Male 61%*.	★ 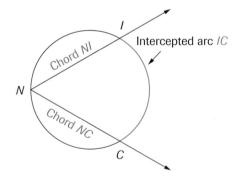 Soccer Participation

258 Inscribed Angles

MORE HELP
See 255, 257

In a circle, an **inscribed angle** is an angle with its vertex on the circle, and with sides that are chords of the circle. In this circle, ∠*INC* is an inscribed angle. The measure of an inscribed angle is half the measure of its intercepted arc.

To inscribe a book, you write a note inside the book. To inscribe an angle, you draw it inside a circle with its vertex on the circle.

EXAMPLE: Arc *IC* measures 120°. What is the measure of ∠*INC*?

$$m\angle INC = \tfrac{1}{2}(120°)$$
$$= 60°$$

★ The measure of ∠*INC* is 60°.

Similarity

Suppose you say that two cars, or movies, or buildings are similar. You probably mean that those two things are alike in one or more ways. In mathematics, **similar** figures are alike in very specific ways:

- Similar figures have the same shape.
- Similar figures may or may not have the same size.

Here are three pictures of a key. The first picture shows the key at actual size. The second picture is an enlargement. The third is a reduction. Because all three keys have the same shape, the pictures of the keys are all similar.

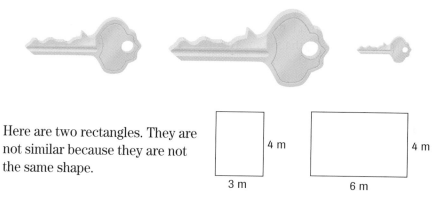

Here are two rectangles. They are not similar because they are not the same shape.

4 m

3 m

4 m

6 m

Corresponding Parts

In geometry, two polygons are in **correspondence** when consecutive vertices of one are matched with consecutive vertices of the other.

For two polygons to be similar, they must have:

- corresponding (or matching) angles that are congruent.
- corresponding (or matching) sides that are proportional.

MORE HELP
See 056, 245, 288–289

The ratios of the lengths of corresponding sides are equal.

MORE ▶

EXAMPLE: Triangle *PQR* is similar to triangle *FED*. Find the length of segment *DF*.

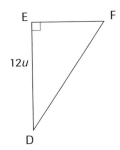

When you write the names of similar figures, you write corresponding vertices in the same order. This means that side *PQ* corresponds to side *FE* and so forth. You know

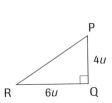

that the lengths of corresponding sides of similar figures are in proportion. You can write a proportion to show what you know and help you figure out what measures you need to find.

$$\text{leg} \longrightarrow \frac{QR}{ED} = \frac{PR}{FD} \longleftarrow \text{hypotenuse}$$
$$\text{corresponding leg} \longrightarrow \qquad\qquad \longleftarrow \text{corresponding hypotenuse}$$

> Remember: $\overline{QR}$ means segment QR. QR with no bar or other label means the distance from Q to R.

You have *QR* and *ED*. You need *PR* and *FD*. Fortunately, you're dealing with right triangles. You have the measures of two sides of a right triangle (*QR* and *PQ*), so the Pythagorean Theorem will help you find *PR*, (*c* in the equation $a^2 + b^2 = c^2$).

$a^2 + b^2 = c^2$

$4^2 + 6^2 = c^2$

$c = \sqrt{52}$

$c = \sqrt{4 \times 13}$

$c = 2\sqrt{13}$

Substitute the values for *PR*, *QR*, and *ED* into your proportion and solve for *FD*.

MORE HELP
See 127, 245

$$\frac{6}{12} = \frac{2\sqrt{13}}{FD}$$

$FD = 4\sqrt{13}$

★ Segment *FD* has a length of $4\sqrt{13}$ units. You can leave your answer like this or find an approximation for $\sqrt{13}$, in which case you could say that segment *FD* has a length of about 14 units.

Scale

To make an accurate model of an object or map of an area, you use a scale. **Scale** is the ratio of a length in the model or drawing to the corresponding length in the actual object or region. Scale is often used to draw or show objects that are too large or too small to be shown in their actual sizes.

Statue of Liberty
Scale: 1 inch = 200 feet

MORE HELP
See 288–289

EXAMPLE 1: How tall is the Statue of Liberty, including its base?

❶ Measure the height of the statue in the drawing.	It is about $1\frac{1}{2}$ inches tall.
❷ Write a proportion.	model inches ⟶ $\dfrac{1\frac{1}{2}}{x} = \dfrac{1}{200}$ ⟵ scale inches actual feet ⟶ ⟵ actual feet
❸ Solve the proportion.	$x = 300$

★ The height of the Statue of Liberty is about 300 feet.

EXAMPLE 2:
How far is it from Memphis to Nashville?

❶ Measure the length on the map.	The length on the map is about 4 cm.
❷ Write a proportion.	scale centimeters ⟶ $\dfrac{4}{x} = \dfrac{1}{50}$ ⟵ scale centimeters actual miles ⟶ ⟵ actual miles
❸ Solve the proportion.	$x = 200$

★ It is about 200 miles from Memphis to Nashville.

MATH ALERT Changing the Scale Causes a Great Change in the Size

EXAMPLE: Make scale drawings of a rectangle with sides of 6 cm and 9 cm. First, use a scale of 1 unit = 3 centimeters. Then, use a scale of 1 unit = 1 centimeter. How does changing the scale change the area of the drawing?

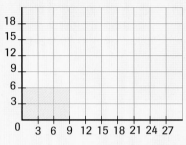

Scale: $\dfrac{1 \text{ unit}}{3 \text{ cm}}$

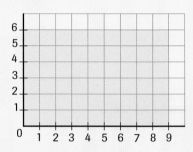

Scale: $\dfrac{1 \text{ unit}}{1 \text{ cm}}$

In this scale, to show sides of 6 centimeters and 9 centimeters, draw sides of 2 units and 3 units. The area is 6 square units.

With this scale, to show sides of 6 centimeters and 9 centimeters, draw sides of 6 units and 9 units. The area is 54 square units.

★ When you made the scale three times as large, from 1 unit = 3 centimeters to 1 unit = 1 centimeter, you multiplied the area of the rectangle in the drawing by nine.

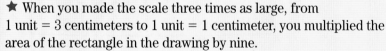

The changes in size forced by a scale change are exponential.

unit × 3 ⟶ area × 3^2
unit × 3 ⟶ volume × 3^3

Using Similarity for Indirect Measurement

There's got to be an easier way.

MORE HELP
See 250, 259

Suppose you want to find the height of a tree or a width of a lake. You could try to stretch a tape measure as you climbed the tree or swam across the lake. Fortunately, there's also an easier way, called **indirect measurement**. One way to make an indirect measurement is to use similar figures.

EXAMPLE: Find the height of the monument.

The angles the sun makes as it causes each object to cast a shadow are the same for each object. The triangles are similar because corresponding angles are congruent.

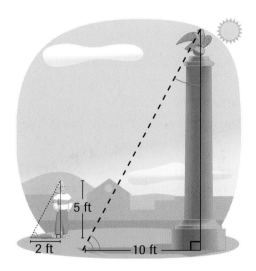

5 ft

2 ft

10 ft

MORE HELP
See 288–289

You can use what you know about similar triangles to solve the problem.

❶ Write a proportion.	❷ Solve the proportion.
boy's shadow ⟶ $\dfrac{2}{10}$ = $\dfrac{5}{x}$ ⟵ boy's height monument's shadow ⟶ $\quad\quad\quad$ ⟵ monument's height	$x = 25$

★ The height of the monument is 25 feet.

Congruence

Congruent figures have the same size and the same shape. To be congruent, sides must have the same length and angles must have the same measure. When two figures are congruent, all corresponding parts of the two figures must be congruent, so the ratios of lengths of corresponding sides will be 1:1.

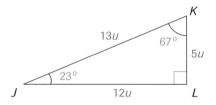

> The three pairs of corresponding sides are congruent.

> The three pairs of corresponding angles are congruent.

Write: $\triangle JKL \cong \triangle TCA$

Say: *Triangle J K L is congruent to triangle T C A.*

Marking Figures to Show Congruence

To help keep track of which lengths and angle measures are equal, you can mark parts of figures with tick marks or arcs to show that they are congruent.

Figure *ABCD* is congruent to figure *EFGH*.

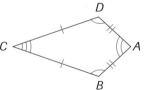

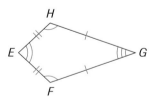

When you are told that two figures are congruent, the way the figures are named tells you what parts correspond to each other.

> All sides with the same number of tick marks are congruent. All angles with the same number of arcs are congruent.

In these two figures, since you were told that $ABCD \cong EFGH$, you know that $AB \cong EF$ even without seeing the tick marks.

Congruent Triangles

SHORTCUT

MORE HELP
See 264–265

When you need to determine whether triangles are congruent, there are shortcuts you can use. A **postulate** is a mathematical statement that is accepted as true without proof.

Side-Side-Side Postulate (SSS)

If each of the three sides of one triangle is congruent to the corresponding side of another triangle, then the triangles are congruent.

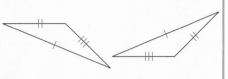

Angle-Angle-Side Postulate (AAS)

If two angles and the side opposite one of them in one triangle are congruent to the corresponding parts of another triangle, then the triangles are congruent.

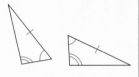

Side-Angle-Side Postulate (SAS)

If two sides and the included angle of one triangle are congruent to two sides and the included angle of another triangle, then the triangles are congruent.

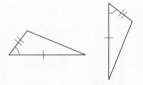

Angle-Side-Angle Postulate (ASA)

If two angles and the included side of one triangle are congruent to two angles and the included side of another triangle, then the triangles are congruent.

The **included angle** is the angle formed by those two sides. The **included side** is the side between the two angles.

MATH ALERT Side-Side-Angle (SSA) Does Not Prove Congruence!

Be careful when you use angles and sides of triangles to prove congruence.

EXAMPLE: Two sides and the angle opposite one of the sides in a triangle are congruent to the two sides and the angle opposite one of the sides in another triangle. Does this prove that the two triangles are congruent?

Look at △*FNP*. Think of side *FN* as a pendulum that you can swing toward point *P*. Eventually, the pendulum forms a vertex with *NP* at point *Q*.

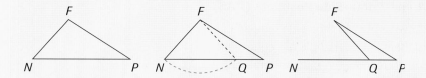

You've created a new triangle, △*FQP*. In △*FNP* and △*FQP*, $\overline{FN} \cong \overline{FQ}$ (both segments are the pendulum); $\overline{FP} \cong \overline{FP}$; and ∠FPN ≅ ∠FPQ. The two triangles have two corresponding sides and an opposite angle (SSA) congruent. However, $\overline{NP}$ is not congruent to $\overline{QP}$, and ∠*FNP* is not congruent to ∠*FQP*.

★ The two triangles are not congruent.

Side-Side-Angle (SSA) does NOT prove congruence. Two triangles with SSA correspondence and congruence CAN be congruent, but you don't know for sure unless you measure other angles and sides to see whether corresponding angles and sides are congruent.

Transformations

Suppose you draw a shape. Then you draw a figure that has the same shape, but dimensions that are twice as large. The second shape is a **transformation** of the first. Whenever you slide, flip, rotate, shrink, or enlarge a figure, you make a transformation of that figure.

If you label a figure with letters, when you transform that figure you can label the corresponding points on the **transformation image** with the same letters and a prime sign that looks a bit like an apostrophe.

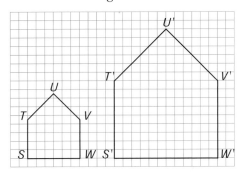

Write: S′ T′ U′ V′ W′

Say: *S prime T prime U prime V prime W prime*

Translations

You can **slide** a figure. This transformation is also called a **translation**. In a translation, every point in the figure slides the same distance in the same direction. The coordinates of the vertices will all change in the same way. You can use a slide arrow to show the direction and distance of the movement.

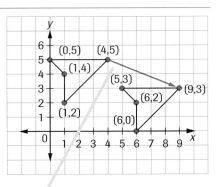

The **slide arrow** shows that every point on the figure moves five units to the right on the x-axis and two units down on the y-axis. Some people consider this two slides.

Rotations

When you rotate an object, you turn it. That's why rotations are sometimes called **turns**. In geometry, rotating a figure means turning a figure around a point. The point can be on the figure, but it doesn't have to be. The point is called the **center of rotation**. The angle that the figure turns is called the **angle of rotation**. When you describe the rotation of a figure, you give the direction, the angle of rotation, and the center of rotation.

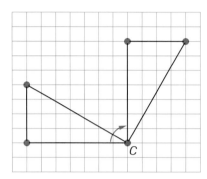

Point C is the center of rotation.
This figure was rotated 90°
clockwise about point C.

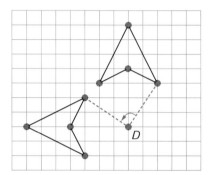

Point D is the center of rotation.
This figure was rotated 90°
counterclockwise about point D.

Polar Coordinates

Polar coordinates are coordinates based on the rotation of a segment about a pole, or center point. Polar coordinates and polar graph paper make it easier to draw rotations. As with rectangular coordinates, you need only two numbers to describe the location of a point:

(distance from origin, angle between x-axis and a ray from origin through point)

The origin is at the center.

Each circle marks an equal distance from the adjacent circles.

The straight lines show equal angles of rotation about the origin. A rotation from one line to the next is 10°.

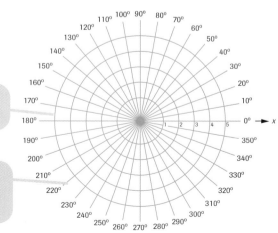

EXAMPLE: Rotate $\triangle HIJ$ 120° counterclockwise about the origin.

Since each space on the grid is 10°, move each vertex of $\triangle HIJ$ counter clock-wise 12 spaces: $12 \cdot 10° = 120°$. Then connect the vertices to draw the rotated triangle. Remember, each vertex stays on its circle as it rotates.

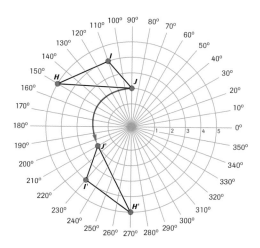

Turn Symmetry

272

A figure that can fit onto itself after rotating less than 360° has **turn symmetry**.

Turn Symmetry   **No Turn Symmetry**

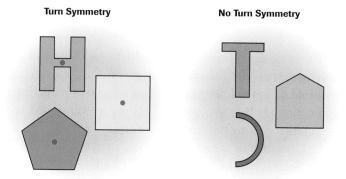

EXAMPLE: Does equilateral $\triangle ABC$ have turn symmetry?

A 120° rotation about point P
rotates $\triangle ABC$ onto itself.

★ $\triangle ABC$ has turn symmetry.

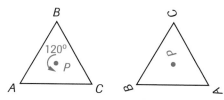

A special case of turn symmetry is **point symmetry**. If a figure can fit onto itself after rotating exactly 180° it has point symmetry. A square has point symmetry.

Reflections

When you look in a mirror, the reflection you see is a reverse image of yourself. When you raise your right hand, your reflection raises its left hand.

In geometry, a **reflection** is a transformation that's also called a **flip** because in a reflection a figure is flipped over a line. Each point in a reflection image is the same distance from the line as the corresponding point in the original shape.

EXAMPLE: Does the diagram show a reflection? How do you know?

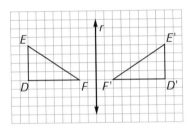

D and D′ are both 8 units from line r.

E and E′ are both 8 units from line r.

F and F′ are both 2 units from line r.

Each vertex in $\triangle D'E'F'$ is the same distance from line r as the corresponding vertex in $\triangle DEF$ and the two triangles are congruent.

★ The diagram shows a reflection.

Line Symmetry

If you can fold a figure along a line so that it has two parts that match exactly, that figure has **line symmetry**. This is sometimes just called symmetry. The fold line is along the **line of symmetry**. A figure can have no lines of symmetry, one line of symmetry, or more than one line of symmetry. A circle, for example, has an infinite number of lines of symmetry.

Line Symmetry

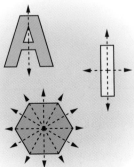

No Line Symmetry

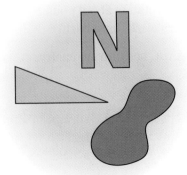

Using the Coordinate Plane to Show Line Symmetry

275

You can use a coordinate plane to show line symmetry.

EXAMPLE: Is line r a line of symmetry for figure $ABCDEFGH$?

To answer the question, check to see whether each vertex on one side of line r is a reflection of a vertex on the other side of the line

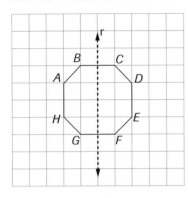

B and C are both one unit from line r. C is a reflection image of B.

The other corresponding vertices are equidistant from the line of reflection.

Each vertex, and so each point, on the right side of line r is a reflection image of a point on the left side of line r.

★ Line r is a line of symmetry for figure $ABCDEFGH$.

Dilations

276

A **dilation** is a transformation that may move a figure, and either enlarges or reduces the figure to make a similar figure. Here's how to make a dilation.

① Draw figure $ABCD$ and point P outside of figure $ABCD$. P is the center of dilation.	
② Draw $\overrightarrow{PA}$, $\overrightarrow{PB}$, $\overrightarrow{PC}$ and $\overrightarrow{PD}$. Choose a factor by which you want to increase the size of figure $ABCD$. We used two here.	
③ Draw points $A'B'C'$ and D'. $PA' = 2PA$ $PB' = 2PB$ $PC' = 2PC$ $PD' = 2PD$	
④ Draw segments $A'B'$, $B'C'$, $C'D'$, and $D'A'$.	

Ratio, Proportion, and Percent

"Six percent unemployment only looks good from the vantage point of the other 94 percent."

–Peter Passell, _New York Times_, 1994.

Who was the best hitter last season? Which college gives out more A's? Questions like these involve comparing different-sized groups. That can be unfair if all you're considering is the total number in each group. Some batters get more chances to hit than others. Some colleges have more students than others.

MORE HELP
See 249

Fortunately, there are ways to level the field when we compare groups of different sizes. **Ratio** and a special ratio called **percent** can be used to even things out. For example, baseball leagues use a number called the batting average that describes how many hits a player gets for every time at bat. Similarly, you can figure out how many A's a college gives out for every grade a student receives. In right triangles, the ratios between the sides adjacent to a given angle depend on the size of the angle. For more on these special ratios, see Trigonometric Ratios (249).

Ratio and percent can do even more than help you make fair comparisons. By using them in **proportions**, you can make models, drawings, and new batches of fruit punch that are just like the original.

You can compare quantities in two different ways. You can think: How *much* greater is one than the other? Or, you can think: How *many times* as great is one compared to the other?

EXAMPLE: Mark is 72 inches tall. His younger brother Jason is 54 inches tall. Compare their heights.

ONE WAY You can subtract to find the difference—*how much* greater.

Mark's height – Jason's height = difference in height
72 in. − 54 in. = 18 in.

★ Mark is 18 inches taller than Jason, or Jason is 18 inches shorter than Mark.

ANOTHER WAY A **ratio** compares two quantities directly—it will tell you *how many times* as great if the units are the same.

$$\frac{\text{Mark's height}}{\text{Jason's height}} \longrightarrow \frac{72 \text{ in.}}{54 \text{ in.}} = \frac{4}{3}$$

★ Mark's height is $\frac{4}{3}$, or $1\frac{1}{3}$, times Jason's height, or Jason is $\frac{3}{4}$ as tall as Mark.

Ratios can be used in many different ways to compare two amounts.

279 ## Writing Ratios

You can write a ratio to compare any two amounts. It doesn't matter whether they are parts, wholes, or even parts of different wholes. Once you decide which amounts you are comparing, you can choose from among several forms to express the ratio.

EXAMPLE: The two bands *Eyes Open* and *Azúl* have different numbers of each type of musician.

MORE HELP
See 012

Here are some different ratios you can use to compare the make-up of the two bands. Each ratio is expressed in four different forms.

Compare part of something to another part of the same thing.

Compare part of something to all of it.

Compare part of one thing to part of another thing.

Compare all of one thing to all of another thing.

	Compare guitarists in *Eyes Open* to horn players in *Eyes Open*.	Compare guitarists in *Eyes Open* to total members in *Eyes Open*.	Compare guitarists in *Azúl* to guitarists in *Eyes Open*.	Compare total members in *Eyes Open* to total members in *Azúl*.
Use *to* (*a to b*)	2 to 4	2 to 8	3 to 2	8 to 12
Use a colon (*a:b*)	2:4	2:8	3:2	8:12
Use fraction form ($\frac{a}{b}$)	$\frac{2}{4}$	$\frac{2}{8}$	$\frac{3}{2}$	$\frac{8}{12}$
Use decimal form	0.5	0.25	1.5	$0.\overline{6}$

To find the decimal form, just use what you know about writing fractions as decimals.

You can write ratios in simplest form, as you do fractions, but you lose track of the original quantities when you do.

MATH ALERT Don't Confuse Ratios with Fractions

Just because a ratio can look like a fraction does not mean it's the same as a fraction. For one thing, the denominator of a fraction always refers to a whole, but the second term of a ratio can refer to a part. For another thing, we often compare ratios for two different wholes. That can make a world of difference when you try to compute. For example, if one class is $\frac{1}{2}$ girls and another class is $\frac{1}{2}$ girls, when the two classes go on a field trip together, it's not true that all the students are girls.

Here's another example:

In the penny group, the ratio of heads to tails is $\frac{1}{3}$.

In the nickel group, the ratio of heads to tails is $\frac{2}{2}$.

If we combine the two groups, the ratio of heads to tails is $\frac{3}{5}$.

total number of heads $\longrightarrow$ $\dfrac{3}{5}$
total number of tails $\longrightarrow$

Even though fractions and ratios are different, they are related. Look at these examples:

Ratio Statement	Related Fraction Statement
The ratio of heads to coins is $\frac{3}{8}$.	$\frac{3}{8}$ of the coins are heads.
The ratio of heads to tails is $\frac{3}{5}$.	There are $\frac{3}{5}$ as many heads as tails.
The ratio of nickels to pennies is $\frac{4}{4}$.	There are $\frac{4}{4}$ or 1 times as many nickels as pennies.

So what's the best advice for not confusing ratios and fractions? Always understand the meaning of the ratios or fractions you're dealing with. Then you can decide whether what you're doing with them makes sense.

Rates

If a ratio compares two different kinds of quantities, it is called a **rate**. You're already familiar with many kinds of rates. Some of them even have their own names, like speed, density, and fuel economy.

Situation	Rate
You type 127 words in 5 minutes.	typing rate $= \dfrac{127 \text{ words}}{5 \text{ min}}$
Your car travels 320 miles using 14.6 gallons of gasoline.	rate of gas consumption $= \dfrac{320 \text{ mi}}{14.6 \text{ gal}}$
Your ring has a mass of 1.5 grams and a volume of 0.08 cubic centimeters.	density $= \dfrac{\text{mass}}{\text{volume}} = \dfrac{1.5 \text{ g}}{0.08 \text{ cm}^3}$
You run a 100-meter race in 12.4 seconds.	speed $= \dfrac{100 \text{ m}}{12.4 \text{ s}}$

Calculating Unit Rates

When the second part of a rate is one unit, the rate is called a **unit rate**. To find a unit rate, divide the first part of the rate by the second part.

EXAMPLE 1: Which of these two bicycle riders rode faster overall?

average speed of rider A $\longrightarrow \dfrac{115 \text{ mi}}{4 \text{ h}} = \dfrac{28.75 \text{ mi}}{1 \text{ h}}$ (or 28.75 mph)

average speed of rider B $\longrightarrow \dfrac{146 \text{ mi}}{5 \text{ h}} = \dfrac{29.2 \text{ mi}}{1 \text{ h}}$ (or 29.2 mph)

$29.2 > 28.75$

★ Rider B rode at a greater average speed.

EXAMPLE 2: Find the unit price of this can of tuna.

6.5 oz
can of tuna
only
$1.25

1 5561 25

unit price $= \dfrac{\$1.25}{6.5 \text{ oz}} \approx \dfrac{\$0.1923077}{1 \text{ oz}}$

★ The unit price is about 19.2 cents per ounce.

MORE ▶

EXAMPLE 3: Population density is the mean number of people per unit of area. Which of the countries listed had the greatest population density in 1997?

Country	1997 Population	Area (km²)
Honduras	5,981,000	112,088
Mexico	94,280,000	1,958,201
United States	271,648,000	9,363,520

Source: United Nations Statistics Division

Calculate the unit rate for each country, then compare.

population density of Honduras → $\dfrac{5{,}981{,}000 \text{ people}}{112{,}088 \text{ km}^2} \approx \dfrac{53 \text{ people}}{1 \text{ km}^2}$

population density of Mexico → $\dfrac{94{,}280{,}000 \text{ people}}{1{,}958{,}201 \text{ km}^2} \approx \dfrac{48 \text{ people}}{1 \text{ km}^2}$

population density of the U.S. → $\dfrac{271{,}648{,}000 \text{ people}}{9{,}363{,}520 \text{ km}^2} \approx \dfrac{29 \text{ people}}{1 \text{ km}^2}$

★ Of the three countries, Honduras had the greatest population density in 1997.

Operating with Ratios

You can simplify ratios just as you would simplify fractions. However, since ratios are not really fractions, they don't follow the same rules for computation. If the ratio of boys to girls in your class is 15 to 15 and the ratio of boys to girls in the class next door is 10 to 20, you do not find the ratio of boys to girls in the combined classes by adding the two ratios in fraction form. Instead, since your ratios both compare boys to girls, think of the *total number of boys* and the *total number of girls* and compare the two as a ratio.

$\dfrac{(15 + 10) \text{ boys}}{(15 + 20) \text{ girls}}$

Simplifying Ratios

It's easier to visualize, remember, and compute with small numbers than with large numbers. It may sometimes make sense to simplify a ratio in the same way you simplify fractions.

EXAMPLE: Cate worked on her history report from 7:00 P.M. to 10:20 P.M., but during that time she took breaks for a total of 25 minutes. Describe how the time Cate spent on breaks compares to the time she actually worked.

break minutes ⟶ $\dfrac{25}{175}$
work minutes ⟶

> From 7:00 to 10:20 is 3 h 20 min, or 200 min.
> 200 − 25 = minutes really working

You can say the ratio is 25 to 175, but smaller numbers would be easier to understand. Simplify the ratio just as you would simplify a fraction. A common factor is 25. Divide both parts by 25.

break minutes ⟶ $\dfrac{25}{175}$ = $\dfrac{1}{7}$ ⟵ break minutes
work minutes ⟶ ⟵ work minutes

★ Overall, Cate took 1 minute of break for every 7 minutes she worked.

> Don't simplify a ratio if you want to preserve the original data. For example, suppose the ratio of boys to girls at last week's dance was 125:140. Since the ratio contains original data, it indicates that there were 125 boys and 140 girls for a total of 265 students. If you simplify the ratio to 25:28, it no longer conveys the actual numbers of boys and girls, so you can't tell the total number of students at the dance.

Using Variables to Express Ratios

You can solve some problems by using variables to represent amounts in a ratio.

EXAMPLE 1: A certain horse feed consists of oats and barley. The ratio of pounds of oats to pounds of barley is 5:7. This means, for every 12 pounds of feed, 5 pounds are oats and 7 pounds are barley. How many pounds of each grain are needed to make 200 pounds of feed?

MORE ▶

To represent two unknown quantities in the ratio 5:7, use $5x$ and $7x$. Let the number of pounds of oats be represented by $5x$. Then the number of pounds of barley is represented by $7x$.

> The ratios $\frac{5x}{7x}$ and $\frac{5}{7}$ are equivalent.

MORE HELP
See 126–129

Since the total weight is 200 pounds, you can write and solve this equation:

$$5x + 7x = 200$$
$$12x = 200$$
$$x = \frac{200}{12} \text{ or } 16\tfrac{2}{3}$$

> The solution to the equation is not the answer to the problem. For that, you need to look back at the original problem.

Find the two measures:

$5x \longrightarrow 5 \times 16\tfrac{2}{3} = 83\tfrac{1}{3}$

$7x \longrightarrow 7 \times 16\tfrac{2}{3} = 116\tfrac{2}{3}$

★ 200 pounds of the feed contains $83\tfrac{1}{3}$ pounds of oats and $116\tfrac{2}{3}$ pounds of barley.

MORE HELP
See 465

EXAMPLE 2: A rectangular prism with a volume of 720 cubic centimeters has sides whose lengths are in the ratio 2:5:9. What are the lengths of the sides?

If the prism had sides of 2 centimeters, 5 centimeters, and 9 centimeters, the volume would be 90 cubic centimeters. Use $2n$, $5n$, and $9n$ to represent the lengths of the three sides in centimeters.

$2:5:9 = 2n:5n:9n$

Since the product of the lengths of the sides is 720, you can write and solve this equation:

$$2n \cdot 5n \cdot 9n = 720$$
$$90n^3 = 720$$
$$n^3 = \frac{720}{90}$$
$$n^3 = 8$$
$$n = \sqrt[3]{8}$$
$$n = 2$$

> Solving an equation is not necessarily the same as solving the given problem. Use the results of your computation to help you solve the problem.

Find the three lengths:

$2n = 4, 5n = 10, 9n = 18$

★ The lengths of the three sides are 4 centimeters, 10 centimeters, and 18 centimeters.

Proportion

If you were a practical joker, you might make a batch of lemonade using half the normal amount of sugar and water and ten times the normal amount of lemon juice. The sour drink would make anyone wince because the ingredients are so far out of proportion. Mathematically speaking, the ratio of lemon juice to water in the normal recipe is different from the ratio of lemon juice to water in the pucker-producing batch.

An equation that shows that two ratios are equal is called a **proportion**. If the ratio $\frac{a}{b}$ is equal to the ratio $\frac{c}{d}$, we call the equation, $\frac{a}{b} = \frac{c}{d}$, a proportion. When ratios are equal they are **in proportion**. On the other hand, when ratios are not equal, they are **out of proportion**.

People generally prefer things like maps, photo enlargements, and thirst-quenching beverages to be in proportion, unless, of course, the people are practical jokers.

Terms of a Proportion

The phrases *extreme terms* and *mean terms* may sound extreme and mean, but in proportions these terms are quite helpful. **Extreme** is a way of saying *at the end*. **Mean** is a way of saying *in the middle*. This matches the *average* meaning of mean.

extremes

$$a{:}b = c{:}d$$

means

Extremes is another word for **extreme terms**, and **means** is another word for **mean terms**.

You know that $\frac{1}{2} = \frac{4}{8}$. If this equation were a proportion, you could write 1:2 = 4:8. The product of the extremes, 1×8 equals the product of the means, 2×4. This is the same as saying the cross products are equal.

MORE ▶

In any proportion, the product of the extremes and the product of the means are equal. You can write that as an algebraic statement:

If $a{:}b = c{:}d$ then $ad = bc$.

MORE HELP
See 089

You can see for yourself why the product of the extremes must equal the product of the means.

> You can also say, if $ad = bc$ then $a{:}b = c{:}d$.

① Write the proportion in fraction form.	$\dfrac{a}{b} = \dfrac{c}{d}$
② Multiply both sides by bd.	$\dfrac{a}{b}(bd) = \dfrac{c}{d}(bd)$
③ Simplify by canceling.	$\dfrac{a\cancel{b}d}{\cancel{b}} = \dfrac{c\cancel{d}b}{\cancel{d}}$ $ad = bc$

You can use cross-products to tell whether an apparent proportion is really a proportion or just an impostor.

EXAMPLE 1: Unit price is total price divided by number of units—the cost for one unit. Do these two packages of cereal have the same unit price?

ONE WAY Find the unit prices and compare.

Find the unit price of the 18-oz box: $4 \div 18 = 0.22\overline{2}$
Find the unit price of the $13\frac{1}{2}$-oz box: $3 \div 13.5 = 0.22\overline{2}$

The unit prices, about $0.22 per ounce, are the same.

ANOTHER WAY Test to see whether $\frac{4}{18} = \frac{3}{13.5}$ is a true proportion.

Find the cross products:

$$18 \times 3 = 54$$
$$\frac{4}{18} \quad \blacksquare \quad \frac{3}{13.5}$$
$$4 \times 13.5 = 54$$

The cross products are equal, so the two ratios are equal.

★ Either way, the two boxes of cereal have the same unit price.

EXAMPLE 2: Are these two rectangles similar?

MORE HELP
See 259–260

If the sides are in proportion, then the rectangles are similar. Test to see whether the statement $\frac{15}{18} = \frac{20}{25}$ is true.

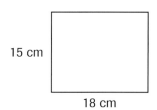

15 cm

18 cm

Find the cross products:

$18 \times 20 = 360$

$$\frac{15}{18} \quad\blacksquare\quad \frac{20}{25}$$

$15 \times 25 = 375$

20 cm

25 cm

The cross products are not equal, so the two ratios are not equal.

★ The rectangles are not similar.

Writing Equivalent Proportions

288

If you're twice as old as your brother, then he is half as old as you. There are always different ways to describe the same relationship. Take any proportion. You can rewrite it in several different ways.

EXAMPLE: In both rectangles, the ratio of width to length is the same. Write that as a proportion.

★ $\dfrac{w}{l} = \dfrac{W}{L}$ $\dfrac{2}{3} = \dfrac{4}{6}$

$w = 2$ ft

$\ell = 3$ ft

If that proportion is true, so are these:

$\dfrac{l}{w} = \dfrac{L}{W}$ $\dfrac{3}{2} = \dfrac{6}{4}$

$\dfrac{w}{W} = \dfrac{l}{L}$ $\dfrac{2}{4} = \dfrac{3}{6}$

$\dfrac{W}{w} = \dfrac{L}{l}$ $\dfrac{4}{2} = \dfrac{6}{3}$

$W = 4$ ft

$L = 6$ ft

You can see for yourself why a proportion has four forms:

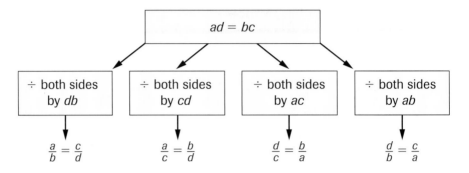

$ad = bc$

÷ both sides by db

÷ both sides by cd

÷ both sides by ac

÷ both sides by ab

$\dfrac{a}{b} = \dfrac{c}{d}$

$\dfrac{a}{c} = \dfrac{b}{d}$

$\dfrac{d}{c} = \dfrac{b}{a}$

$\dfrac{d}{b} = \dfrac{c}{a}$

> Not all arrangements work. For example, $\frac{a}{d}$ does not equal $\frac{b}{c}$ (except in the special case where both ratios equal 1).

289 Solving Proportions

Remember that the cross products of a proportion are equal.

MORE HELP
See 127–129, 261, 287

EXAMPLE 1: For a science fiction movie, a special-effects shop is building a scale model of the Brooklyn Bridge. If the distance between spans is 44 inches, how high above the water should the towers rise?

276.5'

1595'

Source: The Builders: Marvels of Engineering ©1992, National Geographic Society

To answer this, you can write and solve a proportion. Let x represent the distance in inches from the water to the top of the towers.

inches in model ⟶ $\dfrac{44}{1595} = \dfrac{x}{276.5}$ ⟵ inches in model
feet in actual bridge ⟶ $\phantom{\dfrac{44}{1595} = \dfrac{x}{276.5}}$ ⟵ feet in actual bridge

Since the cross products must be equal, set up an equation and solve for x.

$44 \cdot 276.5 = 1595x$

$\dfrac{44 \cdot 276.5}{1595} = x \approx 7.6$

> Be sure to include the correct units in your answer.

★ The towers in the model should rise about 7.6 inches above the water.

EXAMPLE 2: Jennifer used 27 gallons of gasoline to travel 425 miles on the highway. About how many gallons will she use to drive the same car from Seattle to Atlanta, a distance of about 2800 miles?

Let g represent the number of gallons of gas she will need.

miles $\longrightarrow$ $\dfrac{425}{27} = \dfrac{2800}{g}$ $\longleftarrow$ miles
gallons $\longrightarrow$ $\phantom{\dfrac{425}{27} = \dfrac{2800}{g}}$ $\longleftarrow$ gallons

$425g = 27 \cdot 2800$

$g = \dfrac{27 \cdot 2800}{425} \approx 177.9$

★ She will use about 180 gallons of gas to travel from Seattle to Atlanta.

Using Conversion Factors

290

When you travel to another country, you exchange the money used here for the money used there. However, the value of a U.S. dollar changes from day to day. It may be worth 99 Japanese yen one day and 100 yen the next. A **currency exchange rate** is used to figure out how much of another country's money you can get for a dollar.

Currency Exchange Rate Friday, February 12, 1999		
Place and Currency	**Currency per U.S. $**	**U.S. $ Equivalent**
Canada (dollar)	1.4905	0.6709
Japan (yen)	114.05	0.008768
Mexico (peso)	9.9420	0.1006
Europe (Euro)	0.8856	1.1292

Source: Wall Street Journal

This column shows how many dollars you get for one unit of the foreign currency.

This column shows how much foreign currency you get for one U.S. dollar.

CASE 1 Sometimes, you know the number of U.S. dollars and you want to find the amount of foreign currency.

MORE HELP
See 282

EXAMPLE 1: How many Mexican pesos would you have received for 750 U.S. dollars on February 12, 1999?

To answer this, you can set up and solve a proportion. Let p represent the number of Mexican pesos you would have received.

pesos $\longrightarrow$ $\dfrac{p}{750} = \dfrac{9.9420}{1}$ $\longleftarrow$ pesos
dollars $\longrightarrow$ $\phantom{\dfrac{p}{750} = \dfrac{9.9420}{1}}$ $\longleftarrow$ dollars

$1p = 750 \cdot 9.9420 = 7456.5$

According to the table you would get 9.9420 pesos for one U.S. dollar.

MORE ▶

SHORTCUT

The currency per U.S. dollar is a unit rate. You can simply multiply to find the amount of foreign money you get for any number of U.S. dollars.

amount in foreign currency = currency per U.S. $ · amount in U.S. $

number of Mexican pesos $= 9.9420 \cdot 750$

$$= 7456.5$$

★ Either way, you would have received 7456.5 Mexican pesos for 750 U.S. dollars.

CASE 2 Sometimes, you know the amount of foreign currency and you want to find the number of U.S. dollars.

EXAMPLE 2: How many U.S. dollars would you have needed to exchange in order to have received 1000 Euros on February 12, 1999?

The U.S. dollar equivalent is a unit rate (U.S. dollars per 1 unit of foreign currency), so you can simply multiply to find the number of U.S. dollars you need for any amount of the foreign currency.

amount in U.S. $ = U.S. $ equivalent · amount in foreign currency

$$= 1.1292 \cdot 1000$$

$$= 1129.2$$

> The table shows you would get 1.1292 U.S. dollars for 1 Euro.

★ You would have needed $1129.20 U.S. to exchange for 1000 Euros.

Multiple-Step Conversions

Sometimes you need to make more than one conversion because you don't have a single conversion rate you can use.

EXAMPLE: How many feet per second does a car travel when it goes at a speed (or rate) of 60 miles per hour?

You want to change from miles per hour to feet per second. Think about the units. You need to change miles to feet and hours to seconds.

1 mile (mi) = 5280 feet (ft)

1 hour (h) = 3600 seconds (s)

MORE HELP
See 089

❶ Write an equation showing all the changes you need to make.	$speed = \dfrac{60\ mi}{1\ h} \cdot \dfrac{5280\ ft}{1\ mi} \cdot \dfrac{1\ h}{3600\ s}$
❷ Cancel pairs of units in numerator and denominator.	$\dfrac{60\ \cancel{mi}}{1\ \cancel{h}} \cdot \dfrac{5280\ ft}{1\ \cancel{mi}} \cdot \dfrac{1\ \cancel{h}}{3600\ s}$
❸ Cancel the numbers if you can.	$\overset{1}{\cancel{60}} \cdot \overset{88}{\cancel{5280}}\ ft \cdot \dfrac{1}{\underset{1}{\cancel{3600}}\ s} = \dfrac{88\ ft}{1\ s}$

> You can cancel units just as you would numbers or variables. Solving problems this way, by analyzing the units, is called **dimensional analysis.**

★ A car traveling at 60 miles per hour goes 88 feet per second.

Direct Proportion

292

If you work three times as long, you usually earn three times as much. If you buy half as much cheese at the deli, you pay half as much. Many pairs of quantities are related like that. When one quantity always changes by the same factor as another, the two quantities are in **direct proportion**. You can also say they are **directly proportional.** Either way, it means the two quantities always have the same ratio.

MORE HELP
See 146–149, 160

You can express a direct proportion as $\frac{y}{x} = k$, where k is a constant. Usually, the equivalent form is used:

$y = kx$

> The k is called the **constant of proportionality.**

You earn $7.50 per hour. You can write an equation in the form $y = kx$ to relate dollars earned to hours worked.

dollars earned = 7.5 × hours worked
↑
constant of proportionality

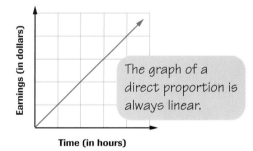

Earnings (in dollars)

Time (in hours)

> The graph of a direct proportion is always linear.

> Just because one quantity increases when the other increases doesn't mean they are in **direct proportion.** For example, suppose you have a brother half your age. As you get older so does he. The ratio of your ages does not stay the same. By next year your brother will be more than half your age.

Inverse Proportion

If you go 3 times as fast, it will take you $\frac{1}{3}$ the time to get where you're going. When one quantity always decreases by the same factor as the other increases, the two quantities are in **inverse proportion**. You can also say they are **inversely proportional**.

MORE HELP
See 144

You can express an inverse proportion as $y = \frac{k}{x}$, where k is a constant. Usually, the equivalent form is used:

$$xy = k$$

As with direct proportions, here k is also called the **constant of proportionality**.

A train travels 240 miles between two cities. The faster it goes, the less time the trip takes. You can write an equation in the form $xy = k$ to relate speed to time.

speed (in miles per hour) · time (in hours) = 240

↑
constant of proportionality

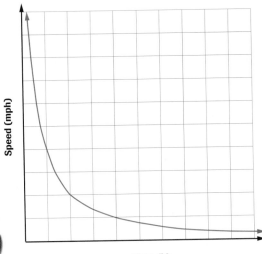

Speed (mph)

Time (h)

The graph of an inverse proportion in the form $y = \frac{k}{x}$ is always a curve with **asymptotes** at the x and y axes. This means the curve approaches each axis, but doesn't actually cross (speed and time must both remain positive numbers).

Just because one quantity decreases when the other increases doesn't mean they are **inversely proportional**. For example, the longer a candle burns, the shorter it gets. Consider a 10-inch tall candle. After 1 hour it may be 8 inches tall. At that rate, after twice that time (2 hours), its height would be 6 inches, which is not half of 8 inches.

Percent

Percents give us a way to talk about parts while using whole numbers. Eighteen percent of college students rent a place to live off campus. Instead of writing 0.18 or $\frac{18}{100}$ and saying *eighteen hundredths*, we can write 18% and say *18 percent*.   Source: Independent Insurance Agents of America

Percents can also be used to show multiples of a number. 200% of a number is twice as large as 100% of that number. If a fraction can't be written as hundredths, the related percent can be written with a decimal or fraction part.

Percent Benchmarks

You can think of percents as a scale, with zero percent standing for no part of the thing and one hundred percent for the whole thing. If you know the percents for common unit fractions, you can just multiply to find the percents for other fractions. Just as $\frac{2}{3}$ is twice $\frac{1}{3}$, $66\frac{2}{3}\%$ is twice $33\frac{1}{3}\%$.

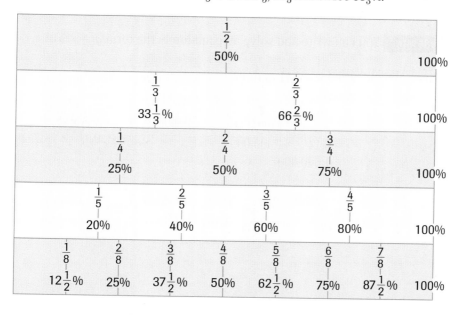

Solving Basic Percent Equations

Since a percent describes a part of a whole, you can think of a percent statement as an equation that says *a part is a certain percent of a whole.*

General percent equation	Examples
$\underset{\substack{\text{part}\\ \text{(percentage)}}}{y} \;\; \text{is} \;\; \underset{\text{percent}}{x\%} \;\; \text{of} \;\; \underset{\substack{\text{whole}\\ \text{(base)}}}{z}$	3 is 25% of 12 48 is 200% of 24 2 is 0.5% of 400

You can also think of a percent statement, $y = x\%$ of z, as a proportion.

part ⟶ $\dfrac{x}{100} = \dfrac{y}{z}$ ⟵ part
whole ⟶ whole

So, *3 is 25% of 12* can be written as $\frac{25}{100} = \frac{3}{12}$;

and *48 is 200% of 24* can be written as $\frac{200}{100} = \frac{48}{24}$,

and *2 is 0.5% of 400* can be written as $\frac{0.5}{100} = \frac{2}{400}$.

Finding the Percentage

Sometimes you know the total and the percent and you need to find the **percentage**, or part of the total.

EXAMPLE: In the largest oil spill in U.S. history, 11 million gallons of oil spilled into Alaska's Prince William Sound. Cleanup crews recovered 14% of that. About how many gallons of oil did they recover?

Source: Newsweek, *March 29, 1999*

ONE WAY You can write and solve an equation in the form $y = x\%$ of z.

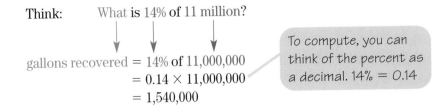

Think:　　What is 14% of 11 million?

gallons recovered = 14% of 11,000,000
= 0.14 × 11,000,000
= 1,540,000

To compute, you can think of the percent as a decimal. 14% = 0.14

ANOTHER WAY Because 14% means 14 out of 100, you can write and solve a proportion.

$$\frac{\text{gallons recovered}}{\text{total gallons spilled}} = \frac{14}{100}$$

$$\frac{x}{11,000,000} = \frac{14}{100}$$

$$x = 1,540,000$$

In general, to find y, in the equation $y = x\%$ of z, multiply $\frac{x}{100}$ by z.

★ Either way, the cleanup crews recovered about $1\frac{1}{2}$ million gallons of oil.

Finding the Percent

298

Sometimes you need to find what percent one number is of another.

EXAMPLE: According to the graph, about what percent of the cost of owning a dog is for food?

Think:

4020 is what % of 14,600?

$$4020 = x\% \text{ of } 14,600$$

$$4020 = \frac{x}{100} \cdot 14,600$$

$$\frac{4020}{14,600} = \frac{x}{100}$$

$$0.275 \cdot 100 \approx x$$

$$27.5 \approx x$$

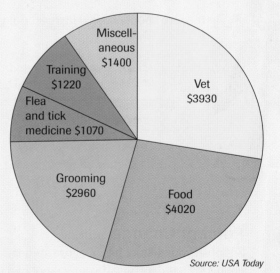

Costs of Owning a Dog for Eleven Years

Miscell-aneous $1400

Training $1220

Flea and tick medicine $1070

Vet $3930

Grooming $2960

Food $4020

Source: USA Today

★ Food accounts for about $27\frac{1}{2}\%$ of the cost of owning a dog.

Total: $14,600 (not including price of puppy)

In general, to find x in the equation $y = x\%$ of z, divide y by z, then multiply the result by 100 so you can write it with a percent symbol. You could also have solved the problem by using a proportion. For example: $\frac{x}{100} = \frac{4020}{14,600}$.

299

Finding the Total

Sometimes you need to find the total when you know the percent and the percentage.

EXAMPLE: There were about 26,600 more high school golfers in 1996 than in 1988, about a 17.4% rise. This means you had n golfers in 1988 and 26,600 more than n golfers in 1996. This 26,600 represents about 17.4% of the 1988 number. How many high school golfers were there in 1988?

Think: 26,600 is 17.4 % of what?

$$26,600 = 17.4\% \text{ of } n$$

$$26,600 = (0.174)n$$

$$\frac{26,600}{0.174} = n$$

Even when a percent has a decimal point, you'll still need to divide by 100 to write it as a decimal number.

$$17.4\% = \frac{17.4}{100} = 0.174$$

$$152,874 \approx n$$

★ There were about 153,000 high school golfers in 1988.

Another good way to find z in the equation $y = x\%$ of z, is to multiply y by $\frac{100}{x}$. You could also have solved the problem by using a proportion. For example: $\frac{26,600}{n} = \frac{17.4}{100}$

300

Percent Change

Suppose your school has 50 more students this year than last. Is that a big change? That depends. If your school had only 50 students last year, 50 more would double the size of the student body. That's a big change. In fact, that change of 50 is 100% of last year's enrollment. If 2000 students attended last year, then going up to 2050 is not such a big change. The same change of 50 is only $2\frac{1}{2}\%$ of the old enrollment, a far cry from a 100% change.

Percent change gives a sense of how big a change really is because it lets you describe a change in comparison to what things were like before. You can use this formula to calculate percent change.

$$\text{percent change} = 100 \times \frac{\text{amount of change}}{\text{original amount}}$$

When you think of percent changes, picture the amount of change compared to the original amount. Here are some examples:

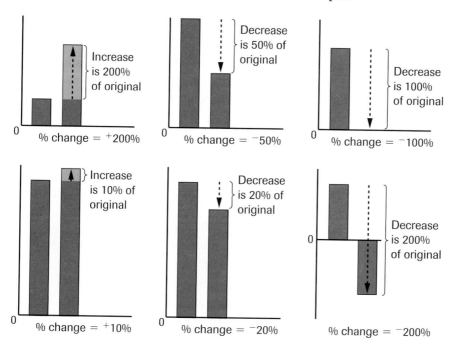

Percent change can be positive or negative. To avoid worrying about positive and negative signs, you can use the terms **percent increase** for positive changes and **percent decrease** for negative changes.

Percent Increase

Percent increase is the percent change when an amount goes up.

$$\text{percent increase} = 100 \times \frac{\text{amount of increase}}{\text{original amount}}$$

EXAMPLE: The average price of gasoline in the U.S. went up from $1.18 in early February, 1999, to $1.38 about a month later. By what percent did the price rise during that time?   *Source: Lundburg Survey Inc.*

% increase $= 100 \times \dfrac{0.20}{1.18}$ ⟵ amount of increase = 1.38 − 1.18
⟵ original amount

$\approx 100 \times 0.169$, or about 16.9

★ The average gasoline price rose about 16.9% during that time.

Percent Decrease

Percent decrease is the percent change when an amount goes down.

$$\text{percent decrease} = 100 \times \frac{\text{amount of decrease}}{\text{original amount}}$$

EXAMPLE 1: The average price of gasoline in the U.S. fell from about $1.24 in early May, 1999 to about $1.19 in early June, 1999. By what percent did the price decrease during that month-long period?

$$\% \text{ decrease} = 100 \times \frac{0.05}{1.24} \quad \begin{array}{l} \longleftarrow \text{ amount of decrease} = \textbf{1.24} - \textbf{1.19} \\ \longleftarrow \text{ original amount} \end{array}$$

$$\approx 100 \times 0.04, \text{ or about } 4$$

★ The average price of gasoline decreased by about 4% during that period.

EXAMPLE 2: During the 1997–1998 school year, students of ages 14–18 said they spent a weekly average of 6.1 hours on homework, down from 6.6 hours the year before. Describe this drop in terms of a percent decrease.   *Source The State of Our Nation and Youth 1998-1999*

$$\% \text{ decrease} = 100 \times \frac{0.5}{6.6} \quad \begin{array}{l} \longleftarrow \text{ amount of decrease} = \textbf{6.6} - \textbf{6.1} \\ \longleftarrow \text{ original amount} \end{array}$$

$$\approx 100 \times 0.076, \text{ or about } 7.6$$

★ According to what students said, they spent about 7.6% less time on homework each week in the 1997-1998 school year than in the year before.

MATH ALERT Be Careful When Combining Percent Changes

Be very careful when you combine percent changes. If sales go up 50% one month and then down 50% the next month, are they back to where they started? You might think that a 50% decrease would exactly cancel a 50% increase, but it doesn't. The first 50% is half of one amount. The second 50% is half of a *different* amount.

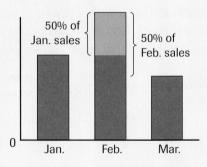

EXAMPLE: A discount is a percent of the original price subtracted from that original price. In this week's special, what is the overall discount? Is it 60%?

The 40% Store

Everyday price of any item is 40% off the msrp*
*(manufacturer's suggested retail price)

This week's special:

Take 20% off our everyday price!

ONE WAY You can use a variable for the suggested price.

Let x represent manufacturer's suggested retail price.

$$\text{price after first discount} = 1x - 0.4x$$
$$= 0.6x$$
$$\text{price after second discount} = 0.6x - 0.2(0.6x)$$
$$= 0.6x - 0.12x$$
$$= 0.48x$$

The final price is 48% of the manufacturer's suggested retail price, so the overall discount is 52% (100% − 48%), not 60%.

ANOTHER WAY You can calculate using a convenient amount for the manufacturer's suggested retail price.

Suppose the manufacturer's suggested retail price for an item is $100.

$$\text{first discount} = 40\% \text{ of } 100, \text{ or } 40$$
$$\text{price after first discount} = 100 - 40, \text{ or } 60$$
$$\text{second discount} = 20\% \text{ of } 60, \text{ or } 12$$
$$\text{total discount} = 40 + 12, \text{ or } 52$$

Fifty-two dollars is 52% of $100. Notice that you don't need to find the final price to answer the question.

★ Either way, a 40% discount followed by a 20% discount is not a 60% discount. It's a 52% discount.

Interest

You can rent almost anything: surfboards, cars, VCRs. You can even rent money. When you borrow money from a bank, it's just like renting. The longer you borrow, the more you pay. The amount you pay to borrow money is called **interest**. Interest is paid when you borrow or invest money. The amount of money borrowed or invested is called the **principal**. The interest is usually a percent of the amount borrowed or invested. That percent is called the **interest rate**.

Simple Interest

You can use this equation to calculate simple interest:

Interest = principal × annual rate of interest × time in years

$I = prt$

EXAMPLE 1: Suppose you borrow $4500 from your aunt to buy a car. You agree to repay the loan at the end of $2\frac{1}{2}$ years with 6% simple annual interest. How much will you need to pay in order to pay off the loan as promised?

$I = prt$

If time is part of a year, write it as a decimal before computing: six months = 0.5, etc.

$= (4500)(0.06)(2.5)$

$= 675$

The interest is $675, so you will need to pay that plus the $4500 you borrowed.

★ You will need a total of $5175 to pay off the loan in full after $2\frac{1}{2}$ years.

In 1805 a Dutch clock maker named Johannes Columbie left $8510 to help the poor. He instructed that the money not be spent until 140 years after his last servant died. Finally, in 1999 his investment, worth about $4.9 million, was distributed.   Source: Ripley's Believe It or Not

EXAMPLE 2: Suppose Johannes Columbie's investment in 1805 earned a constant simple annual interest. What would the rate have been?

Rewrite the equation to solve for r, the rate. $I = prt \longrightarrow r = \frac{I}{pt}$

$r = \dfrac{I}{pt}$

$\approx \dfrac{4{,}891{,}490}{8510 \times 194}$ ← $I \approx 4{,}900{,}000 - 8510$
  ← $t = 1999 - 1805$

≈ 2.96 or 296%

★ The simple annual interest rate would have been about 296%. If you check out the next item, Compound Interest, you'll see a more realistic way the money could have grown from $8510 to almost $4.9 million.

Compound Interest

Suppose you let a bank use your money (which you do if you have a bank account). If you keep the interest in the account, then you are letting the bank use even more of your money. If they pay you interest on that interest, that's called **compound interest.**

You can see how compound interest adds up by looking at this table, which shows a $1000 principal earning interest at a rate of 6% per year compounded quarterly. **Compounded quarterly** means that every three months ($\frac{1}{4}$ year), they figure $\frac{1}{4}$ of your yearly interest, then add it to your balance so that when they figure interest at the end of the next quarter, they're computing with a larger principal. A rate of 6% per year is 1.5% per quarter.

Period	Principal (p)	Interest (I)	New Total ($p + I$)
1st quarter	$1000.00	$15.00	$1015.00
2nd quarter	$1015.00	$15.23	$1030.23
3rd quarter	$1030.23	$15.45	$1045.68
4th quarter	$1045.68	$15.69	$1061.37

With simple interest you would have only 1060.00 at the end of the year.

You can calculate compound interest by using a formula.

$$\text{Total Amount} = \text{Principal}\left(1 + \frac{\text{rate}}{\text{\# yearly compounds}}\right)^{\text{\# yearly compounds} \cdot \text{years}}$$

$A = P\left(1 + \frac{r}{n}\right)^{nt}$ where A is the total amount

P is the principal

r is the yearly interest rate

n is the number of compounding periods per year

t is the number of years.

MORE ▶

EXAMPLE: Remember the Dutch clock maker whose $8510 grew to about $4.9 million? Suppose the interest had been compounded quarterly. Would the yearly interest rate have been more than 4%?

$$A = P\left(1 + \frac{r}{n}\right)^{nt}$$

$$= 8510\left(1 + \frac{0.04}{4}\right)^{4 \times 194}$$

$$\approx 19{,}200{,}636$$

A yearly rate of 4% compounded quarterly would have yielded over $19 million dollars.

★ No, compounded quarterly, the yearly rate would have been less than 4%.

You can see the power of compounding. For the 194 years of growth, a compounded quarterly rate of less than 4% would yield the same amount as a simple annual rate of 296%!

307 Percent Error

MORE HELP
See 097

Someone asks you how far it is from Boston to San Francisco. You'd be doing pretty well if you were only off by 10 miles. But, it would be a very different story if you were off by 10 miles in giving the distance from your house to school. The 10-mile error is the same, but 10 miles is small compared to 3170 miles and huge compared to a few miles. That's why we use percents to describe how far off something is. It gives a better sense of how big the error is.

You can use this equation to calculate percent error:

Percent error $= \frac{\text{amount of error}}{\text{nominal amount}} \times 100$ **Nominal** means **measured.**

EXAMPLE 1: You measure a shelf to the nearest $\frac{1}{8}$ inch and get 20 inches. Because you measured to the nearest $\frac{1}{8}$ inch, your measurement could be off by as much as $\frac{1}{16}$ inch. What percent error would that be?

$$\% \text{ error} = \frac{\text{amount of error}}{\text{nominal amount}} \times 100$$

$$\approx \frac{\frac{1}{16}}{20} \times 100$$

$$\approx \frac{0.0625}{20} \times 100$$

$$\approx 0.3125$$

★ The error would be about 0.3%.

EXAMPLE 2: Using a device you built to measure the speed of light, you get a result of 184,000 miles per second. The actual value is about 186,000 miles per second. What is your percent error?

$$\% \text{ error} = \frac{\text{amount of error}}{\text{nominal amount}} \times 100$$

$$\approx \frac{186,000 - 184,000}{186,000} \times 100$$

$$\approx \frac{2000}{186,000} \times 100$$

$$\approx 1.08$$

★ The error would be about 1.08%.

Percents on a Calculator

308

Many calculators have a $\boxed{\%}$ key, which changes a percent to a decimal to streamline computation with percents.

EXAMPLE: Americans drove 1.12 billion miles in 1970. By 1996, that figure had risen 123%. How many miles did Americans drive in 1996?

Source: Federal Highway Administration

An increase of 123% is a total of 223% of the original amount.

★ Americans drove about 2.5 billion miles in 1996.

On some calculators, you don't even have to press the $\boxed{=}$ key after pressing the $\boxed{\%}$ key. And on some calculators, the percent must be the second factor in the multiplication. Since all calculators do not work the same way, you should check yours to see how it handles percents.

If your calculator does not have a percent key, write the percent as a decimal and multiply.

| 2 | • | 2 | 3 | ✕ | 1 | • | 1 | 2 | = | 2.4976 |

Data Analysis

" 'Obvious' is the most dangerous word in mathematics."

Eric Temple Bell

How long was the average life span of these batteries supposed to be?

Decisions, decisions. Which brand of battery should I buy? What should I eat for breakfast? Should I wear a raincoat to school today?

To make good decisions, you try to find out what you can about the issue. Which brand of battery lasts longer? Will it rain today?

These questions sound simple, but finding reliable answers is not so easy. That's where statistics and probability can play a role. These tools can help you gather information, organize it, analyze it, and make sense of it, so you can answer simple-sounding questions and make better decisions about what to buy, what to eat, and what to wear.

Matrices

Have you ever used a spreadsheet or arranged data in a table? If so, you've worked with something that's much like a matrix. This table shows the results from a survey taken in 1998. For each category of computer program, the table shows the percent of teen-age computer users who use that kind of program.

Percent of Teenage Computer Users					
Computer Games	Music Programs	Educational Programs	Graphics Programs	Spread-sheets	E-Mail
Boys 80	43	43	47	30	29
Girls 74	32	51	54	36	32

Source: The Roper Organization, 1998 Roper Youth Report

Take away the labels and the outlines and you have a rectangular arrangement of values. That's a **matrix**. Call this one Matrix P.

$$P = \begin{bmatrix} 80 & 43 & 43 & 47 & 30 & 29 \\ 74 & 32 & 51 & 54 & 36 & 32 \end{bmatrix}$$

Matrix Terminology

A matrix is a rectangular arrangement of values. A matrix with m rows and n columns has **dimension** $m \times n$. The matrix above has a dimension of 2×6.

Write: 2×6
Say: *two by six*

Each value in a matrix is called an **element** of the matrix. If you're talking about an element, and you want to refer to its position in the matrix, you usually use a system that names each element by its row and column. Be sure you know the system being used before depending on someone else's position-names!

ONE WAY
$$\begin{bmatrix} a_1 & b_1 & c_1 \\ a_2 & b_2 & c_2 \end{bmatrix}$$

ANOTHER WAY
$$\begin{bmatrix} a_1 & a_2 & a_3 \\ b_1 & b_2 & b_3 \end{bmatrix}$$

ANOTHER WAY
$$\begin{bmatrix} a_{11} & a_{12} & a_{13} \\ a_{21} & a_{22} & a_{23} \end{bmatrix}$$

Write: a_{11}
Say: *a one one*

Writing Matrices

If you can show data in a table, you show the data in a matrix.

World Motor Vehicle Production (in millions of vehicles)

Source: Wall Street Journal Almanac

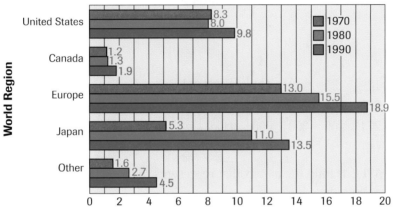

EXAMPLE: Write Matrix *A* to represent the data from the bar graph.

To represent these data in a matrix, think of a way to represent it in a table. Use rows for world regions: United States, Canada, Europe, Japan, Other. Use columns for years: 1970, 1980, 1990.

Think:

	1970	1980	1990
United States	8.3	8.0	9.8
Canada	1.2	1.3	1.9
Europe	13.0	15.5	18.9
Japan	5.3	11.0	13.5
Other	1.6	2.7	4.5

★ Write:

$$\begin{bmatrix} 8.3 & 8.0 & 9.8 \\ 1.2 & 1.3 & 1.9 \\ 13.0 & 15.5 & 18.9 \\ 5.3 & 11.0 & 13.5 \\ 1.6 & 2.7 & 4.5 \end{bmatrix}$$

Adding and Subtracting Matrices _____

You can add or subtract matrices that have the same dimensions. You do this when you have several sets of related data.

A multiplex has three movie theaters. On Saturday and Sunday, each theater has four shows. Matrix *A* represents ticket sales on Saturday. Matrix *B* represents sales on Sunday.

$$A = \begin{array}{c} \text{Show Number} \\ \begin{array}{cccc} 1 & 2 & 3 & 4 \end{array} \\ \begin{bmatrix} 97 & 146 & 151 & 122 \\ 257 & 231 & 194 & 162 \\ 282 & 300 & 300 & 300 \end{bmatrix} \end{array} \begin{array}{l} \text{Theater 1} \\ \text{Theater 2} \\ \text{Theater 3} \end{array}$$

$$B = \begin{array}{c} \text{Show Number} \\ \begin{array}{cccc} 1 & 2 & 3 & 4 \end{array} \\ \begin{bmatrix} 108 & 157 & 149 & 111 \\ 229 & 260 & 234 & 150 \\ 274 & 300 & 300 & 300 \end{bmatrix} \end{array} \begin{array}{l} \text{Theater 1} \\ \text{Theater 2} \\ \text{Theater 3} \end{array}$$

EXAMPLE 1: Find the matrix that represents the total number of tickets sold on both days.

To find the matrix that represents the total number of tickets sold on both days, add the matrices.

MORE HELP
See 311

$$A + B = \begin{bmatrix} 97 + 108 & 146 + 157 & 151 + 149 & 122 + 111 \\ 257 + 229 & 231 + 260 & 194 + 234 & 162 + 150 \\ 282 + 274 & 300 + 300 & 300 + 300 & 300 + 300 \end{bmatrix}$$

$$\bigstar \ A + B = \begin{bmatrix} 205 & 303 & 300 & 233 \\ 486 & 491 & 428 & 312 \\ 556 & 600 & 600 & 600 \end{bmatrix}$$

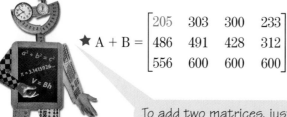

To add two matrices, just find the sum of each pair of corresponding elements. In general $A + B = a_{11} + b_{11}, a_{12} + b_{12}$, etc.

EXAMPLE 2: Find the matrix that indicates the change in ticket sales for the four shows from Saturday to Sunday.

To solve the problem, subtract the matrices.

$$B - A = \begin{bmatrix} 108 - 97 & 157 - 146 & 149 - 151 & 111 - 122 \\ 229 - 257 & 260 - 231 & 234 - 194 & 150 - 162 \\ 274 - 282 & 300 - 300 & 300 - 300 & 300 - 300 \end{bmatrix}$$

To subtract two matrices with the same dimensions, subtract the corresponding elements. In general,

$B - A = b_{11} - a_{11}, b_{12} - a_{12}$, etc.

$$\bigstar\ B - A = \begin{bmatrix} 11 & 11 & ^{-}2 & ^{-}11 \\ ^{-}28 & 29 & 40 & ^{-}12 \\ ^{-}8 & 0 & 0 & 0 \end{bmatrix}$$

314

MATH ALERT   Not All Matrices Can Be Added or Subtracted

If two matrices have different dimensions, you cannot add or subtract them.

$$A = \begin{bmatrix} 6 & 21 & 9 \\ 13 & 2 & ^{-}12 \end{bmatrix} \qquad B = \begin{bmatrix} 21 & ^{-}1 \\ ^{-}18 & 24 \\ 3 & 17 \end{bmatrix} \qquad C = \begin{bmatrix} 41 & 1 & 26 \\ 6 & 5 & 9 \\ ^{-}3 & 8 & 11 \end{bmatrix}$$

EXAMPLE: Can you add Matrix B to Matrix C?

To add two matrices, you find the sum of each pair of corresponding elements.

$$B + C = \begin{bmatrix} 21 + 41 & ^{-}1 + 1 & ? + 26 \\ ^{-}18 + 6 & 24 + 5 & ? + 9 \\ 3 + ^{-}3 & 17 + 8 & ? + 11 \end{bmatrix}$$

There are no numbers from Matrix B to add to the numbers in the last column of Matrix C.

The dimension of Matrix C is 3 by 3. The dimension of Matrix B is 3 by 2. For the third column of C there is no corresponding column in B.

$\bigstar$ You cannot add $B + C$.

Scalar Multiplication _____

You can multiply a matrix by a number. This kind of multiplication is called **scalar multiplication**. When you do scalar multiplication, each element in the matrix is multiplied by the same factor.

A car dealership has three salespeople, Ned, Tanya, and Nate. The number of sales and leases the salespeople made last year is represented by Matrix S.

$$S = \begin{matrix} \text{Ned} & \text{Tanya} & \text{Nate} \\ \begin{bmatrix} 40 & 55 & 25 \\ 60 & 45 & 30 \end{bmatrix} & & \end{matrix} \begin{matrix} \text{Sales} \\ \text{Leases} \end{matrix}$$

MORE HELP
See 294–296

EXAMPLE: The dealership wants to increase the number of sales and leases by 20% this year. Find the matrix that describes that goal.

Last year's results represent 100%. The goal for this year is a 20% increase: 100% + 20% = 120%. To find the matrix that describes that sales goal, multiply Matrix S by 1.2.

$$1.2S = \begin{bmatrix} 1.2 \cdot 40 & 1.2 \cdot 55 & 1.2 \cdot 25 \\ 1.2 \cdot 60 & 1.2 \cdot 45 & 1.2 \cdot 30 \end{bmatrix}$$

$$1.2S = \begin{bmatrix} 48 & 66 & 30 \\ 72 & 54 & 36 \end{bmatrix}$$

In general, $nA = na_{11}, na_{12}$, etc.

★ If the three salespeople are to meet their goals this year, their targets are described by this table:

	Ned	Tanya	Nate	
	48	66	30	Sales
	72	54	36	Leases

Ned's sales must go from 40 to 48 and his leases must go from 60 to 72 to meet his new goals.

The weather forecaster on the evening news says that there's a 60% chance of rain. A sports reporter says that a team has a 50-50 chance of winning the championship. A political analyst says that the odds are against Robinson winning the election. All of these statements are about probability and odds. **Probability** and **odds** are ways of telling how likely it is that an event or series of events will or won't happen. In many situations, you can calculate probability by figuring out how many different, yet equally likely, ways something can happen. These ways are permutations and combinations.

Fundamental Counting Principle

317

The **fundamental counting principle** states that if a first event can occur in a ways and a second event can occur independently in b ways, then the two events can occur together in $a \cdot b$ ways.

EXAMPLE 1: The Z-1 sports car comes in two different body types, convertible and hard top. The Z-1 is available in five different colors. How many choices are there for the Z-1?

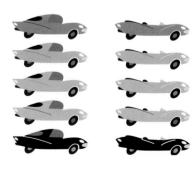

Choices = colors · body types
$$= 5 \cdot 2$$
$$= 10$$

★ There are 10 choices for the Z-1.

MORE ▶

You can use the fundamental counting principle for any number of events.

EXAMPLE 2: You may think you don't have a lot of clothes, but they can be worn in many combinations. If you have three pairs of shoes, six pairs of pants, four shirts, and three belts, how many outfits of shoes-pants-shirt-belt do you have?

$$\begin{aligned} \text{Number of outfits} &= \text{shoe choices} \cdot \text{pant choices} \cdot \text{shirt choices} \cdot \text{belt choices} \\ &= 3 \cdot 6 \cdot 4 \cdot 3 \\ &= 216 \end{aligned}$$

★ You have 216 different outfits. You may refuse to wear some of them, but you have them.

Permutations

Suppose you want to open your locker. You turn left to 28, right to 16, and left to 14. You probably call 28-16-14 your locker combination. However, in math you'd call this a *locker permutation*. That's because a **permutation** is an arrangement of items and events in which each order of items counts as a different arrangement. If you turned to the numbers in a different order, such as 16-14-28, you'd have a different permutation, and your lock wouldn't open!

There are different ways to find all of the possible permutations of a group of items or events.

EXAMPLE: Four cyclists are racing. The first two cyclists win different prizes. How many possible permutations are there for the two prize winners?

ONE WAY You can use a **tree diagram** to find all the possible permutations for a set of items.

You can use special notation to show the number of permutations. For the race finish, each possible permutation includes two of the four cyclists.

Write: $_4P_2 = 12$

Say: *The number of permutations of four items taken two at a time is twelve.*

ANOTHER WAY You can use multiplication to find all the possible permutations for a set of items.

To find the number of possible permutations when there are four cyclists competing for first and second place, multiply the number of choices for each place.

Four choices for first place

Three choices left for second place

$4 \cdot 3 = 12$

Since a cyclist can't finish the race first and second, you have only three possible second-place cyclists for each first-place cyclist. That's why you multiply 4×3 and not 4×4.

ANOTHER WAY You can use the formula $_nP_m = \frac{n!}{(n-m)!}$ where n is the number of items and m is the number of items taken at a time.

MORE HELP
See 022

$$_4P_2 = \frac{4!}{(4-2)!}$$

$$= \frac{4 \times 3 \times 2 \times 1}{2 \times 1}$$

$$= \frac{24}{2} = 12$$

In mathematics, the exclamation point (!) means factorial.

★ Either way, there are 12 possible permutations for the two prize-winners.

EXAMPLE 2: How many different ways can you arrange seven people in a line?

For this situation, you are looking for a permutation of seven items taken seven at a time. $_7P_7$

To find the number of permutations, use the formula.

$$\frac{7!}{(7-7)!} = \frac{7 \times 6 \times 5 \times 4 \times 3 \times 2 \times 1}{0!} = \frac{5040}{1}$$

0! is defined as 1.

★ There are 5040 ways to arrange seven people in a line.

Combinations

Sometimes, you need to count arrangements or groups of items for events. If a different order of items doesn't count as a different arrangement, then each arrangement or group is called a **combination**. The 27 players on a baseball team are a combination of people. No matter what order you arrange them in, the team is still the same team. However, batting order is a permutation, because order matters!

EXAMPLE: There are two seats left on an airplane. Five people still want to get on the flight. How many different possible pairs of passengers can be made from the five who are waiting?

ONE WAY To find all of the possible combinations for a set of items, you can make a list.

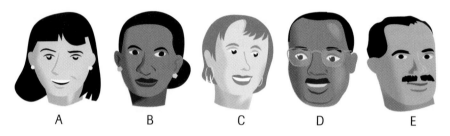

| A | B | C | D | E |

❶ Find the permutations.	❷ Find the combinations.
Here are all the possible pairs if a different order counts as a different pair.	AB and BA are the same two passengers, so cross off one of the pairs. Cross off all the other duplicates.
AB AC AD AE BA BC BD BE $\quad {}_5P_2 = 5 \cdot 4$ CA CB CD CE $\qquad = 20$ DA DB DC DE EA EB EC ED	AB AC AD AE B̶A̶ BC BD BE C̶A̶ C̶B̶ CD CE D̶A̶ D̶B̶ D̶C̶ DE E̶A̶ E̶B̶ E̶C̶ E̶D̶

You can use special notation to show combinations. Here, you are looking for the possible combinations of five passengers taken two at a time.

Write: ${}_5C_2 = 10$

Say: *The number of combinations of five items taken two at a time is ten.*

ANOTHER WAY You can also compute to find all the possible combinations for a set of items.

1 Find the number of possible permutations.	$_5P_2 = 5 \cdot 4$ $= 20$
2 Find the number of ways the items in any one combination can be arranged (the number of permutations).	$2! = 2 \cdot 1$ $= 2$
3 Divide to eliminate duplicates. $\dfrac{\text{number of permutations}}{\text{number of arrangements for each combination}}$	$\dfrac{20}{2} = 10$

ANOTHER WAY You can make a tree diagram to find all the possible combinations for a set of items.

MORE HELP See 318

To make a tree diagram, do a set of branches showing how each passenger can be paired. Give each passenger a letter, so you can keep them straight. Remember, a different order is not a different combination.

Count the branches to find all the combinations.

A — B, C, D, E

B — C, D, E

Don't pair B with A because A has already been paired with B.

C — D, E

D — E

E

E has already been paired with everyone else, so E doesn't get any branches on this tree.

★ Any way you look at it, there are 10 different combinations of two passengers that can take the remaining seats.

In general, $_nC_m = \dfrac{n!}{(n - m)! \cdot m!}$.

How Likely Is An Event?

An **event** is something that may or may not happen. The **probability** of an event can be any number 0 through 1. Probability can be written as a fraction, a decimal, or a percent. If an event is impossible, it has a probability of 0. If an event is certain, its probability is 1. The more unlikely an event is, the closer its probability is to 0. The more likely an event is, the closer its probability is to 1.

Probability

◄——— less likely than not ———►|◄——— more likely than not ———►

0	$\frac{1}{4}$	$\frac{1}{2}$	$\frac{3}{4}$	1
0.0	0.25	0.5	0.75	1.0
0%	25%	50%	75%	100%
impossible	unlikely	as likely as unlikely	likely	certain

A probability cannot be greater than 1 because an event can't be more likely than certain.

EXAMPLE 1: Elvis Presley died in 1977. So, it's *impossible* for that Elvis Presley to give a concert at your school. The probability of the original Elvis Presley performing at your school is 0.

EXAMPLE 2: The weather forecaster says that there's a 10% chance of rain today in Portland, Oregon. This means that it is *unlikely* to rain. It doesn't mean it *won't* rain today in Portland or that it will rain for 10% of the day.

EXAMPLE 3: When you toss a quarter, the chance of tossing heads is $\frac{1}{2}$, or 50%. Tossing heads is *as likely as it is unlikely.*

EXAMPLE 4: In a deck of playing cards, there are 52 cards: 36 number cards, 12 face cards, and four aces.

The chance of picking a number card is $\frac{36}{52}$, or about 69%. This means that if you pick a card at random from a full deck, picking a number card is more likely than picking a card that is not a number card.

EXAMPLE 5: Every week, it is *certain* that Monday will follow Sunday. The probability of Monday following Sunday is 1, or 100%.

Sample Space

A **sample space** is a list of all possible outcomes of an activity.

The Surf Side Snack Shack has a spinner that you can spin when you get your bill. The spinner tells you what part of your bill you must pay.

EXAMPLE: Suppose you spin the spinner. Make a sample space for the spin.

The spinner can land on eight different parts. To make the sample space, list all of the possible outcomes of a spin.

★ The sample space is: full price, 10% off, full price, free meal, full price, 10% off, full price, 25% off.

Probability of an Event

Suppose you want to figure out the likelihood of spinning a 5 on this spinner. Then you would call any space with a 5 a **favorable outcome**. All of the spaces on the spinner (including the ones with a 5) are called **possible outcomes**. All of the spaces on the spinner are the same size and shape. The pointer is just as likely to land on one space as on any other. All of the outcomes are **equally likely.**

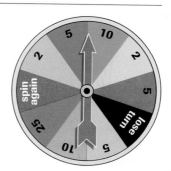

A favorable outcome isn't necessarily one you want to happen. It's just the one for which you're finding probability.

Probability is a measure of likelihood. It is the ratio of favorable outcomes to all possible equally-likely outcomes. When you figure out the likelihood of an event, you figure out the probability of an event.

MORE ▶

Write: $P(\text{event}) = \frac{\text{number of favorable outcomes}}{\text{number of equally-likely outcomes}}$

Say: *The probability of an event is the ratio of the number of favorable outcomes to the number of equally-likely outcomes.*

$$P(\text{spin five}) = \frac{3}{10}$$
← number of favorable outcomes (fives)
← number of equally likely outcomes

MORE HELP
See 320

Since probability is the ratio of favorable outcomes to all possible equally-likely outcomes, all probabilities have values 0 through 1.

If there are zero favorable events in your sample space, the event is impossible and its probability is 0. Since the number of favorable outcomes can't be more than the total number of outcomes, the highest probability possible is 1, or 100%, when the event is certain.

323

Theoretical and Experimental Probability

When you find the probability of an event without doing an experiment or analyzing data, you are finding **theoretical probability**. When you do an experiment or collect and analyze data to find probability, you are finding **experimental probability**.

$$\text{Experimental Probability (event)} = \frac{\text{number of favorable outcomes in experiment}}{\text{number of trials}}$$

You can use theoretical probability to predict the results of a probability experiment. Usually, as the number of attempts in an experiment increases, experimental probability gets closer to theoretical probability.

EXAMPLE: Suppose you toss a fair die. What is the theoretical probability of the die landing on four? Use the theoretical probability to predict how many times you would expect to toss a four if you tossed the die 120 times.

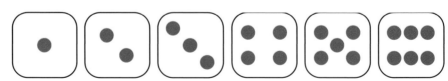

$$P(4) = \frac{\text{number of sides with four}}{\text{number of sides}}$$

$$= \frac{1}{6}$$

You can predict the number of times an outcome will occur by multiplying its probability by the number of trials you plan to complete.

$$\text{Expected number of fours in 120 rolls} = P(4) \cdot \text{number of rolls}$$
$$= \frac{1}{6} \cdot 120$$
$$= 20$$

★ Based on the theoretical probability, you would expect to toss a four 20 times out of 120.

Suppose you toss a fair die 120 times and on 18 of those times you toss a four. The experimental probability is $\frac{18}{120}$ or 0.15. The theoretical probability is $\frac{1}{6}$, or about 0.17. The experimental probability is fairly close to the theoretical probability.

324

Math Alert: When One Event Doesn't Depend on Another, Probability is Not Changed by Previous Events

Don't fall for the old fallacy about an event being *due*. If you toss a fair coin 20 times, and it hasn't landed heads-up yet, the probability of it landing heads up on the next toss is still $\frac{1}{2}$, or 50%.

If you toss a fair coin and it lands heads-up five times in a row, the probability of it landing heads up on the next toss is still $\frac{1}{2}$ or 50%.

The coin doesn't know what's happened so far, so how could the probability be any different?

Populations

325

When you study or gather data about a group, that group is called the **population**. A population is any group of people, objects, or events that fits a particular definition or set of conditions. The population could be limited to a specific group, such as left-handed high-school students who do not watch television. A population could also be as broad as all of the people who live in the United States, which is the population studied by the United States Census.

Sampling

Suppose you want to gather information about a large population, such as all of the teachers in the United States or all of the whales in the world. It would be impractical or even impossible to interview or examine every member of the group. Instead, you take a **sample**. A **representative sample** is a sample whose makeup is similar enough to the whole population that conclusions about the sample can reasonably be applied to the whole population.

To make the results of the sample as accurate as possible, the sample you choose must closely represent the *whole* group. To determine whether a sample is a representative sample, it's important to consider two factors:

- **Sample Size** This is the *number* of members in the sample. It is a small part of the population but should not be an insignificant number.

- **Sample Choice** It's important to select a **random sample**—a sample in which every member of the population has an equal chance of being chosen.

EXAMPLE 1: An ad says that, in a survey, three out of four doctors recommended Painfree Aspirin for controlling headache pain. How might knowing the size of the sample affect how you would respond to the ad?

★ If the sample size was only four or eight or 12 doctors, the results of the survey might not seem convincing. A sample size of 1200 doctors would be much more reliable.

EXAMPLE 2: You want to know what types of television programs are most popular among high school students. How can you choose a representative sample?

Suppose, for convenience, you choose a group, such as the Movie Club or the girls' tennis team. The problem with that is that those groups have special interests that might affect the results. Suppose you narrowed the sample to a particular grade, such as the ninth grade. That wouldn't represent students in other grades, who might have different preferences.

To get a representative sample, it's best to find a way to get a random sample—one that represents the entire population of high school students.

★ One way to get a random sample is to get a computer printout of the names of all of the high school students numbered in alphabetical order. You could then use the random number generator on a calculator or computer to select students to be surveyed.

MATH ALERT Be Wary of Experimental Probability Based on a Few Trials or a Small Sample

When a probability experiment has very few trials or pieces of data, think carefully about how you use the results. For example, suppose you spin this spinner four times and spin a 2 three of the times. You might decide that the probability of spinning a 2 is $\frac{3}{4}$. But it's obvious that you don't have a $\frac{3}{4}$ chance of spinning a 2 *every* time. If you spun the spinner many times, the experimental probability would probably move closer to the theoretical probability, $\frac{1}{8}$.

Probability of Mutually Exclusive Events

Suppose you are playing a word game. You have just used one letter tile and you are going to pick a tile to replace it. You want an S or an E so that you can make a particular word on your next turn. Since you can pick only one tile, the events *pick* S and *pick* E are **mutually exclusive**—one or the other can occur, but not both. If two events are mutually exclusive, you can use this formula to find the probability that one *or* the other will happen.

Probability(A or B) = Probability(A) + Probability(B)

EXAMPLE: You are playing a game and these tiles are left. You want to pick an S or an E. If you choose a tile at random, what is the probability you will pick an S or an E?

These two events are mutually exclusive because if you pick just one tile you can't pick both an S and an E.

MORE HELP
See 294–296

Probability(pick S or pick E) = P(pick S) + P(pick E)

$$= \frac{1}{8} + \frac{2}{8}$$

$$= \frac{3}{8}$$

★ The probability of picking an S or an E is $\frac{3}{8}$, 0.375, or 37.5%.

Probability of Two Events

Suppose you want to find the probability that two events will *both* occur. To make this calculation, you need to know whether the results of one event will affect the other. In other words, you need to decide whether the two events are dependent or independent.

CASE 1 When the outcome of one event does not affect the outcome of another event, the two events are **independent**.

If two events are independent, you can use this formula to find the probability of *both* events occurring.

Probability (A and B) = Probability (A) · Probability (B)

EXAMPLE 1: According to a study done in 1998, 52% of U.S. households had a CD player and 10% of U.S. households had a fax machine. If we assume that having a CD player did not affect whether a household had a fax machine, these two events are independent. What was the probability that a randomly chosen household had a CD player and a fax machine?

Source: Consumer Electronics Manufacturers Association

MORE HELP
See 294–296

$$Probability(CD \text{ and } fax) = P(CD) \cdot P(fax)$$
$$= 0.52 \cdot 0.1$$
$$= 0.052$$

★ The probability that a randomly chosen household had a CD player and a fax in 1998 was 0.052, or 5.2%.

EXAMPLE 2: These are the cards in a deck. Suppose you pick a card, replace it in the deck, shuffle the deck, and pick a second card. What is the probability that you will pick 6, then another 6?

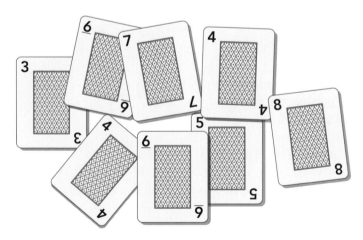

If you pick 6, then *replace* the card in the deck, your first pick doesn't affect your second pick, so the two events are independent.

Probability(6, then 6) = P(6) · P(6)

$$= \frac{2}{8} \cdot \frac{2}{8}$$

$$= \frac{4}{64} \text{ or } \frac{1}{16}$$

★ The probability of picking 6, then 6 again is $\frac{1}{16}$, 0.0625, or 6.25%.

CASE 2 When the outcome of one event affects the outcome of another event, the two events are **dependent**.

Use this formula to find the probability of two dependent events.

Probability $(A$ and $B)$ = Probability (A) · Probability $(B,$ given $A)$

EXAMPLE 3: You are playing cards. These cards are the only ones left and they are face down. If you choose two cards at random, what is the probability you will pick 3 then 8?

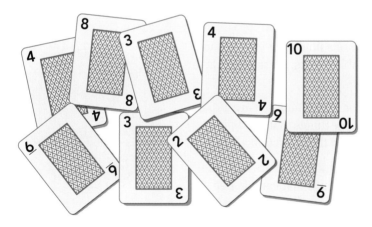

MORE HELP
See 294–296

Since choosing 3 first changes the number of cards that are left to choose from, the two choices are dependent events.

This means the probability of picking 8 if 3 has already been picked.

P(3, then 8) = P(3) · P(8, given 3)

$$\frac{\text{number of 3s}}{\text{number of cards}} \longrightarrow \frac{2}{9} \cdot \frac{1}{8} \longleftarrow \frac{\text{number of 8s left after first pick}}{\text{number of cards left after first pick}}$$

$$= \frac{2}{72} \text{ or } \frac{1}{36}$$

★ The probability that you choose 3, then 8, is $\frac{1}{36}$, about 0.028 or about 2.8%.

330

MORE HELP
See 023–024

Probability of Complementary Events

Either you will get an A on your next test, or you won't. These are two mutually exclusive events. When two mutually exclusive events are the only events that can occur, they are called **complementary events**. If two events are complementary, the sum of their probabilities is 1.

EXAMPLE 1: Suppose you toss two fair dice. Are tossing a sum that is prime and a sum that is composite complementary events?

★ Because each of the possible sums (2–12) is either prime or composite, these two events are complementary.

EXAMPLE 2: Suppose you toss two fair dice. Are tossing a sum of 7 and a sum of 9 complementary?

★ Because there are other possible events (sums of 2, 3, 4, 5, 6, 8, 10, 11, 12), the two events are *not* complementary.

331

Odds

Odds and probability are two different ways of expressing the same thing, **likelihood**.

The **probability** of spinning red is $\frac{1}{4}$ because, out of four possible events, there is one favorable event.

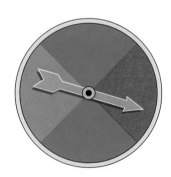

The **odds** in favor of spinning red are 1 to 3 because, of the four things that can happen, one is favorable and three are unfavorable.

The odds against spinning red are 3 to 1 because, of the four things that can happen, three are unfavorable and one is favorable.

MORE HELP
See 041

The odds in favor of an event and the odds against an event are inverses of each other: $\frac{1}{3}$ is the inverse of $\frac{3}{1}$.

When an event has a probability of $\frac{1}{2}$, it has odds of 1 to 1. This is because, of two things that can happen, one is favorable and one is unfavorable. Odds of 1 to 1 are called **even odds** because either event is equally likely.

Odds of 1 to 1 are also called 50-50 because the probability of each possible outcome is 50%.

Computing Odds

You can use these formulas to compute odds.

$$\text{Odds(in favor of an event)} = \frac{\text{probability of favorable outcomes}}{\text{probability of unfavorable outcomes}}$$

$$\text{Odds(against an event)} = \frac{\text{probability of unfavorable outcomes}}{\text{probability of favorable outcomes}}$$

EXAMPLE 1: Suppose the claim in the ad is true. Find the odds in favor of eating your next meal at Hamburger Hank's restaurant.

HAMBURGER HANK'S

If you're like most Americans, you eat one out of every eight meals with us!

Odds(of eating at Hanks)

$$= \frac{\text{probability of favorable outcomes}}{\text{probability of unfavorable outcomes}}$$

$$= \frac{\frac{1}{8}}{\frac{7}{8}} \text{ or } \frac{1}{7}$$

For each eight meals, there is one meal at Hank's. So, there are seven meals that are not at Hank's.

★ The odds in favor of eating at Hank's are $\frac{1}{7}$, 1:7, or 1 to 7.

EXAMPLE 2: A random survey shows that four out of 10 voters will vote for Newman for Senator. Find the odds *against* a voter voting for Newman.

$$\text{Odds(against Newman)} = \frac{\text{probability of unfavorable outcomes}}{\text{probability of favorable outcomes}}$$

$$= \frac{\frac{6}{10}}{\frac{4}{10}}$$

$$= \frac{6}{4} \text{ or } \frac{3}{2}$$

Based on the survey, for each 10 people, there are six who will not vote for Newman and four who will vote for Newman.

★ The odds against a voter voting for Newman are $\frac{3}{2}$, 3:2, or 3 to 2.

Organizing and Summarizing Data with Statistics

You're moving! There are lots of towns to live in near the city where your parents' new jobs are. To help your parents choose a town, you are looking for information about

- the cost of homes in each town,

- the performance of high school students on standardized tests.

Of course, you don't want to look at the sale price of every home, or the test score of every high school student. What you are interested in are **statistics** that summarize each set of data. For example, you may find

- the **median** home price, which is the price that falls exactly in the middle of all of the home prices;

- the **range** of recent home sale prices, which is the difference between the most expensive and least expensive prices;

- the **mean** standardized test scores for high school students;

- the **mode**, or most common, home price.

Statistics such as median, range, mean, and mode summarize data by telling you what's typical in a set of data, how much variation there is in the data, and where one piece of data fits in with the whole set of data.

> The word **average** is not very precise, mathematically speaking, because it can refer to mean, median, or mode.

Range

Sometimes it's useful to know how much numbers in a set of data vary. One way to summarize variation is to find the **range**, the difference between the **maximum** (highest) value and the **minimum** (lowest) value.

EXAMPLE: Find the range for San Francisco's mean monthly temperatures. Why might some people like San Francisco's climate?

Jan.	Feb.	Mar.	Apr.	May	June	July	Aug.	Sept.	Oct.	Nov.	Dec.
51°	54°	55°	56°	56°	58°	59°	60°	62°	62°	57°	52°

Source: http://worldclimate.com

Range = maximum value − minimum value
$$= 62° − 51°$$
$$= 11°$$

★ The range is 11°. That's a pretty narrow range, especially when you compare it to a place like Bismarck, North Dakota, where the mean monthly temperatures have a range of over 60°. Maybe people like San Francisco's weather because it is mild and doesn't vary very much.

Measures of Central Tendency

An **average** is a **measure of central tendency,** a number that summarizes a set of data by giving some sense of the typical (often the middle) value. Measures of central tendency include the **mean**, **median,** and **mode**.

The average that you choose to use depends on the data and your purpose.

- For sets of data with no unusually high or low numbers, *mean* is a good measure to use.

- For sets of data with some points that are much higher or lower than most of the others, *median* may work well.

- For sets of data with many data points that are the same, *mode* may be the most useful measure.

Mean

What does it mean when we find the *mean*? In statistics, *mean* is a type of average. To find the mean, you add all the numbers in a set and divide by the number of values.

$$\text{Mean} = \frac{\text{sum of the values}}{\text{number of values}}$$

CASE 1 When all the data are close to each other, the mean is close to all the data.

Beautiful Books Sales for 8/5 - 8/9

Mon	Tues	Wed	Thurs	Fri
105	96	90	108	116

EXAMPLE 1: What is the mean number of books sold per day at *Beautiful Books?*

❶ Find the sum of the numbers.	❷ Divide by the number of numbers.
105 + 96 + 90 + 108 + 116 = 515	515 ÷ 5 = 103

★ The book store's mean sales were 103 books per day. This means that if the sales were the same every day, but the weekly total stayed at 515 books, each day's sales would be 103 books.

MORE HELP
See 336

CASE 2 When a piece of data is much bigger or smaller than the rest, it is called an **outlier.** It can move the mean away from the main group of data toward the outlier.

EXAMPLE 2: Suppose on the next day, the book store sells only seven books. What happens to the mean?

❶ Find the sum of the numbers.	❷ Divide by the number of numbers.
515 + 7 = 522	522 ÷ 6 = 87

★ One day with very low sales brought the mean sales per day down by nearly 20 books. It made the mean smaller than any of the other pieces of data, so the mean no longer describes a typical day of sales.

337

Median

The **median** is a type of average. It is the number that falls exactly in the middle when a set of data is arranged in order from least to greatest. If there aren't any big gaps in the middle of the data but there are outliers at either end, the median may be a better number than the mean to describe the data.

CASE 1 When there is an odd number of pieces of data, the median is the middle number.

EXAMPLE 1: On August 15, 1999, the top 15 nonfiction bestsellers had been on the bestseller list these numbers of weeks: 95, 35, 7, 6, 30, 10, 3, 122, 4, 10, 17, 37, 19, 8, 17. What is the median number of weeks on the bestseller list? Why might the median be a better measure of central tendency than the mean for these data?   *Source: The New York Times*

① Arrange the numbers in order from least to greatest.	② Find the middle number.
3, 4, 6, 7, 8, 10, 10, 17, 17, 19, 30, 35, 37, 95, 122	3, 4, 6, 7, 8, 10, 10, **17**, 17, 19, 30, 35, 37, 95, 122

★ The median for this set of data is 17. The mean for this set of data, 28, is greater than 10 of the 15 values. The two outliers, 95 and 122 are not typical of most of the list, and, since they do not affect the median as much as they affect the mean, the median better represents the typical values in the list.

CASE 2 When there is an even number of data points in a set of data, there are two middle numbers. In this case you need to find the mean of the two middle numbers. As with the mean, the median does not need to be one of the data points.

EXAMPLE 2: Ted gets these test scores: 82, 86, 39, 91, 84, 80. What is Ted's median test score?

① Arrange the numbers in order from least to greatest. Find the two middle numbers.	② Find the mean of the two middle numbers.
39, 80, **82**, **84**, 86, 91	(82 + 84) ÷ 2 = 83

> A 39 is not a typical test score for Ted. It's nice that this number doesn't affect the median very much. Even if it were a 75 or 80, the median score would still be 83.

★ The median of Ted's test scores is 83.

Mode

The **mode** is the value that occurs most often in a set of data.

CASE 1 Sometimes there is one value that occurs more often than any other.

EXAMPLE 1: For the week of May 3 to 9, 1999, *Variety* listed the maximum weekend ticket prices for 35 Broadway shows. What is the mode? Why is the mode a good measure of central tendency for these data?

MORE ▶

Maximum Weekend Ticket Price	Number of Shows
$55	2
$60	6
$65	4
$67.50	1
$75	15
$80	4
$85	2
$100	1

★ The maximum weekend price that occurs most often is $75, so $75 is the mode for this set of data. It is a good measure of central tendency in this situation because it is a very typical maximum price; nearly half of the shows had a maximum price of $75.

Source: Variety

CASE 2 Sometimes there is more than one mode.

EXAMPLE 2: The chart shows Janine's bowling scores for one season. What is the mode? Why is the mode a good measure of central tendency for this set of data?

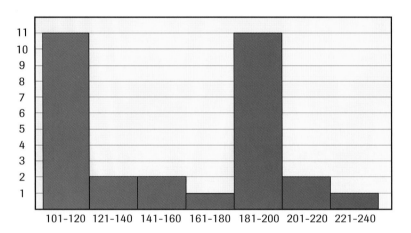

★ Janine's scores are **bimodal** (two modes) because she has 11 scores from 101 to 120 and 11 scores from 181 to 200. The data suggest that Janine has *on games* and *off games*, and infrequently has an *average game* that falls in the middle of the scores. The two modes give a good idea of how Janine bowls.

CASE 3 Sometimes there is no value that occurs more often than the others. In this case, there is no mode and it might be a good idea to use the mean or median to describe the set of data.

Displaying Data in Tables and Graphs

Organizing and displaying data clearly can help you understand data or prove a point. Tables and graphs can help you identify trends, make predictions, and draw conclusions. Knowing how tables and graphs are made can keep you from being fooled by deceptive displays.

When you show data, it's important to think about which type of display best suits your data and your purpose. If you want to show your family's budget, you might use a circle graph. If you want to compare the on-time percentages of various airlines, you might choose a bar graph. To compare the trends in air travel and rail travel, you might try a double-line graph.

Data in Tables

Tables don't give you a picture of data as graphs do, but they help you organize data to make it easy to find the numbers you need.

EXAMPLE: Organize the data in these news clippings into a useful table.

Lake Country Gazette

NEWS FLASH!

Lake Superior is the largest lake in North America!

Its area of 31,700 square miles is almost three times that of Great Slave Lake, whose area is a mere 11,031 square miles.

The lengths of the two lakes are not that different: Superior is 350 miles long and Great Slave is 298 miles long. Great Slave does have the edge in depth, though. It is 2015 feet deep at its deepest point, a full 685 feet deeper than Superior.

More Trivia! The second- and third-largest North American lakes are the shallowest of the top five lakes!

Lake Huron is North America's second-largest lake. It has a surface area of 23,000 square miles. It is 206 miles long, but only 750 feet deep! Lake Michigan is the second longest lake at 307 miles, but it has a smaller surface area than Lake Huron, a mere 22,300 square miles. Its depth is 923 feet.

By contrast, Great Bear Lake, 192 miles long, has about half the area of Huron: 12,096 square miles, but it is about twice as deep: 1463 feet at its deepest point.

MORE ▶

The articles talk about the five largest North American Lakes, so each lake should have its own row of data. As you read the two articles, you'll find categories that will provide your column headings.

★

Name	Area (in mi^2)	Length (in mi)	Maximum Depth (in ft)
Superior	31,700	350	1330
Huron	23,000	206	750
Michigan	22,300	307	923
Great Bear	12,096	192	1463
Great Slave	11,031	298	2015

Source: Geological Survey, U.S. Department of Interior

341

Frequency Tables

A **frequency table** shows how often an item, a number, or a range of numbers occurs.

CASE 1 A frequency table can show how often a particular item occurs.

A class participates in a survey in which they name their main source of news—TV, radio, Internet, newspapers, or magazines.

TV, TV, newspaper, Internet, Internet, TV, magazines, Internet, Internet, TV, TV, radio, TV, newspaper, newspaper, Internet, radio, TV, magazines, TV, magazines, newspaper

To make a frequency table from the raw data, list each item in the data. Then count and record the number of times each item occurs. You may wish to use a tally to help you count.

Source	Tally	Frequency
TV	⦀⦀ |||	8
Radio	||	2
Internet	⦀⦀	5
Newspaper	||||	4
Magazines	|||	3

CASE 2 Another way to make a frequency table is to group the data into intervals. This is called a **grouped frequency table**.

Nolan Ryan holds the record for most career strikeouts by a major league pitcher. Ryan's season strikeout totals were: 6, 133, 92, 125, 137, 329, 383, 367, 186, 327, 341, 260, 223, 200, 140, 245, 183, 197, 209, 194, 270, 228, 301, 232, 203, 157, 46. *Source://www.cnnsi.com/baseball/mlb/players/Nolan.Ryan.001*

❶ Choose a scale that includes all the data (in this case, 6-383).

❷ Divide that range into equal intervals that are easy to picture (0-49, 50-99, 100-149, etc.).

❸ Count the number of data points in each interval. (A tally can help you count.)

Nolan Ryan's Strikeouts		
Interval	**Tally**	**Frequency**
0–49	||	2
50–99	|	1
100–149	||||	4
150–199	⌇⌇⌇	5
200–249	⌇⌇⌇ ||	7
250–299	||	2
300–349	||||	4
350–399	||	2

This frequency table shows that Nolan Ryan's strikeouts were typically between 150 and 250 per season.

Making Graphs on a Coordinate Grid

To create a bar graph, a line graph, or a histogram, you start with a grid. Then, you decide what each axis in the grid stands for. After you choose labels and a scale for the numbers on each axis, you plot data points.

342

MORE HELP
See 219

Labeling the Axes

The **axes** on a graph are the **reference lines**—they tell you what each line in the grid means. The axes are usually a horizontal line and a vertical line that cross where one or both axes is zero. In graphs with no negative numbers, the axes are usually the bottom and left-hand borders of the graph.

MATH ALERT Choose the Proper Axis for Dependent and Independent Variables

To choose axes for line graphs, you have to think about how your data are related. In line graphs, the **dependent variable** is usually shown on the y-axis. The **independent variable** is usually shown on the x-axis. An increase in the dependent variable will be represented by a line that goes up as you read from left to right.

EXAMPLE: Suppose you want to show the change in median family income in the United States from 1975 to 1995. Which of the following two graphs would you use? Why? *Source: U.S. Bureau of Census*

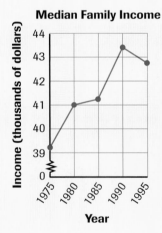

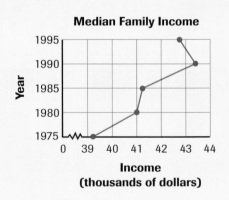

★ In this set of data, median income *depends* on the year. The year is the *independent variable* and should be on the x-axis; median income is the *dependent variable* and should be on the y-axis. You would use the graph on the left.

What makes the graph on the left a better graph than the graph on the right? Look at the points for 1990 and 1995. Since we are used to reading from left to right, the line in the graph at the right appears to go up, even though income goes down. This makes the graph deceptive.

Choosing the Scales

When you make a graph, the first thing you do is choose the axes. Next, you choose the **scale**—the numbers running along a side of the graph. The difference between numbers from one grid line to another is the **interval**. The interval will depend on the lowest and highest values in your data.

CASE 1 When you can, you should choose scales with the numbers starting at zero and increasing by ones or other convenient equal intervals.

EXAMPLE: By the early 1980s, California condors were close to extinction. A program was begun to breed condors in captivity, and later reintroduce them into the wild. The chart shows the number of California condors that were in the wild in given years. Choose scales for a graph of the data.

Wild California Condor Population						
Year	1991	1992	1993	1994	1995	1996
Number	0	7	9	3	13	28

Source: Los Angeles Zoo

Since the year is the independent variable, list years across the horizontal axis. The number of condors ranges from 0 to 28.

★ To cover 0 to 28, there are many options for intervals. Here are a few:

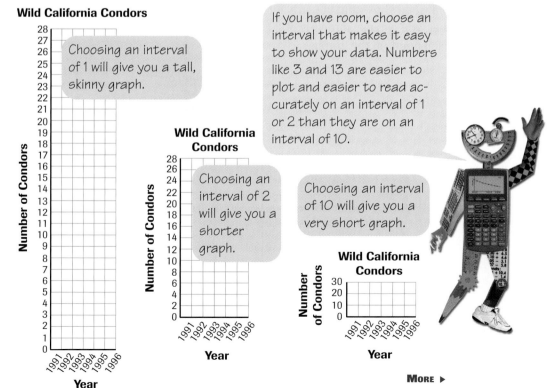

Wild California Condors

Choosing an interval of 1 will give you a tall, skinny graph.

If you have room, choose an interval that makes it easy to show your data. Numbers like 3 and 13 are easier to plot and easier to read accurately on an interval of 1 or 2 than they are on an interval of 10.

Wild California Condors

Choosing an interval of 2 will give you a shorter graph.

Choosing an interval of 10 will give you a very short graph.

Wild California Condors

MORE ▶

CASE 2 Sometimes you don't have enough room to make your scale start at 0 and still have small intervals that are useful.

EXAMPLE 2: Show the scale that you would use to make a line graph of highway taxes that were spent on bike paths and walkways from 1994 to 1997.

Federal Spending on Walking and Biking				
Year	1994	1995	1996	1997
Approximate Spending (in millions of dollars)	110	180	200	240

Source: National Highway and Traffic Administration

After you choose your axes (x–axis for the year and y–axis for the amounts), choose a scale that lets you plot numbers from 110 through 240—the lowest and highest spending totals—in millions of dollars.

MORE HELP
See 139

A scale in which you count by ones from 0 through 240 is impractical. Counting by fives would require 49 lines, and counting by tens would require 24 lines to show 240. Even intervals of 20 might not work. You might not have enough space for 12 lines. What should you do?

★ Since the minimum value is 110, you can use a jagged line to break the scale and show that you are not plotting values between 0 and 110. After that, you can use intervals of 20. You can easily estimate where to plot each point on the graph.

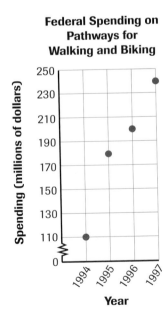

Federal Spending on Pathways for Walking and Biking

MATH ALERT **Broken Scales Can Exaggerate Changes**

Be careful when you make or read a graph with a broken scale. Use a jagged line to show the break in the graph. If a reader doesn't realize a scale is broken, he or she may think that the data show more dramatic changes than they actually do. Look at these two graphs that show changes in median family income between 1975 and 1995. When you don't break the scale, it doesn't look like median family income is changing as much!

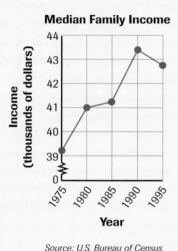

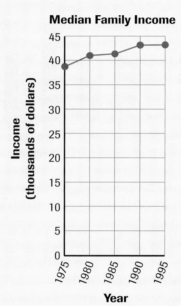

Source: U.S. Bureau of Census

Graphs that Compare

Some graphs make it easy to see comparisons. They may show

- the same kind of data at different times or places (like the population of one city in different years);

- different kinds of data at the same time or place (like the population of different cities at the same point in time);

- the different kinds of data that make up 100% of one group of data (like the different categories of spending in a city's budget).

348

Single-Bar Graphs

On a **bar graph**, solid bars represent quantities. The longer the bar, the greater the quantity.

EXAMPLE: Does this bar graph help you explain why more radio stations have a country format than have a rock format?

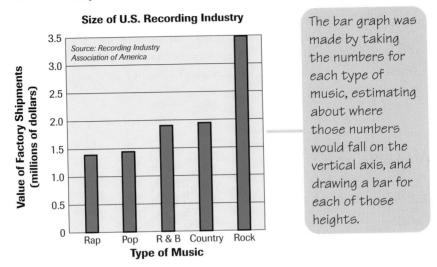

Size of U.S. Recording Industry

Source: Recording Industry Association of America

Value of Factory Shipments (millions of dollars)

Type of Music: Rap, Pop, R & B, Country, Rock

> The bar graph was made by taking the numbers for each type of music, estimating about where those numbers would fall on the vertical axis, and drawing a bar for each of those heights.

The tallest bar, by far, is for rock music, so you would expect that more radio listeners would want to listen to rock music than to country music.

★ The bar graph does not provide an explanation for why more radio stations have a country format than have a rock format.

349

Double-Bar Graphs

Sometimes, placing bars side-by-side in pairs makes it easier to display the kinds of comparisons you want to show. This kind of graph is called a **double-bar** graph.

EXAMPLE: The table and graph show where teenagers get their spending money. What comparisons can you make between the two age ranges?

Sources of Spending Money for Teenagers		
Source	Ages 12-14	Ages 15-17
From parents	88%	79%
Odd jobs	74%	70%
Regular allowance	54%	29%
Full or part-time job	13%	33%

Source: TeenEXCEL survey for Merrill Lynch

MORE HELP
See 342–344

Spending Money for Teenagers

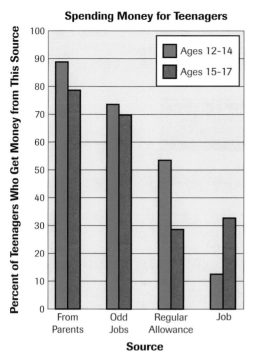

★ The most common source for both age groups is their parents. The percent of teenagers who have jobs is much greater for older than for younger teenagers. The percent of teenagers who get regular allowances is much greater for younger than for older teenagers.

Pictographs

350

A **pictograph** uses pictures or symbols to compare data.

Country	Number of Tourist Arrivals in 1997 (rounded to the nearest million)
France	67,000,000
United States	48,000,000
Spain	43,000,000
Italy	34,000,000

Source: World Tourism Organization

❶ Title your graph and list the items in your data that are being measured in some way.

❷ Choose a symbol for your data and draw a key to show what each symbol represents. In this graph, one suitcase stands for 10,000,000 tourists arrivals. Draw the appropriate number of symbols next to each item.

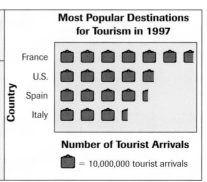

Most Popular Destinations for Tourism in 1997

Number of Tourist Arrivals

= 10,000,000 tourist arrivals

Circle Graphs

A **circle graph** shows how a whole is broken into parts. It makes it easier
to see how the size of each part compares to the whole.

MORE HELP
See 254,
256–257

EXAMPLE: Make a circle graph of the data.

Farmland Usage in the United States 1997	
Use	% of U.S. Farmland
Cropland	46
Conservation Land	3
Woodland	3
Pasture	43
Other	5

Source: U.S. Department of Agriculture

The whole circle will represent the total amount of farmland. Each sector
of the circle will represent the part belonging to a category of farmland.

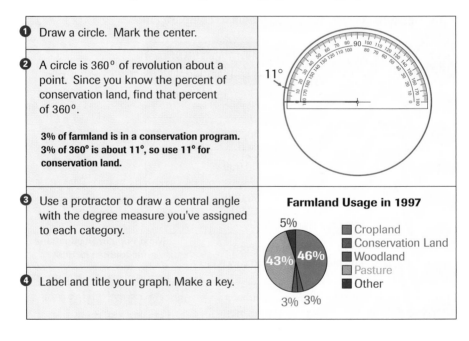

❶ Draw a circle. Mark the center.

❷ A circle is 360° of revolution about a
point. Since you know the percent of
conservation land, find that percent
of 360°.

11°

**3% of farmland is in a conservation program.
3% of 360° is about 11°, so use 11° for
conservation land.**

❸ Use a protractor to draw a central angle
with the degree measure you've assigned
to each category.

❹ Label and title your graph. Make a key.

Farmland Usage in 1997

5%

43%   46%

3%   3%

■ Cropland
■ Conservation Land
■ Woodland
□ Pasture
■ Other

Graphs that Show Change Over Time

Suppose you want to show how quantities change over time. **Line graphs** provide a good way of showing how one or more quantities change over a particular period of time. A line graph is *not* the graph of a line, it's a series of plotted points connected by line segments.

MORE HELP
See 342

Single-Line Graphs

A line graph usually has a measure of time on the horizontal axis. When you look at the line on the graph, you can tell whether a quantity has increased, decreased, or stayed the same over time. All you have to do is look at whether the line goes up or down as you read from left to right.

MORE HELP
See 343–345

EXAMPLE: Look at the table and its related line graph. During which one-year interval did the average salary increase the most? During which one-year interval did the average salary decrease?

To find the one-year interval in which the average salary of NFL quarterbacks increased the most, find the steepest upward segment. This segment is between 1992 and 1993. The average salary increased the most from 1992 to 1993.

To find the one-year interval in which the average salary of NFL quarterbacks decreased, find the segment that goes downward. This segment is between 1993 and 1994, so, the average salary decreased from 1993 to 1994.

Average Salary for NFL Quarterbacks	
Year	Average Salary
1992	$911,000
1993	1,523,000
1994	1,138,000
1995	1,307,000
1996	1,336,000

Source: NFL Players Association

Average Salary for NFL Quarterbacks

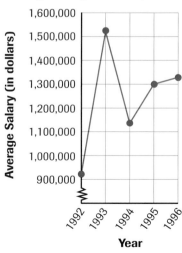

Multiple-Line Graphs

Suppose you want to compare two or more quantities that are changing over time. You can use a multiple-line graph, in which each line shows one set of data.

MORE HELP
See 342–345, 367

The table shows the percent of people who bought jazz recordings and gospel recordings in three recent years. The graph shows information from the table.

Jazz Recordings Versus Gospel Recordings		
Year	% of People Who Bought Jazz Recordings	% of People Who Bought Gospel Recordings
1990	4.8	2.5
1995	3.0	3.0
1997	2.8	4.5

Source: Recording Industry Association of America

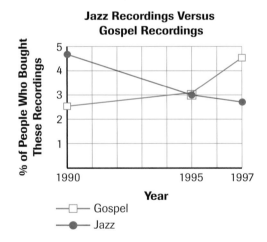

EXAMPLE: What trend does the graph show?

★ The line for gospel recordings is moving up. You can say the percent of people who buy gospel recordings is increasing. The line for jazz recordings is moving down so the percent of people who buy jazz recordings is decreasing. If both trends continue, the percent of people who buy gospel recordings will exceed by an ever greater amount the percent of people who buy jazz recordings.

Graphs that Show How Data Are Clustered _____

Some graphs are designed to show how data points group or cluster together. You can use these graphs to show

- whether some events are related to other events (such as test scores and study time), or

- whether the data are mostly grouped together or are spread out (such as whether there are few 60s and 90s on a test compared to the scores in the 70s and 80s).

Most graphs that show how data clusters are called **plots**. That's because on most of these graphs, all you do is plot individual data points. You don't connect the points.

Line Plots

Suppose you want to show how data points are spread out. One way to do this is to make a **line plot**. When data are shown on a line plot, it's easy to see the mode, the range and any unusually high or low data points. These very high or low points are called **outliers.**

MORE HELP
See 336

EXAMPLE: In 1999, the roster for the WNBA's Phoenix Mercury listed 12 players. Here are their heights, in inches: 77, 74, 68, 73, 75, 73, 73, 64, 69, 80, 67, 70. Show the data on a line plot. Then identify the mode, the range, and any outliers. *Source: http://www.wnba.com*

❶ Title your plot.	❷ Draw a horizontal line segment on grid paper.	❸ Make a scale of numbers. The numbers should include the greatest value and the least value in the set of data.	❹ For each piece of data, draw an X above the corresponding number.

Heights on Phoenix Mercury (in inches)

★ The mode for the data is 73 inches because 73 appears most frequently in the line plot. Since the maximum value is 80 and the minimum value is 64, the range is 80 − 64, or 16 inches. Both 64 and 80 are separated from the rest of the data, but not significantly. There are no outliers.

Box-and-Whisker Plots

Sometimes you want to show an overall picture of how data are grouped, but do not want to show each item. In this situation, a **box-and-whisker plot** may be a good choice. A box-and-whisker plot separates the data into quarters. It also shows the middle 50% of the data, as well as the maximum and minimum values and the median.

The 27 students in a Statistics Class kept a record of the number of hours they spent on homework in one week. Here are their results: 9.5, 14, 7, 7.5, 12, 8.5, 11.5, 10, 7, 16, 10, 11, 9 , 11.5, 8, 14, 10.5, 12.5, 7, 13, 13.5, 10, 6.5, 7, 11, 9 and 6.

To make a box-and-whisker plot for the data follow these steps.

MORE HELP
See 337

❶ Write the data in order from least to greatest. **6, 6.5, 7, 7, 7, 7, 7.5, 8, 8.5, 9, 9, 9.5, 10, 10, 10, 10.5, 11, 11, 11.5, 11.5, 12, 12.5, 13, 13.5, 14, 14, 16**	❷ Draw a number line that can show the data in equal intervals. Mark the median, 10. Mark the medians of the upper half (the **upper quartile**), 12, and the lower half (the **lower quartile**), 7.5. Mark the **upper extreme** (the greatest number), 16, and the **lower extreme** (the lowest number), 6.	❸ Draw a box between the lower quartile and the upper quartile. Split the box by drawing a vertical line through the median. Draw two whiskers from the quartiles to the extremes.

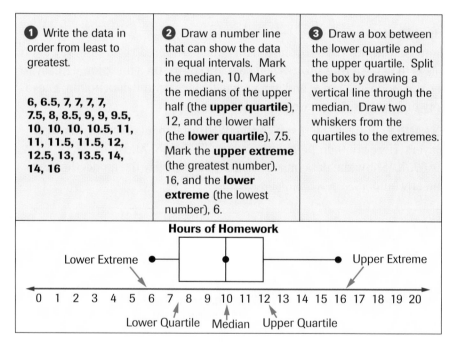

Hours of Homework

Notice that the quarters are not the same length, but each contains one fourth of the data points. The box contains the middle 50% of the data points. If any value is greater than the upper quartile or less than the lower quartile by 50% or more of the range of points in the box, it is an **outlier**.

Histograms

Suppose you want to show how often data fall into different intervals. You could make a histogram. A **histogram** is just like a bar graph, except that each bar represents an interval, and there are no spaces between the bars.

For the week of May 6–May 12, 1999, a particular television network got the following ratings for 44 half-hour nighttime shows: 6.6, 7.2, 7.8, 8.2, 7.6, 8.0, 6.0, 6.7, 6.1, 6.1, 6.2, 8.6, 9.1, 6.1, 6.1, 6.9, 6.5, 7.4, 8.1, 8.9, 9.4, 10.5, 10.9, 12.4, 13.2, 14.0, 14.0, 14.0, 8.3, 8.7, 10.4, 9.6, 8.2, 8.6, 8.9, 9.8, 9.9, 10.9, 10.4, 7.3, 8.9, 8.7, 9.8, 11.0, 11.3 *Source: Nielsen Media Research*

To make a histogram for the data, follow these steps.

❶ Choose a range that contains all the data and divide it into equal intervals.	For these data, we used intervals of 2.0 from 6 to 16.
❷ Make a grouped frequency table. **More ratings fall into the 8.0-9.9 interval than any other interval. The interval with the next greatest amount is 6.0-7.9. This means that most of the shows got ratings of less than ten.**	**Ratings for Nighttime Time Slots** <table><tr><th>Rating</th><th>Frequency</th></tr><tr><td>6.0-7.9</td><td>15</td></tr><tr><td>8.0-9.9</td><td>18</td></tr><tr><td>10.0-11.9</td><td>7</td></tr><tr><td>12.0-13.9</td><td>2</td></tr><tr><td>14.0-15.9</td><td>3</td></tr></table>
❸ Use the table to make a histogram.	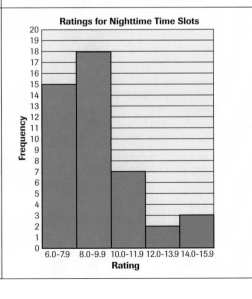

Stem-and-Leaf Plots

Stem-and-leaf plots are a convenient way of displaying every piece of data in a large set of data. When you look at a stem-and-leaf plot, it's easy to see the greatest, least, and median values in a set of data. You can also see how many pieces of data fall into various intervals.

> **DID YOU KNOW** that each year *Forbes*
> magazine lists the earnings of the top 40 entertainers.
> In the 1998 list, the top two earners were Jerry Seinfeld
> and Larry David, with $225,000,000 and $200,000,000.
> Number 40 was Julia Roberts, with $28,000,000.

Here are the top 40 earnings, in millions of dollars, from the Forbes 1998 Top 40 Entertainers list: 225, 200, 175, 125, 115, 77, 65, 58, 57, 56.5, 56, 55.5, 55, 54, 53.5, 53, 53, 52, 49.5, 49, 48, 47.5, 47, 45.5, 45, 44, 42, 41, 40.5, 40, 40, 38.5, 38, 37, 35, 34, 32.5, 32, 31, 28.   *Source: http://www.forbes.com*

To make a stem-and-leaf plot, follow these steps.

	Earnings of the Top 40 Entertainers (in millions of dollars)	
❶ Title your plot.		
❷ If the data are not already written in order, do so.	Stems	Leaves
	22	5
	21	
❸ Choose stem values that will include the extreme values. For this graph, it makes sense to use ten millions: 2, 3, 4, …, 22.	20	0
	19	
	18	
	17	5
	16	
❹ Write the stems vertically from least to greatest. Draw a vertical line to the right of the values.	15	
	14	
	13	
	12	5
	11	5
❺ Separate each number into **stems** (ten millions) and **leaves** (millions). Write each leaf to the right of its stem in order from least to greatest.	10	
	9	
	8	
	7	7
	6	5
	5	2 3 3 3.5 4 5 5.5 6 6.5 7 8
❻ Write a key that explains how to read the stems and leaves.	4	0 0 0.5 1 2 4 5 5.5 7 7.5 8 9 9.5
	3	1 2 2.5 4 5 7 8 8.5
	2	8

Key: 2 | 8 means 28,000,000
        11 | 5 means 115,000,000

You can see from the plot:

- Most of the top earners earned between $30,000,000 and $60,000,000.

- Only five entertainers earned more than $100,000,000.

> Some stem-and-leaf plots are made without ordering the numbers from least to greatest. These are useful, but it's harder to see some patterns. The nicest thing about stem-and-leaf plots is that all your data values are shown.

Double Stem-and-Leaf Plots

360

You can use a **double stem-and-leaf** plot to compare two sets of data.

EXAMPLE: The double stem-and-leaf plot below compares average monthly rainfall in Miami and Chicago. What comparisons can you make with the plot?

In a double-stem-and-leaf plot, the stem is in the middle. The leaves are on the sides. Read from the middle to the left for Chicago. Read from the middle to the right for Miami. In this plot, the stem shows the ones and the leaves show the tenths.

Average Monthly Rainfall in Chicago and Miami (in inches)

Chicago Leaves	Stem	Miami Leaves
9 6	1	9
9 7 6 4	2	0 1 5
7 6 6 6 0	3	1 2
0	4	
	5	9
	6	0
	7	0 8
	8	5
	9	0

Key: |1|9 represents 1.9 inches
9|2| represents 2.9 inches

Source: http://www.worldclimate.com

★ Chicago has more months with less than four inches of rainfall. In fact the average rainfall for every month is four inches or less. Miami has more variation with monthly rainfall averages from 1.9 to 9 inches.

Scatter Plots

Sometimes you want to see how closely two sets of data are related. One way to do this is to make a **scatter plot** (also called a **scattergram**). To make a scatter plot, you take corresponding values from two sets of data and plot them as ordered pairs. The closer they come to forming a straight line, the more closely related are the two sets of data.

MORE HELP
See 365, 367

EXAMPLE: Make a scatter plot for the table. Then describe the relationship between age and participation in sports.

Adult American Participation in Sports							
Age Group	18-24	25-34	35-44	45-54	55-64	65-74	75 and over
Percent Who Play Sports	67%	63%	52%	40%	19%	23%	13%

Source: U.S. National Endowment for the Arts, 1997 Survey of Public Participation in the Arts Research Division Note #70, July 1998

MORE HELP
See 365

❶ Title your plot.	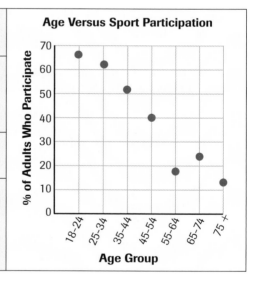
❷ Decide which set of values you will plot on each axis and label the sides.	
❸ Choose a scale for each axis.	
❹ Plot a point for each column in your table. For example, in the table above, plot (18-24, 67%), (25-34, 63%) and so on.	

A scatter plot will help you describe the relationships.

★ The points on the scatter plot are somewhat close to forming a straight line, so there is a correlation between age and participation in sports. As age increases, participation in sports generally decreases.

> When two quantities increase or decrease together, there is a positive correlation. When one quantity increases as another decreases, there is a negative correlation. This graph shows a negative correlation.

Line of Best Fit

If the points on a scatter plot suggest a straight line, you can draw a **line of best fit**, which is also known as a **trend line**. This line is the straight line that comes closest to connecting the points on a scatter plot. You can use this line to identify trends in data and to make predictions.

You can use formulas or graphing calculators to find the exact line of best fit. Or, as in this case, you can just use your eye to approximate it. The dashed line is the line of best fit. It rises about $1700 every five years. You could say that costs are rising about $1700 every 5 years, or about $340 per year.

MORE HELP
See 367

Average Undergraduate Tuition, Room, and Board

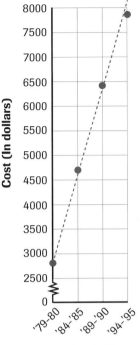

Cost (In dollars)

Academic Year

Venn Diagram

A **Venn diagram** shows relationships among sets of data or objects. It usually consists of intersecting circles. Each circle is named for the data in it. Data that belong in more than one circle go where the interiors of the circles overlap.

EXAMPLE: Make a Venn diagram to show the factors of 30, 36, and 54.

❶ Choose a title for your graph.

❷ Decide on how many groups of data you have and whether they overlap, then draw a circle for each. Since there are three sets of factors and there are overlaps, use three intersecting circles.

❸ Place each piece of data in the proper circle. If a piece fits in more than one circle, be sure to put it where those circles overlap.

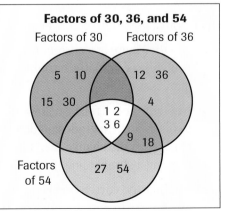

Factors of 30, 36, and 54

Factors of 30   Factors of 36

5   10   12   36

15   30   4

1 2
3 6

9   18

Factors
of 54   27   54

Interpreting Data

Do vegetarians live longer? How will changing the price of a bottle of juice affect its sales? Is global warming really happening?

To answer questions like these, you need to do more than make tables and graphs, and compute averages and ranges. To interpret your data, you need to decide what conclusions you can make and how reliable these conclusions are. Can you

- look for any relationships that exist among sets of data?

- try to find unknown data points between values you already know?

- identify trends, and use them to predict future data?

- predict what might happen if one condition or value is changed?

Correlations

Suppose you want to figure out whether watching TV affects students' grades. You might look for a relationship (**correlation**) between the number of hours of TV watched per week and the average grade received by students watching that amount of TV.

When you analyze the data, you are trying to decide

- whether there is a correlation between the two sets of data (if not, you will see no pattern to the change in grades as TV watching increases);

- whether the correlation is weak or strong (how regular is the pattern to the change in grades; in other words, when you plot the data, how close does the change in grades as TV watching increases come to forming a straight line?); and

- whether the correlation is positive (increases in TV watching are matched with better grades) or negative (increases in TV watching are matched with poorer grades).

An easy way to decide whether there's a correlation is to plot the data in a scatter plot. The closer the points come to forming a straight, slanted line, the stronger the correlation is. However, if the line is horizontal or vertical, that means that as one variable changes, the other variable doesn't. In this kind of situation, it's difficult to see whether there's a correlation.

MORE HELP
See 361

CASE 1 If you plotted amusement park attendance against age for adults aged 20-60 you would probably see a **somewhat negative correlation** and the plot might look like this:

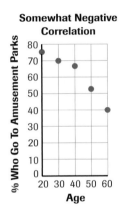

CASE 2 If you were to plot the health care spending for adults aged 20-60 against age you would probably find a **somewhat positive correlation** and the plot might look like this:

Somewhat Positive Correlation

CASE 3 If you plotted average height of girls 8-16 against age, you would see a **strong positive correlation** and the plot might look like this:

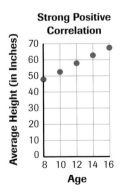

Source: U.S. Agriculture Department

CASE 4 If you were to plot students' average grades against their heights, you would probably see **no correlation** and the plot might look like this:

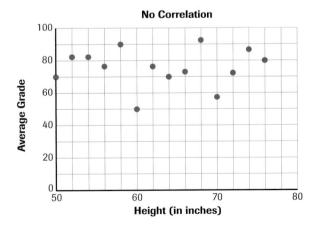

MATH ALERT   Don't Confuse Correlation with Cause and Effect

When you find correlations, be careful not to draw conclusions about cause and effect. A strong correlation indicates that two sets of data are related. It does not tell you *why* the two sets of data are related, or if changes in one set of data are causing changes in the other set of data. For example, there is a somewhat positive correlation between vocabulary and shoe size. But this doesn't mean that a larger shoe size causes a larger vocabulary or even the other way around. In fact, there's a hidden third variable at work in this case, age. As you get older, both your vocabulary and your shoe size increase.

Trends

Suppose you want to know whether sales of different kinds of footwear are increasing, decreasing, or staying the same. This is called identifying **trends**.

EXAMPLE: What trends does the graph show?

To determine the trends, look at the change in the line as you read from left to right.

- The line for walking shoes rises. So, the sales of walking shoes are increasing.

- The line for tennis shoes is nearly horizontal, so the sales of tennis shoes are staying about the same.

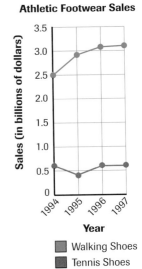

Athletic Footwear Sales

■ Walking Shoes
■ Tennis Shoes

Source: National Sporting Goods Association

Extrapolation

Suppose you have a graph that shows a trend. You may be able to make predictions by extending the graph. This is called **extrapolation.**

MORE HELP
See 361-362

EXAMPLE: Use the data to predict the percent of married women, with children under six years old, in the labor force for the year 2000.

Year	Percent
1960	18.6
1970	30.3
1980	45.1
1995	63.5

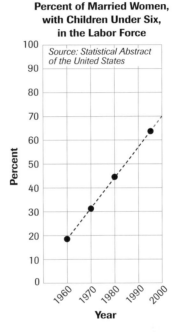

Percent of Married Women, with Children Under Six, in the Labor Force

Source: Statistical Abstract of the United States

★ The points are close to a line that rises at a rate of about 13 percentage points every ten years, or 6.5 percentage points every five years. In 1995, the trend line is at about 63.5%, so, you can predict a figure of about 70% for 2000. Of course, there is a limit to extrapolation—you know there will never be more than 100% of married women, with children under six, in the labor force!

MATH ALERT Use Common Sense When Extrapolating

When you extrapolate to make a prediction, think about whether the past trend is likely to continue.

EXAMPLE: The famous author Juan Yunque autographs copies of his novel. His publicist records the number of copies signed each minute. The graph of the data shows that the points are close to a line where Mr. Yunque autographs six books per minute. Can the publicist predict how long it would take Mr. Yunque to autograph 1000 books? She could use the relation,
Total autographs = number of minutes · 6.

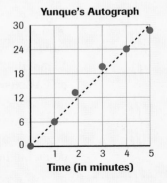

Yunque's Autograph

The data shown on the graph cover only 30 books, but 1000 books is quite a different story. The publicist can't be sure that Mr. Yunque can keep up the pace.

370

Interpolation

Sometimes you can find an unknown value between data points you already know. This is called **interpolation**.

MORE HELP
See 361–362

EXAMPLE: Use the data to estimate the percent of married women, with children under six years old, who were in the labor force in 1990.

Year	Percent
1960	18.6
1970	30.3
1980	45.1
1995	63.5

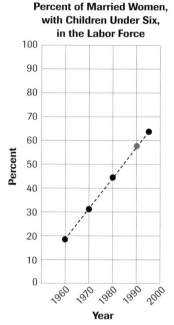

Percent of Married Women, with Children Under Six, in the Labor Force

★ The points are close to a line that rises at a rate of 13 percentage points every ten years. By adding 13% to the 1980 location of the trend line, you get about 58% for 1990.

Source: Statistical Abstract of the United States

371

MATH ALERT   Make Sure Your Graph Has Meaning Between the Data Points

When you extrapolate or interpolate from a graph, be careful. Make sure that your graph has meaning between the data points.

EXAMPLE: Based on the graph, how many homes would the agent sell in 13 months?

★ Based on the data, the real estate agent would sell 6.5 houses in 13 months. But since you can't sell half a house, this data point has no meaning. Based on the existing sales pattern, the real estate agent might sell a seventh house by this point, but he's just as likely not to.

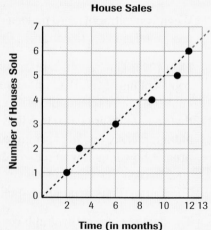

House Sales

Normal Distributions

Suppose you spin this spinner 100 times. You'd expect to spin red close to 50 times. Only three red spins out of 100 would seem a lot stranger than 35 red spins out of 100. The histogram shows the result of such an experiment. There were 100 trials with 100 spins in each trial. In situations like this, as you increase the number of trials, the graph of the frequencies approaches a bell-shaped curve. This type of distribution is called a **normal distribution.**

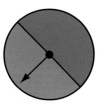

MORE HELP
See 274, 358

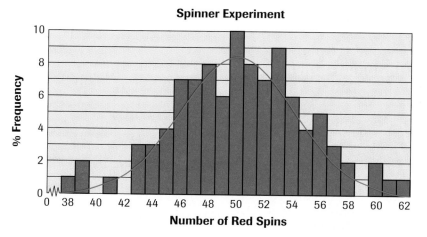

Spinner Experiment

The graph demonstrates a few characteristics of a normal distribution.

- In a normal distribution, an item of data is more likely to be near the center of the data than far from it.

- In a normal distribution, there are about as many values less than the mean as there are values greater than the mean. Another way of saying this is *the mean is close to the median.*

- The mean is a line of symmetry for the curve.

Normal distributions occur often in data sets that describe nature and physical characteristics.

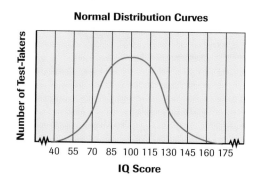

Normal Distribution Curves

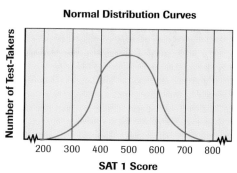

Normal Distribution Curves

Problem Solving

"It isn't that they can't see the solution. It is that they can't see the problem."

G. K. Chesterton, novelist, in
The Scandal of Father Brown

Figuring things out comes naturally for you. As an infant, you figured out how to spin the dials on your activity toys. When you were two, you figured out how to climb out of your crib. Later, you figured out more complicated things like how to turn on the television and change channels.

Now you solve even more complex problems: how to fix your car or bicycle, how to save up for those concert tickets, how to schedule your homework and chores, etc. You seem to be able to just figure things out.

Well, you can just figure out math problems, too. Of course, as with any problem, it helps to know what's going on and what you're supposed to find out. It helps to know methods that have worked for you before. It helps to care about finding a solution. You may be surprised to see how much of what you already do can help you solve math problems.

Don't be too surprised that you know so much about solving math problems. After all, you're a natural-born problem solver.

Keep trying.

Imagine that Sammy Sosa walked away from the plate after one strike. No one's perfect, and that's especially true in problem solving. The best problem solvers make lots of mistakes. Part of what makes them so good is that they don't give up. When you work on a problem, your first try may not work out. That's OK. Just look at what you've done and try again.

Take chances.

There's no reason to be shy when you're solving a math problem. Next time you think you can't solve a problem, just go ahead and give it a shot. You've got nothing to lose. It's like playing chess against your computer. Starting over is just a click away—and the computer doesn't care.

Use what you know.

You go for a car ride and get a flat tire. Uh oh, there's no spare. Now you've got a bigger problem. If you're lucky, that hasn't happened to you. But if it

has, you'll probably always remember to make sure there's a good spare tire in the car. When you solve problems, use your experience. Look for things that are familiar. Maybe the problem you're working on reminds you of one you've solved before. Maybe the method you used then will work now.

Practice.

Do you believe the saying *practice makes perfect*? Well, maybe not perfect, but if you dance, swim, play the guitar, or do any other activity, you know that practice makes you better. It's the same with problem solving. Each time you work on a problem, you learn something new. You become a better problem solver.

Watch what you do.

As you work on a problem, keep an eye on your progress. Take a look at the method you're using. Are you getting closer to a solution? Are you just grinding out calculations that won't help? If you think you're on the right track, stay on it. If you think you're not getting anywhere, stop and look around. You may want to try a different path.

Take a break.

Have you ever worked on a tough problem and felt these signs? You're tired. You're getting nowhere. All your ideas have bombed and you've run out of new ones. These signs may simply be signals that it's time to get away from the problem for a while. Give your brain a chance to refresh itself.

A Four-Step Problem-Solving Plan

Getting stuck on a problem is like being lost. In both cases, a map sure would help. Here is a problem-solving plan that acts like a map. It won't solve the problem for you, but it can help you find your way to a solution.

 You find yourself in a game and you have no clue about the object or the rules. You won't have much chance of winning unless you find out what you're supposed to do. It's like that in problem solving. If you don't understand what's going on, ask yourself, *What do I know? What do I need to find out?*

If you don't understand the problem, use these hints.

- Read the problem again slowly. Take notes or draw pictures to help.

- Try to explain the problem to someone else.

- If there are charts or drawings, study them.

- Look up any words or symbols you don't know.

 When you're not sure how to solve a problem, take a little time to think about what you might do. Drawing diagrams or trying out some numbers may give you ideas. There are many different strategies you can try.

 Go ahead and try the method you picked. Work carefully. Keep thinking while you work, and remember, if your first try doesn't work, try something else.

 After you find an answer, go over what you've done.

- Does your answer make sense?

- Does it really answer what the problem is asking?

- Did you use correct mathematics?

- If you try another way, do you get the same answer?

Problem-Solving Strategies

To get to a friend's house, you might walk. You might take a car or a bike or a bus. You might even combine modes of transportation. There are many ways to get from one place to another. Solving a problem is like going somewhere. There are lots of different methods, or strategies, that you can use to help get an answer.

Keep in mind a few things about strategies:

- Strategies are not recipes; they are more like guides. They will help you find your way, but they won't give you step-by-step directions.

- You can use more than one strategy on a single problem.

- You can use a strategy that's not on the list (even one that you make up yourself).

- You can use whatever strategy works for you. Strategies are not right or wrong. Your friend might work backward to solve a problem. You might write an equation to solve the same problem. It's not necessary for everyone who solves a problem to use the same strategy.

Make a Visual Representation _____

When you draw a diagram to explain a play in soccer or football, you keep it simple. You use *X*s and *O*s to stand for people. You don't have to be an artist to include the important information in a diagram.

EXAMPLE 1: The leader in a bicycle race is $1\frac{1}{2}$ miles from the finish line and $\frac{1}{2}$ mile ahead of the closest opponent. If the leader maintains a speed of 15 mph, what average speed would the second racer need to maintain in order to win the race?

MORE HELP
See 127, 190, 281

 1 ■ You know the location and speed of the rider in first place.

■ You know the location of the rider in second place.

■ What average speed must the second-place rider maintain to pass the leader before the finish?

 2 You could record the information on a diagram to help picture what's going on and to help see how the data are related.

 3 Make a diagram and label it to show the important information.

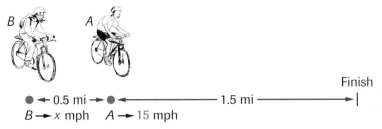

Finish

● ◄ 0.5 mi ► ● ◄————— 1.5 mi —————► |
B ➙ x mph A ➙ 15 mph

The diagram helps show that rider B must cover 2 miles in less time than rider A travels 1.5 miles. You can express that relationship as an inequality:

time for rider B to finish $<$ time for rider A to finish

or $\frac{distance}{speed}$ for rider B $<$ $\frac{distance}{speed}$ for rider A

Distance = rate (or speed) × time,
so time = $\frac{distance}{speed}$

Let x be the speed of rider B in miles per hour:

$$\frac{2}{x} \quad < \quad \frac{1.5}{15}$$

$$30 \quad < \quad 1.5x$$

$$20 \quad < \quad x$$

MORE ►

At 20 miles per hour, B goes one mile every three minutes. That's six minutes to go two miles.

At 15 miles per hour, A goes one mile every four minutes. That's six minutes to go 1.5 miles.

★ The rider in second place has to average more than 20 miles per hour to win.

Sometimes the accuracy of your answer depends on the accuracy of your diagram.

EXAMPLE 2: By measuring shock waves, seismologists can tell the distance to the origin of an earthquake. From the data given, find the **epicenter** of the earthquake (the point on the ground directly above where the quake originated). How far north and how far east of Lab A is the epicenter?

Lab	Location of Lab	Distance to Epicenter
A	---	17 mi
B	20 mi east and 24 mi north of Lab A	15 mi
C	32 mi east and 8 mi north of Lab A	25 mi

- The earthquake originated 17 miles from Lab A, 15 miles from B, and 25 miles from Lab C.

- Where is the epicenter in relation to Lab A?

PLAN
2 Draw a map to help visualize the locations. If the map is accurately drawn to scale, you can draw circular arcs to pinpoint the epicenter.

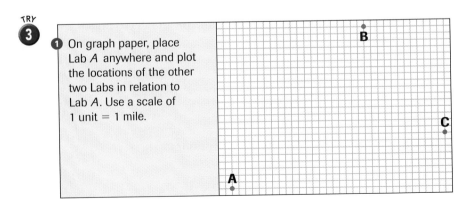

TRY
3
① On graph paper, place Lab A anywhere and plot the locations of the other two Labs in relation to Lab A. Use a scale of 1 unit = 1 mile.

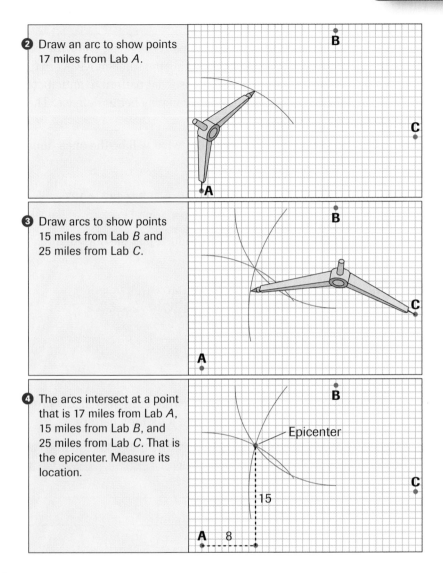

2 Draw an arc to show points 17 miles from Lab *A*.

3 Draw arcs to show points 15 miles from Lab *B* and 25 miles from Lab *C*.

4 The arcs intersect at a point that is 17 miles from Lab *A*, 15 miles from Lab *B*, and 25 miles from Lab *C*. That is the epicenter. Measure its location.

4 Make sure the drawing is accurate.

★ The epicenter is 8 miles east and 15 miles north of Lab *A*.

Find and Use a Pattern _____

You're playing soccer and an opponent keeps getting past you with the ball. Then you notice that the player is making the same move every time. You're seeing a behavior pattern. You can use that pattern to anticipate the move and steal the ball. Patterns can help you play better defense. They can also help you solve math problems.

EXAMPLE: If you compute 127^{100} correctly, what will be the ones (units) digit of the result?

- You're multiplying by 127 over and over: $127 \times 127 \times 127 \ldots$ and so on, with 127 used as a factor 100 times.

- You don't have to give the entire product, just the ones digit.

> If you try to find 127^{100} on a calculator, you may get an error message. $\boxed{2.40089\mathrm{e}+210}$ You definitely won't see the ones digit. So, you need a different method.

Only the ones digits in the factors affect the ones digit in any product. So, try multiplying by 7 a few times and look for a pattern.

Expression	Product of Ones Digits	Ones Digit of Product
127^2	$7 \times 7 = 49$	9
127^3	$9 \times 7 = 63$	3
127^4	$3 \times 7 = 21$	1
127^5	$1 \times 7 = 7$	7
127^6	$7 \times 7 = 49$	9
127^7	$9 \times 7 = 63$	3
127^8	$3 \times 7 = 21$	1

As you keep multiplying by 127, the ones digit changes in a repeating pattern.

When the exponent is 4, 8, or any multiple of 4, the ones digit will be 1. So, when the exponent is 100, the ones digit will be 1.

4 Make sure the pattern you used will really continue. In this case, it will continue because 7×7 is always 49, 9×7 is always 63, and so on.

★ When you compute 127^{100}, the ones digit of the result is 1.

Find and Use a Pattern is often used with other strategies.

Check out:
   Account for All Possibilities [381]
   Start with a Simpler Problem [382]
   Organize the Data [383]
   Model with an Equation [387]

MATH ALERT: Patterns Don't Necessarily Continue

379

Whenever you use a pattern to solve a problem, ask yourself: Can I be sure the pattern will continue? Suppose the high temperatures the past few days were 2°, 4°, 8°, and 16°C. You might see a pattern in the numbers. Should you assume the high tomorrow will be 32°C? Of course not. There's no reason why the pattern must keep going. To convince yourself, imagine the pattern continuing for a few more days: 32°, 64°, 128°! Too hot to be real.

MORE HELP
See 368, 400

Monday	Tuesday	Wednesday	Thursday	Friday

Guess, Check, and Revise

You forget the combination to your locker, so you keep trying different combinations. That strategy can take more time than you have because one guess is as good as another. In many math problems, you can learn a lot from a wrong guess, so your guesses can keep getting better.

Statistics for Winning Team—Final Game of 1999 NBA Finals				
Field Goals		Free Throws		Total Points
Made	Tried	Made	Tried	
27	67	19	25	78

Field goals are worth either two points or three points.

Free throws are worth one point each.

EXAMPLE 1: In the last game of the 1999 NBA finals, how many 2-point field goals and how many 3-point field goals did the winning team make?

- The team scored 78 points. Of those, 19 were from free throws.

- The remaining 59 points were from 27 field goals.

- How many of each kind of field goal did they make?

Make a guess and check it. If it's right, great. If it's not right, see whether it's too high or too low and make your next guess closer.

❶ Guess (sum must be 27)	❷ Check (total must be 59)	❸ Think and revise
2-pointers: 17 3-pointers: 10	$17(2) + 10(3) = 64$	Too high! Make a guess that lowers the total.
2-pointers: 25 3-pointers: 2	$25(2) + 2(3) = 56$	Too low, but close. Make a guess that raises the total a little.
2-pointers: 22 3-pointers: 5	$22(2) + 5(3) = 59$	Just right!

■ Is the total from field goals 59 points? Yes, 22(2) + 5(3) = 59.

■ Are all 78 points accounted for? Yes, 59 from field goals plus 19 from free throws add up to 78.

★ The winning team made 22 two-point field goals and five three-point field goals.

You also could have solved this problem by writing and solving a pair of equations like these:

$3m + 2n + 19 = 78$ m is the number of 3-point shots made;
$m + n$ $= 27$ n is the number of 2-point shots made

To solve: $3m + 2n + 19 = 78$
                                       $m + n$ $= 27$

Solve one equation for n. $m + n = 27$
                                            $n = 27 - m$

Substitute this value into $3m + 2(27 - m) + 19 = 78$
the other equation.

Use the Distributive Property. $3m + 54 - 2m + 19 = 78$

Simplify. $m + 73 = 78$

Solve for m. $m = 5$

Substitute and solve for n. $5 + n = 27$
                                            $n = 22$

MORE HELP
See 161, 387

EXAMPLE 2: Your class is putting up a fence for a rectangular recycling center behind your school. You'll use the back wall of the school for one side and fencing for the other three sides. You have 36 feet of fence. What whole-number dimensions should you use in order to enclose the greatest area possible?

■ You have 36 feet of fence for three sides of a rectangle.

■ The wall will be the fourth side.

■ You want to enclose as much area as you can.

■ How long and how wide should the rectangle be?

Make some guesses and check them. Home in on the answer by evaluating and refining your guesses.

MORE ▶

380

TRY

MORE HELP
See 388

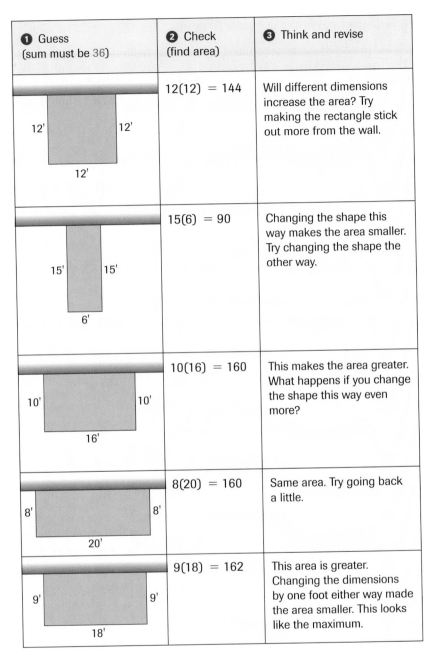

❶ Guess (sum must be 36)	❷ Check (find area)	❸ Think and revise
12' · 12' · 12'	12(12) = 144	Will different dimensions increase the area? Try making the rectangle stick out more from the wall.
15' · 15' · 6'	15(6) = 90	Changing the shape this way makes the area smaller. Try changing the shape the other way.
10' · 10' · 16'	10(16) = 160	This makes the area greater. What happens if you change the shape this way even more?
8' · 8' · 20'	8(20) = 160	Same area. Try going back a little.
9' · 9' · 18'	9(18) = 162	This area is greater. Changing the dimensions by one foot either way made the area smaller. This looks like the maximum.

LOOK BACK
❹

- Is the length of the fence 36 feet? Yes, 2(9) + 18 = 36.
- Is this the greatest area possible using whole-number dimensions? Yes, if you change the dimensions by one foot either way, the area decreases.

★ The rectangle should be 9 feet from the wall and 18 feet long.

Account for All Possibilities

You're planning a surprise party for a friend. You try to account for all the things that could go wrong, so you can plan for them. Accounting for all possibilities can also help you solve some math problems.

When you list possibilities, a pattern can help you make sure you don't leave out items or repeat items. Even with a pattern, however, you have to count carefully. Two items may look different but may actually be the same.

EXAMPLE 1: Five members of a band like to sing. They decide to have a different duet for each song. How many songs can they play without repeating a duet?

- There are five band members.

- A duet is a song performed by two people.

- How many different pairs can be formed?

Make an organized list. Use the letters *A-E* to stand for people.

TRY
3

First, list all the duets with *A*. Then list all the duets with *B*, and so on. Don't list doubles like *AA*; a duet must include two *different* members.

Duets				
With A	**With B**	**With C**	**With D**	**With E**
---	BA	CA	DA	EA
AB	---	CB	DB	EB
AC	BC	---	DC	EC
AD	BD	CD	---	ED
AE	BE	CE	DE	---

There are 20 pairs listed. *AB* and *BA* should not both be listed. They are the same duet. You need to cross out one of each pair that is listed twice.

---	~~BA~~	~~CA~~	~~DA~~	~~EA~~
AB	---	~~CB~~	~~DB~~	~~EB~~
AC	BC	---	~~DC~~	~~EC~~
AD	BD	CD	---	~~ED~~
AE	BE	CE	DE	---

★ The band can play 10 songs without repeating a duet.

Start with a Simpler Problem

Solving the simplest form of a math problem and then changing it little by little may lead you to a solution to the original problem.

EXAMPLE 1: If you stay on the city streets, how many different direct paths are there from A to B?

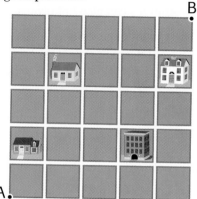

 UNDERSTAND 1

- Move along the lines on the grid, not diagonally. Don't backtrack (move only up and right).

- How many direct routes are there from A to B?

PLAN 2

Look at the simplest grid first. Then, look at grids with more intersections. You may see a relationship you can use.

TRY 3

Start with a 1×1 grid.
Total paths to $B = 2$.
There is one path through P.
There is one path through Q.

Change it to a 2×1 or a 1×2 grid.
Total paths to $B = 3$.
There are two paths through P.
There is one path through Q.

Change it to a 2×2 grid.
Total paths to $B = 6$.
There are three paths through P.
There are three paths through Q.

Change it to a 5×1 or a 1×5 grid.
Total paths to $B = 6$.
There are five paths through P.
There is one path through Q.

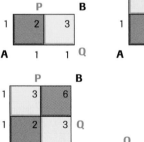

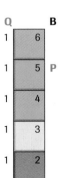

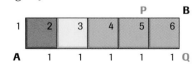

Start filling in the 5×5 grid. A pattern is developing. To get to B, you have to go through either P or Q. So, the number of direct paths to B is the sum of the number of direct paths to P and to Q. You can use that relationship to fill in a 5×5 grid.

MORE HELP
See 319

B				
1	6	21	56	126	252

Grid:

1	6	21	56	126	252
1	5	15	35	70	126
1	4	10	20	35	56
1	3	6	10	15	21
1	2	3	4	5	6

A   1   1   1   1   1

Make sure your reasoning makes sense. Make sure you drew and marked the grid correctly.

★ There are 252 direct paths from A to B.

A simpler problem may have the same answer as the original problem.

EXAMPLE 2: A radio station is having a contest. The DJs will play a certain song on five of the seven days of the week. If you guess which five days, you win. How many combinations of five days are there?

■ How many combinations of five days of the week are there?

■ In the same week, Monday, Tuesday, Friday, Saturday, Sunday is the same as Friday, Saturday, Sunday, Monday, Tuesday.

Listing all of the 5-day combinations is tedious. Instead, you can solve a simpler but equivalent version of the problem. For every five days you list, there are two days you leave out, so find the 2-day combinations.

Use letters *A-G* for the 7 days of the week.

AB	*AC*	*AD*	*AE*	*AF*	*AG*	6 pairs with *A*
	BC	*BD*	*BE*	*BF*	*BG*	5 others with *B* (*BA* is same as *AB*)
		CD	*CE*	*CF*	*CG*	4 others with *C*
			DE	*DF*	*DG*	3 others with *D*
				EF	*EG*	2 others with *E*
					FG	1 other with *F*

There are 21 combinations of two days of the week. These represent all the possible pairs of days *missing* from all the possible groups of five days. One pair is missing from every group of five. That means there must also be 21 combinations of five days.

Make sure your reasoning makes sense. Make sure the listing is complete.

★ There are 21 combinations of five days of the week.

Organize the Data

Imagine that your library kept all its books in one huge pile. Libraries organize their books so that it's easy for you to find the book you need and for the library to keep track of its books. Likewise in math problems, organizing information—using tables, diagrams, and graphs—can make it easy to find and keep track of things.

EXAMPLE 1: In stage 1 of a special fireworks display a flare bursts into a red ball of light and shoots out three other flares. A moment later, in stage 2, each of those flares bursts into a red ball of light and shoots out three more flares. For this effect to occur for 10 stages, how many flares are needed?

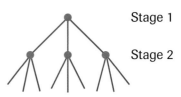

Stage 1

Stage 2

- At every stage, each flare produces three more flares.

- How many flares are needed for 10 stages?

Organize the information in a table to keep track of the flares at each stage.

Stage	1	2	3	4	5
Flares needed for that stage	1	1×3	3×3	$3 \times 3 \times 3$	$3 \times 3 \times 3 \times 3$
Total so far	1	$1 + 3$	$1 + 3 + 9$	$1 + 3 + 9 + 27$	$1 + 3 + 9 + 27 + 81$

Notice the pattern.

The total for 10 stages would be:

$$3^0 + 3^1 + 3^2 + 3^3 + 3^4 + 3^5 + 3^6 + 3^7 + 3^8 + 3^9$$
$$= 1 + 3 + 9 + 27 + 81 + 243 + 729 + 2187 + 6561 + 19{,}683$$
$$= 29{,}524$$

The table makes it easy to check that all the steps make sense.

★ 29,524 flares are needed for 10 stages of the display.

EXAMPLE 2: Based on the article, how many students were surveyed? How many listed only cereal? How many listed only eggs? How many listed only fruit?

MORE HELP
See 363

What's for Breakfast?

Cereal, eggs, or fruit? That is the question.
In a survey, students responded by listing which of those items they ate for breakfast at least once a week. Fifteen included cereal in their list. Eleven included eggs, and six included fruit. Two students listed all three items. Six listed cereal and eggs. Three listed cereal and fruit. Only one listed eggs and fruit.

1 ▪ The article gives some results of a survey of students.

▪ How many students were surveyed?

▪ How many said cereal only? Eggs only? Fruit only?

2 Organize the information with a Venn diagram.

3

❶ Use overlapping circles to show the three choices. Fill in the data from the article.	**❷** So far the diagram shows 11 students who listed cereal. But you know 15 included cereal. So four must have listed cereal only.	**❸** Two students must have listed eggs only for the total to be 11. All six who listed fruit are already shown.
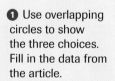	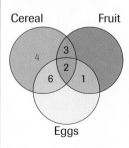	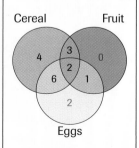

4 Make sure you entered the numbers correctly in the diagram.

★ There were eighteen students in the survey. Four listed cereal only, two listed eggs only, and nobody listed fruit only.

Change Your Point of View

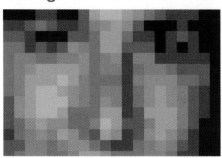

Can you tell what's in the picture? Look closely. Now try looking at it from far away. Sometimes changing your point of view puts things in focus. That's especially true with math problems. You may stare and stare in vain until you look at the problem in a different way.

EXAMPLE 1: You are building a speaker box. Its inside dimensions will be 24 inches high, 12 inches long, and 12 inches wide. You plan to run a wire from a fuse at a bottom corner to the center of the top. The wire cannot hang at all; it must run along the side and top of the speaker box. What is the shortest distance from a lower corner to the top center?

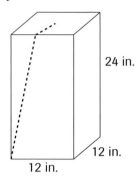

24 in.

12 in.

12 in.

1 Working in two dimensions is sometimes easier than working in three dimensions. Imagine unfolding the box so the side and top are side by side. Then the shortest distance is simply along a straight line from a lower corner to the top center.

Top   **Side**

12 in.

12 in.   24 in.

2 The distance you need to find is the hypotenuse of a right triangle. Use the Pythagorean Theorem.

3

MORE HELP
See 056, 245

The wire ends at the center of a 12-inch square, so it is 6 inches from each side. A perpendicular from the center to a side bisects the side.

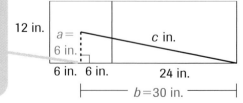

12 in.

$a =$ 6 in.

c in.

6 in. 6 in.   24 in.

$b = 30$ in.

$$c = \sqrt{a^2 + b^2}$$

$$= \sqrt{6^2 + 30^2}$$

$$= \sqrt{936} \text{ or about } 30.6$$

Fold and unfold a sheet of paper to check that the point of view you used makes sense. Make sure all computation is correct.

★ The distance is about 30.6 inches.

EXAMPLE 2: How can you cut this cake into eight congruent pieces with only three straight cuts?

- You need to cut the cake into eight pieces the same size and shape.

- You can make only three cuts, which must be straight.

 If you try cutting only from the top you can't do it. You need to try something different. You need to think about cutting in unusual ways.

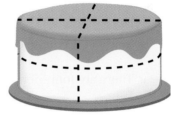

 Once you think about cutting from the side, the solution seems obvious.

 Be sure that all of the conditions of the problem are satisfied.

★ Make one horizontal cut and two vertical cuts as shown.

When you solve problems, don't put unnecessary restrictions on yourself. Think out of the box.

Use Logical Reasoning

Do you ever figure things out, like where you left your keys or who ate the leftover pizza? You often use logic, like a detective, to solve life's daily mysteries. You can use this skill to solve math problems, too.

EXAMPLE 1: Four friends, Ken, Lisa, Marcos, and Nikki, each belong to a different one of the after-school groups listed.

- Nikki and Ken hate sports and they are both older than the friend in the Chess Club.

- Lisa joined the Spanish and Chess Clubs but dropped out of one.

- Ken's choice has more letters than Nikki's.

1 ■ There are four friends, one in each club.

■ Use the clues to figure out who's in which club.

2 Use logical reasoning to eliminate possible answers. Make a chart to keep track.

3 From the first clue, you can tell that Nikki and Ken do not belong to the Chess Club or Soccer Team. Write ✗s in your chart to show that.

	Spanish Club	Chess Club	Soccer Team	Band
Ken		✗	✗	
Lisa				
Marcos				
Nikki		✗	✗	

From the second clue, you can tell Lisa does not belong to the Soccer Team or Band. Write ✗s to show that.

	Spanish Club	Chess Club	Soccer Team	Band
Ken		✗	✗	
Lisa			✗	✗
Marcos				
Nikki		✗	✗	

Look at the column for Soccer Team. Marcos is the only one of the four who could belong to the Soccer Team. Show that with a ✓. Write ✗s to show that he does not belong to the other three clubs.

	Spanish Club	Chess Club	Soccer Team	Band
Ken		✗	✗	
Lisa			✗	✗
Marcos	✗	✗	✓	✗
Nikki		✗	✗	

Lisa is the only one who could belong to the Chess Club. Show that with a ✓. Write an ✗ to show she doesn't belong to the Spanish Club.

	Spanish Club	Chess Club	Soccer Team	Band
Ken		✗	✗	
Lisa	✗	✓	✗	✗
Marcos	✗	✗	✓	✗
Nikki		✗	✗	

Since there are only two choices left, the last clue tells you that Ken must belong to the Spanish Club and Nikki to the Band.

	Spanish Club	Chess Club	Soccer Team	Band
Ken	✓	✗	✗	✗
Lisa	✗	✓	✗	✗
Marcos	✗	✗	✓	✗
Nikki	✗	✗	✗	✓

4 Make sure the reason for each ✗ and ✓ is logical by referring back to the problem.

★ Ken belongs to the Spanish Club, Lisa to the Chess Club, Marcos to the Soccer Team, and Nikki to the Band.

Sometimes, logical reasoning can make a hard problem very easy.

EXAMPLE 2: You are setting up a tournament. The person who wins a match goes on to the next round. The loser is out. There are 128 people in the tournament. How many matches will be played until there is a champion?

Think about the tournament. After each match, one more player is out. To have a champion, 127 players must be out. So you need 127 matches.

★ 127 matches will be played.

Work Backward

If you've ever taken something apart, you know that you have to reverse your steps to put it back together. If the cover was the first thing you re-moved, it will be the last thing you put back. Notice that you not only do the steps in reverse, but each step is the opposite. You can work backward to solve some math problems.

EXAMPLE 1: The population of a certain bacteria colony doubles every 20 minutes. At 1:00 P.M., there are 16 billion bacteria in the colony. What was the size of the population at 11:00 A.M.?

1 UNDERSTAND
- The number of bacteria doubles every 20 minutes.
- The population was 16 billion at 1:00 P.M.
- How many bacteria were in the colony at 11:00 A.M.?

2 PLAN
Since you know the end (the population at 1:00 P.M.) and all the steps (how the population grew), you can work backward to find the begin-ning (the population at 11:00 A.M.).

3 TRY
Start at 1:00 P.M. and work backward in steps of 20 minutes.

MORE HELP
See 127, 387

Time	Population
1:00 P.M.	16,000,000,000
12:40 P.M.	8,000,000,000
12:20 P.M.	4,000,000,000
12:00 Noon	2,000,000,000
11:40 A.M.	1,000,000,000
11:20 A.M.	500,000,000
11:00 A.M.	250,000,000

4 LOOK BACK
Check your answer by working forward: If you start with 250 million and double it 6 times (every 20 minutes for two hours), you get 16 billion.

★ The population was 250,000,000 at 11:00 A.M.

You also could have solved the problem by writing an equation.
$2^6x = 16,000,000,000$ where x is the population at 11:00 A.M.
$x = 250,000,000$

EXAMPLE 2: When you add 79 to the cube of the mystery integer, reverse the digits of that sum, and then divide the result by 3, you get 17. What is the mystery integer?

MORE HELP
See 041, 059, 083

UNDERSTAND 1

- There are four steps: cube the integer, add 79, reverse the digits, divide by 3.

- The result is 17.

- Find the starting integer.

PLAN 2

Since you know the end (17) and all the steps (cube, add, reverse, divide), you can work backward to find the beginning (the mystery integer).

TRY 3

Write steps forward.

mystery integer ⇒ cube it ⇒ ? ⇒ + 79 ⇒ ? ⇒ reverse digits ⇒ ? ⇒ ÷ 3 ⇒ 17

Write steps backward. Use the inverse operation at each step.

17 ⇒ × 3 ⇒ ? ⇒ reverse digits ⇒ ? ⇒ − 79 ⇒ ? ⇒ $\sqrt[3]{\ }$ ⇒ mystery integer

Compute each step.

17 ⇒ × 3 ⇒ 51 ⇒ reverse digits ⇒ 15 ⇒ − 79 ⇒ $^-$64 ⇒ $\sqrt[3]{^-64}$ ⇒ $^-$4

LOOK BACK 4

Check by working forward:

$(^-4)^3 = {}^-64 \rightarrow {}^-64 + 79 = 15 \rightarrow$ reverse 15 to get 51 $\rightarrow 51 \div 3 = 17$

★ The mystery integer is $^-$4.

You could also have solved this problem algebraically. Say x is the mystery integer. Then $x^3 + 79$ is also an integer. Say z is the reverse of the integer $(x^3 + 79)$, then $z \div 3 = 17$ and $z = 51$. This means $x^3 + 79 = 15$. So, $x^3 = {}^-64$ and $x = {}^-4$.

Model with an Equation

Before building bridges, skyscrapers, or roller coasters, engineers and architects make models. Not all models are made of wood, metal, or plastic. Mathematical models are made of equations. These equations can predict how cables, beams, and coaster cars will perform in real life. You can solve many math problems by writing equations to model the situation.

EXAMPLE 1: How many CDs would you need to buy for CompuTune to be cheaper than DiskNet?

 UNDERSTAND **1**
- You pay a greater fee for CompuTune.
- You pay more for each CD with DiskNet.
- At what point does CompuTune become cheaper?

 PLAN **2**
You can write an expression to model the cost of each service. Then, you can set the expressions equal to each other to find out when their costs become equal.

 TRY **3**
Model the cost of each service by using a variable to stand for the number of CDs bought.

Total cost = fee + price per CD · number bought
Total cost in dollars for DiskNet: $15 + 11x$
Total cost in dollars for CompuTune: $24.95 + 9.95x$

Set the two expressions equal to each other and solve for x:

MORE HELP
See 127

$$15 + 11x = 24.95 + 9.95x$$
$$1.05x = 9.95$$
$$x \approx 9.5$$

> You could also have modeled this problem with an inequality:
> $15 + 11x > 24.95 + 9.95x$

You can buy only whole numbers of CDs. Nine CDs would be too few, but after 10 CDs, CompuTune would be cheaper.

Check costs for 9 CDs and 10 CDs by substituting:

MORE HELP
See 435

	9 CDs	**10 CDs**
CompuTune	$24.95 + $9.95(9) = $114.50	$24.95 + $9.95(10) = $124.45
DiskNet	$15 + $11(9) = $114.00	$15 + $11(10) = $125.00

★ You have to buy at least 10 CDs for CompuTune to be cheaper.

You could also have solved this problem by using a graphing calculator to graph
$y = 15 + 11x$ and
$y = 24.95 + 9.95x$
and then finding where the graphs of the two equations intersect.

EXAMPLE 2: If this pattern continues, how many dots will be in the sixty-third figure?

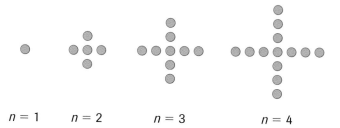

$n = 1$ $n = 2$ $n = 3$ $n = 4$

 ▪ Dots are added to each figure according to a rule.

▪ How many dots are needed for the sixty-third figure?

 You can write an equation to relate the number of dots to the figure number.

 Let n represent the figure number and let d represent the number of dots. For the first figure $n = 1$ and $d = 1$, for the second figure, $n = 2$ and $d = 5$, and so on. Organize some of the data in a table to see whether you notice a pattern.

n	d
1	1
2	5
3	9
4	13

MORE ▶

It looks like the number of dots increases by four with each figure. That makes sense, since with each successive figure one dot is added to each of the four arms.

Each arm of the figure has 1 fewer dot than *n*. The number of dots in each arm is $n - 1$.	$n = 2$	$n = 3$
So, four arms have $4(n - 1)$ dots.	$n = 2$	$n = 3$
You have to add the center dot. So the total number of dots, *d*, is $4(n - 1) + 1$.	$n = 2$	$n = 3$

For the sixty-third figure, $n = 63$, so

$$d = 4(n - 1) + 1$$

$$= 4(63 - 1) + 1 = 249$$

 4 Make sure the equation models the situation. Check your calculations.

★ The sixty-third figure will have 249 dots.

EXAMPLE 3: You have one brand of fruit drink that is 10% juice. You also have another brand that is 25% juice. You want to make five gallons of drink that is 20% fruit juice. How many gallons of each brand should you use?

 1
- One fruit drink is *juicier* than another.

  - How much of each do you need to make five gallons of drink that is 20% juice?

 2 You can write equations for the amount of juice in each drink and in the mixture.

TRY
3 You could first organize the information to help you write the equations:

Drink	% Juice	Volume of Drink (gallons)	Volume of Juice (gallons)
Brand A	10%	x	$0.10x$
Brand B	25%	y	$0.25y$
Mixture	20%	5	$0.20 \cdot 5 = 1$

MORE HELP
See 004, 012, 127, 295

The volume of Brand A used plus the volume of Brand B used must equal the volume of the mixture. ▶ $x + y = 5$

The volume of juice from Brand A plus the volume of juice from Brand B must equal the volume of juice in the mixture. ▶ $0.10x + 0.25y = 1$

Since $x + y = 5$, then $y = 5 - x$.

To find x, substitute $5 - x$ for y in the second equation:

$0.10x + 0.25(5 - x) = 1$

$$x = 1\tfrac{2}{3}$$

Now find y:

$y = 5 - x$

$y = 5 - 1\tfrac{2}{3}$

$y = 3\tfrac{1}{3}$

LOOK BACK
4 Make sure your equations model the situation accurately. Check that $x = 1\tfrac{2}{3}$ and $y = 3\tfrac{1}{3}$ satisfy both equations.

★ You should mix $1\tfrac{2}{3}$ gallons of the brand that is 10% juice with $3\tfrac{1}{3}$ gallons of the brand that is 25% juice.

Model with an Equation is often used with other strategies.

Check out:
  Make a Visual Representation [377]
  Guess, Check, and Revise [380]
  Organize the Data [383]
  Identify Subgoals [388]

Identify Subgoals

You want to play that new song on your guitar but it's too long to learn all at once. First, you learn the introduction. Then you learn the rest, part by part. Breaking up the task makes it more manageable. With math problems, too, what seems complicated can be made simpler by breaking it into smaller tasks.

EXAMPLE: Will a thin, 16-inch long baton fit into a rectangular box that is 9 inches wide, 12 inches long, and 8 inches high on the inside?

- You know the dimensions of the box and the baton.

- The baton cannot fit along either the length or the width of the box.

- Can the baton fit in the box?

PLAN 2

Maybe the baton could fit diagonally along the bottom.

Maybe the baton could fit diagonally from a lower corner to the opposite upper corner.

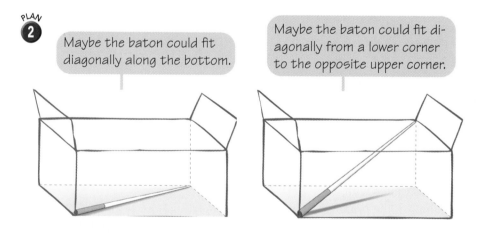

First find the diagonal distance along the bottom of the box. Then, if necessary, find the diagonal distance from the lower corner to the opposite upper corner.

MORE HELP
See 056, 245

TRY
3

Find the first diagonal:

The diagonal (d_1) forms a right triangle with two edges of the box (9 in. and 12 in.).

Use the Pythagorean Theorem:

$d_1 = \sqrt{9^2 + 12^2}$

$\quad = \sqrt{225}$

$\quad = 15$

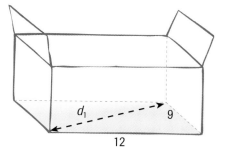

The baton will not fit diagonally on the bottom of the box.

Find the second diagonal:

The diagonal (d_2) forms a right triangle with the first diagonal (15 in.) and the height of the box (8 in.).

$d_2 = \sqrt{15^2 + 8^2}$

$\quad = \sqrt{289}$

$\quad = 17$

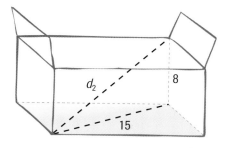

LOOK BACK
4

The solution works if the baton has no thickness. But, in reality, the greater the diameter of the baton, the less it will be able to reach into a corner. The baton will fit only if it is thin enough.

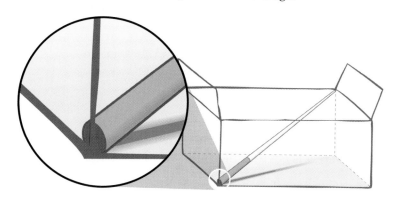

★ If the baton is thin enough, it will fit if tilted.

Consider Special Cases

Every number is special in some way, but some numbers, like 0 and 1, are special more often. Looking at special numbers or special conditions can help make a complicated problem more understandable.

EXAMPLE 1: If x is a real number, which of the following describes the inequality $x^2 \geq x$?

    a) always true
    b) sometimes true
    c) never true

UNDERSTAND **1**

- Is the statement true for every real value of x?

- Is the statement true for at least one real value of x and false for at least one real value of x?

- Is the statement true for no real values of x?

PLAN **2**

Try different values for x to get a handle on what happens. Be sure to try a wide range of types of real numbers.

TRY **3**

Value to test	Result
0	$0 \geq 0$ ✓
A positive number, like 3	$9 \geq 3$ ✓
A negative number, like $^-2$	$4 \geq {}^-2$ ✓
An irrational number, like $\sqrt{5}$	$5 \geq \sqrt{5}$ ✓
A number between 0 and 1, like $\frac{1}{2}$	$\frac{1}{4}$ is not greater than $\frac{1}{2}$

Although they weren't needed in this solution, 1 and $^-$1 are often useful numbers to consider.

LOOK BACK **4**

Since you found at least one case where the statement is true and one case where it is not true, then it is sometimes true.

★ Choice b best describes the inequality.

Extreme cases may help you see what's going on in a mathematical situation, even if the extreme cases are not realistic.

MORE HELP
See 316

EXAMPLE 2: An auto manufacturer once claimed that 90% of the cars it had sold during the last 10 years were still on the road. Does that statement mean that these cars have a 90% chance of lasting 10 years?

■ Can you conclude from the manufacturer's claim that the probability of one of these cars lasting 10 years is 0.9?

To get a handle on the meaning of the manufacturer's claim, consider some extreme examples of when the cars might have been sold.

For simplicity, suppose a total of 1000 cars were sold. One extreme case is that all the cars were sold this past year.

10 years ago   this past year

Year	1	2	3	4	5	6	7	8	9	10
Cars sold	0	0	0	0	0	0	0	0	0	1000

If only 90%, or 900, of these cars are still on the road, that doesn't indicate a very reliable car. Since the chance of lasting only one year was 90%, the chance of lasting 10 years would be much less.

Another extreme case is that all the cars were sold the first year of the 10-year period.

Year	1	2	3	4	5	6	7	8	9	10
Cars sold	1000	0	0	0	0	0	0	0	0	0

In this case, 90%, or 900, of the cars lasted 10 years. That would indicate a 90% chance of lasting 10 years.

The real figures lie somewhere between the extreme cases.

★ Unless they were all sold 10 years ago and none since, these cars probably have less than a 90% chance of lasting 10 years. Without more data, you cannot safely conclude that the cars have a 90% chance of lasting 10 years.

Create a Simulation

You're on a simulation ride, one moment racing through a jungle and the next moment plunging mid-air into a deep canyon. You know it's just a ride, but it sure feels real. Simulations imitate reality because reality is not always practical. You can use simulations to solve math problems that are not practical to act out.

EXAMPLE 1: To choose a captain, the 10 members of a debate team line up and count off 1, 2, 3, 4, 1, 2, 3, 4, and so on. Each person who says *four* is out. When the end of the line is reached, the next number in the count-off is assigned to the first person still in line, until only one person—the new captain—remains. Which person will be captain?

- Ten people line up.

- They count off 1, 2, 3, 4 and the fourth person is out.

- They continue until one person is left.

- In which position was that person originally?

PLAN
2

If you don't have 10 people to help, then you can simulate the count-off process using any handy objects, like two-colored counters, coins, or paper clips, to represent people.

Place 10 counters in a line.	● ● ● ● ● ● ● ● ● ●
Count off. When you say *four* turn over that counter.	● ● ● ◑ ● ● ● ◑ ● ● 1 2 3 **4** 1 2 3 **4** 1 2
When you reach the end of the line, go to the front. Skip people who are already out.	● ● ● ◑ ● ● ● ◑ ● ● 1 2 3 4 1 2 3 4 1 2 3 **4** 1 2 3 **4** 1 2
Keep going till there is only one counter left in the line.	● ● ● ◑ ● ● ● ◑ ● ● 1 2 3 4 1 2 3 4 1 2 3 **4** 1 2 3 **4** 1 2 3 **4** 1 2 3 **4** 1 2 3 **4** 1 2 3 **4** 1 2 3 **4**

Make sure the simulation reproduces the actual event closely enough for the answer to be valid.

★ The fifth person in line will be the captain.

EXAMPLE 2: A basketball player makes about half of her free throws. In 100 attempts, about how many times would you expect her to make three or more shots in a row?

- The probability of the player making a free throw is $\frac{1}{2}$.
- She takes 100 shots.
- About how many streaks of three or more baskets would you expect?

 You could use a random number table or a calculator or computer that generates random numbers.

 On the random number table, pick a starting digit at random. Let even digits (e) count as a hit and odd digits (o) as a miss. Mark the streaks of three or more even digits in a row.

Here's a sample of what you might get:

```
09533 43722 03856 52830 93540 13284 96496 45541 54976 17508
eoooo eooee eoeoe oeeoe oooee ooeee oeeoe eooeo oeooe oooee
18367 22814 36752 10707 48774 39615 03102 02834 04116 00112
oeoeo eeeoe oeooe oeoeo eeooe ooeoo eooee eeeoe eeooe eeooe
```

There are six streaks of three or more even digits.

 Repeat the simulation several times because you know that random numbers will not generate exactly the same results every time. You're looking for a general sense of what you can expect.

```
49554 30825 38185 42234 76401 65095 53934 36559 85347 42306
eoooe oeeeo oeoeo eeeoe oeeeo eoeoo ooooe oeooo eooeo eeoee
09411 22337 63725 18280 32248 86091 17368 66843 62596 83667
eoeoo eeooo eooeo oeeee oeeee eeeoo oooee eeeeo eeooe eoeeo
```

In this set of 100, there are seven streaks of three or more even digits.

★ You might expect about six or seven streaks of three or more baskets in 100 shots.

Problem-Solving Skills

It takes more than one skill to play a sport. In basketball, for example, you need to know how to pass, dribble, shoot, rebound, and play defense. In problem solving, too, you need many skills. The more skills you have, the better all-around problem-solver you'll be.

392

Be Ready for Multiple Answers

You miss the bus to school. Maybe you ask your parents for a ride. Maybe you call a friend. Maybe you bike, skate, or walk. There's more than one answer to the question, *how will I get to school?* Some math problems are like that. They may have more than one correct answer.

EXAMPLE 1: An explorer travels due south for one mile, then due east for one mile, and then due north for one mile. She is then back where she started. Where did she start?

One answer is the North Pole.

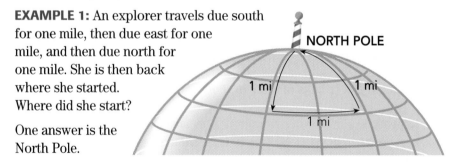

Another answer is, near the South Pole.
The explorer could also have started a little more than a mile north of the South Pole. After traveling one mile South she is so close to the South Pole that when she walks east one mile, she walks in a complete circle.

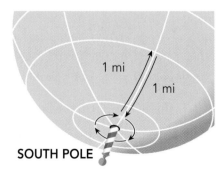

She also might have started a little further south. So, after walking one mile south, she gets close enough to the South Pole that walking one mile east makes two complete circles.

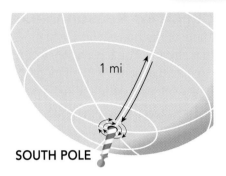

1 mi

SOUTH POLE

★ Mathematically, there are an infinite number of answers to this problem. Depending on her starting point, she could make any number of complete circles when she walks one mile east.

EXAMPLE 2: It's early in the season. A baseball player has four hits so far. If he gets hits in his next two times at bat, his batting average will jump 100 points (.100). How many official times at bat could he have so far?

MORE HELP
See 336

	Times At Bat So Far	Average So Far	Average After Hits in Next 2 Times at Bat	Increase
One Answer	8	$\frac{4}{8} = .500$	$\frac{6}{10} = .600$	.100
Other Answer	10	$\frac{4}{10} = .400$	$\frac{6}{12} = .500$	.100

★ The player might have batted eight times or 10 times.

Initial zeros are not normally used with batting averages.

EXAMPLE 3: What digits would make this addition example true?

```
  O N E
+ O N E
  T W O
```

You might use logical reasoning to limit the possible values of the letter O.

- O is even because it is the ones digit of a double (E + E).

- O is less than 5, because O + O is a 1-digit number.

- So, O must stand for 2 or 4.

★ There are many sets of possible values for the letters. For example:

```
  216        457        281
+ 216      + 457      + 281
  432        914        562
```

Check for Reasonableness

Many of the things you see in movies cannot happen in real life. You know that already. You have a sense of what's reasonable and what's not. You can use that sense with math problems. After you have solved a problem, look over your solution. Ask yourself:

- Does the answer match what I know about the world?
- Does the answer fit the question that was asked?
- Is the size of the answer about right?

Number of Children in U.S. by Age Group (in millions)				
Age group	1950	1995	1996	1997
Ages 0–5	19.1	23.5	23.4	23.2
Ages 6–11	15.3	22.6	23.0	23.4
Ages 12–17	12.9	22.3	22.6	23.0
Total under 18	47.3	68.4	69.0	69.5

Source: U.S. Bureau of the Census

MORE HELP
See 316

EXAMPLE 1: If you picked, at random, a U.S. resident under 18 years of age in 1997, what would be the probability that the person would be over the age of 5? Suppose you ended up with an answer of 1.2. Could that be right?

★ No, it couldn't be right. A probability of 1 means something is certain. A probability cannot be greater than 1. The probability is $\frac{69.5 - 23.2}{69.5}$ or about 0.67 or about $\frac{2}{3}$.

EXAMPLE 2: From 1950 to 1997, by what percent did the number of people under the age of 18 increase? Suppose you ended up with an answer of 146%. Is that reasonable?

Percents can be over 100. But an increase of 100% means the amount doubled. You can see that the total for 1997 (69.5 million) is less than twice the total for 1950 (47.3 million). The percent increase in this case must be less than 100%.

★ An answer of 146% is not reasonable. $\frac{69.5 - 47.3}{47.3} \approx 0.469$, so the number of people under the age of 18 increased about 46.9% from 1950 to 1997.

MORE HELP
See 097, 241,
465

EXAMPLE 3: The perimeter of an isosceles triangle with integral sides is 16 centimeters and the area is 12 square centimeters. How long are the sides?

Suppose you used the guess, check, and revise strategy and thought that the three sides could be 10 cm, 3 cm, and 3 cm. Is that reasonable?

Try to sketch a triangle with those sides. You can't. You know that one side of a triangle cannot be greater than the sum of the other two sides. (The shortest distance between two points is along a straight line.)

★ The answer could not be right. Revise your guesses to reflect the Triangle Inequality Theorem. The sides are 5, 5, and 6 centimeters long.

EXAMPLE 4: A bicycle wheel has a diameter of 26 inches. How far will the bike travel when the wheel turns 100 times?

Suppose you use a calculator to solve the problem this way:

$C = \pi d$

$\approx$ | π | $\times$ | 2 | 6 | $=$ | 81.681409

Is an answer of about 82 inches reasonable?

No, because that's the distance for one turn of the wheel, not 100 turns.

Suppose you then calculate further.

$81.681409 \times 100 = 8168.1409$

$$\frac{8168.1409 \text{ in.}}{(12 \text{ in./ft})} \approx 680.67841 \text{ ft}$$

You write the answer as 680.67841 feet. Is that reasonable?

Could you really determine the distance to the hundred-thousandth of a foot? No, even if the value for π is correct to 9 decimal places, the diameter measurement is not nearly that precise.

★ The bike will travel about 681 feet.

You could also say it will travel about 680 feet.

Choose an Estimate or Exact Amount

Suppose you worked for New York City and needed to report how many people had watched a parade. Could you find out the exact number? Sometimes, you have to estimate because you cannot get an exact amount. Sometimes, you estimate because it makes things easier and you don't need an exact amount. And sometimes, an estimate just won't do.

When you solve math problems, think about the situation before deciding whether you can estimate or whether you need an exact amount.

CASE 1 You can often estimate when you are finding whether one amount is greater or less than another amount.

1998 Total Mint Production (thousands)				
	1¢	5¢	10¢	25¢	50¢
Jan	753,200	71,280	152,500	102,200	3,400
Feb	685,200	84,960	158,500	116,600	7,500
Mar	938,600	108,720	190,500	129,400	13,500
Apr	876,000	98,880	165,500	132,600	6,200
May	872,000	110,640	208,000	144,400	0
Jun	772,400	90,240	199,000	110,800	110
Jul	871,200	128,160	202,000	145,200	0
Aug	1,092,400	119,040	217,500	133,000	0
Sep	962,000	121,152	215,500	162,200	0
Oct	964,000	123,360	205,500	249,200	0
Nov	646,400	151,440	213,500	230,200	0
Dec	824,000	115,800	207,300	211,600	0
Total	10,257,400	1,323,672	2,335,300	1,867,400	30,710

Source: U.S. Mint

EXAMPLE 1: In 1998, did the U.S. mint more than a half billion dollars worth of coins?

You are trying to find out whether one amount (total value) is greater than a specified amount ($500,000,000). So, maybe you can estimate.

coin	approx. number	approx. value
1¢	10.3 billion	$130 million
5¢	1.3 billion	$65 million
10¢	2.3 billion	$230 million
25¢	1.8 billion	$450 million

You can see that the total so far is already over $500 million, so you don't have to include the half dollars.

★ Yes, the U.S. minted more than a half billion dollars worth of coins in 1998.

CASE 2 You can estimate when you just need to know *about how many* or *about how much.*

EXAMPLE 2: In January 1998, about how many more pennies were minted than all other coins combined?

You just need to know the approximate difference. You might estimate by rounding each amount to the nearest ten million.

pennies	other coins		difference
≈ 750 million	nickels	≈ 70 million	750 million
	dimes	≈ 150 million	− 320 million
	quarters	≈ 100 million	430 million
	half dollars ≈	0 million	
	Total	≈ 320 million	

★ In January 1998, about 430 million more pennies were minted than all other coins combined.

CASE 3 Of course, you often do need to find an exact amount.

EXAMPLE 3: In a budget report, the Treasury Department is going to list the total value of nickels minted in 1998. What is that amount?

In this situation, you need an exact amount.

$1,323,672,000 \times 0.05 = 66,183,600$

★ In 1998, the total value of nickels minted by the U.S. Government was $66,183,600.

Check by Using Another Method

When you add, maybe you check your answer by adding again. You are more likely to catch an error if you change your method when you add again, perhaps by putting the addends in a different order. In more complicated math problems, you can check your result by solving the problem a different way. If you get the same result, you can be more sure it's right.

EXAMPLE: How many cubic feet of concrete will be in the foundation shown in the diagram? The top of the foundation is open.

MORE HELP
See 465

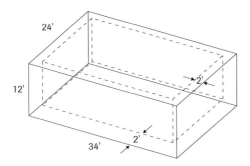

You might find the volume by thinking of the foundation in parts. (You have to be careful not to overlap parts.)

Volume of left and right wall
= 2(24 ft)(12 ft)(2 ft)
= 1152 ft³

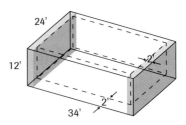

Volume of front and back wall
= 2(30 ft)(12 ft)(2 ft)
= 1440 ft³

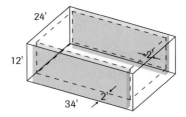

Volume of bottom
= (30 ft)(20 ft)(2 ft)
= 1200 ft³

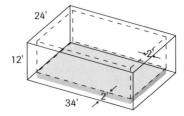

Total volume

= 1152 ft³ + 1440 ft³ + 1200 ft³

= 3792 ft³

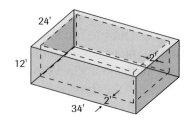

To check your answer, you could use a different method to find the volume. Find the total volume enclosed by the outside walls and subtract the empty space inside.

Volume enclosed by outer walls

= (34 ft)(24 ft)(12 ft)

= 9792 ft³

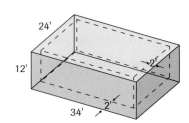

Volume of empty space inside

= (30 ft)(20 ft)(10 ft)

= 6000 ft³

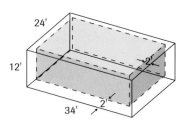

Difference

= 9792 ft³ − 6000 ft³

= 3792 ft³

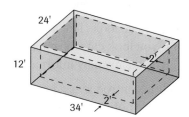

★ Since both methods give the same result you can be more sure of your answer, 3792 cubic feet.

Find Information You Need _____

You're going to a movie. You know where it's playing but you don't know when it starts. You've been in situations like this where you need more information. To find out when the movie starts, you could look in the newspaper or call the theater. Knowing what information you need and how to find it can come in handy when you solve math problems, too. Ask yourself:

- What information could help me solve the problem?

- Can I look up the information?

- Can I ask someone?

- Can I take a measurement?

- Can I use an estimate?

EXAMPLE: Which of the choices would provide the information you need to find the roots of the equation $x^2 + bx - 6 = 0$?

MORE HELP
See 174

a) $x < 10$

b) $x^2 + bx = 6$

c) $b = 2d$

d) $2bx = 4$

The first choice limits the possible values of x but doesn't give you enough information to find the roots.

The second choice looks like it provides another relationship between x and b, but if you look closely you'll see it's the same equation. So, choice b does not give you any new information about the roots of the equation.

The third choice introduces a new variable, d. Since you know nothing about d, you are not getting any useful information about b.

★ The last choice gives you information relating b and x. In fact, it gives you a numerical value for the middle term in the equation.

If $2bx = 4$, then $bx = 2$

Substituting 2 for bx in the original equation, you get:

$x^2 + 2 - 6 = 0$

or $x^2 = 4$

The roots are $x = 2$ and $x = {}^-2$.

$x = \{2, {}^-2\}$

Almanac 397

"To speak algebraically, Mr. M is execrable, but Mr. G is $(x + 1)$-ecrable."

Edgar Allen Poe

Prefixes are added at the beginning of words or suffixes to provide consistent meaning.

Prefix	Definition	Example
bi-	two	binomial: an expression with two terms
centi-, cent-	one hundredth	centimeter: a unit of length equal to one hundredth of a meter
circum-	around	circumference: distance around a circle
co-	joint, jointly, together	coplanar: lying in the same plane
dec-, deca, deka	ten	decahedron: polyhedron with ten faces
deci-	one tenth	deciliter: one tenth of a liter
di-	two, twice, double	dihedral: having two plane surfaces
dodeca-	twelve	dodecagon: polygon with 12 sides
equi-	equal, equally	equiangular: having all angles equal
giga-	10^9, or one billion	gigabyte: one billion bytes
hecto-	100	hectometer: metric unit of length equal to 100 meters
hemi-	half	hemisphere: half of a sphere
hepta-	seven	heptagon: polygon with seven sides
hex-, hexa-	six	hexagon: polygon with six sides
in-	not, without	inequality: not equal $5 \neq 8$ or $9 > 4$
inter-	between, mutual	intersecting: lines or planes that cross or meet

Prefix	Definition	Example
iso-, is-	equal	isosceles triangle: a triangle that has two congruent sides
kilo-	1000	kilogram: 1000 grams
mega-	10^6, or one million	megavolt: one million volts
mid-	middle	midpoint: point on a line segment that cuts it into two congruent segments
milli-	one thousandth	millimeter: one thousandth of a meter
multi-	many	multinomial: an expression with many terms
nona-	ninth, nine	nonagon: polygon with nine sides
octa-, octo-, oct-	eight	octagon: polygon with eight sides
para-, par-	beside, along-side	parallel: being an equal distance apart at every point
penta-, pent-	five	pentagon: polygon with five sides
per-	for each	percent: a ratio that compares a number to 100
poly-	many	polynomial: an expression with many terms
quad-	four	quadrants: the four sections of a coordinate plane that are separated by the x- and y-axes
semi-	half	semiannually: happening once every half year
septi-, sept-	seven	septennial: occurring every seven years
sexa-, sex-	six	sexcentenary: pertaining to a six-hundred-year period
tera-	10^{12}, or one trillion	terahertz: 10^{12} cycles per second
tri-	three	triangle: polygon with three sides

Suffixes are added at the end of prefixes or words to provide consistent meaning.

Suffix	Definition	Example
-centenary	of or pertaining to a 100-year period	tercentenary: of or pertaining to 300 years
-gon	having a specified number of interior angles	polygon: many-angled figure hexagon: 6-angled figure
-hedral	surfaces or faces of a given number	dihedral: formed by two plane figures
-hedron	having a given number of faces or surfaces	polyhedron: a solid whose faces are polygons heptahedron: polyhedron with seven faces
-lateral	of, at, or relating to sides	equilateral: having all sides equal
-metry	science or process of measuring	geometry: mathematics of properties, measurement, and relationships of points, lines, angles, surfaces, and solids
-nomial	term in a mathematical expression	binomial: an expression with two terms $ax^2 + bx$
-sect	cut, divide	bisect: cut or divide into two equal parts

Imagine a house of cards. All the cards look new and rigid and capable of supporting the cards above them. But, if one of the cards is weak or torn, the whole structure could come tumbling down.

Mathematics is built like a house of cards. If you know something is true (for example, the measures of the angles of a triangle must add up to 180°), then you can show that other things have to be true. But, if you're not extremely careful with your reasoning, all the things you thought you were proving could topple in a moment.

A mathematical **proof** usually starts with something that is generally accepted as true and moves step by carefully justified step to show that something else is also true. You can also use some of the techniques of mathematical proof to show that something is not true.

Postulates   401

A proof is not possible without some statements which are accepted as true. These statements are the **postulates**. We accept them without proof. Notice that this means that a postulate is an assumption made up by someone (usually a mathematician). **Axiom** is another word for postulate.

In general, postulates must be *consistent, complete,* and *independent.* **Consistency** means that proofs using the same postulates cannot contradict each other. **Completeness** means that all theorems in the system can be deduced from the same set of postulates. **Independent** means that no postulate is a consequence of another postulate.

MORE ▶

You can build a whole mathematical system on one set of postulates, and you can build a different system on another set. For example, Euclidean geometry (the geometry with which you're familiar) uses the *postulate of the unique parallel*: one and only one line through a given point not on the line can be drawn parallel to a given line. However, a whole new type of geometry (hyperbolic geometry) arises when you use a different postulate: infinitely many straight lines can be drawn parallel to a given line through an external point.

A **theorem** is a mathematical statement or proposition that is derived from previously accepted results. Theorems are based on postulates and definitions or on other established theorems.

Statements

Statements in mathematics often take an *If . . . , then . . .* form. The statement in the *if* part of the sentence is the **hypothesis** (or what you are given or taking as your starting point). The **conclusion** that follows is the statement in the *then* part.

Here are some examples of statements:

- If it is March, then there are 31 days in the month.
- If the pet is an iguana, then it is a reptile.
- If $x = 3$, then $x + 3 = 6$.
- If the polygon is a hexagon, then it has six sides.
- In a function, the value of the dependent variable *depends* on the value of the independent variable. In $y = 3x$, if $x = 2$, then $y = 6$.

A proof of a statement can be direct and follow consecutive steps that lead to a conclusion. Consider this: *If it is sunny, then I wear a hat outside.* A direct proof would show: *It is sunny outside.* You would conclude that I wear a hat outside.

A proof of a statement can also be indirect and reach the conclusion in a roundabout way. Consider this: *If it is raining, then I will carry my umbrella.* In an indirect proof you might notice that I am not carrying my umbrella and conclude that it is not raining.

Converses

You can think of a statement as *If A, then B*. The **converse** of the statement is *If B, then A*.

The converse of a statement may or may not be true.

EXAMPLE 1: Statement: If today is Monday, then yesterday was Sunday.

Converse: If yesterday was Sunday, then today is Monday.

In this case, both the statement and its converse are true.

EXAMPLE 2: Statement: If Toto is a dog, then Toto is a mammal.

Converse: If Toto is a mammal, then Toto is a dog.

This converse is false. While all dogs are mammals, not all mammals are dogs.

Because converses of true statements may be either true or false, converses can easily be used to mislead you. In advertising especially, beware of claims made by using the converse of a statement.

Inverses

You can think of a statement as *If A, then B*. The **inverse** of the statement is *If not A, then not B*.

Notice that in the inverse of a statement, both *A* and *B* are negated, while in the converse of a statement, *A* and *B* change position. Just as you must test to see whether the converse of a statement is true, you must also test to see whether the inverse of a statement is true.

MORE HELP
See 403

EXAMPLE: Statement: If 8 is a factor of a number, then 4 is a factor of the number.

Inverse: If 8 is not a factor of a number, then 4 is not a factor of the number.

While the statement is true, the inverse is not true. Consider the number 12: 8 is not a factor and 4 is.

405 ## Contrapositives

Think of a statement as *If A, then B.* The **contrapositive** of the statement is *If not B, then not A.*

MORE HELP
See 126

If a statement is true, the contrapositive of the statement must also be true.

EXAMPLE 1: Statement: If today is Saturday, then tomorrow is Sunday.

Contrapositive: If tomorrow is not Sunday, then today is not Saturday.

EXAMPLE 2: Statement: If x is divisible by 4, then it is divisible by 2.

Contrapositive: If x is not divisible by 2, then it is not divisible by 4.

406 ## Using Inductive Reasoning

Every morning at about 9 A.M. a certain jogger passes your house. If you see the jogger pass your house in the morning, you may conclude that it is about 9 A.M. This is using **inductive reasoning**. When you use inductive reasoning, you make a generalization from specific cases. You use inductive reasoning whenever you think up a general rule after considering a pattern. While it often suggests statements or relationships between patterns that you can prove in other ways, inductive reasoning is not an acceptable way to prove things by itself.

407 ## Transformational Proof

In a **transformational proof**, you change the form of a statement while keeping it true.

MORE HELP
See 044–048,
127–129,
181–182

For example, $3a^2 + 3a = 6$ transforms into $3(a + 2)(a - 1) = 0$. Transforming the statement makes it easier to solve the equation.

Statement:	$3a^2 + 3a = 6$
First transformation: Use the Equality Properties to subtract 6 from both sides.	$3a^2 + 3a - 6 = 6 - 6$ $3a^2 + 3a - 6 = 0$
Second transformation: Use the Distributive Property to factor.	$3(a^2 + a - 2) = 0$
Third transformation: Factor again to arrive at your conclusion.	$3(a + 2)(a - 1) = 0$

Another example of a transformational proof involves translating a set of parallel lines cut by a transversal in the direction of the transversal to prove that corresponding angles are congruent.

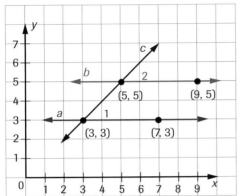

Line *a* is parallel to line *b*. Line *c* is a transversal intersecting *a* and *b*.

If you translate line *a* by moving every point on it two units along *x* and two units along *y*, it becomes collinear with *b*. Its slope hasn't changed, so its relationship to *c* hasn't changed. $\angle 1 \cong \angle 2$

Using Deductive Reasoning

You use **deductive reasoning** when you apply a general rule to a specific case. It is the process of reasoning where specific cases are tested against a specific rule.

Deductive reasoning uses accepted facts and lists them step-by-step. Definitions, postulates, statements, and theorems that have already been proved are often used. Each reason follows the other to reach the desired conclusion.

EXAMPLE: Prove for real numbers a and b, $b \neq 0$, that $\left(\frac{a}{b}\right)^{-n} = \left(\frac{b}{a}\right)^{n}$.

★ $\left(\frac{a}{b}\right)^{-n} = \frac{1}{\left(\frac{a}{b}\right)^{n}}$, using the definition of a negative exponent.

Rewriting the complex fraction, $\frac{1}{\left(\frac{a}{b}\right)^{n}} = 1 \cdot \left(\frac{b}{a}\right)^{n} = \left(\frac{b}{a}\right)^{n}$.

The proof is direct.

Using Contradiction

You can use a contradiction to prove that a statement is not true.

MORE HELP
See 106–107

When you show that a rule isn't true for all examples, you are using **contradiction,** or *proof by counterexample*. All it takes is one counterexample to prove that a statement is not true.

Consider the Commutative Property of Addition. This property states that changing the order in which you add two numbers will not change the sum. Now suppose that someone thinks the commutative property is also true for subtraction. All you need is one counterexample to show that the commutative property is not valid for subtraction: $1 - 2 \neq 2 - 1$ because $^-1 \neq 1$.

Counterexamples can disprove something, but no matter how many examples satisfy a hypothesis, examples alone won't prove that a hypothesis is true for all cases.

To disprove a statement, you only need one counterexample, but how do you choose values for a and b? Think of the different kinds of values a and b can have: positive/negative, integral/rational, relative size, and so forth.

EXAMPLE: Prove that the statement $|a| - |b| = |a - b|$ is not true.

Try positive values:

$$|6| - |4| = 6 - 4$$
$$= 2$$
$$|6 - 4| = 2$$
$$2 = 2$$

Try one negative and one positive:

$$|6| - |^-4| = 6 - 4$$
$$= 2$$
$$|6 - {}^-4| = 10$$
$$2 \neq 10$$

★ Since $|^-6| - |^-4| \neq |6 - {}^-4|$, the statement is false.

Believe it or not, the way you study can be more important than how long you study. If you don't like to study, or don't have very much time, you can use the tips in this section to make the most of your study time.

Taking Notes and Keeping a Journal _____

Think of notes as your personal customized review book. Notes can help you remember what you learned in class. They can guide you when you try exercises on your own. A math notebook is a good place to record examples that you think are especially helpful. You can also include fun facts about mathematics and describe your own accomplishments, just as you would in a personal journal. Write about new vocabulary, use symbols with examples, and draw diagrams or illustrations. Include descriptions or discussions of how mathematics is used in the world around you. There is often more than one way to solve a problem. Try to include alternate methods when you can.

Some students like to use a two-column format for their notes.

Use your math journal to chart your course through different math challenges. It can help you see how much you have learned.

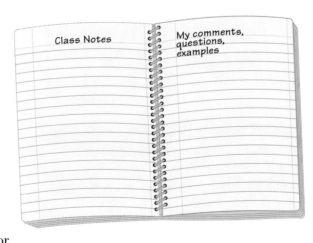

Wherever you take notes, have a good set of tools with you: a pencil or two with good erasers, a highlighter, colored pens or pencils, plenty of lined paper, and graph paper, too, when you need it.

How to Take Notes

Your math notebook can take different forms. You can write math notes on cards and keep them in an envelope. To keep this card journal handy, punch holes in the envelope and place it in your loose-leaf binder. You can also write your notes in a separate notebook. Date your notes to keep track of the order in which topics were introduced, studied, or reviewed in class.

MORE HELP

See 182

Your notes can take different forms. You can use an outline form or write full sentences. You can even draw diagrams. You don't have to use the same form all the time. Just try to make your notes as useful as possible.

Try to make connections in class. Try to reflect the connections in your notes so you can make the same connections outside of class. Your notes are your connection back to your teacher and to your math class.

Solve: $x^4 = 17x^2 - 16$

$x^4 - 17x^2 + 16 = 0$ Put the terms of equation in descending order of powers; set the expression equal to zero.

Let: $w = x^2$ Make the equation look like a quadratic.

$w^2 - 17w + 16 = 0$

$(w - 1)(w - 16) = 0$ Factor to solve.

$w = 1$ or $w = 16$

$x^2 = 1$ or $x^2 = 16$ Remember: need to solve for x.

$x = \pm 1$ or $x = \pm 4$ Substitute $x^2 = w$, then solve again.

Listen as actively as possible to explanations and include in your notes any comments that might be helpful to you later.

It's hard to remember everything covered in class, so copy all notes written on the board. If an example is worked out in detail, try to include in your notes the comments your teacher makes.

Listen carefully. That means, think about what the teacher is saying and how the problem is being solved. Reword what the teacher is saying in terms that you understand and can apply. If you are uncertain about a particular step or part of a solution and have a question, ask. Don't be afraid to ask, since others probably have the same question in mind. Remember to include specific answers in your notes. Try to work through similar problems on your own as soon as you can.

Evaluating Your Notes

The easier to read and more complete your notes are, the more they can help you study for tests. If one way of taking notes isn't as helpful as you'd like it to be, try something new.

- If writing in paragraphs doesn't work, write in outline form instead.

- If you can't find what you need in your notes because they are too brief, try to fill in some of the details. When you copy a problem from the board, define new symbols and explain the steps in the problem. Try to record comments that help you understand the procedure.

- If you have too many details, concentrate on only the most important points, but be careful here. Too many details are better than too few. Use your class time to understand new concepts being taught and record what you think is most important. When you read through your notes you can always use a highlighter to mark the most important details.

- Try to look over your notes every day while the material is still fresh in your mind. Try to use them to help you with a few practice problems. If you don't understand what you've written, you'll need to improve your notes by checking another source and filling in the gaps.

- Look over your notes before you do your homework. If something is unclear, check your textbook and this handbook, too. If you still have a question, write it in the margin of your notebook so you'll remember to ask your teacher.

- Don't wait until just before a test to look through all of your notes. Regularly look back at what you did earlier in the week, last week, or last month.

Guidelines for Improving Note-Taking Skills

Taking effective notes is tricky. Sure, you're writing to yourself, but you can't be sure how much you'll remember when you read your notes. A short word or phrase that seems clear when you write it may be a mystery when you read it sometime later. In a sense, you're writing for someone else. If you act as if that were true, you'll be more careful to be clear.

- **Be attentive.** Listen carefully as your teacher explains how to solve a problem or an equation or how to use a procedure. Carefully read explanations in your textbook or this handbook. Write down parts of the explanation that seem to particularly help you understand the problem and its solution.

- **Keep it simple.** Write only things that help you understand how to solve problems.

- **Be organized.** Number all items presented in a list or a time order. Highlight items that you do not understand so that you can look them up or ask about them later.

- **Summarize.** Try to write a brief summary after the class. Do it before you forget what went on. Just a few sentences might be what you need to jog your memory later on and give you insight into how much you really understood.

- **Use discussions, questions, and answers.** Class discussions, questions, and answers all help you find out how much you understand. Questions can clarify difficult concepts and help you out when you get stuck.

- **Communicate.** Mathematics is about reasoning. Use your notes to communicate with yourself. Your thoughts, ideas, and insights are valuable. Don't take them for granted.

- **Look for another way.** Is there another way to solve it? There often is more than one way to solve a problem. If a different method is used, write it down. It makes you more mathematically flexible and it may give you another point of view.

Reading Mathematics Materials

Mathematics materials require a different kind of reading than you're used to in other subjects because the text doesn't flow in the same way and much of the information you need is found in diagrams, tables, graphs, and examples. Much of the information is symbolic rather than textual. Some exercises may require you to use answers or other information from previous exercises. You need to pay careful attention to all the information provided to you and this may require that you read a section more than once.

Greatest Common Factor

021

The greatest number that is a factor of two or more whole numbers is the **greatest common factor (GCF)** of the numbers. GCF is very useful in simplifying fractions and algebraic expressions. When looking for GCF or prime factors, you do not need to count 1 as a factor.

EXAMPLE 1: Find the GCF of $4x^3$, $12x^2$, and $8x$.

ONE WAY Use a Venn Diagram to help you understand the GCF.

> Often, the book will show a worked-out procedure. Work out the same example yourself, then try a different one to be sure you understand. Refer back to these procedures in the book or your notes when you do homework exercises.

> Terms and symbols are defined and then used right away.

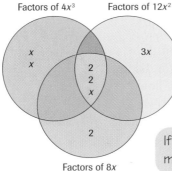

Factors of $4x^3$ Factors of $12x^2$

Factors of $8x$

> If you've forgotten what a term or symbol means, look it up in your glossary.

ANOTHER WAY Find the GCF of the terms by listing the **prime factors** of each expression. Identify the common factors.

Factors of $4x^3$ $= 2 \cdot 2 \cdot x \cdot x \cdot x$
Factors of $12x^2 = 2 \cdot 2 \cdot 3 \cdot x \cdot x$
Factors of $8x$ $= 2 \cdot 2 \cdot 2 \cdot x$

> The text will assume you know certain procedures. If you don't understand a conclusion in the text, look up the procedure to refresh your memory.

★ Either way, the greatest common factor (GCF) of $4x^3$, $12x^2$, and $8x$ is $2 \cdot 2 \cdot x$ or $4x$.

Factorials

022

Take any whole number and call it n.

Multiply all the positive integers from 1 through n.

$1 \times 2 \times 3 \times ... \times (n - 1) \times n$

This product is called **n factorial (n!)**.

> Here is a strange mathematical definition. 0! is defined as 1. 1! is also defined as 1.

MORE ▶

Managing Your Time

Do you have trouble getting things done on time (or at all)? The bad news is that you can't add more hours to the day. The good news is that you *can* get more things done in the hours you have. Time management will help you organize both your study time and your free time.

- **Keep a weekly schedule.** A weekly planner helps you organize your assignments and plan for time to complete them. The planner makes it easier for you to prepare for tests and get projects and other homework done well and on time. Keep this schedule in your notebook or in your math journal.

- **Make a daily list.** Write down things you need to do today and must do tomorrow. Don't put off assignments until the last minute. Prioritize them in order of importance. Place the list someplace where you won't forget it. Check off items as you complete them.

- **Have a homework schedule.** Set aside a specific time for doing homework assignments. Allow yourself short breaks between each assignment. Don't make the breaks longer than five minutes.

- **Set goals.** Be realistic. Make sure the tasks you set for yourself and the time you allow are reasonable. Reward yourself for completing tasks that you set. Try to learn from goals or tasks that you don't quite achieve.

- **Get it done and turn it in on time.**

  - Go over any instructions your teacher has given for an assignment.

  - Pick an easy thing to do first, just to get started.

  - Carefully read the directions.

  - Check your notes and your textbook to make sure that you know how to do your homework as accurately as possible.

  - Keep a list of things you don't understand to ask your teacher about.

  - After you're finished, check the directions again to make sure your homework is really complete.

  - Keep your completed assignments someplace safe!

The nice thing about writing math ideas is that you can use symbols and diagrams to save time and effort. A symbol is shorter than a word or phrase. A diagram, like any picture, can be worth a thousand words.

The slope of the line below is 2. Remember, the slope is given by $\frac{\text{change in } y}{\text{change in } x}$. The diagram should help you understand the meaning of slope.

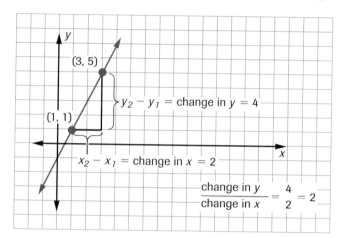

MORE HELP
See 221–222

418

Using a Rubric to Plan and Evaluate Your Writing

You can use the outline below to help you organize your thoughts to write clearly in mathematics.

Statement of problem	
	Detail: Step 1
	Detail: Step 2
Solution	. . .
	. . .
	Detail: last step
Conclusion/Answer	

MORE ▶

Use the following outline, or **rubric**, to help you when you are writing in mathematics. It tells you what you need to include in your writing to get a top grade. You can improve your ability to write in mathematics by using the rubric to evaluate your own work. Check to see how much you understand from your own writing. Decide which level you think your solution would be. Then ask a parent, teacher, or friend to evaluate the solution. Discuss any differences. Keep in mind that it takes a lot of effort to reach the top level, but if you keep trying, you'll get there.

Rubric Level:

- **Excellent.** The writing shows a full understanding of the topic. It shows how you think through a problem. Each step is explained with both examples and words. The examples are worked out correctly and in detail. There may be sketches or diagrams. The problem is organized so that steps are in order. It is more than just calculations.

- **Well done.** The writing is clear, most procedures and calculations are correct, and a full written explanation supports the work. The answer is correct and correctly labeled.

- **Adequate.** The writing shows a good understanding of the topic. You include examples, calculations, and maybe even diagrams. Steps are followed in order with each example or diagram explained. There may be some errors in computation, but your descriptions show that you can think through the details of the problem.

- **Weak.** The writing does not really explain what is going on in the problem. There are errors in both understanding and in calculations. While there may be examples or calculations, there is nothing to explain what the examples mean or why the calculations were made. Steps may not be in order. There is not much language used in the solution.

- **Inadequate.** The writing is unclear and it is not well-organized. Examples and computation are not explained. There are many errors in both understanding and computation. Very little language is used in the solution.

- **Too brief to evaluate.**

- **Blank.**

EXAMPLE: What rubric level should be assigned to this exercise? Explain.

A car travels an average of 70 miles in $2\frac{1}{2}$ hours. How much faster must the car average to make the trip in 45 fewer minutes?

This is a distance problem, so I used the distance formula:

rate · time = distance or $r \cdot t = d$. Also, since this problem is about average rate, I assumed a constant rate of speed, r, for the car.

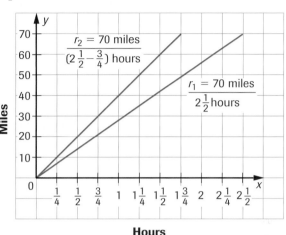

$r_1 \cdot t = d$
$r_1 = \frac{d}{t}$
$r_1 = \frac{70}{2.5} = 28$ mph

I used the distance formula and solved for r when $t = 2\frac{1}{2}$ hours and $d = 70$ miles. The car travels 28 mph.

$2\frac{1}{2} - \frac{3}{4} = 1\frac{3}{4}$

To find the time a 45 minute faster trip would take, I subtracted. Before subtracting, I converted the minutes to a fraction of an hour: 45 minutes $= \frac{3}{4}$ hour.

Substitute:
$r_2 = \frac{70}{1.75} = 40$ mph

The new trip needs to take $1\frac{3}{4}$, or 1.75 hours. I converted from a fraction to a decimal to make the division easier in the next step. I used the new time and the old distance in the formula ($r = \frac{d}{t}$) to find the new average rate. The new average rate should be 40 mph.

$40 - 28 = 12$

To find how much faster the new rate is, I subtracted the old rate from the new rate. The car must average 12 mph faster to make the trip in 45 fewer minutes.

★ Excellent. Good explanations. Correct answer. Well organized. Useful diagram.

419 Test-Taking Skills

Success on a test depends on how well you prepare along the way. Keep up with assignments, try practice problems, ask questions when you don't understand something. To do well, organize your approach to studying and give yourself ample time to develop confidence.

420 Reviewing Test Material

Even before you begin studying for a test, you should find out the rules of the test and what the test will cover.

- **What will be on the test?** Ask the teacher to be as specific as possible. Write a list of all the topics the test might cover.

- **What will the test questions be like?** Will there be short answer computation, word problems, multiple-choice or true/false questions, or a combination of these? Will it include definitions? Will you need to show your work?

- **Make an outline of problem types.** Find an example for each type of problem that will be on the test.

- **Do I understand the topics?** List each kind of problem separately. Then you can focus on each type of problem individually. Make sure that everything makes sense to you. If it doesn't, study more and get help if you need it.

- **Use index cards.** Use index cards to list and illustrate formulas you need to memorize and/or use. Write the formula on one side and how to identify it and use it on the other side. Include an example.

- **Think about how things fit together.** The more you understand, the less you'll have to memorize. For example, if you understand why a formula works, you'll have an easier time remembering it.

■ **Review your notes carefully.** Compare your class notes and examples with those in your math book. Go over your homework.

■ **Get any notes or assignments that you may have missed.** If you've missed any classes, you may have missed something important. Make sure you find out what you missed. Get copies of notes and do any homework that was assigned. Your teacher or classmates will help if you ask ahead of time.

■ **Make a list of questions.** If you are uncertain about anything, talk to your teacher several days before the test.

■ **Start reviewing early.** Don't wait until the night before the test to study. Work out problems one at a time—don't rush through them. By studying a little each day for several days, you will gain confidence in your abilities, and you will remember more than if you try to study everything the night before the test.

■ **Find a good place to study.** Find a quiet place. Make sure there's room to spread out your notes, open your textbook and your handbook, and try some sample problems.

■ **Make sure you get enough rest.** If you get tired, take a break or get some sleep. If you're tired on test day, you'll have trouble concentrating and that could hurt your grade.

■ **Remember to eat well.** If you're hungry, it's hard to concentrate. If you've eaten too much, you may be sleepy.

■ **Set up a specific time to study.** Review your notes, look through your textbook, and try sample problems.

■ **Practice, practice, practice.** Redo old homework problems or quiz problems. Try different examples to prepare for the test. You can even make yourself a practice test.

■ **Use study aids.** Silly sayings, called mnemonic devices, can help you remember complicated rules or procedures. See 069 for an example.

MORE HELP
See 069

■ **Study with others.** By talking about how to work through problems, you will test your own understanding.

■ **Study by yourself.** You will be taking the test alone, so you need to be able to do the problems on your own.

Taking the Test

■ **Try to arrive early for the test.** Allow yourself time to put your books down, get comfortable in your seat, and get out whatever materials you need for the test.

MORE ▶

■ **Try to unwind before the test.** Breathe deeply and try to relax. Think of the problems as puzzles or mysteries that you want to solve.

■ **Check that you have all the materials you need for the test.** You may need a ruler, sharp pencils, paper, a calculator, and so on.

■ **Know the rules of the test.** How long is the test? Do all the questions count equally? Is your textbook, handbook, notes, or a formula sheet allowed? Is there partial credit for short-answer items? If it's a multiple-choice test, is a *guessing factor* used? Is a calculator allowed?

■ **Look over the entire test quickly.** Try to get an idea of the length of the test and the points each type of problem is worth. Think about how much time you can allot for each problem. Then begin the test. Check the time once in a while. If you are not allowed a formula sheet and you need to know formulas, you may want to write them down at the beginning of the test while they're still fresh in your mind.

■ **Read the directions carefully.** If you don't understand the directions, ask your teacher. Follow all instructions.

■ **Answer the questions you are sure of first.** If you are stuck, move on to the next question. Mark the questions you skip.

■ **Read the problems carefully.** Even if a problem seems easy, read it over a couple of times. Make sure your answer is reasonable.

■ **If time is running out, try not to panic.** Panicking will only waste time that you could be using to finish a problem or move on to another problem.

■ **Never leave an answer blank.** Try to do some work on every question. You may receive partial credit. Take a fresh look at any problems you skipped the first time. You may see something that you overlooked the first time through. An exception to this rule is when a guessing factor is used in scoring a multiple-choice test. In that case, give an answer only when you can positively eliminate at least one choice.

■ **Only change your answers if you are sure they are wrong.** Do not rush through a problem a second time and quickly change your answer. You are often right the first time, but rethinking an answer you are uncertain about might allow you to come up with a better choice.

■ **Double-check.** Make sure that you have answered all the questions that you can and that all of your answers make sense. Recheck your work carefully if you have time. Don't be in a rush to leave or you might miss some errors that you have made!

■ **Check that all your answers are readable.** You may need to show your work for all the questions you answer—be neat.

How to Use a Calculator on a Test _____

If a calculator is allowed during an exam, remember that it is only a tool. You are the problem solver. Do not fail to study before a test or read carefully during a test just because you can use a calculator.

In general, whether or not you use your calculator will depend on what type of answer you need. You should use your understanding of the material covered on the test to help you decide whether using the calculator will help you or whether it will slow you down (for example, you might have to convert an answer to a different form or your answer may not be a number at all).

- Before you start pressing keys, ask yourself, *Can I do the problem in my head? Can I estimate?* These methods can be even faster and more reliable than using a calculator. Look at the numbers and think about the operations involved. Ask yourself questions such as, *Can I use compatible numbers? Are there benchmark fractions (0, $\frac{1}{2}$, 1) or benchmark percents (25%, 50%, 75%) that I can use?*

  MORE HELP
  See 072

- When you do use the calculator, be sure to check all the calculator answers for reasonableness by estimating the answers.

- For fractions, the choice may depend on the form required for the answer and the kind of calculator you have. It may be quicker to just add, subtract, multiply, or divide the fractions directly if you are supposed to write the answer in simplest form. If a decimal answer is acceptable or you can easily recognize the fraction from its decimal form, the calculator might be quicker.

  MORE HELP
  See 004

- If you are going to use your calculator for special operations, make sure you know how to use your calculator to produce correct answers.

- Your calculator may be able to find the roots of a quadratic equation. However, if you need an answer in radical form, it is probably better to use the quadratic formula.

  MORE HELP
  See 051, 184

- If you have a graphing calculator, it may help you make quick decisions about the graphs of various functions. If pictures help you more than words, the graph may even help you decide whether a relation is a function.

  MORE HELP
  See 134, 436

Tips for Multiple-Choice Tests

In a multiple-choice problem, there is usually one correct answer. If you read the problem carefully, think logically, and use your math sense, you can often eliminate one or two choices easily.

If you get stuck on a multiple-choice problem, skip it and go on to another problem. Make sure you mark it for later. Go back to these problems after you have completed the ones that you know. When you go back, if you have time, go through each choice to see whether it could be correct.

MORE HELP
See 118–119

1. Use number sense to save time and work. Problems that look like they have time-consuming calculations can often be solved by using a shortcut.

Compute. $\dfrac{11 \times 10 \times 9 \times 8 \times 7 \times 6}{12 \times 11 \times 10 \times 9 \times 8 \times 7} = \blacksquare$

A. $\frac{7}{12}$ B. $\frac{1}{2}$

C. $\frac{11}{12}$ D. $1\frac{1}{2}$

In this problem, you can cancel $11 \times 10 \times 9 \times 8 \times 7$ in the numerator with the same factors in the denominator. Now it's easy: $\frac{6}{12} = \frac{1}{2}$.
The answer is B.

2. Use estimation when you can. Check for reasonableness. You can also use clues to help you solve a problem. Think about units, decimal places, and signs (positive or negative) to help you eliminate choices.

MORE HELP
See 465

What is the approximate length of the diameter of a circle that has an area of 28.26 square centimeters? Use 3.14 for π.

A. 3 cm   B. 6 cm

C. 9 cm   D. 9 cm²

The answer is a length, so it must be in centimeters; you can eliminate D. Now you can estimate using 3 for π in the formula for the area of a circle, $A = \pi r^2$.

$3 \times 3^2 = 27$, so choice A is the radius. The diameter is about $2 \times 3 = 6$ cm. The answer is B.

3. Eliminate obviously wrong choices. Try the easier choices first.

$\frac{-1}{4}$ and 0 are the solutions to which equations?

A. $4x^2 + 1 = 0$

B. $4x^2 - x = 0$

C. $4x^2 + x = 0$

D. $4x - 1 = 0$

Try testing zero first—it's easier than $\frac{-1}{4}$. Zero is obviously not a solution to A or D. So, you need to decide between B and C. You can substitute $\frac{-1}{4}$ into each equation and find which one works.

$4\left(\frac{-1}{4}\right)^2 - \left(\frac{-1}{4}\right) = \frac{1}{4} + \frac{1}{4} = \frac{1}{2} \neq 0$

$4\left(\frac{-1}{4}\right)^2 + \left(\frac{-1}{4}\right) = \frac{1}{4} - \frac{1}{4} = 0$ The answer is C.

Tips for Short-Answer Tests

- Answer the question that was asked. Show your solution.

- These questions are often either right or wrong with no partial credit, so you want to be very careful with your computation.

- Know and use the order of operations.

- Remember to include units of measure whenever needed.

MORE HELP
See 069

- If the directions ask for a fraction in simplest form, make sure that the answer really is in simplest form.

- If you are asked for a diagram, make sure you clearly label it.

Problem	Solution/Check	Answer
A. If $x + x + x = y + y$, then $3x - 2y = [\blacksquare]$	$x + x + x = 3x$ and $y + y = 2y$, so $3x = 2y$ or $3x - 2y = 0$.	0
B. 8 is 30% of what number?	$8 = 0.30n$ $n = \frac{8}{0.30}$ or $26\frac{2}{3}$	$26\frac{2}{3}$
C. A rectangular field 38 feet long is twice as long as it is wide. How many feet of fencing are needed to go around the field?	[diagram: rectangle labeled 19 ft on right side, 38 ft below] $P = 2l + 2w$ $= 2 \times 38 + 2 \times 19 = 114$	114 ft
D. Factor: $x^2 - 6x + 8$	$(x - 4)(x - 2) = x^2 - 2x - 4x + 8$ $= x^2 - 6x + 8$	$(x - 4)(x - 2)$
E. Simplify: $(\sqrt{18})(\sqrt{2})$	$(\sqrt{18})(\sqrt{2}) = \sqrt{18 \times 2} = \sqrt{36} = 6$	6
F. Solve for x. $3x + 2 = 4x - 5$	$3x + 2 \quad = 4x - 5$ $3x + 2 + 5 \quad = 4x - 5 + 5$ $3x - 3x + 7 = 4x - 3x$ $\quad\quad 7 = x$	$x = 7$
G. Town A is 30 miles due west of Town B and Town C is 40 miles due south of Town A. What is the shortest distance from Town B to Town C? Illustrate your solution with a diagram.	Use the Pythagorean Theorem: $30^2 + 40^2 \quad = c^2$ $900 + 1600 = c^2$ $\sqrt{2500} = \sqrt{c^2}$ $\quad\quad 50 = c$	The shortest distance from B to C is 50 miles. [diagram: right triangle with A top-left, B top-right (30 mi between), 40 mi down left side to C, 50 mi hypotenuse, north arrow]

MORE HELP
See 104

MORE HELP
See 182

MORE HELP
See 245

Tips for Constructed-Response Tests

If a problem asks you to explain your answer, include all the details needed to understand your thinking process. Grading is usually based on how you do *and* how you explain each step of the problem.

MORE HELP
See 418

SAMPLE PROBLEM: For $x > 1$, which of the following expressions decrease as x increases? Increase as x increases? Explain your thinking.

I. $x + \frac{1}{x}$ II. $x^2 - x$ III. $\frac{1}{x + 1}$

1. First consider what happens to $x + \frac{1}{x}$ as x increases. But don't stop here. Remember, you must investigate all three expressions. If you stop here you will only receive partial credit.

As x increases, $\frac{1}{x}$ decreases since a unit fraction decreases as the denominator increases. Also, since $x > 1$, $x > \frac{1}{x}$.

Even though as x increases $\frac{1}{x}$ decreases, the increase is greater than the decrease, so the sum increases. $x + \frac{1}{x}$ increases as x increases.

2. Now consider $x^2 - x$. Don't forget to explain your thinking here.

If you factor $x^2 - x$, you get $x(x - 1)$. As x increases, $(x - 1)$ also increases. If both factors increase, the product must also increase. So, $x^2 - x$ increases as x increases.

3. You must also consider how $\frac{1}{x + 1}$ behaves as x increases. Don't be fooled into thinking this expression increases just because the other two expressions increase as x increases.

For all unit fractions, as the denominator increases, the value of the fraction decreases. Since $x > 1$, $x + 1$ is always greater than x. So, as x increases, $\frac{1}{x + 1}$ decreases.

4. After solving the problem, use the original question to form your answer.

For $x > 1$, as x increases, the expressions $x + \frac{1}{x}$ and $x^2 - x$ increase while the expression $\frac{1}{x + 1}$ decreases.

After a Test

■ **Keep a record.** Record in your math notebook how you study for tests. Compare how you prepared for the test with how the test turned out.

  ■ *Did you study all the topics for the test?*

  ■ *Did you cover each topic thoroughly?*

  ■ *Were you able to do different types of problems?*

  ■ *What types of practice exercises worked the best for you?*

  Think about how you could improve your study habits, the way you study for a test, and how you actually take a test.

■ **Correct the test and fill in the details.** When the teacher goes over the test in class, correct your errors. Use a different-color pencil or pen to write the corrections. Don't erase your original answer. Keep it there so you can figure out what went wrong. If you don't understand why your answer is wrong, ask your teacher after you've tried to figure it out yourself.

■ **Evaluate the methods you used.** As you look through your test, consider whether you used appropriate strategies to solve problems. Think about whether alternate solution methods might have been easier or even possible.

  ■ *Did you use logical reasoning and math sense whenever you could?*

  ■ *Did you use a calculator and/or estimation when appropriate?*

  ■ *Whether your mistakes were computational or conceptual, do you understand your error(s)?*

  ■ *Did you skip harder problems or only partially solve them when you studied?*

Use your test as a guide to how well you understand the topics tested. If you can identify what went wrong on your test and in your studying, you will be less likely to repeat the mistakes on future tests.

Before computers, people had to make tables, charts, and graphs by hand. If one number changed, they might have to calculate everything all over again and rewrite all the entries. Before computers, people could not store information electronically—they used only cards, folders, and other tedious systems. If they wanted to research information, they went to the library. Now people can access all kinds of information on the Internet.

428) ## Spreadsheets

Spreadsheet programs are great tools for organizing, analyzing, managing, sorting, and retrieving data. They are quick, efficient, and accurate. If data change, the spreadsheet can automatically recalculate with any data that are affected by the change. Spreadsheet programs contain powerful formulas and functions that can be used to analyze data. They are easy to edit and to customize. They even let you display data on charts and graphs.

429) ### Spreadsheet Terminology

A document or file that is created by a spreadsheet program is called a **worksheet**. The labels on the sample worksheet on the next page explain different parts of the worksheet and how to refer to and locate an element in the worksheet.

A **cell** is a box where you can enter data. The **cell address** gives the location of the cell. The cell address includes the column letter followed by the row number. A2 refers to the cell in column A row 2.

When you type an entry into an active cell, it shows here. When you make that cell active again, what you entered before shows here.

Information is entered into the **active cell**. It has a dark border or looks shaded.

A **row** is a horizontal line of cells.

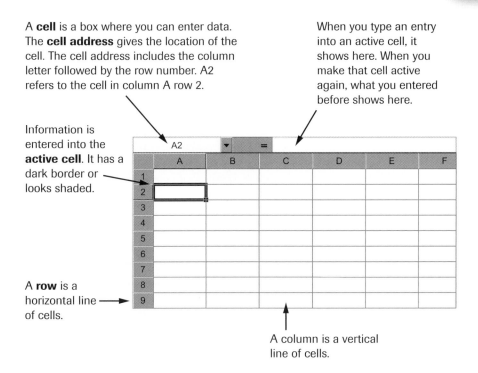

A column is a vertical line of cells.

Average is a function that finds the mean of a list of numbers. Cell B8 contains this function: = Average (B1:B6). This means it will find the **mean** of the numbers in cells B1 through B6. When you press Enter after typing the function, the computer finds the mean. It puts the value in cell B8.

MORE HELP
See 465

Labels are words or abbreviations entered into cells to identify information used in the spreadsheet. Labels are descriptive and are never involved in the computation.

Values are numbers. Values may be entered as data in the worksheet or they may be computed for you by the program.

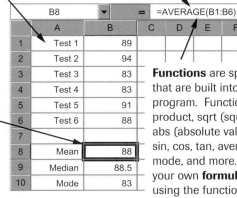

Functions are specific formulas that are built into the spreadsheet program. Functions include sum, product, sqrt (square root), abs (absolute value), fact (factorial), sin, cos, tan, average, median, mode, and more. You can define your own **formulas** in addition to using the functions that come with the spreadsheet program.

What-If Analysis

Spreadsheets allow you to change the relationships among cells and see what happens. Results which could take a very long time to compute by hand are given almost instantaneously on your worksheet. That makes it easy to get answers to *what if?* questions. *What if the interest rate were 5% instead of 6%? What if the dimensions were 4 × 6 instead of 3 × 7?*

For example, suppose you are interested in how the volume of a sphere increases as the radius of the sphere increases. By entering different values for the radius, you can immediately see how the volume changes.

C5		▼		=	4/3* PI( )*B5^3	
	A	B	C	D	E	F
1					You can tell	
2		Radius	Volume		the spread-	
3		(in.)	(in.^3)		sheet how to	
4		1	4.19		round all the	
5		2	33.51		numbers in a	
6		3	113.10		column. This	
7		4	268.08		column's	
8		5	523.60		numbers are	
9		6	904.78		rounded to	
					hundredths.	

To compute the volume in the worksheet above, notice that you must define the formula for the volume of a sphere, $V = \frac{4}{3}\pi r^3$. When you do this, you must also define the radius, r. You can define the radius by referring to the column of cells that correspond to the lengths of the radii.

Notice that * means multiplication and that ^ means to raise the base (each radius in this example) to the power (cubed, or to the third power, for volume). PI( ) is a function that supplies the value of pi to 15 decimal places.

Graphs from a Spreadsheet

Most spreadsheet programs can automatically create graphs and charts like bar graphs, scatter plots, pie charts, line graphs, and three-dimensional graphs. Of course, you have to decide which graph would best show the data so you can tell the program which graph to make. The program makes the graph. It allows you to give the graph a title and to label the axes. It even creates a legend that explains the colors or symbols used in the graph.

The program leads you through steps to create the graph. However, it does not check to see whether your graph makes sense. You have to do that. You must be careful to choose the kind of graph that applies to the data you have. Keep in mind that after creating a chart or graph, you can still try different options that might better suit the data.

Suppose you want to graph the data about the volume of spheres from the previous section. You may decide to plot several points and then connect them with a smooth curve. Even though this is not strictly a scatterplot because a scatterplot consists of discrete points, the scatterplot spreadsheet function will do this for you.

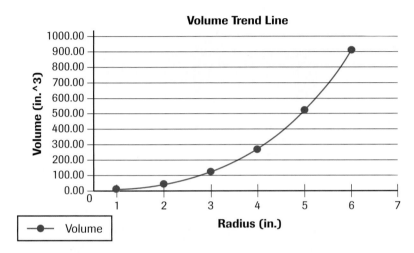

You may want to make a bar graph of the data in the spreadsheet.

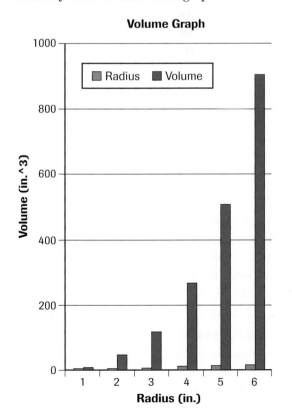

MORE ▶

Remember, the computer will let you select a graph that doesn't make sense. If you selected a pie chart for these data, you'd get a pie chart like this. But it still doesn't make sense because the set of data doesn't represent 100% of anything.

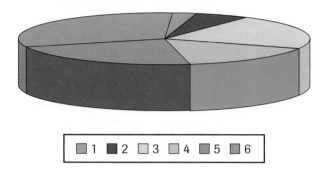

☐ 1 ■ 2 ☐ 3 ☐ 4 ■ 5 ☐ 6

432   Databases

A **database** is a collection of information. While spreadsheets organize numerical data, databases can handle any type of information. Database programs are commonly used to manage phone directories, mailing lists, product listings, and payroll information. You might want to use a database to manage your address book or to keep track of all your CDs. You can easily update and view the information stored in a database, and you can quickly find information of interest.

Databases and spreadsheets can sometimes replace each other. You can compute in both programs. If the fields in a database are mostly numbers, a spreadsheet might work better. If a spreadsheet contains more labels, a database might be a better choice.

433   Parts of a Database

A **file**, or **table**, is a collection of information about a specific topic, such as an address book. It is made up of a collection of fields and records. The **field** is a specific category of information, such as last names. You may think of each column in the table as a field. Each field might be limited in size. You can type in only as many letters or numbers as the size of the field allows. If you have a very long name, and the name field is not long enough, some of the letters may get cut off!

The **record** contains information about a single subject. You may think of each record as a row in the table. It is like an index card containing information about the subject.

Each piece of data is stored in a **field**. Each field has its own name to keep it separate from other fields. In an address book, there are different fields for the name, the address, and so on. If you set a field to *numeric*, you may only enter the digits 0–9. This will guarantee that you do not write names in number-only fields. It will also guarantee that if you want to use data from this field to compute, there won't be an impossible calculation. If you set a field to *alphanumeric*, you can enter both numbers and letters in the field.

ID	First Name	Last Name	Age	Weight	Zip Code
1	Greg	Brown	15	104	10020
2	Brenda	Kim	14	86	02117
3	Lonnie	Kelton	17	110	82060
4	Jacob	Smith	16	89	22901
5	Maria	Gonzales	15	92	84092
6	Devin	Roberts	16	102	92122
7	Leah	Nygen	15	84	30374
8	Natalie	Walters	16	81	32253
9	Luke	Harris	16	95	88001

A **record** is a collection of information about one thing in a table. A record in an address book would contain the full name and address of one person.

A database stores and manages a large collection of information related to a particular subject. The following features are part of most database programs and can be used to help you quickly add, delete, view, organize, and update information stored in the database.

- **Browse** You can browse, or scan, a database for information. If a database is very large, browsing may be limited to certain records.

- **Query** The process of letting the database know which records you need is called a query. It can be used with the browse, search, and sort features.

- **Search** You can instantly locate information of interest in a database. If you know what you need, the database will search the records for the desired information and display it on the screen.

- **Sort** A database can sort information using different orders. For example, you can sort names in alphabetical order, friends by state, clients by last name, zip codes in numerical order, or telephone numbers by area code. Sorting can be especially powerful with statistical applications such as making a stem-and-leaf plot from unordered data.

You can print out the information stored in your database. Most programs also allow you to perform calculations to analyze the data stored in the database.

The Internet

The **Internet** links **servers** and telephone lines worldwide. A home computer must have a **modem** to access the Internet. The modem and special software use telephone lines to connect to a server and its services. Internet Service Providers (ISP) have giant computers with large data banks to store and process information. They usually provide **electronic mail** (e-mail), access to the World Wide Web, weather reports, and many other services. They usually charge a monthly fee for the service.

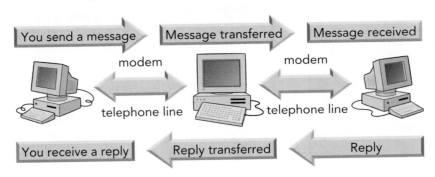

The **World Wide Web (WWW)** allows Internet users to interact with each other. It is a place where you can go from one page to another by just clicking on an icon or on highlighted words. It includes text, pictures, and sound and video. You can look up any kind of information, from archives to world news (both past and current). Basic ways of communicating on the Internet include e-mail, chatting, group chatting, and newsgroups.

Search engines can help you navigate the Web. A search engine is a program designed to access the Internet and search for whatever information you request. Often, you can do a search by just selecting **key words** that identify the type of documents you need. Key words can return thousands of entries, so you should try to be as specific as possible in a search. On the other hand, if an exact entry does not turn anything up, try to be more general in your description. For example, by typing *sports or football or helmets*, you will find entries related to items containing one or more of the three words. If you type *sports and football and helmets*, you will find entries related to all three words.

Another way to find your way around the Web is to use a directory. The directory is organized like a big index broken into categories. Choosing a category (such as sports) often brings you into a subcategory (such as a list of specific sports) or it may bring you to an individual page.

One of the most exciting aspects of the World Wide Web is multimedia, a combination of text, pictures, sound, and video. You can even find movie clips or listen to a speech.

This section shows you how to use some of the features available on a graphing calculator.

The Graphing Calculator

436

A graphing calculator is an amazing tool. It allows you to perform a large variety of mathematical operations. You can see the graph of a function or a scatter plot of data points by just pressing the right keys. The trick is knowing how to use your graphing calculator. It will probably look similar to the calculator below.

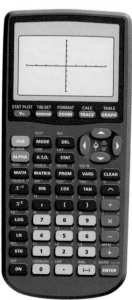

The best way to learn how to use your graphing calculator is to use it. Use this section as a guide only. Consult your manual often. Try different commands and work through some of the specific examples that are shown in the manual. Read through the table of contents and examine the index. Just being familiar with these sections will help you locate specific instructions when you want to try something new. The commands in your manual may be different than those shown in this handbook, but your calculator will most likely perform the functions.

A word of advice about consulting your calculator manual. Don't be intimidated by it. It's just a tool, too. If the instructions confuse you, try the examples that are shown in the manual. They will help you understand how to use the commands.

MORE ▶

A graphing calculator is set up much like a regular calculator. The display or screen is at the top of the calculator. All of the operations (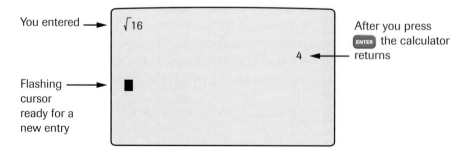 + , − , × , ÷) are located near each other along the right side of the calculator. Similarly, the numbers are together in their standard calculator order. The ENTER key replaces = found on other calculators. Notice the (−) key next to the ENTER key. You press this key to enter the negative sign for a negative number (not the − key or the +/− key).

The ∧ key is used to raise a number to a power. To evaluate 2^3 on this calculator, use the keystrokes 2 ∧ 3 ENTER . The answer, 8, will be displayed on the right side of the screen.

A graphing calculator has many more keys and symbols than an ordinary calculator. It is color coded to show more than one function for each key. The 2nd key in the left hand corner is a different color than the other keys. So is the ALPHA key below it. These keys allow you to access commands built into the calculator by pushing buttons whose primary use is for something else. The different commands or functions are color coded on the calculator above the key that they correspond to. So, if your 2nd key is yellow, the yellow characters above the keys become active for the next keystroke after you press 2nd .

The graphing keys are the keys directly beneath the screen. On this calculator they are the, Y= , WINDOW , ZOOM , TRACE , and GRAPH keys. These keys allow you to access the graphing features of the calculator.

The arrow keys on the upper right of the calculator are editing keys and allow you to move up, down, left, or right on the screen.

Now suppose you want to find the square root of a number. On this calculator, the square root is color coded yellow above the x^2 key. To find $\sqrt{16}$, press the yellow 2nd key, then x^2 1 6 ENTER .

A typical screen might look like this:

You entered → | $\sqrt{16}$

4 ←

After you press ENTER the calculator returns

Flashing → ▪
cursor
ready for a
new entry

MATH ALERT Check Your Manual

Your calculator may look different or have different keys that do the same thing. Check the directions in the manual for your calculator.

Math Functions and Operations

A graphing calculator can do so many things that it is not practical to have a separate key for each function.

In addition to the keyboard mathematical functions, such as ⊞ , 𝑥² , and SIN , there are other functions built into the calculator. If you press MATH , the screen might display a menu similar to this one:

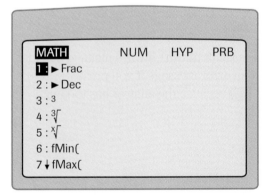

This is the math menu. Using the arrow keys to move up and down the list, you can change an answer to a fraction, find the cube of a number, or find the cube root of a number. Using the arrow keys to move across the top line will change the active menu. For example, NUM accesses the MATH NUM menu. You can use this menu to find the absolute value of a number or to round a number. You can even find the least common multiple or the greatest common factor from a list of numbers. PRB accesses the MATH PRB or the probability menu. You can use this menu to compute a factorial, a combination, or a permutation.

If you are trying to find a specific function, remember to look it up directly in the index of your calculator manual. If you want a more general discussion, the table of contents may have a chapter about *MATH Operations* that will explain how to access each function. There may also be an appendix with tables and reference information.

439

MATH ALERT Clear the Home Screen

As you use your calculator, remember to clear the home screen before starting a new calculation. The table of contents may address this in the very first section of the manual. There will probably also be an entire chapter on *Memory*. Check the index under *memory*, with a subentry for *reset* or *resetting*.

440

Variables on a Graphing Calculator

Suppose you want to use a value or a numerical expression more than once. Instead of entering the number (or expression) over and over again, you can store the value (or expression) to a variable letter. A key such as **STO→** is usually used to store the value. The variable letters used to name the value may be activated with the **ALPHA** key. There is also a special key for commonly-used variables, **X,T,θ,n**. You can even store an answer to a variable. Check your manual for details on how to *store*, *display*, and *recall* the variables. The initial chapter on operating instructions should have details or check the index under *store*.

441

MATH ALERT Error Messages

Don't panic if you get an error message. It doesn't always mean you made a mistake. For example, you'll get an error message if you press **2** **7** **^** **1** **0** **0** **ENTER** because the answer has too many digits to fit on the calculator display.

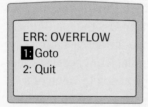

ERR: OVERFLOW
1: Goto
2: Quit

If you can't figure out what the error message means, check your manual. Error conditions will probably be covered in the first chapter of the manual. An appendix may explain each type of error in detail. Looking in the index under *error* should direct you to help.

Formulas on a Graphing Calculator

442

Suppose you want to use a formula to solve an equation or to make a calculation. Use variable names to store the values. Then all you have to do is enter the formula and the calculator will calculate the answer.

MORE HELP
See 221

For example, suppose you want to find the slope of a line that goes through the points $(2, 5)$ and $(8, 9)$. You should be able to store each value to a letter name. A set of keystrokes similar to the following should store 2 for the variable A:

Now suppose you store 5 in B, 8 in C, and 9 in D. Using the slope formula $\frac{(D - B)}{(C - A)}$ may display a decimal: .6666666667. Use the **MATH** menu to select fraction and display the answer as a fraction: $\frac{2}{3}$. Notice that you must understand how to use a formula in order to use the calculator to solve problems with the formula.

Programming a Graphing Calculator

443

Many graphing calculators are programmable. This means that you can store a set of instructions, such as a formula, in the calculator to make specific calculations as the values of the variables change. Each line in the program is executed in the order in which it is entered, so you must understand how your input works to produce the desired output.

This feature of the calculator is especially useful for formulas that you might use over and over. For example, programs to find the volumes of figures such as cones, cylinders, and spheres are both easy to write and easy to use. Consult your manual for specific details. Check the table of contents for a chapter on *Programming* or look up *programming* in the index.

Equation Solver

444

Your graphing calculator may have an equation solver in which you can solve for any variable in an equation. The *Solver* might be listed in the *MATH* menu. The equation solver can be used to try to find the roots of an equation written in standard form. If you wanted to solve the equation, $x^2 = 4$, you would have to rewrite it as $x^2 - 4 = 0$. If there is more than one solution, the equation solver will probably find only one solution at a time.

MORE HELP
See 152

Function Graphing on a Graphing Calculator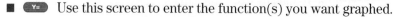

Here are some of the most common keys used to graph a function.

■ **Y=** Use this screen to enter the function(s) you want graphed.

■ **WINDOW** Use this screen to set the viewing window. Xmin, Xmax, Ymin, and Ymax define the coordinate plane displayed in the window. Xscl and Yscl define the distance between the tick marks on the x- and y-axes.

> In math jargon, MIN means *minimum*, MAX means *maximum*, and SCL means *scale*.

■ **ZOOM** Use the ZOOM menu to adjust the viewing window of the graph. With the Zoom feature you can look more closely at a particular section of the graph or at a larger portion of the graph. *ZBox* draws a box to define the viewing window. You can move the zoom cursor to define a box around the part of the graph in which you want to use the Zoom feature. *Zoom In* magnifies the part of the graph around the cursor. *Zoom Out* views more of a graph around the cursor. *Zoom factors* define the magnification used to *Zoom In* or *Zoom Out* around a point.

■ **TRACE** You can use the cursor to trace along the graph of a function. It will display variable values for its location as you move it along the graph. When using Trace to find points on a graph, be aware that rounding errors may affect the coordinate values being displayed on the screen.

■ **GRAPH** Displays the graph screen. It graphs the selected functions entered in **Y=** .

Make sure you check your manual to find out exactly which keys you need to use to enter a function, to graph the function, and to access options available with the graph. In particular, your graphing calculator probably has a menu that will allow you to calculate a y-value for a given x-value of a function, find a zero (x-intercept) of a function, and find a maximum and/or minimum of a function. Check the table of contents under *Function Graphing* or look in the index for specific entries under *zero, x-intercept, maximum* (or *minimum*) *operation on a graph*. Be sure to check all subentries in the index under *function graphing* for other references.

What if you are interested in how a periodic function changes as the amplitude and/or the frequency of the function changes? The graphing calculator will graph more than one function simultaneously on the same set of axes. The **Y=** key may display a list in the form $y_1 =$, $y_2 =$, and so on. All you have to do is enter the different functions and then select **GRAPH** to see how the functions look and are related.

MORE HELP
See 449

Consider $y_1 = \sin(x)$, $y_2 = 2\sin(x)$, and $y_3 = \sin(2x)$. You can see what happens when there is a numerical change in a parent function such as $y = \sin(x)$. The calculator will graph y_1 first, y_2 second, and y_3 third. Typical graphing calculator screens will look similar to these:

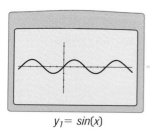

$y_1 = \sin(x)$

The first function $y_1 = \sin(x)$ is graphed on the screen.

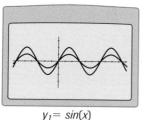

$y_1 = \sin(x)$
$y_2 = 2\sin(x)$

The second function, $y_2 = 2\sin(x)$, is graphed on the same set of axes as the first function. Notice that the amplitude of the second function is greater than that of the first function. In this case, the coefficient, 2, changes the amplitude of $y = \sin(x)$.

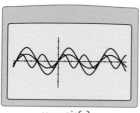

$y_1 = \sin(x)$
$y_2 = 2\sin(x)$
$y_3 = \sin(2x)$

The third function, $y_3 = \sin(2x)$, is graphed on the same set of axes as the other two functions. Notice that the graph of $y = \sin(x)$ corresponds to two cycles of $y = \sin(2x)$. In this case, the coefficient of x, 2, changes the frequency of $y = \sin(x)$.

You may be able to graph a family of curves using a list with the function. Consider $y_1 = \{1, 2, 4\}\cos(x)$. The family of curves will look similar to this on a graphing calculator:

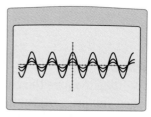

$y_1 = \{1, 2, 4\}\cos(x)$

MORE ▶

Using similar methods, you can explore how the graph of a quadratic function looks as you change the coefficients. The coefficients of $y = ax^2 + bx + c$ are a, b, and c. To investigate the effect of changes in a, set $b = 1$ and $c = 0$. To investigate the effect of changes in b, set $a = 1$ and $c = 0$. To investigate the effect of changes in c, set $a = 1$ and $b = 0$. For example, the screen on the left shows the graphs of $y_1 = x^2$, $y_2 = {}^-x^2$, $y_3 = 10x^2$, and $y_4 = 0.5x^2$. The screen on the right shows the graphs of $y_1 = x^2 + x$; $y_2 = x^2 + 0.5x$; $y_3 = x^2 + 2x$; and $y_4 = x^2 - x$.

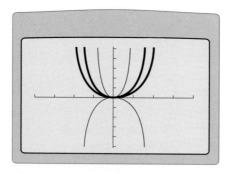
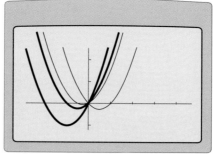

You can differentiate among graphs drawn on the same set of axes by using different line styles. These may be selected by setting different graph styles. You can also shade the area above or below a graph to graph an inequality. Check your manual for specific details. The chapter on *Function Graphing* should show steps to use the different styles. In the index, look under *graph style*. *Graph style* may be listed as a subentry under *function graphing* in the index.

There are many types of graphs you can investigate quickly and easily. Try changing the slope of a line, graphing lines with the same slope and different intercepts, or lines with slopes that are negative reciprocals. Does the graph confirm what you think should or will happen?

Trace

Use (TRACE) to move the cursor from one point to the next along a function. When you press (TRACE), the trace cursor will be on the first function in the (Y=) editor. To move the cursor along the curve, use the left and right arrows on the calculator. To change from one function to another, use the up and down keys. When the trace cursor moves along a function, the y-value is calculated from the x-value displayed. Both values are displayed at the bottom of the screen.

You can use TRACE to explore exponential growth from the graph of an exponential function. Suppose you put \$25 into a savings account that pays 5% interest compounded quarterly. Enter the equation $A = P\left(1 + \frac{r}{n}\right)^{nt}$ into the graphing calculator as $y = 25\left(1 + \frac{0.05}{4}\right)^{4x}$ and graph. You can use TRACE to find values for y by moving the trace cursor along the graph. The graph itself will show you how quickly exponential functions increase. Remember that rounding errors may affect the coordinate values being displayed on the screen.

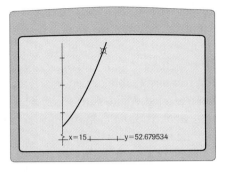

x=15   y=52.679534

MORE HELP
See 306

Tables and Lists on a Graphing Calculator
447

You might not think of using a calculator to make and use tables and lists, but the graphing calculator is perfect for these tasks.

Tables on a Graphing Calculator
448

The graphing calculator can usually display function values in a table. The function (or functions) displayed in the table are defined in the Y= editor. You can use the arrow keys to scroll up and down or left and right in the table to highlight specific values. You can even edit the equation from the table directly by moving the cursor to the y_1 cell in the table. When the equation is changed, new y-values will automatically be calculated and displayed. Using a TABLE SETUP screen, most graphing calculators will let you decide whether you want independent and dependent variables calculated automatically or whether you want values calculated only when you move the cursor to a specific location in the table. They also let you choose the value to start the table and the increment for the independent variable. Generally, you only select the increment if the table automatically generates the values of the independent variable.

In the table, after each x-value was entered, the corresponding y-value was calculated for the function $y_1 = x^4 + 2x^2 - 5$.

Check your manual to find out how to set up and use tables. The table of contents may have an entire chapter on *Tables*. You might also look in the index under *tables*.

X	Y_1	
1	−2	
2	19	
3	94	
4	283	
5	670	

$Y_1 = x^4 + 2x^2 - 5$

449

Lists on a Graphing Calculator

Suppose you want to evaluate an expression, such as $3x^2 + 5$, for $x = 6, 7,$ and 8. You can use a table or you can use a list. Make sure you check your calculator manual to find out which symbols you must use to define a list. Some calculators use braces, { and }, to enclose lists.

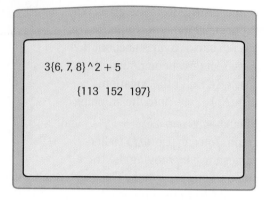

3{6, 7, 8}^2 + 5

{113 152 197}

You can use lists for many other things. There is often a separate List Menu available from which you can find a sum, the mean, or the median of a list of numbers. In fact, your manual will probably have an entire chapter on *Lists*. Look under *lists* in the index.

450

Matrices on a Graphing Calculator

MORE HELP
See 310, 313, 315

Many graphing calculators allow you to define matrices using a Matrix Menu. A **matrix** is a two-dimensional array. Before you can define the matrix, you may have to first select the matrix name from the Matrix Menu. The name might be a variable name, such as A or B. You will also have to define the dimensions of the matrix before you can enter the matrix elements. The dimensions of a matrix are given by the number of rows and the number of columns in the matrix using the form *row* $\times$ *column*. After you set the dimensions of the matrix, you can view the matrix and enter matrix values.

To add or subtract matrices, the dimensions of the matrices must be the same. You can also multiply a matrix by a real number. Check your manual for details on how to select, view, and display a matrix on the screen. Once you are able to display the matrix on the screen, it should be very easy to add or subtract matrices and to multiply a matrix by a scalar or by another matrix. The table of contents will probably have a chapter called *Matrices*. In the index, look under *matrices* and any subentries that address specific questions you might have.

Probability and Statistics on a Graphing Calculator

Many graphing calculators have features built in to make probability and statistics computation quick and easy.

The Math Menu may have a separate probability menu that will have features that will generate random numbers, and that will calculate permutations (nPr), combinations (nCr), and factorials (!).

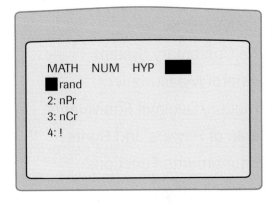

For details on how to use these built-in functions, check the table of contents for a chapter on *Math Operations*. In the index, look up each term individually (*random number, permutation, combination, factorial*).

The statistical features of many graphing calculators can be quite impressive. Check your manual to learn how to use these features. If your graphing calculator does statistics, the manual will likely have at least one chapter devoted to *Statistics*. For specific functions that you want to use, look up each term under its own heading in the index (look for *mean, first quartile, median, third quartile,* and *minimum* or *maximum*).

One of the nicest features available on graphing calculators is the statistical plotting. After you store statistical data in a list, you can often choose from a variety of statistical plots to view the data. You may have to enter the data to create an Xlist and a Ylist using a STAT EDIT MENU. Some possible options are listed below.

Scatter makes a scatter plot of data points from Xlist and Ylist.

xyLine is a scatter plot in which points from Xlist and Ylist are plotted and connected.

Histogram makes a histogram of one-variable data.

Boxplot makes a boxplot of one-variable data.

When you make a scatter plot of data points, you may want to find a line (or other type of curve) of best fit. Your calculator may even be able to do this for you. Look in the index under *LinReg, regression model,* or subentries under *regression model,* to find the full details.

453

Plane Figures

A **polygon** is any closed plane figure whose sides are line segments that do not cross. It has the same number of interior angles as it has sides. A **regular polygon** is a polygon with all sides the same length and all angles the same measure. A square is a regular quadrilateral. A circle is a special plane figure that doesn't count as a polygon.

Plane Figure	Number of Sides	Sum of the Measures of Interior Angles of Each n–gon: $(n-2)180°$	Example(s)
triangle	3	180°	equilateral isosceles scalene acute right obtuse
quadrilateral	4	360°	quadrilateral trapezoid parallelogram rhombus rectangle square
pentagon	5	540°	regular
hexagon	6	720°	regular
heptagon or septagon	7	900°	regular
octagon	8	1080°	regular
nonagon	9	1260°	regular
decagon	10	1440°	regular

Geometric Solids

A **polyhedron** is a solid figure made up of flat surfaces called **faces**. Each face is a polygon. A **regular polyhedron** is a solid figure with congruent regular polygons for all faces. A cube is a regular polyhedron—each of its faces is a square. A **right** polyhedron prism has its faces perpendicular to its bases. A **right circular** cylinder has circular bases and a segment between the centers of the bases is perpendicular to them. A **right circular** cone has a circular base and a segment from its vertex to the center of its base is perpendicular to the base.

Polyhedron	Example	Net
cube		
rectangular prism		
triangular prism		
triangular pyramid		
rectangular pyramid		
pentagonal pyramid		
tetrahedron		
octahedron		
dodecahedron		

Geometric Solid	Example	Net
sphere		
cone		
cylinder		

The Metric System

Linear Measure (length)		
1 centimeter	0.01 meter	0.3937 inch
1 decimeter	0.1 meter	3.937 inches
1 meter		39.37 inches
1 dekameter	10 meters	32.8 feet
1 hectometer	100 meters	328 feet
1 kilometer	1000 meters	0.621 mile
1 myriameter	10,000 meters	6.21 miles

Capacity Measure		
1 centiliter	0.01 liter	0.338 fluid ounce
1 deciliter	0.1 liter	3.38 fluid ounces
1 liter		1.0567 liquid quarts or 0.9081 dry quart
1 dekaliter	10 liters	2.642 gallons or 0.284 bushel
1 hectoliter	100 liters	26.42 gallons or 2.84 bushels
1 kiloliter	1000 liters	264.2 gallons or 35.315 cubic feet

MORE ▶

Volume Measure		
1 cubic centimeter	1000 cubic millimeters	0.06102 cubic inch
1 cubic decimeter	1000 cubic centimeters	61.02 cubic inches
1 cubic meter	1000 cubic decimeters	35.315 cubic feet

Mass		
1 centigram	0.01 gram	0.0003527 ounce
1 decigram	0.1 gram	0.003527 ounce
1 gram		0.03527 ounce
1 dekagram	10 grams	0.3527 ounce
1 hectogram	100 grams	3.527 ounces
1 kilogram	1000 grams	2.2046 pounds
1 myriagram	10,000 grams	22.046 pounds
1 quintal	100,000 grams	220.46 pounds
1 metric ton	1,000,000 grams	2204.6 pounds

Land Measure (area)		
1 centare	1 square meter	1.196 square yards
1 are	100 square meters	119.6 square yards
1 hectare	10,000 square meters	2.471 acres
1 square kilometer	1,000,000 square meters	0.386 square mile

The Customary System

Linear Measure (length)		
1 inch		2.54 centimeters
1 foot	12 inches	0.3048 meter
1 yard	3 feet	0.9144 meter
1 rod, (pole, or perch)	16.5 feet	5.029 meters
1 (statute) mile	5280 feet	1609.3 meters
1 (land) league	15,840 feet	4.83 kilometers

Square Measure (area)		
1 square foot	144 square inches	929.0304 square centimeters
1 square yard	9 square feet	0.8361 square meter
1 acre	43,560 square feet	4046.86 square meters

Cubic Measure		
1 cord foot	16 cubic feet	0.4531 cubic meter
1 cord	128 cord feet	3.625 cubic meters

Dry Measure (capacity, volume)			
1 pint		33.60 cubic inches	0.5505 liter
1 quart	2 pints	67.20 cubic inches	1.1012 liters
1 peck	16 pints	537.61 cubic inches	8.8096 liters
1 bushel	64 pints	2150.42 cubic inches	35.2383 liters

MORE ▶

Liquid Measure			
1 fluid ounce	0.25 gill	1.8047 cubic inches	0.0296 liter
1 gill	4 fluid ounces	7.219 cubic inches	0.1183 liter
1 cup	8 fluid ounces	14.438 cubic inches	0.2366 liter
1 pint	16 fluid ounces	28.875 cubic inches	0.4732 liter
1 quart	32 fluid ounces	57.75 cubic inches	0.9463 liter
1 gallon	128 fluid ounces	231 cubic inches	3.7853 liters

Circular (or Angular) Measure			
60 seconds	1 minute	90 degrees	1 quadrant or 1 right angle
60 minutes	1 degree	4 quadrants or 360 degrees	1 complete rotation about a point

Weight (avoirdupois)		
1 grain	0.0001426 pound	0.0648 gram
1 dram	0.003907 pound	1.772 grams
1 ounce	0.0625 pound	28.3495 grams
1 pound	16 ounces	453.59 grams
1 hundredweight	100 pounds	45.359 kilograms
1 ton	2000 pounds	907.18 kilograms

General Measurement

Benchmark Measures		
1 inch	≈	width of tip of your thumb
1 centimeter	≈	width of the tip of your index finger
1 foot	≈	length of your notebook
1 kilogram	≈	mass of a small textbook
1 minute	≈	time it takes to count to 60 saying *one thousand* between each number
1 pound	≈	weight of a loaf of bread
1 ounce	≈	weight of a slice of bread
1 gram	≈	mass of a paper clip

Additional Units of Measure	
Astronomical Unit (A.U.)	93,000,000 miles: the average distance of Earth from the sun; used in astronomy
Bible cubit	21.8 inches
board foot (bd. ft)	144 cubic inches (12 in. × 12 in. × 1 in.); used for lumber
bolt	40 yards; used for measuring cloth
Btu (British thermal unit)	amount of heat needed to increase the temperature of one pound of water by one degree Fahrenheit
small calorie	0.00399 Btu
food calorie	1000 small calories
cubit	18 inches
1° of great circle (Equator)	60 nautical miles
furlong	220 yards
gross	12 dozen, or 144
hand	4 inches

MORE ▶

More Additional Units of Measure	
knot	rate of speed of one nautical mile per hour
light, speed of	186,281.7 miles per second
light-year	5,880,000,000,000 miles: the distance light travels in a year at the rate of 186,281.7 miles per second
parsec	3.086×10^{13} km or 1.918×10^{13} mi
pi (π)	3.14159265358979323846 ...; the ratio of the circumference of a circle to its diameter
Röentgen	dosage unit of radiation exposure produced by X rays
score	20 units
sound, speed of	about 1088 feet per second at 32°F at sea level through air
span	6 inches
short ton	2000 pounds
long ton	2240 pounds

458

Common Abbreviations

Common Abbreviations			
c	cup	mg	milligram
cm	centimeter	mi	mile
cos	cosine	min	minute
d	day	mL	milliliter
dm	decimeter	mm	millimeter
fl oz	fluid ounce	mo	month
ft	foot	pt	pint
gal	gallon	qt	quart
g	gram	s or sec	second
h or hr	hour	sin	sine
in.	inch	t	ton
kg	kilogram	tan	tangent
km	kilometer	trig	trigonometry
L	liter	wk	week
lb	pound	yd	yard
m	meter	y or yr	year

Conversion Factors

(Note: the conversion factor for meters to feet is the reciprocal of the conversion factor for feet to meters.)

Conversion Factors					
To change	to	multiply by	To change	to	multiply by
acres	hectares	0.4047	liters	quarts (liquid)	1.0567
acres	square feet	43,560	meters	feet	3.2808
acres	square miles	0.001563	meters	miles	0.0006214
centimeters	inches	0.3937	meters	yards	1.0936
centimeters	feet	0.03281	metric tons	tons (long)	0.9842
cubic meters	cubic feet	35.3147	metric tons	tons (short)	1.1023
cubic meters	cubic yards	1.30795	miles	kilometers	1.6093
cubic yards	cubic meters	0.7646	miles	feet	5280
feet	meters	0.3048	miles (nautical)	miles (statute)	1.1516
feet	miles (nautical)	0.0001645	miles (statute)	miles (nautical)	0.8684
feet	miles (statute)	0.0001894	miles/hour	feet/min	88.00
feet/second	miles/hour	0.6818	millimeters	inches	0.0394
furlongs	feet	660	ounces	grams	28.3495
furlongs	miles	0.125	ounces	pounds	0.0625
gallons	cubic feet	0.13368	pecks	liters	8.8096
gallons (U.S.)	liters	3.7853	pints (dry)	liters	0.5506
grains	grams	0.0648	pints (liquid)	liters	0.4732
grams	grains	15.432	pounds	kilograms	0.4536
grams	ounces	0.0353	pounds	ounces	16
grams	pounds	0.002205	quarts (dry)	liters	1.1012
hectares	acres	2.471	quarts (liquid)	liters	0.9463
horsepower	watts	745.7	square feet	square meters	0.0929
hours	days	0.04167	square kilometers	square miles	0.3861
inches	millimeters	25.4	square meters	square feet	10.7639
inches	centimeters	2.54	square meters	square yards	1.196
kilograms	pounds	2.2046	square miles	square kilometers	2.59
kilometers	miles	0.6214	square yards	square meters	0.8361
kilowatts	horsepower	1.341	tons (long)	metric tons	1.016
knots	nautical mi/hr	1.0	tons (short)	metric tons	0.9072
knots	statute mi/hr	1.151	tons (long)	pounds	2240
liters	gallons (U.S.)	0.2642	tons (short)	pounds	2000
liters	pecks	0.1135	watts	Btu/hr	3.4121
liters	pints (dry)	1.8162	watts	horsepower	0.001341
liters	pints (liquid)	2.1134	yards	meters	0.9144
liters	quarts (dry)	0.9081	yards	miles	0.0005682

Fraction/Decimal Equivalents

(Note: For percents, multiply the decimal by 100.)

Fraction/Decimal Equivalents

Fraction	Decimal	Fraction	Decimal	Fraction	Decimal	Fraction	Decimal
$\frac{1}{2}$	0.5	$\frac{1}{8}$	0.125	$\frac{1}{11}$	$0.\overline{09}$	$\frac{1}{16}$	0.0625
$\frac{1}{3}$	$0.\overline{3}$	$\frac{2}{8}$	0.25	$\frac{2}{11}$	$0.\overline{18}$	$\frac{2}{16}$	0.125
$\frac{2}{3}$	$0.\overline{6}$	$\frac{3}{8}$	0.375	$\frac{3}{11}$	$0.\overline{27}$	$\frac{3}{16}$	0.1875
$\frac{1}{4}$	0.25	$\frac{4}{8}$	0.5	$\frac{4}{11}$	$0.\overline{36}$	$\frac{4}{16}$	0.25
$\frac{2}{4}$	0.5	$\frac{5}{8}$	0.625	$\frac{5}{11}$	$0.\overline{45}$	$\frac{5}{16}$	0.3125
$\frac{3}{4}$	0.75	$\frac{6}{8}$	0.75	$\frac{6}{11}$	$0.\overline{54}$	$\frac{6}{16}$	0.375
$\frac{1}{5}$	0.2	$\frac{7}{8}$	0.875	$\frac{7}{11}$	$0.\overline{63}$	$\frac{7}{16}$	0.4375
$\frac{2}{5}$	0.4	$\frac{1}{9}$	$0.\overline{1}$	$\frac{8}{11}$	$0.\overline{72}$	$\frac{8}{16}$	0.5
$\frac{3}{5}$	0.6	$\frac{2}{9}$	$0.\overline{2}$	$\frac{9}{11}$	$0.\overline{81}$	$\frac{9}{16}$	0.5625
$\frac{4}{5}$	0.8	$\frac{3}{9}$	$0.\overline{3}$	$\frac{10}{11}$	$0.\overline{90}$	$\frac{10}{16}$	0.625
$\frac{1}{6}$	$0.1\overline{6}$	$\frac{4}{9}$	$0.\overline{4}$	$\frac{1}{12}$	$0.08\overline{3}$	$\frac{11}{16}$	0.6875
$\frac{2}{6}$	0.3	$\frac{5}{9}$	$0.\overline{5}$	$\frac{2}{12}$	$0.1\overline{6}$	$\frac{12}{16}$	0.75
$\frac{3}{6}$	0.5	$\frac{6}{9}$	$0.\overline{6}$	$\frac{3}{12}$	0.25	$\frac{13}{16}$	0.8125
$\frac{4}{6}$	$0.\overline{6}$	$\frac{7}{9}$	$0.\overline{7}$	$\frac{4}{12}$	$0.\overline{3}$	$\frac{14}{16}$	0.875
$\frac{5}{6}$	$0.8\overline{3}$	$\frac{8}{9}$	$0.\overline{8}$	$\frac{5}{12}$	$0.41\overline{6}$	$\frac{15}{16}$	0.9375
$\frac{1}{7}$	$0.\overline{142857}$	$\frac{1}{10}$	0.1	$\frac{6}{12}$	0.5		
$\frac{2}{7}$	$0.\overline{285714}$	$\frac{2}{10}$	0.2	$\frac{7}{12}$	$0.58\overline{3}$		
$\frac{3}{7}$	$0.\overline{428571}$	$\frac{3}{10}$	0.3	$\frac{8}{12}$	$0.\overline{6}$		
$\frac{4}{7}$	$0.\overline{571428}$	$\frac{4}{10}$	0.4	$\frac{9}{12}$	0.75		
$\frac{5}{7}$	$0.\overline{714285}$	$\frac{5}{10}$	0.5	$\frac{10}{12}$	$0.8\overline{3}$		
$\frac{6}{7}$	$0.\overline{857142}$	$\frac{6}{10}$	0.6	$\frac{11}{12}$	$0.91\overline{6}$		
		$\frac{7}{10}$	0.7				
		$\frac{8}{10}$	0.8				
		$\frac{9}{10}$	0.9				

Table of Powers and Roots

n	n^2	$\sqrt{n}$	n^3	$\sqrt[3]{n}$	n	n^2	$\sqrt{n}$	n^3	$\sqrt[3]{n}$
1	1	1.000	1	1.000	51	2601	7.141	132,651	3.708
2	4	1.414	8	1.260	52	2704	7.211	140,608	3.733
3	9	1.732	27	1.442	53	2809	7.280	148,877	3.756
4	16	2.000	64	1.587	54	2916	7.348	157,464	3.780
5	25	2.236	125	1.710	55	3025	7.416	166,375	3.803
6	36	2.449	216	1.817	56	3136	7.483	175,616	3.826
7	49	2.646	343	1.913	57	3249	7.550	185,193	3.849
8	64	2.828	512	2.000	58	3364	7.616	195,112	3.871
9	81	3.000	729	2.080	59	3481	7.681	205,379	3.893
10	100	3.162	1000	2.154	60	3600	7.746	216,000	3.915
11	121	3.317	1331	2.224	61	3721	7.810	226,981	3.936
12	144	3.464	1728	2.289	62	3844	7.874	238,328	3.958
13	169	3.606	2197	2.351	63	3969	7.937	250,047	3.979
14	196	3.742	2744	2.410	64	4096	8.000	262,144	4.000
15	225	3.873	3375	2.466	65	4225	8.062	274,625	4.021
16	256	4.000	4096	2.520	66	4356	8.124	287,496	4.041
17	289	4.123	4913	2.571	67	4489	8.185	300,763	4.062
18	324	4.243	5832	2.621	68	4624	8.246	314,432	4.082
19	361	4.359	6859	2.668	69	4761	8.307	328,509	4.102
20	400	4.472	8000	2.714	70	4900	8.367	343,000	4.121
21	441	4.583	9261	2.759	71	5041	8.426	357,911	4.141
22	484	4.690	10,648	2.802	72	5184	8.485	373,248	4.160
23	529	4.796	12,167	2.844	73	5329	8.544	389,017	4.179
24	576	4.899	13,824	2.884	74	5476	8.602	405,224	4.198
25	625	5.000	15,625	2.924	75	5625	8.660	421,875	4.217
26	676	5.099	17,576	2.962	76	5776	8.718	438,976	4.236
27	729	5.196	19,683	3.000	77	5929	8.775	456,533	4.254
28	784	5.292	21,952	3.037	78	6084	8.832	474,522	4.273
29	841	5.385	24,389	3.072	79	6241	8.888	493,039	4.291
30	900	5.477	27,000	3.107	80	6400	8.944	512,000	4.309
31	961	5.568	29,791	3.141	81	6561	9.000	531,441	4.327
32	1024	5.657	32,768	3.175	82	6724	9.055	551,368	4.344
33	1089	5.745	35,937	3.208	83	6889	9.110	571,787	4.362
34	1156	5.831	39,304	3.240	84	7056	9.165	592,704	4.380
35	1225	5.916	42,875	3.271	85	7225	9.220	614,125	4.397
36	1296	6.000	46,656	3.302	86	7396	9.274	636,056	4.414
37	1369	6.083	50,653	3.332	87	7569	9.327	658,503	4.431
38	1444	6.164	54,872	3.362	88	7744	9.381	681,472	4.448
39	1521	6.245	59,319	3.391	89	7921	9.434	704,969	4.465
40	1600	6.325	64,000	3.420	90	8100	9.487	729,000	4.481
41	1681	6.403	68,921	3.448	91	8281	9.539	753,571	4.498
42	1764	6.481	74,088	3.476	92	8464	9.592	778,688	4.514
43	1849	6.557	79,507	3.503	93	8649	9.644	804,357	4.531
44	1936	6.633	85,184	3.530	94	8836	9.695	830,584	4.547
45	2025	6.708	91,125	3.557	95	9025	9.747	857,375	4.563
46	2116	6.782	97,336	3.583	96	9216	9.798	884,736	4.579
47	2209	6.856	103,823	3.609	97	9409	9.849	912,673	4.595
48	2304	6.928	110,592	3.634	98	9604	9.899	941,192	4.610
49	2401	7.000	117,649	3.659	99	9801	9.950	970,299	4.626
50	2500	7.071	125,000	3.684	100	10,000	10.000	1,000,000	4.642

(Roots are rounded to the nearest thousandth.)

Trigonometric Functions

Trigonometric Functions							
Angle	Sine	Cosine	Tangent	Angle	Sine	Cosine	Tangent
0°	0.000	1.000	0.000	50°	0.766	0.643	1.192
5°	0.087	0.996	0.087	55°	0.819	0.574	1.428
10°	0.174	0.985	0.176	60°	0.866	0.500	1.732
15°	0.259	0.966	0.268	65°	0.906	0.423	2.145
20°	0.342	0.940	0.364	70°	0.940	0.342	2.747
25°	0.423	0.906	0.466	75°	0.966	0.259	3.732
30°	0.500	0.866	0.577	80°	0.985	0.174	5.671
35°	0.574	0.819	0.700	85°	0.996	0.087	11.430
40°	0.643	0.766	0.839	90°	1.000	0.000	–
45°	0.707	0.707	1.000				

(Trigonometric values are rounded to the nearest thousandth.)

Prime Numbers

Here are the prime numbers between 1 and 500.

Prime Numbers								
2	3	5	7	11	13	17	19	23
29	31	37	41	43	47	53	59	61
67	71	73	79	83	89	97	101	103
107	109	113	127	131	137	139	149	151
157	163	167	173	179	181	191	193	197
199	211	223	227	229	233	239	241	251
257	263	269	271	277	281	283	293	307
311	313	317	331	337	347	349	353	359
367	373	379	383	389	397	401	409	419
421	431	433	439	443	449	457	461	463
467	479	487	491	499				

Yellow Pages

The numbers in black at the end of many entries refer you back to topic numbers. You will find topic numbers at the top of each page and next to each new piece of information.

Term   Abbreviation or Symbol   Definition

cosine ratio (cos): In a right triangle, the cosine of an angle is the ratio of the length of the leg adjacent to that angle to the length of the hypotenuse. The value of the cosine of an angle depends upon the measure of the angle.   Item Reference ⟶ **(250)**

$$\cos A = \frac{4}{5} = 0.8$$

Example

Illustration

Glossary of Mathematical Symbols   510

Glossary of Mathematical Formulas

Perimeter: The distance around a plane figure.

Figure	Formula	Variables	Example
Polygon	$P = s_1 + s_2 + s_3 + \ldots$	P: Perimeter s_1: length of one side s_2: length of another side s_3: length of a third side	4 cm, 3 cm, 5 cm, 4 cm, 6 cm $P = 4 + 3 + 4 + 5 + 6$ $= 22$ Perimeter = 22 cm
Any regular n-sided polygon	$P = ns$	P: Perimeter n: number of equal-length sides s: length of side	16 ft, 16 ft, 16 ft, 16 ft, 16 ft $P = 5(16)$ $= 80$ Perimeter = 80 ft
Rectangle	$P = 2l + 2w$ or $P = 2(l + w)$	P: Perimeter l: length w: width	12 m 15 m $P = 2(15) + 2(12)$ $= 54$ Perimeter = 54 m
Rhombus	$P = 4s$	P: Perimeter s: length of side	8.2 cm $P = 4(8.2)$ $= 32.8$ Perimeter = 32.8 cm
Square	$P = 4s$	P: Perimeter s: length of side	3.25 in. $P = 4(3.25)$ $= 13$ Perimeter = 13 in.
Circle	$C = \pi d$ or $C = 2\pi r$	C: Circumference π: pi (about 3.14, or $\frac{22}{7}$) d: diameter r: radius	38 mm $C \approx 2(3.14)(38)$ ≈ 238.64 Circumference ≈ 238.64 mm

Area: The number of square units contained by a plane figure.

Note that 4 square inches is not the same as a 4-inch square. A 4-inch square has an area of 4×4, or 16 square inches.

Figure	Formula	Variables	Examples
Triangle	$A = \frac{1}{2}bh$	A: Area b: base h: height **The height is the length of the perpendicular line segment from the vertex to the opposite base. You can choose any side as the base as long as you use the height perpendicular to that side.**	 $A = \frac{1}{2}(9)(6)$ $= 27$ Area $= 27$ ft^2
Parallelogram	$A = bh$	A: Area b: base h: height **You can choose any side as the base, as long as you use the height that is perpendicular to that side.**	 $A = 16(8)$ $= 128$ Area $= 128$ m^2
Rectangle	$A = lw$	A: Area l: length w: width	 $A = (8.5)(5.2)$ $= 44.2$ Area $= 44.2$ cm^2
Square	$A = s^2$ or $A = \frac{1}{2}d^2$	A: Area s: length of side d: diagonal	 $A = 4.6^2$ $= 21.16$ Area ≈ 21.2 ft^2
Trapezoid	$A = \frac{1}{2}h(b_1 + b_2)$	A: Area h: height b_1: one base b_2: other base **The bases are the two parallel sides and the height is perpendicular to both.**	 $A = \frac{1}{2}(4)(6 + 14.7)$ $= 41.4$ Area $= 41.4$ yd^2

MORE ▶

Area: (continued)

Figure	Formula	Variables and Symbols	Examples
Circle	$A = \pi r^2$	A: Area π: pi (about 3.14 or $\frac{22}{7}$) r: radius	7.25 m $A \approx 3.14(7.25^2)$ ≈ 165.05 Area ≈ 165.05 m^2
Sector	$A = \frac{1}{2}r^2\,\theta$	A: Area r: radius θ: central angle (in radians, $\frac{\pi}{2}$ radians = 90°)	8 cm $\frac{\pi}{2}$ $A \approx \frac{1}{2}(8^2)(\frac{3.14}{2})$ ≈ 50.24 Area ≈ 50.24 cm^2

Surface Area: The total area of the faces (including the bases) of a solid figure.

MORE HELP
See 097

Figure	Formula	Variables and Symbols	Example
Rectangular prism	$SA = 2lw + 2lh + 2wh,$ or $2(lw + lh + wh)$	SA: Surface Area l: length w: width h: height	8 ft, 7 ft, 24 ft $SA = 2(24 \cdot 7) + 2(24 \cdot 8)$ $+ 2(8 \cdot 7)$ $= 832$ Surface Area = 832 ft^2
Cube	$SA = 6s^2$	SA: Surface Area s: length of side	4.7 cm $SA = 6(4.7^2)$ ≈ 132.5 Surface Area ≈ 132.5 cm^2

Surface Area: (continued)

Figure	Formula	Variables and Symbols	Example
Square pyramid	$SA = b^2 + 2bh$	*SA*: Surface Area *b*: base *h*: height of triangular face	 15 in. 8 in. 8 in. $SA = 8^2 + 2(8)(15)$ $= 304$ Surface Area = 304 in.^{2}
Cylinder	$SA = 2\pi r^2 + 2\pi rh$ **$2\pi r^2$ is the area of the two circular bases.** **$2\pi r$ is the circumference of a circular base.**	*SA*: Surface Area π: pi (about 3.14 or $\frac{22}{7}$) *r*: radius *h*: height	 4 cm 12 cm $SA \approx 2(3.14)(4^2) +$ $2(3.14)(4)(12)$ ≈ 401.92 Surface Area = 401.92 cm^2
Right circular cone	$SA = \pi r\sqrt{r^2 + h^2}$ $+ \pi r^2$ *or* $\pi rs + \pi r^2$	*SA*: Surface Area π: pi (about 3.14 or $\frac{22}{7}$) *r*: radius *h*: height *s*: slant height	 9 ft 17.5 ft 15 ft $SA \approx (3.14 \cdot 9 \cdot 17.5) +$ $(3.14 \cdot 9^2)$ ≈ 748.89 Surface Area = 748.89 ft^2
Sphere	$SA = 4\pi r^2$	*SA*: Surface Area π: pi (about 3.14 or $\frac{22}{7}$) *r*: radius	 14 in. $SA \approx 4(3.14)(14^2)$ ≈ 2461.76 Surface Area = 2461.76 in.^{2}

Volume: The number of cubic units a figure contains.

Note that 4 cubic centimeters is not the same as a 4-cm cube. A 4-cm cube has edges four centimeters long and a volume of 4 cm × 4 cm × 4 cm or 64 cm³.

MORE HELP

See
097

Figure	Formula	Variables and Symbols	Example
Rectangular prism	$V = lwh$	V: Volume l: length w: width h: height	 16 m 15 m 34 m $V = (34)(15)(16)$ $= 8160$ Volume = 8160 m³
Cube	$V = s^3$	V: Volume s: length of side	 8.5 cm $V = 8.5^3$ ≈ 614.1 Volume ≈ 614.1 cm³
Prism	$V = Bh$	V: Volume B: area of base h: height	 4 ft 8 ft 3 ft $V = Bh$ and $B = \frac{1}{2}(b)h$ $B = \frac{1}{2}(3)(4) = 6$ So, $V = 6(8)$ $= 48$ Volume = 48 ft³
Rectangular pyramid	$V = \frac{1}{3}Bh$	V: Volume B: area of base h: height **The height is the perpendicular distance from the vertex to the base.**	 15 cm 12 cm 14 cm $V = \frac{1}{3}Bh$ and $B = lw$ $B = 12(14) = 168$ So, $V = \frac{1}{3}(168)(15)$ $= 840$ Volume = 840 cm³

Volume (continued)

Figure	Formula	Variables and Symbols	Example
Cylinder	$V = \pi r^2 h$	V: Volume π: pi (about 3.14 or $\frac{22}{7}$) r: radius h: height	29 m, 56 m $V \approx 3.14\,(29^2)(56)$ $\approx 147{,}881.44$ Volume $\approx 147{,}881.44$ m^3
Cone	$V = \frac{1}{3}\pi r^2 h$, or $V = \frac{1}{3}Bh$	V: Volume π: pi (about 3.14 or $\frac{22}{7}$) r: radius h: height B: area of base	18 ft, 9 ft $V \approx \frac{1}{3}(3.14)(9^2)(18)$ ≈ 1526.04 Volume ≈ 1526.04 ft^3
Sphere	$A = \frac{4}{3}\pi r^3$	V: Volume π: pi (about 3.14 or $\frac{22}{7}$) r: radius	14 m $A \approx \frac{4}{3}\left(\frac{22}{7}\right)(14^3)$ $\approx 11{,}498.7$ Volume $\approx 11{,}498.7$ m^3

Theorem for Polyhedra: Relationships among the numbers of faces, vertices, and edges of solids.

Formula	Variables	Example
$F + V = E + 2$	F = number of faces V = number of vertices E = number of edges	$F = 7$, $V = 10$, $E = 15$ $F + V = E + 2$ $7 + 10 = 15 + 2$ $17 = 17$

Economics Formulas

MORE
HELP
See
112,
304–306

	Formula	Variables	Example
Simple interest	$I = prt$	I: Interest p: principal (investment) r: annual rate of interest t: time (in years)	Interest accumulated if $1500 is invested at 4% for three years: $I = prt$ $= 1500(0.04)(3)$ $= 180$ Interest $= \$180$
Compound interest	$A = P(1 + \frac{r}{n})^{nt}$	A: Amount of money after t years P: Principal r: interest rate if compounded annually t: time (in years) n: number of yearly compounds	Money in an account if $200 is invested at 4% interest compounded quarterly for five years: $A = P(1 + \frac{r}{n})^{nt}$ $= 200(1 + \frac{0.4}{4})^{4 \cdot 5}$ $= 200(1.01)^{20}$ $\approx 200(1.22)$ ≈ 244 Amount $\approx \$244$

Temperature

Formula	Variables	Example
$C = \frac{5}{9}(F - 32)$	C: degrees Celsius F: degrees Fahrenheit	$F = 68$ $C = \frac{5}{9}(F - 32)$ $= \frac{5}{9}(68 - 32)$ $= \frac{5}{9}(36)$ $= 20$ Temperature $= 20°C$
$F = \frac{9}{5}C + 32$	C: degrees Celsius F: degrees Fahrenheit	$C = 15°$ $F = \frac{9}{5}(15) + 32$ $= 27 + 32$ $= 59$ Temperature $= 59°F$

Probability

MORE
HELP
See
316–332

Formula	Example
Probability of an event when all outcomes are equally likely Probability (event) = $\dfrac{\text{number of favorable outcomes}}{\text{number of possible outcomes}}$	A bag is filled with 3 yellow marbles and 9 green marbles. Pick a yellow marble at random. $P(\text{yellow}) = \frac{3}{12} \text{ or } \frac{1}{4}$
Probability of A and B, if A and B are independent $P(A \text{ and } B) = P(A) \cdot P(B)$	Roll a red die and a blue die. A red one and a blue five land face up. $P(1 \text{ and } 5) = P(1) \cdot P(5)$ $P(1 \text{ and } 5) = (\frac{1}{6})(\frac{1}{6}) = \frac{1}{36}$
Probability of A or B **Probability Event A occurs or Event B occurs or they both occur** $P(A \text{ or } B) = P(A) + P(B)$ $\qquad\qquad - P(A \text{ and } B)$ **Note: P(A and B) = 0 if events A and B are mutually exclusive** *This makes sense because the 13 clubs plus the three other 3s total 16 of the 52 cards in the deck.*	Select a 3 or a Club from a deck of cards. $P(3) = \frac{4}{52}$ $P(C) = \frac{13}{52}$ $P(3 \text{ and } C) = \frac{1}{52}$ $P(3 \text{ or } C) = P(3) + P(C)$ $\qquad\qquad - P(3 \text{ and } C)$ $= \frac{4}{52} + \frac{13}{52} - \frac{1}{52}$ $= \frac{16}{52} \text{ or } \frac{4}{13}$
Probability of not A $P(\text{not } A) = 1 - P(A)$	Select any card but an ace from a deck of cards. $P(\text{ace}) = \frac{4}{52} \text{ or } \frac{1}{13}$ $P(\text{not ace}) = 1 - P(\text{ace})$ $P(\text{not ace}) = 1 - \frac{1}{13} = \frac{12}{13}$
Odds of A occuring when all outcomes are equally likely Odds = $\dfrac{\text{number of favorable outcomes}}{\text{number of unfavorable outcomes}}$	There are eight cards numbered from 1 through 8. The odds of choosing the 5 card are 1 to 7.
Different permutations of n things $n! = n(n-1)(n-2)\ldots \cdot 1$	$9! = 9 \cdot 8 \cdot 7 \cdot 6 \cdot 5 \cdot 4 \cdot 3 \cdot 2 \cdot 1$ $\qquad = 362,880$
Different combinations of n things taken r at a time $\dfrac{n!}{(n-r)!\,r!} = {}_nC_r$	There are six people. The number of groups of four people that can be formed is $\dfrac{6!}{2!\,4!} = 15$

Statistics

MORE
HELP
See
333–338

	Formula	Example
Mean	$\dfrac{\text{sum of numbers}}{\text{number of numbers}}$	Find the mean test score: 83, 82, 94, 89, 92 $\dfrac{83 + 82 + 94 + 89 + 92}{5} = \dfrac{440}{5}$ Mean = 88
Median	(a) middle piece of data when a set of data is arranged from least to greatest.	The median daily high temperature: (a) 68°F, 72°F, 65°F, 58°F, 66°F Order the data: 58, 65, 66, 68, 72 Median is the middle piece of data: 66°F
	(b) When a set has two middle pieces of data, the median is halfway between them.	(b) 76°F, 75°F, 80°F, 82°F, 73°F, 78°F Order the data: 73, 75, 76, 78, 80, 82 Median is halfway between middle two: $\dfrac{76 + 78}{2} = \dfrac{154}{2}$ $= 77$ Median = 77°F
Mode	piece of data that appears most frequently in a set of data	The mode of the temperatures: (a) 23°C, 25°C, 18°C, 23°C, 21°C mode: 23°C (b) 16°C, 18°C, 19°C, 18°C, 20°C, 16°C Mode: 16°C and 18°C (called bimodal) (c) 21°C, 15°C, 17°C, 14°C Mode: none
Range	difference between the greatest and least values in a set of data	The range of the temperatures: 12°C, 8°C, 15°C, 17°C, 14°C high − low = 17 − 8 $= 9$ Range = 9°C
Quartiles	medians of lower and upper half of a set of data.	The lower quartile of the test scores: 70, 70, 72, 75, 79, 80, 80, 84, 89, 95 lower quartile = 72 upper quartile = 84

Finding Missing Measures in Right Triangles

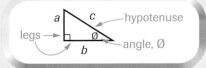

MORE HELP
See
245–250

	Formula	Variables and Symbols	Example
Pythagorean theorem	$a^2 + b^2 = c^2$	a = length of one leg of right triangle b = length of other leg of right triangle c = length of hypotenuse of right triangle	The length of the hypotenuse of this triangle: 9 ft 12 ft $9^2 + 12^2 = c^2$ $81 + 144 = c^2$ $225 = c^2$ $15 = c$ The hypotenuse is 15 feet long.
Sine ratio	$\sin \theta =$ $\dfrac{\text{length of opposite leg}}{\text{length of hypotenuse}}$	θ: theta, Greek letter indicating angle measure	10, 8, 6, θ $\sin \theta = \dfrac{\text{opposite}}{\text{hypotenuse}}$ $\sin \theta = \dfrac{8}{10}$ or 0.8
Cosine ratio	$\cos \theta =$ $\dfrac{\text{length of adjacent leg}}{\text{length of hypotenuse}}$	θ: theta, Greek letter indicating angle measure	10, 8, 6, θ $\cos \theta = \dfrac{\text{adjacent}}{\text{hypotenuse}}$ $\cos \theta = \dfrac{6}{10}$ or 0.6
Tangent ratio	$\tan \theta =$ $\dfrac{\text{length of opposite leg}}{\text{length of adjacent leg}}$	θ: theta, Greek letter indicating angle measure	10, 8, 6, θ $\tan \theta = \dfrac{\text{opposite}}{\text{adjacent}}$ $\tan \theta = \dfrac{8}{6}$ or $1.\overline{3}$

Algebraic Formulas

	Formula	Variables	Example
MORE HELP See 184–185, 187 Quadratic formula: Used for finding the roots or zeros of $ax^2 + bx + c = 0$.	$x = \dfrac{-b \pm \sqrt{b^2 - 4ac}}{2a}$	a: coefficient of x^2 b: coefficient of x c: constant (number)	Find the roots of $x^2 + x - 1 = 0$. $a = 1, b = 1, c = {}^-1$ $x = \dfrac{{}^-1 \pm \sqrt{1^2 - 4(1)({}^-1)}}{2(1)}$ $= \dfrac{{}^-1 \pm \sqrt{1 + 4}}{2}$ $= \dfrac{{}^-1 \pm \sqrt{5}}{2}$ The two solutions to $x^2 + x - 1 = 0$ are $x = \dfrac{{}^-1 + \sqrt{5}}{2}$ and $x = \dfrac{{}^-1 - \sqrt{5}}{2}$
Discriminant: Used to determine whether the quadratic formula can be used to find real roots to solve $ax^2 + bx + c = 0$.	$b^2 - 4ac$	a: coefficient of x^2 b: coefficient of x c: constant (number)	In $x^2 + x - 1 = 0$, the discriminant is $b^2 - 4ac = 1^2 - 4(1)({}^-1)$ $= 1 + 4$ $= 5$ $5 \geq 0$, so the two roots of this equation are real.

Discriminant	Roots
> 0	2 real
$= 0$	double
< 0	no real

Formulas Used in Graphing

	Formula	Variables	Example
MORE HELP See 150–159, 175, 184–185, 221–222 Slope	$m = \dfrac{(y_2 - y_1)}{(x_2 - x_1)}$, or $m = \dfrac{\text{change in } y}{\text{change in } x}$	m: slope (x_1, y_1) and (x_2, y_2): coordinates of two points on a line	Slope of line connecting $(3, 5)$ and $(6, 9)$: $m = \dfrac{9 - 5}{6 - 3}$ $m = \dfrac{4}{3}$
Straight line Slope-intercept form	$y = mx + b$	m: slope b: y-intercept	$y = 3x - 2$

Formulas Used in Graphing (continued)

	Formula	Variables	Example
Straight line Standard form	$ax + by + c = 0$	a: coefficient of x b: coefficient of y c: constant	$3x - y - 2 = 0$
Parabola	$y = ax^2 + bx + c,$ $a \neq 0$	a: coefficient of x^2 b: coefficient of x c: constant (number) positive $a \rightarrow$ parabola opens up negative $a \rightarrow$ parabola opens down	$y = x^2 + 2x + 1$
Parabola: special case vertex at (0, 0)	$y = x^2$	$a = 1$ b and $c = 0$	$y = x^2$
Circle (center at the origin)	$x^2 + y^2 = r^2$	r: radius $(r, 0), (^-r, 0), (0, r),$ and $(0, ^-r)$ are on the graph	$x^2 + y^2 = 16, r = 4$ $(0, 4)$, $(4, 0)$, $(^-4, 0)$, $(0, ^-4)$
Hyperbola: special case	$xy = 1$, or $y = \dfrac{1}{x}$, or $x = \dfrac{1}{y}$		$y = \dfrac{1}{x}$

A

abacus: Computation device, usually a frame that allows beads to slide along rods that represent different place values.

abscissa: *See x-coordinate*

absolute value (| |)**:** The distance of a number from zero on the number line. For a complex number $(a + bi)$, the absolute value is the distance from the origin of point (a, b). Absolute value is never negative. $|^{-}28| = 28; |28| = 28$ **(009)**

abundant number: A number whose factors (except for the number itself) have a sum greater than the number. 12 is an abundant number because $1 + 2 + 3 + 4 + 6 > 12$. 10 is not abundant because $1 + 2 + 5 < 10$. No prime number is abundant.

accurate: An approximate number is accurate (correct) to the last decimal place shown if all of its digits are significant and if the true value is within $\frac{1}{2}$ of the value of the last place. You could say that 3.14 is π accurate to the hundredths place because π (3.14159…) is between 3.135 and 3.145.

acute angle: An angle with a measure less than 90° and greater than 0°. **(226)**

acute triangle: A triangle with no interior angle measuring 90° or more. **(243)**

add (+): Combine. **(078)**

addend: Any number being added. **(078)**

Addition Property of Equality: If you add equals to equals you get equals. If $a = b$, then $a + c = b + c$. **(045)**

additive identity: Zero. $a + 0 = a$ **(039)**

additive inverse: The opposite of a number. When a number is added to its additive inverse, the sum is zero. 15 and $^{-}15$ are additive inverses because $15 + ^{-}15 = 0$. **(041)**

adjacent: Next to.

adjacent angles: Any two non-overlapping angles with the same vertex and a side in common. In both diagrams $\angle a$ and $\angle b$ are adjacent **(236)**

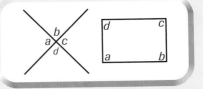

algebra: A branch of mathematics that includes the use of variables to express rules about numbers, number relationships, and operations.

algebraic expression: A group of numbers, symbols, and variables that express an operation or a series of operations. $5x^2 + 6$ is an expression. **(099)**

algebraic fraction: *See rational expression*

algorithm: A step-by-step method for computing or carrying out any mathematical procedure.

alternate exterior angles: Angles whose interior points are on opposite sides of a transversal line and on the *outside* of the lines it intersects. Angles 1 and 7 are alternate exterior angles. So are angles 8 and 2. **(237)**

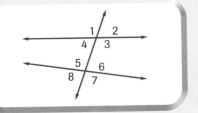

alternate interior angles: Angles whose interior points are on the opposite sides of a transversal line and on the *inside* of the lines it intersects. Angles 4 and 6 are alternate interior angles. So are angles 3 and 5. **(237)**

altitude: *See height*

amplitude: Half the difference between the maximum and the minimum values of a periodic function. **(145)**

angle (∠): (1) The figure formed by two rays that share an endpoint. (2) The measure of a turn about a point. *See also angle of rotation* **(225)**

angle bisector: A ray that separates an angle into two congruent angles. **(235)**

angle of depression or elevation: The angle between a horizontal and the line of sight. If you're looking up, the angle is an angle of **elevation**. If you're looking down, it's an angle of **depression**.

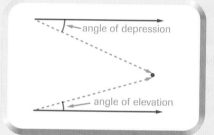

angle of rotation: If you rotate or turn a geometric figure, the angle that the figure is rotated or turned is called the angle of rotation. The angle of rotation of the triangle is 90°. **(270)**

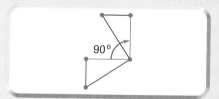

apex: The point on a figure farthest from the base line or base plane. The apex of a pyramid is its vertex.

apothem: The perpendicular line segment (or the length of a perpendicular line segment) from the center of a regular polygon to a side.

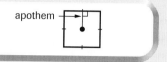

approximate number (≈): A number that describes another number without specifying it exactly. 3.1416 is an approximate number for π.

approximation: (1) A method for obtaining an approximate number. (2) An approximate number.

Arabic numerals: The digits used in our base ten (decimal) number system: 0, 1, 2, 3, 4, 5, 6, 7, 8, 9.

arc (⌒): Part of a curve between any two of its points. **(257)**

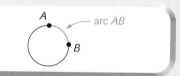

area (A): The measure, in square units, of the interior region of a two-dimensional figure or the surface of a three-dimensional figure. **(466)**

arithmetic: Calculation using addition, subtraction, multiplication, or division.

arithmetic mean: *See mean*

arithmetic progression: A set of numbers in which the difference between any two consecutive numbers is the same. 3, 6, 9, 12, ... is an arithmetic progression because the difference between any two consecutive numbers is 3. The series 3, 9, 27, 81, ... is not an arithmetic progression, because each item in the series is a power of three.

arithmetic sequence: *See arithmetic progression*

arithmetic series: The sum of the numbers in an arithmetic progression.

arm: (1) One of the sides, or legs, of a right triangle, not the hypotenuse. (2) One of the rays forming an angle.

Associative Law: *See Associative Property of Addition/Multiplication*

Associative Property of Addition: The sum stays the same when the grouping of addends is changed. $(a + b) + c = a + (b + c)$, where a, b, and c stand for any real numbers. **(035)**

Associative Property of Multiplication: The product stays the same when the grouping of factors is changed. $(a \cdot b) \cdot c = a \cdot (b \cdot c)$, where a, b, and c stand for any real numbers. **(036)**

asymptote: A line to which the graph of a curve gets increasingly closer but never touches or crosses. In the graph of $y = \frac{1}{x}$, the axes are asymptotes. **(293)**

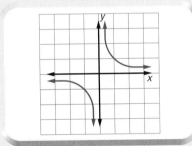

average: A single number that describes all the numbers in a set. Usually, the average refers to the mean, but sometimes it refers to the median or the mode.

average deviation: The average of the absolute values of all the deviations in a set of data. The average deviation indicates by how much the data points tend to differ from the mean.

axes: Plural of *axis*.

axiom: *See postulate*

axis: A reference line from which distances or angles are measured on a coordinate grid. **(219)**

axis of symmetry: *See line of symmetry*

B

bar graph: A graph in which quantities are represented by bars. **(347)**

base of an exponent: The number used as the factor in exponential form. In 4^6, the base is 4 and the exponent is 6. **(051)**

base of a parallelogram (b): The side of a parallelogram that contains one end of the altitude or height (h).

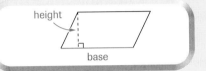

base of a percent: The number for which the percent is found. In 15% of 82, the base is 82. **(294)**

base of a solid figure (B): A special face of a solid figure. If the solid is a cylinder or prism, there are two bases that are parallel and congruent.

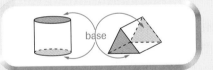

base ten: A number system in which each digit has ten times the value of the same digit one place to its right. $8888 = 8$ thousands + 8 hundreds + 8 tens + 8 ones

base of a triangle (b): The side of a triangle that contains one end of the height (h). Every triangle has three bases and three corresponding heights. **(240)**

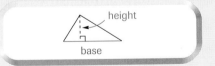

best-fit line: *See line of best fit*

biased sample: A sample that is not representative of a population.

bimodal: Having two modes. The set of data: 72, 85, 75, 81, 85, and 72 is bimodal. There are two modes: 72 and 85. *See also mode* **(338)**

binomial: A polynomial with two terms. In $5x + 3$, the terms are $5x$ and 3. *See also monomial, polynomial* **(101)**

binary number system: A number system in which each digit has two times the value of the same digit one place to its right. The only digits this system uses are zero and 1. 10100 in binary is 1 sixteen + 0 eights + 1 four + 0 twos + 0 ones, or 20 in base ten.

bisect: To cut or divide into two congruent parts. The midpoint of a line segment bisects the segment.

bit: Abbreviation for binary digit—a zero or a one in the binary number system. 1110 in binary contains four bits (three ones and a zero).

borrow: Regroup from one place value to another place value in order to subtract. *See regroup*

boundary line: In the graph of an inequality, a graph of a related equation which divides the plane. **(202)**

box plot: *See box-and-whisker plot*

box-and-whisker plot: A graph that uses a rectangle (or box) to represent the middle 50% of a set of data (the midquartile range) and line segments (or *whiskers*) at both ends to represent the remainder of the data. **(357)**

braces ({ }): (1) Grouping symbols used to enclose items that should be regarded as a single expression or to indicate that an expression between them should be evaluated first. **(070)**

(2) Braces are often used for set definitions. $\{a, b, c\}$ means the set that contains three things, a, b, and c.

brackets ([ ]): (1) Grouping symbols used to indicate that an expression between them should be evaluated first. (2) Grouping symbols used to set off a matrix. (3) Used to indicate greatest integer function. **(143)**

byte: A group of eight binary digits. *See also bit*

cancel: To simplify by dividing out equal factors from both sides of an equation or from the numerator and denominator of a fraction. The equation $8x = 48y$ is the same as $8x = 8 \cdot 6 \cdot y$. Since both sides of the equation have eight as a factor, the eights can be canceled to simplify the equation to $x = 6y$. **(089)**

capacity: The maximum amount that can be contained by an object. Often refers to the measurement of liquids.

cardinal number: A whole number that names how many objects are in a group. If there are 12 oranges, the cardinal number is 12. *See also ordinal number*

cardinality: The number of elements in a set.

carry: Regroup from one place value to another in order to add. *See regroup*

Cartesian coordinate system: A two- or three-dimensional system for naming the precise location of a point. *See also coordinate grid*

Celsius (C): The metric-system scale for measuring temperature. 0°C is the freezing point of fresh water at sea level. 100°C is the boiling point of fresh water at sea level.

center: (1) Occupying a middle position. (2) A point that is the same distance from all the vertices of a regular polygon. (3) A point that is the same distance from all points on a circle or a sphere. **(254)**

center of rotation: The point that a geometric figure is rotated or turned around. The point can be on the figure, but does not have to be. **(270)**

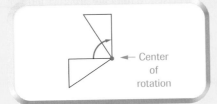

← Center
of
rotation

centigrade: *See Celsius*

central angle: An angle that has the center of a circle as its vertex. $\angle ACB$ is a central angle. **(256)**

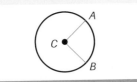

central tendency: *See measure of central tendency*

century: 100 years.

certain event: An event that will *definitely* happen. A certain event has a probability of 1. **(320)**

characteristic: The integer part of a common logarithm. $\log 38 \approx 1.579784$. The characteristic of this logarithm is 1. *See also mantissa*

chord: A line segment that joins two points on a circle. $\overline{QR}$ is a chord. **(255)**

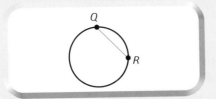

circle: A closed curve in one plane with all its points the same distance from a fixed point (the center). **(254)**

circle graph: A graph that divides a circle into sectors in order to compare different parts of a data set to the entire set. **(351)**

circulating decimal: *See repeating decimal*

circumference (C): (1) The perimeter of a circle. (2) The length of the boundary line of a circle. **(465)**

circumscribed: A plane figure whose sides are tangent to a circle is circumscribed about the circle. A circle containing a plane figure whose vertices are on the circle is circumscribed about the figure. Solid figures may be circumscribed about other solid figures. Not all figures can be circumscribed.

clearing an equation: When working with an equation that contains fractions or decimals, multiplying both sides of the equation by some number that will eliminate all denominators.

$$\frac{x}{3} + \frac{5y}{6} = 15$$

$$6\left(\frac{x}{3} + \frac{5y}{6}\right) = 6(15)$$

$$2x + 5y = 90 \qquad \textbf{(129)}$$

clockwise: In the same direction that the hands of a clock rotate.

closed figure: A figure that completely surrounds a region in a plane.

clustered: Grouped together.

coefficient: A numerical factor in a term of an algebraic expression. In $3a$, the coefficient of a is 3. **(100)**

collecting terms: *See combining like terms*

collinear: On the same line. **(209)**

combination: A group of items or events. Placing these items or events in a different order does not create a new combination. Red, blue, and green are a combination of colors. Blue, red, and green are the same combination. **(319)**

combining like terms: When working with an expression, combining terms that have the same variable raised to the same power. **(104)**

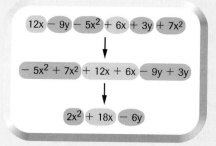

common: Shared.

common divisor: *See common factor*

common factor: A number that is a factor of two or more numbers. 1, 2, and 4 are the common factors of 28 and 36. **(020)**

common fraction: Any fraction whose numerator and denominator are integers. $\frac{9}{10}$ and $\frac{12}{5}$ are both common fractions.

common logarithm: (1) Logarithm to the base 10. (2) An exponent showing the number of times 10 is used as a factor to find another number. $\log 1000 = 3$ means $10^3 = 1000$, so 3 is the common logarithm of 1000. **(066)**

common multiple: A number that is a multiple of two or more numbers. The numbers 15, 30, 45, and 60 are some of the common multiples of 3 and 5. **(028)**

commutativity: *See Commutative Property of Addition/Multiplication*

Commutative Property of Addition: The sum stays the same when the order of the addends is changed. $a + b = b + a$, where a and b are any real numbers. $78 + n = n + 78$ **(031)**

Commutative Property of Multiplication: The product stays the same when the order of the factors is changed. $a \cdot b = b \cdot a$, where a and b are any real numbers. $25n = n \cdot 25$ **(032)**

compass: A tool used to draw a circle or arc.

compatible numbers: A pair of numbers that are easy to work with mentally. The numbers 90 and 30 are compatible numbers for estimating $91.3 \div 29.7$. **(074)**

complementary angles: Two angles with measures whose sum is 90°. **(234)**

complementary events: Two or more mutually exclusive events that together cover all possible outcomes. The sum of the probabilities of complementary events is 1. If you toss a coin, heads and tails are complementary events. **(330)**

completeness: All theorems in a system can be deduced from the same set of postulates. **(400)**

complete the square: A method used to solve a quadratic equation when factoring is possible, but the factors are not immediately obvious. **(183)**

complex fraction: A fraction with a fraction in the numerator and/or denominator.

$\frac{5\frac{2}{3}}{12}$ and $\frac{\frac{3}{8}}{\frac{7}{9}}$ are complex fractions.

$\frac{7}{8}$ is not a complex fraction. **(005)**

composite figure: A figure made up of two or more figures.

composite number: A natural number that has more than two factors. Nine is a composite number because it has three factors: 1, 3, and 9. **(024)**

compound event: A combination of simple events. If you select a marble from a bag containing red, blue, green, and yellow marbles, selecting a blue or a green marble is a compound event. **(329)**

compound inequalities: Two inequalities combined using *and* or using *or*. **(195)**

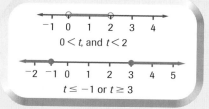

compound interest: Interest earned on the sum of the principal and any previous interest payments. **(306)**

compounded quarterly: Every three months ($\frac{1}{4}$ year) interest on an amount of money is computed at $\frac{1}{4}$ of the yearly interest and added to the original amount. This sum is used to compute the interest for the next quarter. **(306)**

computation: *See compute*

compute: To find a numerical result, usually by adding, subtracting, multiplying, or dividing.

concave polygon: A polygon with one or more diagonals that have points outside the polygon.

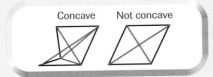

Concave   Not concave

concurrent: With a common point.

cone: A three-dimensional figure with a circular base and one vertex.

congruent ($\cong$): Having exactly the same size and shape. **(264)**

congruent angles: Angles that have exactly the same measure. **(232)**

congruent segments: Line segments that have exactly the same length.

conjugate complex numbers: Complex numbers that differ only in the sign of their imaginary parts. $6 + 8i$ and $6 - 8i$ are conjugates of each other.

consecutive: In order, with none missing. 24, 25, 26 are consecutive integers. 29, 31, 33 are consecutive odd numbers.

consistency: Proofs using the same postulates cannot contradict each other. **(400)**

constant: A quantity that always stays the same. In $12y + 5$, 5 is a constant. **(100)**

constant of proportionality: Also called constant of variation. The constant factor by which a proportion increases or decreases. In a direct proportion, $y = kx$ and in an indirect proportion, $y = \frac{k}{x}$, where $k \neq 0$, k is the constant of proportionality. **(292)**

constant of variation: *See constant of proportionality*

continuous graph: A graph in which there are no gaps, jumps, or holes. The graph of a straight line is continuous, while the graph of the greatest integer function is not. **(139)**

contrapositive: Think of a statement as *If A is true, then B is true.* The contrapositive of the statement is *If B is not true, then A is not true.* **(405)**

converse: Think of a statement as *If A is true, then B is true.* The converse of the statement is *If B is true, then A is true.* **(403)**

convex polygon: A polygon with each interior angle measuring less than 180°. All diagonals of a convex polygon lie inside the polygon.

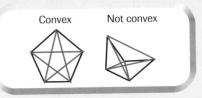

Convex   Not convex

coordinate grid: A two-dimensional system in which a location is described by its distances from two intersecting, usually perpendicular, straight lines, called axes. **(219)**

coordinate plane: *See coordinate grid*

coordinate system: *See coordinate grid*

coordinates: An ordered pair of numbers that give the location of a point. In a coordinate plane, the order of numbers in the pair is (direction and distance along x, direction and distance along y). $(3, {}^-2)$ describes a point three units to the right on the x-axis and two units down on the y-axis. **(219)**

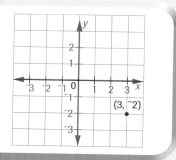

coplanar: In the same plane.

correlation: An association between two variables used in statistics. *See also positive correlation, negative correlation* **(365)**

corresponding angles: (1) When a transversal crosses two lines, corresponding angles are in the same position from one line to the other. They are congruent if the two lines are parallel. **(237)** (2) When comparing two figures, angles in the same relative position from one figure to the other are corresponding angles. If the figures are similar or congruent, the corresponding angles are congruent.

cosine ratio (cos): In a right triangle, the cosine of an angle is the ratio of the length of the leg adjacent to that angle to the length of the hypotenuse. The value of the cosine of an angle depends upon the measure of the angle. **(250)**

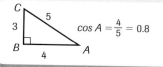

counterclockwise: In a direction opposite to the direction that the hands of a clock rotate.

counterexample: A specific case that shows that a rule isn't true for all examples. It only takes one counterexample to prove that a statement is not true. A says: *All blooters are red.* B says: *Here is a green blooter.* B's statement is a counterexample of A's statement. **(409)**

counting principle: See *fundamental counting principle*

cross multiplication: A method for finding a missing numerator or denominator in equivalent fractions or ratios by making the cross products equal. **(287)**

cross product: The product of one numerator and the opposite denominator in a pair of equivalent fractions or ratios. The cross products of equivalent fractions or ratios are equal. Related to the statement, *the product of the extremes equals the product of the means.*

$$\frac{A}{B} = \frac{C}{D} \longrightarrow AD = BC$$

$$A : B = C : D \longrightarrow AD = BC \qquad \textbf{(287)}$$

cross section: A plane shape formed when a plane cuts through a three-dimensional figure.

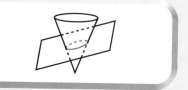

cube: (1) A regular solid having six congruent square faces. (2) The third power of a number. $20^3 = 20 \times 20 \times 20 = 8000$ **(059)**

cube root: A number whose cube is equal to a given number. $\sqrt[3]{729} = 9$ **(059)**

cubic measure: See *cubic unit*

cubic unit: A unit such as a cubic meter used to measure volume or capacity.

cuboid: A prism with six rectangular faces.

currency: The official money issued by a government.

currency exchange rate: The rate at which currency between countries is exchanged. **(290)**

curve: (1) An infinite set of points having length but no other dimensions. (2) A smooth line, often one that is continuously not straight. (3) A line representing data on a graph. **(217)**

customary system: A system of measurement used in the U.S. The system includes units for measuring length, capacity, weight, and temperature. **(456)**

cylinder: A three-dimensional figure with two parallel and congruent curves (usually circles) as bases, which are joined by a curved surface.

data: Information, especially numerical. Usually organized for analysis.

database: A collection of information. A computer database stores and manages a large collection of information related to a particular subject. **(432)**

decade: (1) 10 years. (2) The numbers from $10n + 1$ through $10n + 10$.

decile: The nine deciles divide ordered data into 10 groups with 10% of the data points in each group.

decimal (decimal number): (1) A number written using base ten. (2) A number containing a decimal point. **(006)**

decimal point: A dot separating the ones and tenths places in a decimal number. **(006)**

deductive reasoning: The process of reasoning where specific cases are tested against a specific rule. **(408)**

deficient number: A number whose factors (except for the number itself) have a sum less than the number. Nine is a deficient number because $1 + 3 < 9$.

degree (angle measure): A unit of angle measure. 1° equals the central angle of a circle formed by rays that cut $\frac{1}{360}$ of its circumference.

degree Celsius (°C): The metric unit of measure for temperature. *See also Celsius*

degree Centigrade: *See degree Celsius*

degree Fahrenheit (°F): The customary unit of measure for temperature. *See also Fahrenheit*

degree of a polynomial: The highest power of any term of a polynomial. A quadratic is a second degree polynomial. **(174)**

denominate number: A number used with a unit. 18 kg or 12 ft

denominator: The quantity below the bar in a fraction. It tells the number of equal parts into which a whole is divided. In the fraction $\frac{5}{6}$, the denominator is 6. **(004)**

Density Property: Between every two real numbers there is another real number. **(050)**

dependent events: Two events in which the outcome of the first event affects the outcome of the second event. A bag contains 3 red marbles and 3 blue marbles. Draw a marble from the bag at random and don't put it back. The color that you draw will affect the probability of picking a given color in a second draw. **(329)**

dependent variable: In a function, a variable whose value is determined by the value of the related independent variable. **(131)**

determine: Provide sufficient information. We say *two points determine a line* because a line can be drawn through any two points: The two points provide sufficient information to draw a line.

deviation: The difference between a number in a set of data and the mean of all the numbers in the set.

diagonal: A line segment that joins two vertices of a polygon but is not a side of the polygon. $\overline{BE}$ and $\overline{CE}$ are two of the diagonals of this pentagon. **(117)**

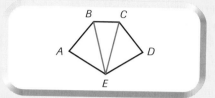

diagram: A drawing that represents a mathematical situation.

diameter: (1) A line segment that passes through the center of a circle and has endpoints on the circle. (2) The length of such a line segment. **(255)**

dice: Two or more prisms with numbers or dots on each face. The most common dice are cubes numbered 1–6.

die: Singular of dice.

difference: The amount that remains after one quantity is subtracted from another. The difference between 198 and 152 is 46. **(078)**

digit: Any one of the ten symbols: 0, 1, 2, 3, 4, 5, 6, 7, 8, or 9.

dihedral angle: Angle formed by two intersecting planes. **(218)**

dilation: A proportional shrinking or enlargement of a figure. **(276)**

dimensional analysis: Solving a problem by analyzing the units. Suppose you are solving a problem using the equation $r \cdot t = d$. If you know that the rate is $\frac{miles}{hour}$ and the time is hours then you know that the distance is $\frac{miles}{hour} \cdot hours$, or miles. **(291)**

dimensions: (1) The lengths of the sides of a geometric figure. (2) The number of coordinates needed to locate a point in space. Cones, prisms, and other three-dimensional figures occupy more than one plane; three coordinates are needed to locate a point on a three-dimensional figure.

dimension of a matrix: If a matrix has m rows and n columns, then its dimension is $m \times n$. **(311)**

direct proportion: Two quantities that always have the same ratio. In $y = kx$, where k is a constant, y is directly proportional to x. **(292)**

direct variation: *See direct proportion*

directed number: A number with a positive or negative sign to show its direction from zero. Temperatures are directed numbers. Distance is always positive, so distances are not directed numbers.

discount: The amount by which an original price was reduced. **(303)**

discrete: Discontinuous, made up of distinct parts.

discrete function: A function that takes on distinct values not connected by intermediate values. **(139)**

discriminant: An algebraic expression related to the coefficients of a quadratic equation that gives information about the roots of the equation. For $ax^2 + bx + c = 0$, the discriminant is $b^2 - 4ac$. The discriminant is non-zero if the two roots are distinct. It is equal to zero when the two roots are equal. If the discriminant is less than zero, there are no real roots. **(187)**

disprove (a statement): Show that a statement is not true for all numbers.

distance: (1) The length of the shortest line segment joining two points. (2) The length of a line segment perpendicular to two parallel lines is the distance between those lines.

Distributive Property: The product of a number and the sum or difference of two numbers is equal to the sum or difference of the two products. $a \cdot (b + c) = (a \cdot b) + (a \cdot c)$ and $a \cdot (b - c) = (a \cdot b) - (a \cdot c)$, where a, b, and c stand for any real numbers. **(037)**

divide (÷): (1) To separate into equal groups. (2) To separate equally into a given number of groups. (3) To be an exact divisor of.

dividend: A quantity to be divided.

dividend ÷ divisor = quotient

$$\text{divisor}\overline{)\text{dividend}}^{\text{quotient}}$$ **(085)**

divisible: One number is divisible by another if their quotient is an integer. 24 is divisible by four but is not divisible by five.

division: The operation of making equal groups or of making equal amounts within each given group. There are 12.8 groups of 15 in 192. **(085)**

divisor: The quantity by which another quantity is to be divided.

dividend ÷ divisor = quotient

$$\text{divisor}\overline{)\text{dividend}}^{\text{quotient}}$$ **(085)**

domain: In a function, $f(x)$, the possible values for x in the given situation. It is the set of values of the independent variable of a given function. *See also range* **(131)**

double bar graph: A bar graph that uses pairs of bars to compare data. **(349)**

double root: The solution to a quadratic equation whose roots are the same. **(187)**

double stem-and-leaf plot: A stem-and-leaf plot that compares two sets of data. In a double stem-and-leaf plot, the stem is in the middle and the leaves are on either side. **(360)**

E ―――――――――――――

edge: The line segment where two faces of a solid figure meet.

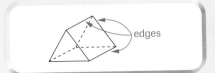
edges

elapsed time: The amount of time between two given clock times or events.

element: (1) One of the objects in a set. Also called a *member*. (2) Any of the terms in a matrix. **(311)**

elimination: *See linear combination method*

ellipse: A closed curve shaped like an oval and symmetric about two axes of different lengths.

endpoint: (1) A point marking either end of a line segment. (2) A point marking the end of a ray. **(211)**

equal (=): Having the same value.

equal ratios: *See proportion*

Equality Properties: If $a = b$, then

$$a + c = b + c$$
$$a - c = b - c$$
$$a \cdot c = b \cdot c$$
$$\frac{a}{c} = \frac{b}{c}, c \neq 0$$ **(044)**

equally likely outcomes or events: Having the same chance, or probability. If you toss a fair die, the six outcomes are equally likely. **(322)**

equation: A statement that two mathematical expressions are equal. $y \div 3.9 = 42.8$ means that $y \div 3.9$ must have the same value as 42.8 in order for the statement to be true. **(124)**

equiangular: All angles have the same measure. In an equiangular quadrilateral, each angle measures 90°. **(243)**

equidistant: Equally distant. All points on the surface of a sphere are equidistant from its center.

equilateral: All sides have the same measure. A triangle whose sides are all the same length is equilateral. **(243)**

equivalent: Having the same value. 0.08 and 0.080 are equivalent decimals. $\frac{5}{9}$ and $\frac{15}{27}$ are equivalent fractions. 12:3 and 4:1 are equivalent ratios. $4x + 4y$ and $4(x + y)$ are equivalent expressions.

estimate (es´ ti mate, verb): To find a number close to an exact amount. **(072)**

estimate (es´ ti met, noun): A number close to an exact amount; an estimate tells *about* how much or *about* how many. An estimate of 5.8×3.7 is 24. **(072)**

evaluate: To find the value of a mathematical expression. **(114)**

evaluate an algebraic expression for given values: Substitute the given values for the variables and compute to find a value for the expression. **(114)**

even number: A whole number that can be represented by the expression $2n$ where n is a whole number. The ones digit of any even number is 0, 2, 4, 6, or 8. **(018)**

event: A possible result, or outcome, in probability. **(320)**

expanded form: A way to write numbers that shows the place value of each digit. $3024 = (3 \times 1000) + (0 \times 100) + (2 \times 10) + (4 \times 1)$

expected value: The sum of probabilities of each outcome multiplied by the value of the outcome.

experimental probability: A statement of probability based on the results of a series of trials.

experimental probability (event) = $\frac{\text{number of trials resulting in favorable outcomes}}{\text{number of trials in experiment}}$ **(323)**

exponent: The number that tells how many equal factors there are. In $8 \times 8 \times 8 \times 8 \times 8 = 8^5$, the exponent is 5. **(051)**

exponential form: A way of writing a number using exponents. $28,063 = (2 \times 10^4) + (8 \times 10^3) + (6 \times 10^1) + (3 \times 10^0)$ **(066)**

exponential function: The function $y = a^x$, for a (greater than 0 but not equal to 1) and exponent, x.

exponential growth: The increase of a quantity x with time t according to the equation $x = Ca^t$; a is a constant greater than 1, C is a constant greater than 0.

expression: A variable or combination of variables, numbers, and symbols that represents a mathematical relationship. $16\pi r^3$; $4x^2 + 2x + 9$; $8^{\frac{2}{3}}$ **(099)**

exterior angle: If you extend one side of a polygon, the angle between the extension and the adjacent side of the polygon is called an exterior angle. **(229)**

exterior angle

extraneous solutions: Solutions to a transformed equation that are not solutions to the original equation or problem.

extrapolation: Making predictions by extending a graph that shows a trend beyond the range of the data available. **(368)**

extremes: The first and last terms in the ratios of a proportion. In $4:5 = 20:25$, the extremes are 4 and 25. *See also means* **(287)**

extreme terms: *See extremes*

F

face: A plane figure that serves as one side of a solid figure. The faces of a prism are parallelograms.

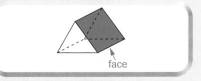

face

factor: An integer that divides into another with no remainder. In $9 \times 4 = 36$, 9 and 4 are factors of 36. *See also factorization, factoring* **(017)**

factor tree: A method used to find the prime factorization of a number. **(026)**

factored form: *See factoring*

factorial (!): The product of a whole number and every natural number less than itself. Note: 0! is defined as 1. $6! = 6 \times 5 \times 4 \times 3 \times 2 \times 1 = 720$ **(022)**

factoring: Rewriting a polynomial expression as a product.
$$x^2 - 6x + 5 = 0$$
$$(x-1)(x-5) = 0.$$ **(182)**

factorization: (1) Finding the factors of a number or expression. (2) A number or expression written as a product of its factors. *See also prime factorization*

Fahrenheit (F): The customary system scale for measuring temperature. 32°F is the freezing point of fresh water at sea level. 212°F is the boiling point of fresh water at sea level.

favorable outcome: In probability, the outcome being measured. **(322)**

Fibonacci sequence: A series of numbers in which each number is the sum of the two numbers before it. 1, 1, 2, 3, 5, 8, . . .

figure: (1) Joined line segments or curves in two or three dimensions. (2) Diagram. (3) Number.

finite: Having bounds; limited. **(007)**

five-number summary: The minimum score, maximum score, median, and the two hinges of a set of data. Used in creating box-and-whisker plots.

flat angle: *See straight angle*

flip: *See reflection*

formula: A general mathematical statement, equation, or rule.

fraction: A way of representing part of a whole (or a group) by telling the number of equal parts in the whole and the number of those parts you are describing.

$\frac{3}{8}$ ← numerator (3 parts)
← denominator (8 equal parts) **(004)**

frequency: The number of times something occurs in an interval or set of data.

frequency table: A table that shows how often each item, number, or range of numbers occurs in a set of data. **(341)**

function (f(x)): A relation in which every value of x has a unique value of y.

If $y = x + 5$
then f(x) = $x + 5$ **(134)**

fundamental counting principle: If one event can happen in a ways and a second, independent, event can happen in b ways, the two can occur together in $a \cdot b$ ways. **(317)**

Fundamental Theorem of Arithmetic: Any composite number can be written as a unique product of prime numbers. $6 = 2 \cdot 3$ *See also prime factorization* **(023)**

 G

geometric: Having to do with geometry.

geometric progression: A sequence of terms in which each term is created by multiplying the previous term by a constant. 1, 8, 64, 512, ...

geometry: The mathematics of the properties and relationships of points, lines, angles, surfaces, and solids. **(207)**

gradient: *See slope*

graph: A pictorial device that shows a relationship between variables or sets of data.

graphing calculator: A calculator with the capacity to graph and display functions on a screen. Also sometimes called *graphics calculator.* **(435)**

greatest common factor (GCF): The greatest number that divides into two or more numbers with no remainder. The greatest common factor of 16, 20, and 36 is 4. **(021)**

greatest integer function ([ ]): The function f(x) = [x] where [x] is the greatest integer less than or equal to a real number, x. When $x = 2.7$, [x] = 2 and when $x = {}^-2.7$, [x] = $^-3$. **(143)**

greatest possible error (GPE): One half the unit of measure used in making a measurement. If you use an inch ruler marked in eighths to make a measurement, the GPE is $\frac{1}{16}$ inch.

grid: A pattern of horizontal and vertical lines, usually forming squares.

grouping symbols: Parentheses, braces, or brackets indicating grouping of terms in an expression. **(070)**

half line: Ray. In some texts, a half-line is defined as a ray without an endpoint.

half planes: In the graph of an inequality, the two regions separated by the plane divider. **(204)**

half turn: A rotation of 180° (or half of one revolution) about a point.

height (altitude, *h*): (1) The perpendicular distance from a vertex to an opposite, parallel, side of a trapezoid or parallelogram. (2) The perpendicular distance from the vertex to the base of a triangle, pyramid, or cone. (3) The perpendicular distance between the bases of a prism or cylinder. If there is more than one side or edge that can be used as a base in a figure, then the figure has more than one possible height. **(240)**

hexagon: A polygon with six sides. **(453)**

hinge: The median value of the bottom or top half of a set of ordered data. *See also upper quartile, lower quartile*

histogram: A bar graph in which the labels for the bars are numerical intervals, so the bars touch each other. **(358)**

horizontal: Parallel to or in the plane of the horizon. In a coordinate grid, the x-axis is a horizontal line. **(221)**

hyperbola: The graph of an equation in the form of $\frac{x^2}{a^2} + \frac{y^2}{b^2} = 1$. **(144)**

hypotenuse: The longest side of a right triangle. This side is always opposite the right angle. **(240)**

Identity Elements: For any real number, a: $a + 0 = a$ and $0 + a = a$;
$a \cdot 1 = a$ and $1 \cdot a = a$. **(039)**

image: *See transformation image*

imaginary number: The square root of a negative real number. It cannot be shown on the number line. **(016)**

imaginary unit (*i*): $i = \sqrt{-1}$. $i^2 = -1$. Can be used to write the square root of any negative number.
$$\sqrt{-9} = \sqrt{9 \cdot -1}$$
$$= \sqrt{9} \cdot \sqrt{-1}$$
$$= 3i$$

impossible event: An event with a probability of zero. **(320)**

improper fraction: A number with a value greater than 1 or less than -1 which is not written as a mixed number. $\frac{9}{4}$ is an improper fraction. **(004)**

in proportion: Having equivalent ratios. **(286)**

included angle: Angle formed by two adjacent sides. **(266)**

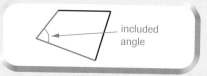
included angle

included side: The side between two angles. **(266)**

included side

independent: No postulate is a consequence of another postulate. **(400)**

independent events: Two events in which the outcome of the first event does not affect the outcome of the second event. **(329)**

independent variable: A variable in a mathematical equation whose value determines that of the dependent variable. **(131)**

index: The number indicating what root you are looking for. In $\sqrt[3]{343}$, the index is 3. **(063)**

indirect measurement: Finding a measurement by measuring something else and then using relationships to find the measurement you need. **(250)**

inductive reasoning: Making a generalization from specific cases. Used whenever you formulate a general rule after considering a pattern. **(406)**

inequality: A mathematical sentence that compares two unequal expressions using one of these symbols: $<, >, \leq, \geq,$ or $\neq$. **(190)**

infinite: Having no boundaries or limits.

inflection: A change of curvature at a point from positive to negative or from negative to positive. In the graph of a function, a point of inflection is a point at which the graph changes its curvature. *See also maximum and minimum*

inscribed: An angle or polygon whose vertices are part of another figure is inscribed in that figure. A circle or other curved figure tangent to all surfaces of another figure is inscribed in that figure.

inscribed angle of a circle: An angle with its vertex on the circle and with sides that are chords of the circle. **(258)**

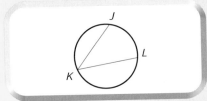

integers: The set of whole numbers and their opposites. . . . , $^-2, ^-1, 0, 1, 2, \ldots$ **(002)**

integral: Refers to an integer. An integral solution to a problem cannot be a decimal or fractional solution.

interest: The amount you pay to borrow money. Likewise, the amount you get paid for lending money. **(304)**

interest rate: The percent of the amount borrowed or invested that you will pay or be paid. **(304)**

interior angle: An angle on the inside of a polygon, formed by the sides of the polygon. **(228)**

interpolation: The process of finding an unknown value between data points using known data points. **(370)**

interquartile range: The difference between the upper quartile and the lower quartile.

intersect: To meet or cross. **(209)**

intersecting lines: Lines that have one point in common or all points in common. **(214)**

interval: On a graph, the distance between numbers from one grid line to another. **(345)**

inverse: Think of a statement as *If A is true, then B is true.* The inverse of the statement is *If A is not true, then B is not true.* **(404)**

inverse elements:
(1) For any real number, a
$$a + {^-a} = 0$$
$${^-a} + a = 0$$
(2) For any real number $a \neq 0$
$$a \cdot \frac{1}{a} = 1$$
$$\frac{1}{a} \cdot a = 1 \qquad \textbf{(041)}$$

inverse function: A function in which two variables are inversely proportional. $xy = k,$ or $y = \frac{k}{x},$ where $k \neq 0.$ **(144)**

inverse proportion: *See inverse function*

inverse relation: An operation that is the opposite of another operation. Addition and subtraction are inverse relations. Multiplication and division are also inverse relations. **(078)**

inverse variation: *See inverse function*

inversely proportional: Two variables whose products are always the same are inversely proportional.
$$xy = 2 \quad x = \frac{2}{y} \quad y = \frac{2}{x} \qquad \textbf{(293)}$$

irrational numbers: Numbers that cannot be written as a ratio of two integers. If you try to write an irrational number as a decimal, the digits never terminate and never repeat. $\sqrt{2} = 1.41421356\ldots$ **(013)**

irrational root: The square root of a number that is not a perfect square. The cube root of a number that is not a perfect cube, etc. **(054)**

irregular polygon: A polygon whose sides are not all the same length or whose angles are not all congruent.

isolate the variable: Get the variable of an equation on one side of the equation by itself. **(127)**

isosceles triangle: A triangle that has exactly two congruent sides. Some mathematicians define an isosceles triangle as having *at least* two congruent sides. **(243)**

kite: A quadrilateral with two distinct pairs of adjacent, congruent sides. **(253)**

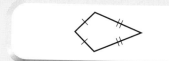

lateral face: A face that is not a base in a prism or a pyramid.

leading coefficient: The coefficient of the term of the highest degree in a polynomial with a single variable. In $3x^4 + 2x^2 + x + 8$, the leading coefficient is 3.

leap year: A year which has 366 days; usually occurs every 4 years. Leap years are years which are multiples of 4, unless the year is a multiple of 100. Then, the year must be a multiple of 400. 2000 was a leap year, but 2100 will not be.

least common denominator (LCD): The least common multiple of the denominators of two or more fractions. The LCD of $\frac{1}{8}$ and $\frac{7}{12}$ is 24.

least common multiple (LCM): The smallest number, greater than zero, found in all of the lists of multiples of two or more numbers. The LCM of 6 and 9 is 18. **(028)**

leg: (1) In a right triangle, one of the two sides that form the right angle. **(240)** (2) In an isosceles triangle, one of the two congruent sides. (3) In a trapezoid, one of the non-parallel sides.

length (l): (1) The distance along a line or figure from one point to another. (2) One dimension of a two- or three-dimensional figure.

like terms: Terms that have the same variables with the same corresponding exponents. In $9x^2 + 5y^2 + 6y^2$, $5y^2$ and $6y^2$ are like terms. **(104)**

line ($\longleftrightarrow$): An infinite set of points forming a straight path extending in two directions. **(210)**

line graph: A graph that uses line segments, a curve, or a ray to show how one or more quantities change over a period of time. **(353)**

line of best fit: A line, segment, or ray drawn on a scatter plot to estimate the relationship between two sets of data. Also called a linear regression. **(362)**

line of reflection: The line over which two figures are mirror images of each other. **(273)**

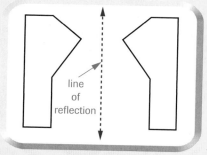

line of reflection

line plot: A diagram showing frequency of data on a number line. **(356)**

line segment (‾): A part of a line defined by two endpoints. **(212)**

line symmetry: A figure that can be folded along a line so that the two halves match exactly has line symmetry. **(274)**

line of symmetry: A line that divides a figure into two congruent halves that are mirror images of each other. *See also line of reflection.* **(178)**

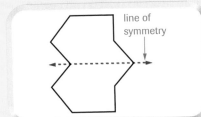

line of symmetry

linear combination method: Adding, subtracting or multiplying a system of equations to help solve the system. **(167)**

linear equation: An equation in two variables whose graph in a coordinate plane is a straight line. It is a first degree polynomial equation. $y = x + 1$ is a linear equation. **(146)**

linear function: *See linear equation* **(140)**

linear regression: *See line of best fit*

logarithm (log): An exponent. The number of times a factor is used to produce another number. The logarithm to the base 6 of 1296 is 4 ($\log_6 1296 = 4$) means $6^4 = 1296$. *See also common logarithm* **(066)**

logic: (1) Formal structure for reasoning. (2) The mathematical study of ways to reason through problems.

lower bound: A value less than or equal to all the values of a set. *See minimum*

lower bound of a parabola: The y-coordinate of the vertex on a parabola that opens upward. The lower bound of $y = x^2$ is 0. **(177)**

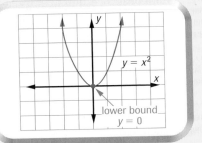

lower quartile: The median of the lower 50% of a set of data. **(357)**

lowest terms: *See simplest form*

 M ———————————————

major arc: An arc greater than a semicircle (greater than 180° or π radians). $\overset{\frown}{ADB}$ is a major arc of circle C. **(257)**

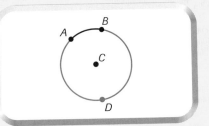

mantissa: The positive decimal part of a common logarithm. $\log 25 = 1.3979$. The mantissa of this logarithm is .3979. *See also characteristic*

mass: The amount of matter in an object. Usually measured by balancing against an object of known mass. Gravity influences weight, but it does not affect mass. **(455)**

matrices: Plural of *matrix*.

matrix: A rectangular arrangement (array) of numbers. A matrix with m rows and n columns has dimension $m \times n$. **(310)**

maximum: The greatest value of a function. A function can have a local maximum or an absolute maximum or both. A **local maximum** is a value greater than any other in its neighborhood. The **absolute maximum** is the greatest value a function attains. **(142)**

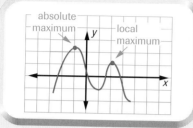

maximum point of a function: The point at which a function attains its greatest value. **(142)**

maximum value: The greatest number in a group of data. **(334)**

mean: The sum of a set of numbers divided by the number of elements in the set. Often referred to as the average. **(336)**

mean terms: *See means*

means: The two middle terms in the ratios of a proportion. In 8:15 = 24:45, the means are 15 and 24. *See also extremes* **(287)**

measure: (1) The dimensions, quantity, length, or capacity of something. (2) To find the dimensions of something.

measure of central tendency: Value intended to indicate the typical value in a collection of data. The mean, median, and mode are measures of central tendency. **(335)**

measure of dispersion: Measures that reflect the amount of variability in a set of data. The variance and standard deviation are measures of dispersion.

median: When the numbers are arranged from least to greatest, the middle number of a set of numbers. The mean of two middle numbers when the set has an even number of numbers. **(337)**

member: *See element*

metric system: A system of measurement based on tens. The basic unit of capacity is the liter. The basic unit of length is the meter. The basic unit of mass is the gram. Temperature is measured in degrees Celsius. **(455)**

midpoint: The point on a line segment that divides it into two congruent segments. **(213)**

midquartile range: The middle 50% of an ordered set of data.

millennium: 1000 years.

minimum: The least value of a function. A function can have a local minimum or an absolute minimum or both. A **local minimum** is a value less than any other in its neighborhood. The **absolute minimum** is the least value a function attains. **(142)**

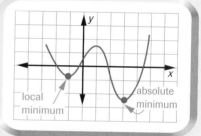

minimum value: The least number in a group of data. **(334)**

minimum point of a function: The point at which a function attains its least value. **(142)**

minor arc: An arc less than a semicircle. AB is a minor arc of circle C. **(257)**

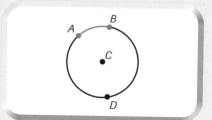

minuend: In subtraction, the minuend is the number you subtract from.

$$\begin{array}{r} 90{,}000 \quad \longleftarrow \text{ minuend} \\ - \ 3{,}456 \quad \longleftarrow \text{ subtrahend} \\ \hline 86{,}544 \quad \longleftarrow \text{ difference} \end{array}$$ **(078)**

minute (′): (1) $\frac{1}{60}$ of an hour. (2) $\frac{1}{60}$ of a degree of angle measure.

mirror image (flip): *See reflection*

mixed decimal: A decimal number with an integer part and a decimal part. 16.94

mixed fraction: A number with an integer part and a fraction part. $8\frac{7}{9}$

mixed measures: Measures that mix two units together to specify the measure of one thing. 5 ft 3 in. **(095)**

mixed number: *See mixed decimal, mixed fraction*

mode: The number that appears most frequently in a set of numbers. There may be one, more than one, or no mode. **(338)**

monomial: The product of constants and variables is a monomial. This product may be a term in a longer algebraic expression. $26r^3s^4$ is a monomial. **(101)**

multinomial: A sum of monomials (terms). *See also polynomial* **(101)**

multiple: The product of a whole number and any whole number. A multiple of 16 is 64 ($4 \times 16 = 64$). **(027)**

multiple-line graph: A graph that compares two or more quantities that are increasing or decreasing, usually over time. Each line shows one set of data. **(354)**

multiplicand: In multiplication, the multiplicand is the factor being multiplied.

$$\begin{array}{r} 83.9 \quad \longleftarrow \text{ multiplicand} \\ \times \ 3.06 \quad \longleftarrow \text{ multiplier} \\ \hline 256.734 \quad \longleftarrow \text{ product} \end{array}$$ **(086)**

multiplication: The operation of repeated addition. **(085)**

multiplication principle: *See fundamental counting principle*

Multiplication Property of Equality: If $a = b$, then $ac = bc$. **(046)**

multiplicative identity: One. $a \cdot 1 = a$

multiplicative inverse: Reciprocal of a number. When a number is multiplied by its multiplicative inverse, the product is always one. Zero is the only number with no multiplicative inverse.

$a \cdot \frac{1}{a} = 1$ where $a \neq 0$ **(041)**

multiplier: In multiplication, the multiplier is the factor being multiplied by.

$$\begin{array}{r} 83.9 \quad \longleftarrow \text{ multiplicand} \\ \times \ 3.06 \quad \longleftarrow \text{ multiplier} \\ \hline 256.734 \quad \longleftarrow \text{ product} \end{array}$$ **(086)**

multiply (× or ·): *See multiplication*

mutually-exclusive events: Two events that cannot occur at the same time. If you toss a fair coin, heads and tails are mutually exclusive events. **(328)**

natural numbers: The counting numbers: 1, 2, 3, 4, 5, . . . **(002)**

negative correlation: A relationship between two sets of numerical data in which one set generally increases as the other decreases. **(365)**

negative exponent: A base raised to a negative exponent is equivalent to the reciprocal of the base raised to the absolute value of that exponent. $2^{-3} = \left(\frac{1}{2}\right)^3$; $\left(\frac{2}{3}\right)^{-3} = \left(\frac{3}{2}\right)^3$; $\left(\frac{1}{3}\right)^{-3} = 3^3$ **(061)**

negative numbers (⁻x): Numbers less than zero. **(002)**

negative slope: A line that slants downward from left to right has negative slope. **(221)**

net: A two-dimensional shape that can be folded into a three-dimensional figure is a net of that figure. **(454)**

nominal: Measured.

non-linear equation or function: A function whose graph is not a straight line. **(169)**

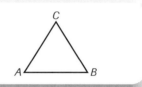

non-repeating, non-terminating decimal: A decimal that continues without end and doesn't have a repeating pattern. *See also irrational number* **(008)**

normal distribution: A bell-shaped probability distribution. There are as many values that are less than the mean as there are values that are greater than the mean. **(372)**

number line: A diagram that represents numbers as points on a line.

number theory: The mathematical theory that studies the properties and relations of integers and their relationships. **(001)**

numeral: A symbol (not a variable) used to represent a number.

numerator: The number or expression written above the line in a fraction. It tells how many equal parts of a total number of parts are described by a fraction. In $\frac{9}{20}$, the numerator is 9. **(004)**

oblique: A relationship between lines and/or plane figures that is not perpendicular or parallel.

obtuse angle: An angle with a measure greater than 90° and less than 180°. **(226)**

obtuse triangle: A triangle whose largest angle measures greater than 90°. **(243)**

octagon: A polygon with eight sides. **(453)**

odd number: A whole number represented by the expression, $2n + 1$ where n is a whole number. The ones digit of any odd number is 1, 3, 5, 7, or 9. **(018)**

odds: The ratio of favorable outcomes to unfavorable outcomes if all outcomes are equally likely. **(331)**

operation: An action performed on some set of quantities. Addition $(+)$, subtraction $(-)$, multiplication $(\times)$, division $(\div)$, raising to a power, and taking a root $(\sqrt{})$ are mathematical operations.

opposite: (1) Directly across from. (2) Having a different sign but the same numeral. $^{-}58$ is the opposite of $^{+}58$; side BC is opposite $\angle A$. **(003)**

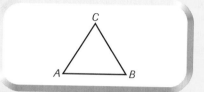

order of operations: Rules describing what sequence to use in evaluating expressions:

(1) Evaluate within grouping symbols.

(2) Evaluate powers or roots.

(3) Multiply or divide in order from left to right.

(4) Add or subtract in order from left to right. **(068)**

Order Property of Addition: *See Commutative Property of Addition*

Order Property of Multiplication: *See Commutative Property of Multiplication*

ordered pair: A pair of numbers that gives the coordinates of a point on a grid in this order: (horizontal coordinate, vertical coordinate). **(219)**

ordinal number: A whole number that names the position of an object in a sequence. First, fifth, and tenth are ordinal numbers. *See also cardinal number*

ordinate: *See y-coordinate*

origin: The intersection of the x- and y-axes in a coordinate plane. It is described by the ordered pair (0, 0). **(219)**

out of proportion: Not having equal ratios. **(286)**

outcome: One of the possible events in a probability situation. **(322)**

outlier: A piece of numerical data that is much smaller or larger than the rest of the data in a set. **(336)**

overestimate: An estimate greater than the exact numerical answer. **(075)**

parabola: The graph of a quadratic function. It is a symmetric curve. **(142)**

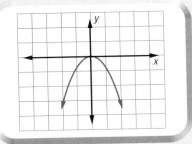

parallel (∥): Always the same distance apart. **(214)**

parallel lines: Lines in the same plane that never intersect and are always the same distance apart. **(214)**

parallelepiped: A prism whose bases and faces are all parallelograms.

parallelogram: A quadrilateral with two pairs of parallel and congruent sides. **(252)**

parameter: (1) An arbitrary constant whose value affects an expression, such as a and b in $ax^2 + bx + c = 0$. (2) A measured characteristic of a population. Suppose that 35% of the students play an instrument in a particular high school. This is a parameter since it is based on the entire population of that high school.

parent function: A function that generates a family of functions. The parent function of a quadratic function, $y = ax^2 + bx + c$, is $y = x^2$.

pattern: A design or sequence that is quantitatively predictable because some aspect of it repeats. Numbers in the sequence 1, 3, 5, 7, 9, … do not repeat but the difference between successive elements in the sequence does, so this is a number pattern. **(378)**

pentagon: A polygon that has five sides. **(453)**

pentomino: A plane figure made up of five congruent squares with each square having at least one side shared with another square.

per: For each.

percent (%): A special ratio that compares a number to 100. The word *percent* means *per hundred* or *out of 100*. 59% of 100 is 59, 59% of 200 is 118. **(294)**

percent change: A way to describe a change in a quantity by expressing it as a percent of the original quantity.
Percent change = $\frac{\text{amount of change}}{\text{original amount}} \times 100$. **(300)**

percent decrease: The absolute value of the percent change when an amount goes down.
Percent decrease = $\frac{\text{amount of decrease}}{\text{original amount}} \times 100$.
Suppose a coat that costs $30 originally cost $40. The percent decrease is $\frac{10}{40} \times 100$, or 25. You would say there was a 25% decrease in the price. **(302)**

percent error: A percent used to describe the difference of a measured or computed quantity from the actual quantity.
Percent error = $\frac{\text{amount of error}}{\text{nominal amount}} \times 100$. **(307)**

percent increase: The percent change when an amount goes up.
Percent increase = $\frac{\text{amount of increase}}{\text{original amount}} \times 100$. **(301)**

percentage: A number that is a given percent of another number. In 85% of 3000 is 2550, the percentage is 2550. **(297)**

percentile: A division of ordered data into 100 equal parts. About 1% of the data are in each part.

perfect number: A whole number that is equal to the sum of its factors (excluding the number itself). 28 is a perfect number because
$1 + 2 + 4 + 7 + 14 = 28.$

perfect power: Any number that is the product of repeated integral factors. 36 is a perfect square, 343 is a perfect cube, 81 is a perfect square and a perfect fourth power. **(053)**

perfect square: The product of an integer and itself. 144 is a perfect square because $12 \times 12 = 144$ and
$^-12 \times {}^-12 = 144.$ **(053)**

perfect square trinomial: Result of squaring a binomial.
$(x + 1)^2 = x^2 + 2x + 1$ **(111)**

perimeter (*P*): The distance around a figure. **(465)**

period: A group of three places used for the digits in numbers greater than 99. Periods are usually separated from each other by commas.

period of a function (p): Length of one repetition in a periodic function. **(145)**

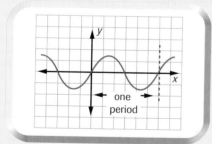

one
period

periodic: Occurring at regular intervals.

periodic decimal: *See repeating decimal*

periodic function: A function that repeats itself at regular intervals. The trigonometric functions are periodic functions. **(145)**

permutations: Possible orders, or arrangements, of a set of events or items. If you put the items or events into a different order, you have a different permutation. Three different permutations of the same combination (the letters *n*, *o*, and *w*) are own, now, and won. **(318)**

perpendicular (⊥): Forming right angles. **(215)**

perpendicular bisector: A line, line segment, ray, or plane that divides a line segment into two congruent segments and intersects the segment to form right angles. **(216)**

perpendicular distance: (1) The length of a segment from a point to a line, perpendicular to the line. (2) The length of a segment between two lines, perpendicular to both.

perpendicular lines: Lines that form right angles when they intersect. **(215)**

pi (π): The ratio of the circumference of any circle to its diameter; approximately equal to 3.14, or $\frac{22}{7}$.

pictograph: A graph that uses pictures or symbols to represent data. **(350)**

pie chart: *See circle graph*

place value: (1) The value of the position of a digit in a number. In the number 1,234,567, the three is in the ten-thousands place, so it stands for 30,000. (2) A system of writing numbers such that the value of a digit depends on its position.

plane: A surface with infinite length and width but no thickness. **(218)**

plane divider: A graph of an equation which divides a plane. **(203)**

plane figure: Any two-dimensional figure. Arcs, sectors, polygons, circles, and angles are all plane figures. **(453)**

point: An exact location in space. **(209)**

point of tangency: The one and only point at which a tangent line intersects a circle or curve. **(255)**

point-slope form: The equation of a line in the form $y - y_1 = m(x - x_1)$ where m represents the slope of the line and (x_1, y_1) is a known point on the line. **(156)**

point symmetry: A geometric property. A figure that can be turned exactly 180° about a point and fit exactly on itself has point symmetry. **(272)**

polar coordinates: Coordinates based on the rotation of a segment about a pole, or center point. **(271)**

polygon: A closed figure formed from line segments that meet only at their endpoints. **(227)**

polyhedra: Plural of polyhedron.

polyhedron: A closed three-dimensional figure in which all the surfaces are polygons. A pyramid is a polyhedron. **(454)**

polynomial: The sum of monomials (terms). $18r^4 + 9r^2 + 5r$ is a polynomial. **(102)**

polynomial long division: A method of dividing one polynomial into another. **(118)**

population: (1) A group of people (or objects or events) that fit a particular description. (2) In statistics, the complete collection of elements to be studied. **(325)**

population density: The number of items in a given region. The population density of Alabama is 79.6 people per square mile. **(074)**

positive correlation: Two sets of data are positively correlated if, as the numbers in one set tend to increase, the numbers in the other set tend to increase. **(365)**

positive numbers: Numbers that are greater than zero. **(002)**

positive slope: A line that slants upward from left to right has a positive slope. **(221)**

possible outcomes: All of the outcomes that can occur. If there are three colors on a spinner, each color is a possible outcome. **(322)**

postulate: A mathematical statement that is accepted as true without proof. Also called an axiom. **(266)**

power: (1) A number with a base and an exponent. 8^5 can be read as *the fifth power of eight.* (2) An exponent. **(051)**

power of 10: A number with 10 as a base and an integral exponent. **(065)**

precision: An indication of how finely a measurement was made. When you calculate with measured values, you may need to round to the smallest place in the roughest actual measurements. Suppose you ride 62.5 miles in 6.0 hours. To find the hourly rate, divide. A calculator will show the result, 10.41666667. Since the original measurements were in tenths of an hour and tenths of a mile, the hourly rate is precise only to the tenths place: 10.4 miles per hour. **(097)**

prime factorization: The expression of a number as the product of prime factors. The prime factorization of 36 is $2^2 \times 3^2$. **(026)**

prime number: (1) A positive integer that has exactly two different positive factors, itself and 1. (2) A negative integer that has exactly four different factors, itself, its opposite, 1, and ⁻1. **(023)**

prime polynomial: A polynomial that cannot be factored.

principal: The amount of money borrowed or invested. **(304)**

principal square root: The positive square root of a number. The principal square root of 16 is 4. **(057)**

prism: A three-dimensional figure that has two congruent and parallel faces that are polygons. The remaining faces are parallelograms. Prisms are named by their bases. A triangular prism has two triangular bases. **(454)**

probability: The measure of the likelihood of an event occurring. The probability of an event is the ratio of the number of favorable outcomes to the number of equally likely possible outcomes:

$P(\text{event}) = \frac{\text{number of favorable outcomes}}{\text{number of possible outcomes}}$ **(320)**

product: The result of multiplication. **(085)**

proper divisor: a factor of a number other than the number itself.

proper fraction: A fraction, the absolute value of whose numerator is an integer less than its integer denominator. $\frac{15}{22}$ is a proper fraction; $\frac{22}{15}$ is not. $\frac{-2}{5}$ is a proper fraction, $\frac{-5}{2}$ is not.

proportion: An equation showing that two ratios are equal. $\frac{3}{8} = \frac{15}{40}$ **(286)**

proportional: Having equivalent ratios. **(286)**

protractor: A tool used to measure angles.

pyramid: A polyhedron whose base is a polygon and whose other faces are triangles that share a common vertex. A pyramid is named by its base. The base of a square pyramid is a square. **(454)**

Pythagorean Theorem: The sum of the squares of the lengths of the two legs of a right triangle is equal to the square of the length of the hypotenuse.
$a^2 + b^2 = c^2$ **(245)**

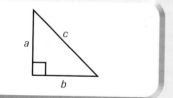

Pythagorean triple: A set of three positive integers that name the lengths of the sides of a right triangle. 5, 12, and 13 are a Pythagorean triple because
$5^2 + 12^2 = 13^2$. **(246)**

quadrangle: A figure formed by four points and the four line segments that join them in order. All quadrilaterals are quadrangles. In some quadrangles, the sides intersect and these are not quadrilaterals.

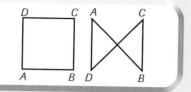

quadrants: The four sections of a coordinate grid that are separated by the axes. By convention, they are numbered counterclockwise from the upper right, I, II, III, IV. **(219)**

quadratic: (1) Of the second degree. (2) Containing one or more terms in which the variable is raised to the second power, but no variable is raised to a higher power.

quadratic equation: A polynomial equation containing one or more terms in which the variable is raised to the second power but no higher. The standard form of a quadratic equation is $ax^2 + bx + c = 0$, where a and c can be any nonzero rational number, and b can be any rational number, including 0. **(174)**

quadratic formula: Formula used to solve any quadratic equation:
If $ax^2 + bx + c = 0$ and $a \neq 0$, then $x = \frac{-b \pm \sqrt{b^2 - 4ac}}{2a}$. See also discriminant **(184)**

quadratic function: A function with a second degree variable. $y = 2x^2$ and $y = x^2 + 4x + 2$ are quadratic functions. **(142)**

quadrilateral: A four-sided polygon. **(251)**

quantity: An amount.

quarter turn: One-fourth of a revolution (90°) about a given point (turn center).

quartile: *See lower quartile, upper quartile*

quotient: The result of the division of one quantity by another.

dividend ÷ divisor = quotient

$$\frac{\text{quotient}}{\text{divisor} \overline{)\text{dividend}}}$$ **(085)**

R

radical ($\sqrt{}$): A symbol that indicates the root to be taken. The symbol $\sqrt{}$ with no index indicates the square root.

radians: Real number angle measure; $180° = \pi$ radians.

radical equation: An equation that contains a radical.

radical expression: An expression that contains a radical.

radicand: The number or expression under a radical. In $\sqrt{2.5}$, the radicand is 2.5. In $\sqrt[3]{5x}$, the radicand is $5x$.

radii: Plural of radius.

radius (r): (1) A line segment from the center of a circle to any point on the circle. (2) The length of such a segment. **(255)**

random: By chance, with no outcome any more likely than another. **(326)**

random sample: A sample in which every person, object, or event in the population has an equal chance of being selected for the sample. **(326)**

range: (1) The difference between the greatest and the least values in a set of data. (2) The possible values for a variable in a given situation. In the volume formula, $V = lwh$, the variables must be positive numbers, so the range for the variables is all positive numbers. (3) The possible values for y in a function. *See also domain* **(131)**

ranked data: Data that are arranged in a sequence, especially in terms of the ordering of their numeric elements.

rate: A ratio comparing two different units. Inches per second and cents per pound are rates. **(281)**

rate of change: The ratio of change in one quantity to the corresponding change in another quantity. *See also slope* **(223)**

ratio: A comparison of two numbers or measures using division. **(278)**

rational expression: An algebraic expression that can be written as a fraction whose numerator and denominator are polynomials. $\frac{x}{5}; \frac{a^2 - 3a - 4}{9a\,(a - 2)}; \frac{b^2 - 4}{b - 2}$ **(170)**

rational equation: An equation involving a rational expression. $\frac{x}{5} + \frac{1}{x^2} - 4 = \frac{1}{4}$ **(170)**

rational number: A number that can be expressed as a ratio of two integers (a fraction). **(003)**

rationalize: Write an equivalent expression or equation without radicals. $\sqrt{a^2} \rightarrow a; \sqrt{a + 1} = 5 \rightarrow a + 1 = 25$

ray ($\rightarrow$): A part of a line that has one endpoint and extends indefinitely in one direction. **(211)**

real numbers: The combined set of the rational and irrational numbers. **(002)**

reciprocals: Two numbers that have a product of 1. Also called multiplicative inverses. $\frac{5}{9}$ and $\frac{9}{5}$ are reciprocals because $\frac{5}{9} \times \frac{9}{5} = 1$. **(041)**

rectangle: A quadrilateral with two pairs of congruent, parallel sides and four right angles. **(252)**

recurring decimal: *See repeating decimal*

reduce: Write a fraction in simplest form. $\frac{9}{12} = \frac{3}{4}$

redundant number: *See abundant number*

reference angle: The acute angle being referred to in a trigonometric ratio. **(249)**

reflection (flip): A transformation creating a mirror image of a figure on the opposite side of a line. **(273)**

reflex angle: An angle that measures more than 180°. **(226)**

Reflexive Property of Equality: Any real number is equal to itself. **(047)**

region: A part of a plane.

region of feasible solutions: The portion of a graph that shows the possible solutions to a problem. **(206)**

regression line: *See line of best fit*

regroup: Use place value to think of a number in a different way to make addition and subtraction easier. 425 can be thought of as 300 + 120 + 5 in order to make subtracting 172 easier.

regular polygon: A polygon with all sides the same length and all angles the same measure. **(453)**

regular polyhedron: A solid figure with congruent regular polygons for all faces.

regular solid: *See regular polyhedron*

relation: A set of ordered pairs for which all x and y are related in the same way. **(131)**

relatively prime: Two numbers are relatively prime if they have no common factors other than one. 9 and 16 are relatively prime.

remainder: In whole-number division, when you have divided as far as you can without using decimals, what has not been divided yet is the remainder. The final remainder must be less than the divisor.

repeating decimal: A decimal that has an infinitely repeating sequence of digits. $4.7272\ldots = 4.\overline{72}$ **(008)**

replacement set: The set of meaningful values that can be substituted for a variable. In $y = \frac{1}{x}$, the replacement set for x is all real numbers except zero. **(115)**

representative sample: A sample that closely represents the whole group. The sample must consider the sample size and the sample choice. **(326)**

revolution: A 360° turn about a point.

rhombi: Plural of rhombus.

rhombus: A parallelogram with all four sides equal in length. **(252)**

right angle (∟): An angle that measures exactly 90°. **(226)**

right triangle: A triangle that has one 90° angle. **(243)**

rise: The change in y-value between two points in the graph of a line. **(222)**

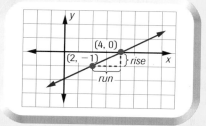

Roman numerals: The Roman number system based on addition and subtraction rather than on place value:

I	1	L	50	M 1000
V	5	C	100	$\overline{V}$ 5000
X	10	D	500	

root: The inverse of a power. In $a^x = b$ or $\sqrt[x]{b} = a$, a is the xth root of b. **(051)**

rotation (turn): A transformation in which a figure is turned a given angle and direction around a point. **(270)**

round: To approximate a number by analyzing a specific place value:

• If the digit in the first place after the specified place is five or greater, add one to the digit in the specified place and delete all digits to the right. This is rounding up.

• If the digit in the first place after the specified place is less than five, do not change the digit in the specified place and delete all digits to the right. This is rounding down.

rubric: (1) A rule, direction, or explanation. (2) A detailed explanation of how a piece of work will be evaluated or scored. **(418)**

Rule of Three: From ancient Hindu mathematics: In a proportion, the product of the means equals the product of the extremes, so if you have three terms for a proportion, you can find the fourth.

run: The change in x-value between two points in the graph of a line. **(222)**

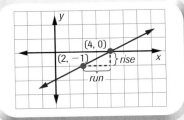

S

sample: The people, objects, or events chosen from a given population to represent the entire group. **(326)**

sample size: The number of members in the sample. **(326)**

sample space: A list of all possible outcomes of an activity. **(321)**

scalar multiplication: Multiplying a matrix by a number. **(315)**

scale: (1) An instrument used for weighing. (2) A system of marks at fixed intervals used in measurement or graphing. (3) The ratio of length used in a drawing, map, or model to the length of the object in reality. **(261)**

scale factor: The ratio of the lengths of corresponding sides of two similar figures.

scalene triangle: A triangle that has no congruent sides. **(243)**

scatter plot: A graph with one point for each item being measured. The coordinates of a point represent the measures of two attributes of each item. **(361)**

scattergram: *See scatter plot*

scientific notation: A form of writing numbers as the product of a power of 10 and a decimal number greater than or equal to 1 and less than 10. 8,905,000 is written as 8.905×10^6 in scientific notation. **(065)**

score: Twenty years.

secant: (1) The reciprocal of the cosine function. (2) A line that contains a chord of a circle. **(255)**

second: (1) (") $\frac{1}{60}$ of an angle minute ($\frac{1}{3600}$ of a degree). (2) (") $\frac{1}{60}$ of a minute of time ($\frac{1}{3600}$ of an hour). (3) The number two position in a row of items.

sector: The region formed by a central angle and an arc. **(257)**

segment: (1) *See line segment* (2) A region of the interior of a circle bounded by a chord and the arc that shares its endpoints.

semicircle: An arc that is exactly half of a circle. A diameter intersects a circle at the endpoints of two semicircles. **(255)**

sequence: An ordered set of objects or numbers.

series: Sum of a finite or infinite sequence of terms. $1 + \frac{1}{2} + \frac{1}{3} + \frac{1}{4} + \ldots$

set: A collection of distinct elements or items.

short radius: *See apothem*

side: (1) One of a number of line segments, each connected to two other line segments to form a polygon. (2) An edge of a polyhedron.

Sieve of Eratosthenes: A way of finding prime numbers in a sequential list of natural numbers.

signed number: A positive or negative number. ⁺5.06 and ⁻8.99 are signed numbers. Zero is not a signed number.

significant digit: In measurement, the significant digits tell how much of a measured value can be used with confidence. The most significant digit is the first non-zero digit in the number. The least significant digit may be a rounded digit. In 87.0405, the most significant digit is 8. If the least significant digit is 5, you know the true value is at least 87.04045 and less than 87.04055.

significant figure: *See significant digit*

similar figures (~): Figures whose corresponding sides are proportional and whose corresponding angles are congruent. **(259)**

similar terms: *See like terms*

simple event: An experimental outcome that cannot be broken down any further.

simple interest: The amount of interest determined by the following formula:
Interest = principal × annual rate
× time in years. **(305)**

simplest form: (1) A fraction whose numerator and denominator have no common factor greater than one. The simplest form of $\frac{16}{36}$ is $\frac{4}{9}$. (2) A number under the radical sign that is not a product with a perfect square factor.
$\sqrt{80} \longrightarrow \sqrt{16 \times 5} \longrightarrow 4\sqrt{5}$ **(118)**

simplify: Combine like terms and apply properties to an expression to make computation easier. $\frac{6x^2}{2x} = 3x$, $x \neq 0$ **(104)**

simplify a fraction: To divide the numerator and denominator of a fraction by a common factor. $\frac{15}{12} \longrightarrow \frac{15 \div 3}{12 \div 3} = \frac{5}{4}$

simulation: A model of an experiment that might be impractical to carry out.

sine ratio (sin): In a right triangle, the ratio of the length of the leg opposite the given angle to the length of the hypotenuse. The value of the sine of the angle depends upon the measure of the angle. **(250)**

single line graph: *See line graph*

skew lines: Lines that are not parallel and do not intersect. If two lines are skew, then there is no single plane that contains them both. **(214)**

slant height: (1) The perpendicular distance from the vertex of a pyramid to one edge of its base. (2) The shortest distance from the vertex of a right circular cone to the edge of its base.

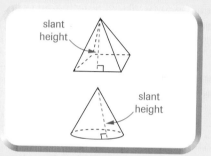

slide: *See translation*

slope: The measure of steepness of a line as you look at it from left to right. A numerical value for slope is found using two points on the line and dividing the change in y-value by the change in x-value (slope $= \frac{\text{change in } y}{\text{change in } x}$, or $\frac{\text{rise}}{\text{run}}$). **(221)**

slope-intercept form: A form of a linear equation, $y = mx + b$, where m is the slope of the line and b is the y-intercept. **(150)**

solid: *See solid figure*

solid figure: A closed three-dimensional figure. **(454)**

solution: Any value for a variable that makes an equation or inequality true. The solutions of $8x^2 = 72$ are $x = 3$ or $x = {}^-3$. **(160)**

solution set ({ }): The set of values that make an equation or inequality true. $\{3, {}^-3\}$ is the solution set for $8x^2 = 72$. **(127)**

space figure: *See solid figure*

sphere: A three-dimensional figure made up of all points in space that are equally distant from a point called the center.

spreadsheet: A table of rows and columns used for organizing, analyzing, managing, sorting, and retrieving data. **(428)**

spreadsheet program: A computer program that allows a person to create and manipulate spreadsheets. **(428)**

square: A parallelogram with four congruent sides and four right angles. **(252)**

square measure: A unit, such as a square meter, or a system of units used to measure area.

square number: (1) The number of dots in a square array. The first four square numbers are 1, 4, 9, and 16. (2) The product of two identical factors. *See also perfect square* **(056)**

square root ($\sqrt{\ }$): *See root*

square unit: *See square measure*

standard deviation: The measure of dispersion equal to the square root of the variance. One standard deviation on either side of the mean will encompass $\frac{2}{3}$ of the data in a normal distribution.

standard form: A number written with one digit for each place value. 123.45 is written in standard form.

standard form of a linear equation: $ax + by + c = 0$, where a, b, and c are integers and a > 0. *See also slope-intercept form* **(152)**

standard form of a quadratic equation: $ax^2 + bx + c = 0$, where a, b, and c are integers (not multiples of each other) and a > 0. **(175)**

standard score: *See z score*

stanine: Scores that divide a normal distribution into nine parts, each of which is $\frac{1}{2}$ standard deviation wide.

statement: (1) A mathematical sentence that describes a relationship between two numbers, expressions, or concepts. $9 > 5$; $3x \le 8$; $5x + 2 = 7$ (2) Statements in mathematics often take an *If . . . , then . . .* form. The statement in the *if* part of the sentence is the hypothesis (or what you are given or taking as your starting point.) The conclusion that follows is the statement in the *then* part. If $a = b$, then $b = a$. **(402)**

statistic: A measured characteristic of a sample. The mean of a sample is a statistic.

statistics: (1) The collection, organization, description, and analysis of data. (2) Quantitative data. **(333)**

straight angle: An angle with a measure of 180°. **(226)**

subtract ($-$): *See subtraction*

subtraction: An operation that gives the difference between two numbers. Subtraction is also used to compare two numbers or sets. The difference between 9.83 and 2.64, $9.83 - 2.64$, is 7.19. **(078)**

subtrahend: In subtraction, the subtrahend is the number being subtracted.

750.2 ⟵ minuend
$-$ 84.5 ⟵ subtrahend
665.7 ⟵ difference **(078)**

sum: The result of addition. **(078)**

supplementary angles: Two angles with measures whose sum is 180°. **(233)**

surface: A two- or three-dimensional region.

surface area: The total area of the faces (including the bases) and curved surfaces of a solid figure. **(467)**

symbol: A sign used to represent something, such as an operation, quantity, or relation. $\times$ means *multiply*, $\div$ means *divided by*, x is an unknown quantity, and $\ge$ means *is greater than or equal to*. **(510)**

symmetric: Having symmetry. *See also line symmetry, point symmetry, and turn symmetry.*

Symmetric Property of Equality: For any real numbers a and b, if $a = b$, then $b = a$. **(048)**

symmetry: *See line symmetry, point symmetry, and turn symmetry.*

system of linear equations: Two or more related linear equations for which you seek a common solution. A system of linear equations can have no common solutions, one common solution, or many common solutions. **(162)**

system of inequalities: Two or more related inequalities for which you seek a common solution. The system may have no common solutions, one common solution, or many common solutions. **(206)**

table: A way of organizing many pieces of data about a topic into categories. **(339)**

tangent (tan): In a right triangle, the ratio of the length of the leg opposite an angle to the length of the adjacent leg. **(250)**

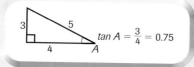

$$\tan A = \frac{3}{4} = 0.75$$

tangent line: A line that touches a circle or curve at just one point. **(255)**

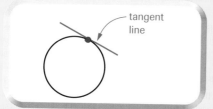

tangent line

term: (1) A number, variable, product, or quotient in an expression. A term is not a sum or difference. In $35x^4 + x^2 + 18x + 1$, there are four terms, $35x^4$, x^2, $18x$, and 1. **(101)** (2) Each element of a fraction is a term. In $\frac{7}{12}$, 7 and 12 are both terms. (3) Each element of a proportion is a term. In 3:7 = 15:35, 3, 7, 15, and 35 are terms. *See also means and extremes* **(287)**

terminating decimal: A decimal that contains a finite number of digits. A terminating decimal can be written as a fraction with a denominator of 10, 100, 1000, and so on. 0.876452, 0.5, and 0.625 are terminating decimals. **(007)**

tessellation: A covering of a plane without overlaps or gaps using combinations of congruent figures.

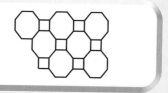

theorem: A mathematical statement or proposition derived from previously accepted results. **(401)**

theoretical probability: Finding the probability of an event without doing an experiment or analyzing data.
$$P = \frac{\text{number of favorable outcomes}}{\text{number of equally likely possible outcomes}}$$
(323)

three-dimensional: Existing in three dimensions; having length, width, and height.

time line: A number line with dates showing when events happened and/or when they will happen.

topologically equivalent: Figures that can be made into one another by stretching, bending, and shrinking without cutting.

topology: The study of those properties of a figure that remain unchanged when the figure is distorted.

transformation: A rule for moving every point in a plane figure. *See also dilation, reflection, rotation, and translation* **(268)**

transformation image: The figure created when a figure undergoes a transformation. **(268)**

transformational proof: Changing the form of a statement while keeping it true.

$5x + 3 = 28$
$5x = 25$
$x = 5$

Each new statement has the same solution set as the previous statement. **(407)**

Transitive Relation: If $a = b$ and $b = c$, then $a = c$. Also called transitive property or transitive axiom. **(049)**

translation (slide): A transformation that moves every point on a figure a given distance in a given direction. **(269)**

transpose: Appear to change the sign and move a number from one side of an equation to the other.

$x - 5 = y$
$\downarrow$
$x = y + 5$

transversal: A line that intersects two or more other lines at different points. **(237)**

trapezium: A quadrilateral with no parallel sides. **(251)**

trapezoid: A quadrilateral with exactly one pair of parallel sides. Some mathematicians define a trapezoid as having *at least* one pair of parallel sides. **(251)**

tree diagram: A diagram used to find all the possible permutations for a set of items or the prime factorization of a number. **(318)**

trend: A general pattern in a set of data; for example, if a line graph moves generally upward from left to right, the trend is increasing. **(367)**

trend line: *See scatter plot*

triangle: A three-sided polygon. **(239)**

Triangle Inequality Theorem: In any triangle, no side can be equal to or longer than the sum of the lengths of the other two sides. **(241)**

triangular number: The number of dots in a triangular array. The first four triangular numbers are 1, 3, 6, and 10.

trigonometric ratios: Sine, cosine, and tangent are ratios among the sides of right triangles. **(249)**

trigonometry: The branch of mathematics based on properties of right triangles.

trinomial: A polynomial with three terms. The three terms of $2x^2 - 5x + 11$ are $2x^2$, ^-5x, and 11. **(102)**

truncate: (1) To make numbers with many digits easier to read and use by ignoring all digits to the right of a chosen place. 3.1416 truncated to the thousandths place is 3.141 (2) To cut off part of a geometric figure.

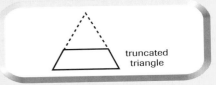
truncated triangle

turn: *See rotation*

turn center: The point around which a figure is rotated. **(270)**

turn symmetry: A figure that can fit onto itself after rotating less than 360° has turn symmetry. **(272)**

twin primes: Two prime numbers that are also consecutive odd numbers. 17 and 19 are twin primes but 2 and 3 are not, nor are 13 and 17.

two-dimensional: Existing in two dimensions; having length and width.

undefined slope: The slope of a vertical line (a line with an x-value that does not change) is undefined. The slope of the line is undefined because division by zero is undefined. **(159)**

underestimate: An estimate less than the exact numerical answer. **(075)**

Unique Factorization Theory: *See Fundamental Theorem of Arithmetic*

unit: A precisely fixed quantity used to count or measure.

unit fraction: A fraction with a numerator of one.

unit price: The price of one unit. The total price divided by the number of units. **(287)**

unit rate: A rate with a denominator of one. 60 mph or $\frac{60 \text{ miles}}{1 \text{ hour}}$ is a unit rate. **(282)**

units digit: The numeral in the ones place. *See also place value*

upper bound: (1) The maximum value of a set. (2) The y-coordinate of the vertex on a parabola that opens downward. **(177)**

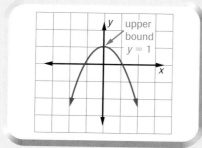

upper quartile: The median of the upper 50% of a set of data. **(357)**

V

value: (1) The number assigned to a variable. (2) The quantity that is the result of applying one or more operations.

variability: Measures that show how items in a data set differ from one another. *See also measures of dispersion.*

variable: (1) A quantity that changes or that can have different values. (2) A symbol, usually a letter, that can stand for different values. In $72n^3$, the variable is n. **(100)**

variable expression: An expression that represents an amount that can have different values. $6m^2$ has a different value for every value assigned to m.

variance: A measure of dispersion of data centered about the mean.

Venn diagram: A diagram that shows relationships among sets of objects. **(363)**

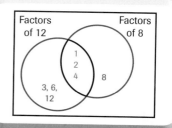

vertex: (1) The point at which two line segments, lines, or rays meet to form an angle. (2) A point on a polyhedron where three or more faces intersect. (3) The fixed point that is generated by a cone. **(225)**

vertical: At right angles to the horizon. In a coordinate grid, the y-axis is a vertical line. **(221)**

vertical angles: The non-adjacent angles formed when two lines intersect. Vertical angles are congruent. $\angle a$ and $\angle c$ are vertical angles. So are $\angle b$ and $\angle d$. **(236)**

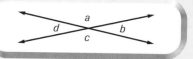

vertical line test: If you draw a vertical line through the graph of any function, it will intersect the graph at no more than one point. **(136)**

vertices: Plural of vertex.

vinculum: The bar separating the numerator and denominator of a fraction.

volume (V): The number of cubic units it takes to fill a three-dimensional space. **(469)**

vulgar fraction: *See common fraction*

W

weight: A measure of the heaviness or the force of gravity on an object.

weighted average: *See weighted mean*

weighted mean: Mean of a collection of values that have been assigned different degrees of importance.

whiskers: *See box-and-whisker plot*

whole number: Any of the numbers 0, 1, 2, 3, 4, 5, and so on. **(002)**

width (*w*): One dimension of a two-dimensional or three-dimensional figure.

X

x-axis: On a coordinate grid, the horizontal axis. **(219)**

x-coordinate (abscissa): The signed horizontal distance from the *y*-axis on a coordinate grid. In an ordered pair, the value that is always written first. In (6, 15), 6 is the *x*-coordinate. **(220)**

x-intercept: The value of *x* in an ordered pair describing the point at which a line or the graph of a function intersects the *x*-axis. If a graph intersects the *x*-axis at (6, 0), the *x*-intercept is 6. In some texts, the *x*-intercept is defined as the point whose *y*-coordinate is zero. **(186)**

Y

y-axis: On a coordinate grid, the vertical axis. **(219)**

y-coordinate (ordinate): The signed vertical distance from the *x*-axis on a coordinate grid. In an ordered pair, the value that is always written second. In (6, 15), 15 is the *y*-coordinate. **(220)**

year: The amount of time it takes for the earth to make one complete revolution around the sun, about 365.25 days. Since it is more convenient to have a whole number of days each year, each year has 365 days except leap years which have 366. *See also leap year*

y-intercept: The value of *y* in an ordered pair describing the point at which a line or the graph of a function intersects the *y*-axis. If a graph intersects the *y*-axis at (0, 6), the *y*-intercept is 6. In some texts, the *y*-intercept is defined as the point whose *x*-coordinate is zero. **(150)**

Z

zeros of a function: Values of the variable for which the value of a function is zero. Also called the roots of a function. $x^2 + 4x$ has zeros at $x = {}^-4$ and $x = 0$ because $x^2 + 4x = x(x + 4)$, ${}^-4({}^-4 + 4) = 0$ and $0(0 + 4) = 0$.

zero pair: A pair of numbers whose sum is zero. ${}^-4 + 4 = 0$ **(082)**

Zero Product Property: The product of any number and zero is zero. $a \cdot 0 = 0$ and $0 \cdot a = 0$, where a is any real number. **(042)**

z-score: The number of standard deviations that a given value is above or below the mean. Also called the standard score.

Glossary of Mathematical Symbols _____

Symbol	Meaning	Example
$+$	plus (addition)	$5.9 + 8.4 = 14.3$
$+$	positive	$^{+}24$: the integer 24 units to the right of zero on a number line
$-$	minus (subtraction)	$60.3 - 12.8 = 47.5$
$-$	negative (additive inverse)	$^{-}35$: the integer 35 units to the left of zero on a number line
$\times, \cdot, a(b), *$	multiplied by or times	$1.2 \times 7.5 = 9$; $6 \cdot 18 = 108$; $51(3) = 153$; $2 * 7 = 14$
$\div$ or $\overline{)}$	division	$8.1 \div 9 = 0.9$ $\quad 9\overline{)8.1}^{\,0.9}$
$=$	is equal to	$45 + 37 = 82$
$\neq$	is not equal to	$36 - 6 \neq 12$
$\cong$	is congruent to	$\overline{AB} \cong \overline{BC}$
$\sim$	is similar to	$ABCDE \sim FGHIJ$
$\approx$ or $\doteq$	is approximately equal to	$\pi \approx 3.14$
$<$	is less than	$58 + 16 < 100$
$\leq$	is less than or equal to	$8.79 \leq 9$
$>$	is greater than	$5\frac{3}{8} > 5.1$
$\geq$	is greater than or equal to	$7.2 \geq 7.2$
$\pm$	plus or minus	$15 \pm 12 = 27$ or 3
$(\,)$	parentheses: used as grouping symbols	$(5.7 + 3.2) - (4.1 - 1.2)$ $= 8.9 - 2.9$ $= 6$

Mathematical Symbols (continued)

Symbol	Meaning	Example
[ ]	brackets: used as grouping symbols	$6[(9 + 2) - (38 - 25)]$ $= 6[11 - 13]$ $= 6(^-2) = ^-12$
{ }	braces: used as grouping symbols *See also* {} set	$0.1\{8[(48 + 9) - (6 \times 5)]\}$ $= 0.1\{8[57 - 30]\}$ $= 0.1\{8[27]\}$ $= 0.1\{216\}$ $= 21.6$
%	percent	75%: 75 percent
°	degree	360° is the number of degrees in a circle
°F	degrees Fahrenheit	85°F
°C	degrees Celsius	23°C
:	is to (ratio)	9:11; say: *9 is to 11*
π	the irrational number pi $\pi \approx$ 3.14159265358979323846...	usually use $\pi \approx 3.14$, or $\pi \approx \dfrac{22}{7}$
| |	absolute value	$\|^-123\| = 123$ and $\|123\| = 123$
$\sqrt{}$	prinicipal square root	$\sqrt{144} = 12$
$\sqrt[3]{}$	cube root	$\sqrt[3]{64} = 4$
$5.\overline{12}$	repeating decimal symbol	$5.\overline{12} = 5.121212...$
{ }	set; braces	{*M*}: the set containing the letter M
∠	angle	
Δ	triangle	
$\overleftrightarrow{CD}$	line *CD*	
$\overline{ST}$	line segment *ST*	

Mathematical Symbols (continued)

Symbol	Meaning	Example
$\overrightarrow{AB}$	ray AB	
$\overarc{JK}$	arc JK	
⌐	right angle	$\angle WXY$ is a right angle.
$\perp$	is perpendicular to	$\overline{CD} \perp \overline{EF}$
$\parallel$	is parallel to	$\overline{QR} \parallel \overline{ST}$
$\therefore$	therefore	$m\angle ABC$ is 30°, $\therefore$ $\angle ABC$ is an acute angle.
∞	infinity	
$!$	factorial	$7! = 7 \cdot 6 \cdot 5 \cdot 4 \cdot 3 \cdot 2 \cdot 1$ $= 5040$
a^0	1	$32^0 = 128^0 = 1$
a^n	using the number a as a factor n times	$2^6 = 2 \cdot 2 \cdot 2 \cdot 2 \cdot 2 \cdot 2$ $= 64$
a^{-n}	$\frac{1}{a^n}$, or using $\frac{1}{a}$ as a factor n times	$4^{-4} = \frac{1}{4^4}$ $= \frac{1}{256}$
$a^{\frac{1}{n}}$	$\sqrt[n]{a}$, or the nth root of a	$216^{\frac{1}{3}} = \sqrt[3]{216} = 6$ since $6 \cdot 6 \cdot 6 = 216$
$a^{\frac{b}{n}}$	$\left(\sqrt[n]{a}\right)^b$, or the nth root of a raised to the b power	$343^{\frac{2}{3}} = 7^2$ $= 49$
$y = \log_a x$	y equals the logarithm to the base a of the number x	$4 = \log_3 81$ is equivalent to $81 = 3^4$

This index contains topic numbers, not page numbers. You will find topic numbers at the top of each page and next to each new piece of information.

515

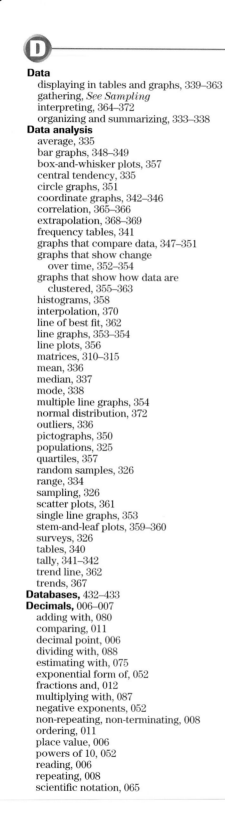

G

H

523

Illustration Credits

Part opener illustrations by Joe Spooner: pp. 001, 067, 098, 146, 169, 190, 207, 230, 277, 309, 373, 397
All remaining creative illustration: Rob Dunleavy
Technical Art: Nesbitt Graphics, Inc.
Robot Characters: Bill SMITH STUDIO with Jon Conrad
Map Art: Joe Lemonnier